English Language Arts
Lesson Guide

Book Staff and Contributors

Kristen Kinney-Haines   *Director, English Language Arts*
Amy Rauen   *Director, Instructional Design*
Mary Beck Desmond   *Senior Text Editor*
Allyson Jacob   *Text Editor*
Tricia Battipede   *Senior Creative Manager*
Julie Jankowski   *Senior Visual Designer*
Caitlin Gildrien   *Visual Designer*
Sheila Smith   *Print Designer*
Tricia Battipede, Mike Bohman, Shannon Palmer   *Cover Designers*
Robyn Campbell, Heather Evans, Alane Gernon-Paulsen, Tara Gleason, Tim Mansfield, Melisa Rice,
      Tisha Ruibal   *Writers*
Amy Eward   *Content Specialist; Senior Manager, Writers and Editors*
Dan Smith   *Senior Project Manager*

Doug McCollum   *Senior Vice President, Product Development*
Kristin Morrison   *Vice President, Design, Creative, and User Experience*
Rohit Lakhani   *Vice President, Program Management and Operations*
Kelly Engel   *Senior Director, Curriculum*
Christopher Frescholtz   *Senior Director, Program Management*
Erica Castle   *Director, Creative Services*
Lisa Dimaio Iekel   *Senior Production Manager*

Illustrations Credits

All illustrations © Stride, Inc. unless otherwise noted
Characters: Tommy DiGiovanni, Matt Fedor, Ben Gamache, Shannon Palmer
Cover: Spiral © Silmen/iStock; Polygon © LPETTET/iStock
Program Overview: xxiv Used by permission of HarperCollins Publishers

At Stride, Inc. (NYSE: LRN)—formerly K12 Inc.—we are reimagining lifelong learning as a rich, deeply personal experience that prepares learners for tomorrow. Since its inception, Stride has been committed to removing barriers that impact academic equity and to providing high-quality education for anyone—particularly those in underserved communities. The company has transformed the teaching and learning experience for millions of people by providing innovative, high-quality, tech-enabled education solutions, curriculum, and programs directly to students, schools, the military, and enterprises in primary, secondary, and post-secondary settings. Stride is a premier provider of K-12 education for students, schools, and districts, including career learning services through middle and high school curriculum. Providing a solution to the widening skills gap in the workplace and student loan crisis, Stride equips students with real world skills for in-demand jobs with career learning. For adult learners, Stride delivers professional skills training in healthcare and technology, as well as staffing and talent development for Fortune 500 companies. Stride has delivered millions of courses over the past decade and serves learners in all 50 states and more than 100 countries. The company is a proud sponsor of the Future of School, a nonprofit organization dedicated to closing the gap between the pace of technology and the pace of change in education. More information can be found at stridelearning.com, K12.com, destinationsacademy.com, galvanize.com, techelevator.com, and medcerts.com.

ISBN: 978-1-60153-574-0

Printed by Walsworth, Marceline, MO, USA, May 2021.

English Language Arts

Lesson Guide

Book Staff and Contributors

Kristen Kinney-Haines   *Director, English Language Arts*
Amy Rauen   *Director, Instructional Design*
Mary Beck Desmond   *Senior Text Editor*
Allyson Jacob   *Text Editor*
Tricia Battipede   *Senior Creative Manager*
Julie Jankowski   *Senior Visual Designer*
Caitlin Gildrien   *Visual Designer*
Sheila Smith   *Print Designer*
Tricia Battipede, Mike Bohman, Shannon Palmer   *Cover Designers*
Robyn Campbell, Heather Evans, Alane Gernon-Paulsen, Tara Gleason, Tim Mansfield, Melisa Rice,
      Tisha Ruibal   *Writers*
Amy Eward   *Content Specialist; Senior Manager, Writers and Editors*
Dan Smith   *Senior Project Manager*

Doug McCollum   *Senior Vice President, Product Development*
Kristin Morrison   *Vice President, Design, Creative, and User Experience*
Rohit Lakhani   *Vice President, Program Management and Operations*
Kelly Engel   *Senior Director, Curriculum*
Christopher Frescholtz   *Senior Director, Program Management*
Erica Castle   *Director, Creative Services*
Lisa Dimaio Iekel   *Senior Production Manager*

Illustrations Credits

All illustrations © Stride, Inc. unless otherwise noted
Characters: Tommy DiGiovanni, Matt Fedor, Ben Gamache, Shannon Palmer
Cover: Spiral © Silmen/iStock; Polygon © LPETTET/iStock
Program Overview: xxiv Used by permission of HarperCollins Publishers

At Stride, Inc. (NYSE: LRN)—formerly K12 Inc.—we are reimagining lifelong learning as a rich, deeply personal experience that prepares learners for tomorrow. Since its inception, Stride has been committed to removing barriers that impact academic equity and to providing high-quality education for anyone—particularly those in underserved communities. The company has transformed the teaching and learning experience for millions of people by providing innovative, high-quality, tech-enabled education solutions, curriculum, and programs directly to students, schools, the military, and enterprises in primary, secondary, and post-secondary settings. Stride is a premier provider of K-12 education for students, schools, and districts, including career learning services through middle and high school curriculum. Providing a solution to the widening skills gap in the workplace and student loan crisis, Stride equips students with real world skills for in-demand jobs with career learning. For adult learners, Stride delivers professional skills training in healthcare and technology, as well as staffing and talent development for Fortune 500 companies. Stride has delivered millions of courses over the past decade and serves learners in all 50 states and more than 100 countries. The company is a proud sponsor of the Future of School, a nonprofit organization dedicated to closing the gap between the pace of technology and the pace of change in education. More information can be found at stridelearning.com, K12.com, destinationsacademy.com, galvanize.com, techelevator.com, and medcerts.com.

ISBN: 978-1-60153-574-0

Printed by Walsworth, Marceline, MO, USA, May 2021.

Table of Contents

Mystery!

Frontiers of Flight

Pax

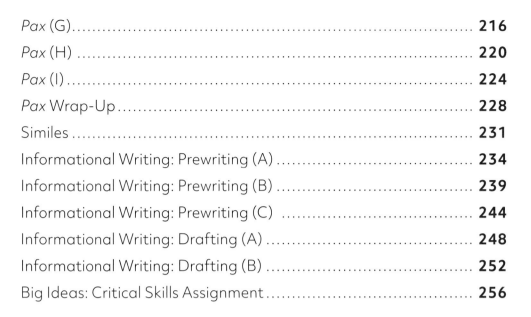

Childhood Classics

Quilting Bee

Choice Reading Project

Men and Women of Character

Healthy and Safe

Underwater Adventures

Life Choices

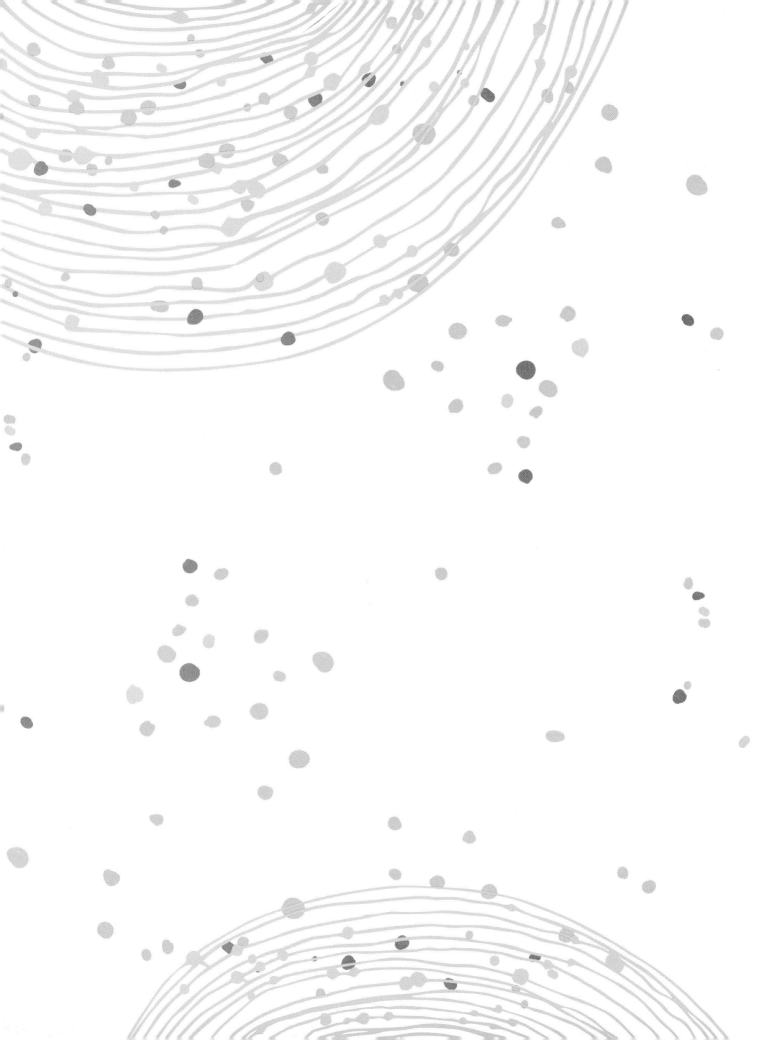

K12 Summit English Language Arts 4 Overview

Welcome to Summit English Language Arts 4. We are grateful for this opportunity to play a role in the English language arts education of your students. We offer this overview of the content and structure of the course as part of our effort to help you best support them. At any time, if you have questions or would like further clarification, please reach out to us. Let's begin.

Summit English Language Arts 4 encourages students to learn independently. As a Learning Coach, your role is to support and enhance the learning experience. Each lesson includes rich interactivity to ensure that students build the depth of understanding they need to succeed on state assessments. Online interactions provide a wealth of data, so teachers know exactly where students are struggling. Offline practice, during which students write directly in an activity book, offers variety. With rich content that engages and motivates students, and enough practice to reinforce each concept, this course includes the tools and technology that students need to succeed.

Course Components

Online Lessons

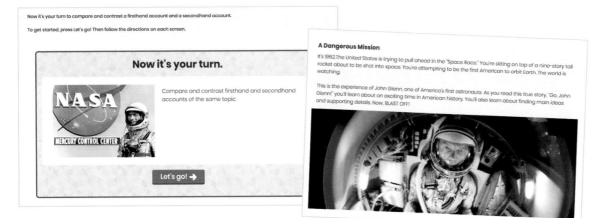

The online lessons make up the core instruction and multiple opportunities for practice in Summit ELA 4. These lessons include

- Instruction in reading, writing, word study, and spelling in a predictable lesson structure

- Interactive activities and assessments that challenge students to use higher-order thinking skills

- A carefully thought-out progression from guided to independent practice

- Computer-scored practice with instant and meaningful feedback

- Learning experiences that support struggling students

- Independent practice using Stride, an adaptive tool that offers individualized practice based on specific need

- Student-friendly learning goals

- Engaging games to review and practice skills

- Access to Big Universe, a digital library of thousands of fiction and nonfiction texts

Rich offline print materials support learning with ample opportunity for students to demonstrate mastery of concepts taught online. Contemporary literature, timely and engaging nonfiction, and a digital library give readers a variety of reading experiences.

Lesson Guide

The lesson guide that accompanies the course makes it quick and easy for Learning Coaches to understand each lesson at a glance—without logging in. The lesson guide provides an overview of a lesson's content, activities, and materials; answer keys for activity book pages; alerts when special Learning Coach attention is needed; and other features to aid the Learning Coach in supporting students.

Activity Book

Summit ELA 4 includes an activity book where students can put pencil to paper every instructional day. Key activity book features:

- Full color pages with sufficient space for students' answers

- Activities that require students to write explanations, analyze and reflect on readings through extended responses, and work through the writing process from brainstorming to publishing

- Custom drafting paper with built-in space for revising

- Spelling Pretest pages that double as study aids

- Spelling Activity Bank pages that offer students choice in how to practice their Spelling words

- A glossary of keywords from the course

Reading Materials

Summit ELA 4 offers students diverse perspectives through both classic and contemporary fiction and nonfiction texts. Print and digital formats are offered. The following materials are included.

Expeditions in Reading: Fiction and nonfiction readings are brought to life through full-color illustrations and photographs. Select words and phrases are defined to support comprehension. While this collection is provided in both print and digital formats, K12 recommends that students read the print format whenever possible and use the digital format on those occasions when learning may need to take place on the go. Research continues to show that students are better able to comprehend their reading when holding a book in their hands.

Trade books: Students receive printed copies of contemporary, high-quality trade books that span genres.

Nonfiction magazines: A full-color magazine, in both print and digital formats, is included with the course and focuses on high-interest topics while teaching students important skills for comprehending a wide variety of text features.

Big Universe: Access to Big Universe, a leveled e-book library, is built into the course. In Big Universe students have at their fingertips over 14,000 fiction and nonfiction texts from more than forty publishers on countless topics.

Course Structure

Summit ELA 4 uses a well-balanced approach to literacy that connects reading, writing, grammar, vocabulary, and spelling into one integrated course. Dedicated time for keyboarding practice is also included. The course is designed to lead students through concepts based on current state and national academic standards. The material is structured to fit a typical 180-day school year, but it can also be easily adapted to fit individual needs.

Summit ELA 4 is divided into **units**. Units are divided into a series of **workshops**, which are in turn divided into **daily lessons**. Each unit contains workshops, and a workshop centers on a major focus (reading, writing, or word study) and also includes spelling practice. Each workshop ends with time dedicated to review and a quiz or graded writing assignment. A separate **Big Ideas** lesson synthesizes the course content and occurs at the end of each unit.

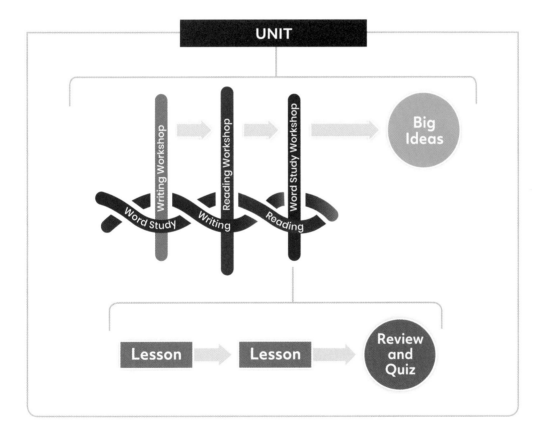

Lesson Model Overview

Reading and writing workshops in Summit ELA 4 follow a multiday learning cycle, consisting of an initial lesson, one or more middle lessons, and a final lesson. Word study workshops, however, are each made up of one lesson only. Regardless of length, each workshop follows a consistent, predictable instructional formula.

GET READY

Get Ready activities introduce and orient students to the lesson content. Spelling activities are also located in the Get Ready section.

LEARN AND TRY IT

Learn and Try It activities include one or more cycles of bite-size instruction coupled with guided practice, followed by opportunities to apply new skills. Reading workshops also contain a Read section, in which students read from the workshop text and answer comprehension questions.

WRAP-UP

Wrap-Up activities include one or two ungraded questions that serve to gauge students' understanding as they exit the lesson. These activities may also include independent practice in Stride, independent reading, and keyboarding practice. On the final day of each workshop, the Wrap-Up section is preceded by a graded quiz or graded written assignment.

Initial and Middle Days   During the initial and middle days, students learn, practice, and apply the core content.

As students work through these lessons, they are asked to work more and more independently. They progress from explicit instruction, through guided practice, to independent practice and application.

Final Day   In reading, word study, and writing skills workshops, the final day of the workshop includes a computer-graded quiz based on the workshop's key objectives. Activities in those lessons prepare students for the quiz. In Planning and Drafting, and Revising and Publishing writing workshops, the final day includes a submitted writing assignment—either students' written drafts or their final published writing pieces.

		INITIAL DAY	MIDDLE DAYS	FINAL DAY
READING WORKSHOP	**GET READY**	Lesson Introduction	Lesson Introduction	Lesson Introduction
		Spelling	Spelling	
		60-Second English	Recall	
		Look Back	Before You Read	
		Before You Read		
	READ	Read	Read	
		Check-In	Check-In	
	LEARN AND TRY IT	**LEARN**	**LEARN**	**TRY IT** Activity Book
		TRY IT Guided	**TRY IT** Guided	Read and Record
		TRY IT Apply	**TRY IT** Apply	Review
		TRY IT Activity Book	**TRY IT** Activity Book	
		TRY IT Vocabulary	**TRY IT** Vocabulary	
	QUIZ			Reading Quiz
				Spelling Quiz
	WRAP-UP	Formative Assessment	Formative Assessment	Stride
WRITING SKILLS WORKSHOP	**GET READY**	Lesson Introduction	Lesson Introduction	Lesson Introduction
		Spelling	Spelling	
		Look Back		
	LEARN AND TRY IT	**LEARN** Grammar, Usage, and Mechanics	**LEARN** Grammar, Usage, and Mechanics	**TRY IT** Activity Book
		TRY IT Grammar, Usage, and Mechanics	**TRY IT** Grammar, Usage, and Mechanics	**Review:** Grammar, Usage, and Mechanics
		LEARN Writing Skills	**LEARN** Writing Skills	
		TRY IT Writing Skills	**TRY IT** Writing Skills	
		TRY IT Activity Book	**TRY IT** Activity Book	
	QUIZ			Writing & Grammar, Usage, and Mechanics Quiz
				Spelling Quiz
	WRAP-UP	Formative Assessment	Formative Assessment	Stride
		Go Read!	Go Read!	

		INITIAL DAY	MIDDLE DAYS	FINAL DAY
PLANNING AND DRAFTING WORKSHOP	**GET READY**	Lesson Introduction	Lesson Introduction	Lesson Introduction
		Spelling	Spelling	
		Look Back		
	LEARN AND TRY IT	**LEARN** Grammar, Usage, and Mechanics	**LEARN** Grammar, Usage, and Mechanics	**Review:** Grammar, Usage, and Mechanics
		TRY IT Grammar, Usage, and Mechanics	**TRY IT** Grammar, Usage, and Mechanics	
		LEARN Writing Skills	**LEARN** Writing Skills	
		TRY IT Writing Skills	**TRY IT** Activity Book	
		TRY IT Activity Book		
	QUIZ			Grammar, Usage, and Mechanics Quiz
				Spelling Quiz
				Submit Draft
	WRAP-UP	Formative Assessment	Formative Assessment	Stride
			Go Read!	
REVISING AND PUBLISHING WORKSHOP	**GET READY**	Lesson Introduction	Lesson Introduction	Lesson Introduction
		Look Back	Look Back	
	LEARN AND TRY IT	**LEARN** Writing Skills	**LEARN** Writing Skills	**LEARN** Writing Skills
		TRY IT Activity Book	**TRY IT** Activity Book	**TRY IT** Writing Skills
	QUIZ			Submit Published Writing
	WRAP-UP	Formative Assessment	Formative Assessment	Stride
		Go Read!	Go Read!	

WORD STUDY WORKSHOP		SINGLE LESSON DAY
	GET READY	Lesson Introduction
		Look Back
	LEARN AND **TRY IT**	**LEARN**
		TRY IT Guided
		TRY IT Activity Book
		Go Write!
		Review
	QUIZ	Word Study Quiz
	WRAP-UP	Stride
		Go Read!

Activity Descriptions

This table describes each activity type in Summit ELA 4.

GET READY	Description
Unit Overview	The Unit Overview briefly introduces students to the content that will be covered in the unit.
Lesson Introduction	The Lesson Introduction introduces the content of each lesson within an engaging context. It also presents the objectives as student-friendly goals, defines new keywords that students will encounter in the lesson, and lists the key state standards covered in the lesson.
Spelling	Spelling activities include pretests, offline practice in the activity book, online practice activities or games, and graded quizzes.
60-Second English	The 60-Second English gets students excited about upcoming content and prompts curiosity.
Before You Read	Before You Read activities introduce vocabulary from the reading by way of online flashcards, provide background information to set context for the upcoming reading, and ask guiding questions to help students set a purpose for reading.
Recall	Recall activities prepare students to continue reading by refreshing their knowledge of what they read in the previous lesson.
Look Back	Look Back activities provide a quick review of the prerequisite skills that are essential to understanding the new content. Students who struggle with the Look Back should seek additional help before proceeding.

LEARN AND TRY IT	Description
Read	Read activities direct students to complete an independent reading assignment.
Check-In	Check-In activities evaluate students' basic comprehension of what they just read. These activities are not graded, but results are visible to the teacher.
Learn	Learn activities are direct instruction. The format of this instruction varies, including guided exploration of a text or writing sample with narrated animation, or video featuring an expert teacher and interactive questions.
Try It	Learn activities are followed by a series of Try It activities. Try It activities differ depending on topic and specific purpose, but all share the purpose of allowing students to practice and apply what they've learned.
Read and Record	Read and Record activities allow students to practice reading fluently. Students record themselves reading text aloud, listen to their recording, and evaluate their reading using a fluency checklist.
Review	Students review the workshop content either by answering questions or playing a game, after which they take a graded quiz.
Go Write!	Go Write! activities provide dedicated time for freewriting.

WRAP-UP	Description
Formative Assessment	Formative assessments are those activities with "Questions About" in the activity title. These include 1–2 ungraded questions that gauge students' understanding at the end of the lesson. Although the questions are ungraded, the results are available to teachers.
Quiz	Final days of workshops include graded online quizzes, and/or graded writing assignments that students must submit.
Stride	Additional independent practice with ELA concepts is provided in Stride.
Go Read!	Go Read! activities allow for free reading time at the end of Writing and Word Study workshops.

A Balance of Online and Offline Time

Summit ELA 4 online activities make up about 60 percent of core lesson time. Equally critical to learning is that students spend time reading (for both instruction and pleasure), and put pencil to paper. Summit ELA 4 incorporates daily reading, and offline activities in a predictable place in each lesson sequence. After completing online practice in which instant feedback can help to address any misunderstandings, students complete an activity in their activity book or continue to work on a longer writing assignment.

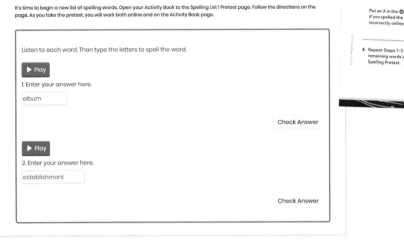

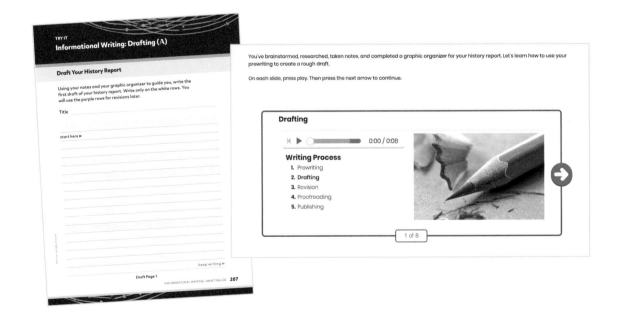

Special Features

In addition to the standard units and lessons, Summit ELA 4 has these special features.

Big Ideas Lessons

A Big Ideas lesson occurs at the end of each unit. In these lessons, students keep their skills fresh by reviewing prior content, practice answering the types of questions they will encounter on state assessments, and complete an assignment that allows them to connect and apply what they have learned. Note that some of these assignments are graded assessments.

Choice Reading Projects

Summit ELA 4 contains one Choice Reading Project unit. In this unit, students encounter a unique reading workshop designed to build their comprehension and critical-thinking skills as they read a work or works of their choice and complete a related project. Research indicates that opportunities for choice enhance student performance and motivate readers.

Students will select a project and corresponding book or books from a bank of options. All but one of the projects will require you to acquire a book on your own. The remaining project option will use a book or books available in Big Universe. To help students make a choice, the online lessons include synopses of the books and descriptions of the related projects. Review the options with students well enough in advance so that, if selecting a project whose related reading is not in Big Universe, you can acquire the necessary book in time for students to begin the unit.

Embedded Keyboarding Practice

On Your Choice days, students will practice their keyboarding skills using an external website or program. You will need to work with students to select an appropriate keyboarding practice website or program; K12 does not specify which resource to use. A few suggestions are provided in the online activity, including a program that is navigable by keyboard and screen-reader accessible. Depending on which program is chosen, students may need to set up an account to save their progress. You should assist with this, if needed.

Assessment Overview

To ensure that students can show what they have learned and to support high academic outcomes, students need exposure to the types of questions they will see on state assessments.

Online Interactive Questions

Online interactive questions, similar in style and format to today's digital state assessments, provide powerful opportunities for students to demonstrate deep understanding. For this reason, a variety of online question types, including drag-and-drop and fill-in-the-blank, are used throughout Summit ELA 4.

Correctly fill in the blank.

I wouldn't have believed that a dog could surf, but I was at the beach this summer and I saw a collie catch a wave _____. It was one of the most incredible things I've ever witnessed.

dedicated   segregation   firsthand

Check Answer

← 1 2 3 →

Which word or phrase **best** completes the passage?

I was just waking up when I heard the [✓ Choose... / whoosh / slurp / squelch / pitter patter] of little feet outside in the hallway. Then came the gentle taps on my door and more so... huffling behind it, and I knew my youngest cousins had arrived.

Check Answer

← 1 2 3 4 5 6 7 8 9 →

Graded Assessments

Summit ELA 4 includes both online computer-scored quizzes and teacher-graded assignments.

Assessment Type	How Many?
Workshop Quizzes	52
Spelling Quizzes	27
Writing Assignments - Drafts	4
Writing Assignments - Published	4
Big-Ideas: Mini-Projects	4
Big Ideas: Critical Skills Assignments	4
Big Ideas: Responses to Prompts	4
Choice Reading Project	1
Mid-Year Assessment	1
End-of-Year Assessment	1

Instructional Approach: Reading Workshops

Close Reading and Textual Analysis

Summit ELA 4 uses a close-reading approach: students read first for comprehension and then reread to support further study of texts. Research shows that students who participate in repeated readings of instructional-level texts demonstrate better outcomes.

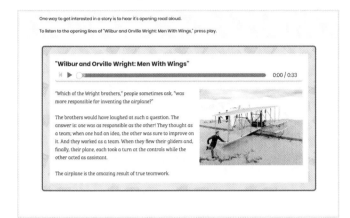

Students are first introduced to a reading selection by listening to a brief reading from it.

Students then spend dedicated time reading independently.

In the Learn activity, students engage in guided analysis of the text.

A Mix of Contemporary and Classic Literature and Engaging Informational Texts

The reading workshops engage students in works of literature and nonfiction texts from various genres. In grade 4, the program is an even split between fiction and nonfiction. The fiction selections provide students with contemporary novels to enjoy and picture books to savor, as well as classic tales retold in a new way. Nonfiction topics are wide and varied; students interact with magazines, biographical stories, websites, and even videos.

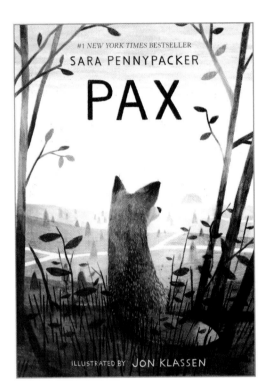

Reading List

TITLE	AUTHOR	DELIVERY	GENRE
Adelita	Tomie dePaola	trade book	fiction
Baseball Saved Us	Ken Mochizuki	trade book	fiction
Bed in Summer	Robert Louis Stevenson	*Expeditions in Reading*	poetry
Cinderella	K12	*Expeditions in Reading*	fiction
Coral Reef Food Chains	Rebecca Pettiford	trade book	nonfiction
Coral Reefs	Kristin Baird Rattini	trade book	nonfiction
Coral Reefs	Jason Chin	trade book	nonfiction
Counterfeit Money: Then and Now	K12	nonfiction magazine	nonfiction
Dangerous Adventure! Lindbergh's Famous Flight	Ruth Belov Gross	*Expeditions in Reading*	nonfiction
Elizabeth Blackwell: Pioneering Physician	Vanessa Wright	*Expeditions in Reading*	nonfiction
From Cave Paintings to Emoji	K12	nonfiction magazine	nonfiction
Glass Slipper, Gold Sandal: A Worldwide Cinderella	Paul Fleischman and Julie Paschkis	trade book	fiction
Go, John Glenn!	Brian Floca	*Expeditions in Reading*	nonfiction
Grace	K12	*Expeditions in Reading*	fiction
Ibrahim	K12	*Expeditions in Reading*	fiction
John Glenn and Friendship 7	adapted from NASA.org	*Expeditions in Reading*	nonfiction
Keeping Safe from Rabies	adapted from kids.gov	website	nonfiction
Louis Pasteur: Battle With Death	Dorothy Haas	*Expeditions in Reading*	nonfiction
Maria Gonzalez, Modern Hero	K12	*Expeditions in Reading*	fiction
Pax	K12	trade book	fiction, novel
Pink and Say	K12	trade book	fiction
Project Mercury Fiftieth Anniversary	from Interview with John Glenn by Audie Cornish	*Expeditions in Reading*	nonfiction
Rikki Tikki Tavi	from *The Jungle Book* by Rudyard Kipling	*Expeditions in Reading*	fiction

Reading List (continued)

TITLE	AUTHOR	DELIVERY	GENRE
Staying Safe While Being Active	adapted from kids.gov	website	nonfiction
Still Standing: The Leaning Tower of PIsa	K12	nonfiction magazine	nonfiction
Sweet Clara and the Freedom Quilt	Deborah Hopkins	trade book	fiction
Tayo's Wishes	K12	*Expeditions in Reading*	fiction
The Challenge: Bessie Coleman's Story	Margaret Roberts	*Expeditions in Reading*	nonfiction
The Ecchoing Green	William Blake	*Expeditions in Reading*	poetry
The Gold Coin	Alma Flor Ada	*Expeditions in Reading*	fiction
The Grateful Stork	a Japanese folktale retold by Yoshiko Uchida	*Expeditions in Reading*	fiction
The Green Glass Ball	an Irish folktale dramatized by Hazel W. Corson	*Expeditions in Reading*	fiction, drama
The Keeping Quilt	Patricia Polacco	trade book	fiction
The Many Colors of Birds	K12	*Expeditions in Reading*	nonfiction
The Mystery of the Missing Hamburger	K12	*Expeditions in Reading*	fiction, mystery
The Mystery of the Topaz Heart	K12	*Expeditions in Reading*	fiction, mystery
The Quilting Bee	Gail Gibbons	trade book	nonfiction
Try, Try Again	T.H. Palmer	*Expeditions in Reading*	poetry
Two Views of Project Mercury	K12	*Expeditions in Reading*	nonfiction
Why Kids Should Eat Healthy and Exercise	adapted from kids.gov	website	nonfiction
Wilbur and Orville Wright: Men with Wings	Dorothy Haas	*Expeditions in Reading*	nonfiction
Wynken, Blynken, and Nod	Eugene Field	*Expeditions in Reading*	poetry
Yeh Shen	retold by Ai Ling Louie	trade book	fiction

Instructional Approach: Writing Workshops

A Balance of Explicit Instruction and Authentic Writing Experiences

Summit ELA 4 writing workshops prepare students to express themselves as educated people in the twenty-first century. Students analyze model writing samples and then work through the writing process to develop original compositions of their own. An emphasis on thoughtful planning takes the fear out of writing as students learn tangible strategies to make the process manageable. Grammar, usage, and mechanics activities focus on grammatical terms, sentence construction, recognizing and fixing errors, punctuation, and using precise language. Students practice these skills in editing activities and apply them to their own writing assignments.

An Organized Approach to Teaching Process

Students will complete four major assignments by following the writing process: prewriting, drafting, revising, proofreading, and publishing. Assignments include a personal narrative, a science report, an editorial, and a history presentation. Each assignment is completed over a series of two workshops, with both the rough draft and the final work submitted to the teacher. Additional writing skills workshops break down the skills needed using model writing samples and short writing assignments.

Research skills, including how to do research online ethically and effectively, are an integral part of the writing workshops. Students will conduct and incorporate research into their informational, opinion, and presentation writing.

UNITS 1-3	UNITS 4-6	UNITS 7-9	UNITS 10-12
NARRATIVE	INFORMATIONAL	OPINION	PRESENTATION
Writing Skills	Writing Skills	Writing Skills	Writing Skills
Plan and Draft	Plan and Draft	Plan and Draft	Plan and Draft
Revise and Publish	Revise and Publish	Revise and Publish	Revise and Publish

Instructional Approach: Word Study Workshops

A Focus on Words and Strategies

Word study workshops expose students to a wide variety of vocabulary words, which in turn helps them with reading comprehension and writing. In each word study workshop, students are taught a set of vocabulary words and definitions while also learning about word relationships and using context clues to figure out unfamiliar words. Students look at synonyms, antonyms, and etymology to expand on the core word set. Workshop topics run from understanding nuance and shades of meaning to using Greek and Latin roots and affixes to determine word meanings. Several workshops are dedicated to figurative language and homonyms, providing a thorough word study experience that helps grow students' speaking, reading, listening, and writing vocabularies.

Instructional Approach: Spelling

A Focus on Patterns

In Summit ELA 4 students learn to spell words quickly by studying spelling patterns that are common to many words. Throughout the word lists, students develop an understanding of sound-symbol relationships and spelling patterns, identify affixes and how they affect the meaning of words, and recognize base words and roots in related words.

However, some words do not follow conventional spelling patterns. Spelling lists in Summit ELA 4 include words that follow the spelling pattern being studied, as well as "Heart Words" (words we must learn to spell by heart).

Repetition, Variety, and Choice

In nearly all lessons, students are given opportunities to practice and master the spelling words. Each spelling list begins with a pretest, showing which words the student may already know and which require more practice. Pretests are followed by offline practice in which students complete an activity of their choice from a supplied bank. From there, students continue with online practice and a review game before wrapping up the spelling cycle with a graded quiz.

Individualized Learning

Summit ELA 4 is designed to help all students succeed.

Branching Pathways Particularly difficult concepts include practice with branching pathways for struggling students. These interactions are designed to uncover misconceptions and common errors to create a "tighter net" that catches struggling students at the point of instruction. Students receive feedback targeted to their individual responses and are then led through a reteaching activity that corrects the misconception or common error, if they need it.

Stride An engaging teaching tool that motivates students toward mastery and rewards learning with games, Stride offers students individualized practice. Following each workshop's quiz, students will practice related concepts based on their specific needs. Time to use Stride is integrated right into the course to ensure sufficient independent practice time.

Stride's adaptive technology guides students to practice where they need it most—and then serves up a variety of content that is lively and engaging. Stride's vast database of questions, video lessons, and printable resources delivers grade-level appropriate content aligned to the rigor of the Common Core and individual state standards. Stride's assessments identify where students are performing on specific grade-level standards throughout the year and help identify critical foundational gaps missed in prior grade levels. Test prep capabilities pinpoint student strengths and weaknesses for improved student outcomes on end-of-year assessments.

The Help Me Button Located on the lesson menu, this is an additional personalization feature that lets students opt into activities that are dynamically chosen based on the concept they are studying. Recommendations are powered by a sophisticated engine designed to serve up the activities most likely to be effective for the individual student.

How to Use This Guide

This lesson guide contains information that will be helpful to you as you begin Summit English Language Arts 4 and daily as you work through the program. Here is what the lesson guide contains and how to use it.

Lesson Title

The lesson title indicates the lesson topic and matches the title you will see in the online course.

Learning Coach Check-In

This label indicates that your participation is particularly important for the activity it appears in. A description of how to support your student is included with the specific activity in the Activities section of the lesson guide.

Content Background

This information will help you better understand the content students will be learning.

Synopsis

In reading lessons, this section gives a brief summary of the reading selection.

Lesson Goals

The goals indicate what students will do in the lesson.

Lesson Overview Table

This table shows an overview of the lesson's activities, their approximate times, and whether students complete them offline or online.

Materials

This box lists all materials needed for the lesson and indicates whether each material is Supplied or Also Needed.

Keywords

The definitions of key terminology specific to lesson concepts are given here.

Activities

Each lesson is broken down into three or more main sections Get Ready, Read, Learn and Try It, Quiz and Wrap-Up. Each section is broken down into individual activities.

Answer Key

The lesson guide includes answer keys for activity book pages.

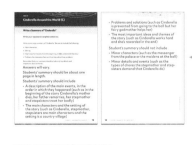

Lessons with Graded Assessments

Check in with students when a lesson has a graded assessment.

- The final lesson of every workshop has a computer-scored quiz. Check to make sure students have completed and submitted this quiz.

- Teacher-graded assignments appear throughout the course. You may need to help students submit these assignments to their teacher. Discuss with the teacher the best method of turning in students' work.

Remember

Academic support at home is critical to student success. While Summit ELA 4 empowers students to work independently, this guide is designed help you support your students each day to help them maximize their learning.

Cinderella
Around the World

Cinderella Around the World (A)

Lesson Overview

ACTIVITY	ACTIVITY TITLE	TIME	ONLINE/OFFLINE
GET READY	Cinderella Around the World Unit Overview	**1** minute	online
	Introduction to Cinderella Around the World (A)	**1** minute	online
	Spelling List 1 Pretest **LEARNING COACH CHECK-IN**	**10** minutes	online and offline
	Cinderella Around the World in 60 seconds	**1** minute	online
	Look Back at Theme	**4** minutes	online
	Before You Read *Yeh-Shen*	**14** minutes	online
READ	*Yeh-Shen*	**30** minutes	offline
	Check-In: *Yeh-Shen*	**5** minutes	online
LEARN AND **TRY IT**	Theme in *Yeh-Shen*	**10** minutes	online
	Determine Theme in *Yeh-Shen*	**10** minutes	online
	Apply: Theme	**15** minutes	online
	Write About Theme **LEARNING COACH CHECK-IN**	**10** minutes	offline
	Practice Words from *Yeh-Shen*	**7** minutes	online
WRAP-UP	Question About *Yeh-Shen*	**2** minutes	online

Content Background

Students will complete a spelling activity and read *Yeh-Shen: A Cinderella Story from China* retold by Ai-Ling Louie. They will then complete activities in which they learn about themes, how to distinguish topics from themes, and how to determine themes from evidence in a text.

Themes, the big ideas that authors convey in text, emerge and develop over the course of a story. To identify a theme, good readers pay attention to what the characters in a story say and do. Themes and topics are related, but topics are a single word while themes are complete thoughts or statements. Identifying a topic can lead a reader to identify a theme.

MATERIALS

Supplied

- *Yeh-Shen: A Cinderella Story from China* retold by Ai-Ling Louie
- *Summit English Language Arts 4 Activity Book*
  - Spelling List 1 Pretest
  - Write About Theme

Topic: love

Theme: Love is more important than money.

KEYWORDS

theme – the author's message or big idea

Yeh-Shen Synopsis

In this Chinese version of the Cinderella tale, Yeh-Shen is a young woman being raised by her cruel stepmother. Her only friend is a large fish, which her stepmother kills and eats. But the bones of Yeh-Shen's fish are magical. They help her attend the festival where young men and women meet possible partners. At the festival, Yeh-Shen believes she has been recognized, so she runs away but leaves behind a golden sandal. The king seeks the owner of the tiny shoe, which Yeh-Shen attempts to retrieve in the dark of night. The king follows Yeh-Shen home and asks her to try on the sandal. Her identity is revealed, and the king and Yeh-Shen are married.

Lesson Goals

- Take a spelling pretest.
- Read *Yeh-Shen: A Cinderella Story from China* retold by Ai-Ling Louie.
- Examine theme and vocabulary in *Yeh-Shen*.

GET READY

Cinderella Around the World Unit Overview

Students will read a summary of what they will learn in the Cinderella Around the World unit.

Introduction to Cinderella Around the World (A)

Students will get a glimpse of what they will learn about in the lesson. They will also read the lesson goals and keywords. Have students select each keyword and preview its definition.

Spelling List 1 Pretest

Students will take a spelling pretest.

LEARNING COACH CHECK-IN   Have students turn to Spelling List 1 Pretest in *Summit English Language Arts 4 Activity Book* and open the online Spelling Pretest activity. Online, students will listen to the spelling word, type the word in the space indicated, and then check their answer. In the activity book, students will write the correct spelling of the word in the tables provided and indicate with a ✓ or an ✗ if they spelled the word correctly or incorrectly online. Students will repeat this process with the remaining words.

As needed, help students with the interaction between the online activity and the activity book page until they become comfortable with what they need to do. As students practice their spelling words throughout the workshop, they should pay special attention to words they spelled incorrectly on the pretest.

This is the complete list of words students will be tested on.

Short Vowels	Base *magnet*	Prefix *re–*	Heart Words
album	magnet	rewind	Connecticut
establishment	magnetic	renew	Wisconsin
admit	magnetism	replace	could
insect	magnetize	revise	people
object			
optimist			
planet			
subject			
absent			
habitat			
system			
witness			
contest			

NOTE Have students keep their completed activity page in a safe place so they can refer to it later.

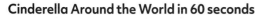

Cinderella Around the World in 60 seconds
Students will watch a short video designed to spark their interest in upcoming topics.

Look Back at Theme
Students will practice the prerequisite skill of determining themes.

Before You Read *Yeh-Shen*
Students will be introduced to some key vocabulary words that they will encounter in the upcoming reading, learn some cultural and historical background related to the reading, and answer questions to help them set a purpose for their reading.

READ

Yeh-Shen
Students will read the book *Yeh-Shen: A Cinderella Story from China* retold by Ai-Ling Louie.

Check-In: *Yeh-Shen*
Students will answer questions to demonstrate their comprehension of *Yeh-Shen*.

LEARN AND TRY IT

LEARN   Theme in *Yeh-Shen*
Students will learn about theme and how to determine themes in a story.

SUPPORT   Check that students are able to distinguish topics from themes. For students having difficulty with this, select a passage from the book and think aloud to model determining a topic and that topic's relationship to a theme. For example, when the king hides as he watches women try on the shoe at the pavilion, he is very patient. Patience is a topic. It can be used in a sentence to express a theme, such as, "patience pays off in the end."

TRY IT   Determine Theme in *Yeh-Shen*
Students will analyze passages and answer questions related to the story's themes.

TRY IT   Apply: Theme
Students will apply to a new work what they've learned about theme.

TRY IT   Write About Theme
Students will complete Write About Theme from *Summit English Language Arts 4 Activity Book*.

LEARNING COACH CHECK-IN This activity page contains open-ended questions, so it's important that you review students' responses. Give students feedback, using the sample answers provided to guide you.

TRY IT
Cinderella Around the World (A)

Write About Theme

Read the passage from *Yeh-Shen: A Cinderella Story from China* retold by Ai-Ling Louie. Then answer the questions in complete sentences.

> The old man sighed and said, "Yes, my child, your fish is no longer alive, and I must tell you that your stepmother is once more the cause of your sorrow." Yeh-Shen gasped in horror, but the old man went on. "Let us not dwell on things that are past," he said, "for I have come bringing you a gift. Now you must listen carefully to this: The bones of your fish are filled with a powerful spirit. Whenever you are in serious need, you must kneel before them and let them know your heart's desire. But do not waste their gifts."

1. To determine the themes of a story, readers must consider the characters' actions.

   a. Based on the passage, what word best describes the actions of Yeh-Shen's stepmother? Identify a sentence from the passage that

   Answers will vary. Students' answer should demonstrate an understanding that the stepmother's actions are cruel or hurtful to Yeh-Shen. This is indicated by this sentence: "The old man sighed and said, 'Yes, my child, your fish is no longer alive, and I must tell you that your stepmother is once more the cause of your sorrow.'"

   CINDERELLA AROUND THE WORLD (A) **3**

---

   b. What lesson might readers learn from the stepmother's actions?

   Students' answer should indicate a lesson that conveys the consequences of cruel or unkind actions. Readers might learn that unkind actions are often punished.

2. A theme is a message an author wants to share with readers. It is something the author wants readers to learn about life.

   a. What is one of the themes of *Yeh-Shen: A Cinderella Story from China?*

   Answers will vary.
   Possible answers: Looks can be deceiving; kindness and generosity are rewarded.

   b. What evidence from the text supports this theme?

   Answers will vary.
   Possible evidence for "Looks can be deceiving" is the king believing Yeh-Shen is a thief because she is wearing ragged clothes. Possible evidence for "Kindness and generosity are rewarded" is the fish bones rewarding Yeh-Shen or Yeh-Shen's marrying the king in the end.

   4 CINDERELLA AROUND THE WORLD (A)

TRY IT   Practice Words from *Yeh-Shen*

Students will answer questions to demonstrate their understanding of the vocabulary words from the reading.

WRAP-UP

Question About *Yeh-Shen*

Students will answer a question to show that they understand themes in *Yeh-Shen*.

Cinderella Around the World (B)

Lesson Overview

ACTIVITY	ACTIVITY TITLE	TIME	ONLINE/OFFLINE
GET READY	Introduction to Cinderella Around the World (B)	**1** minute	
	Spelling List 1 Activity Bank	**10** minutes	
	Recall *Yeh-Shen*	**5** minutes	
	Before You Read *Adelita*	**9** minutes	
READ	*Adelita*	**30** minutes	
	Check-In: *Adelita*	**5** minutes	
LEARN AND **TRY IT**	Summarizing *Adelita*	**10** minutes	
	Practice Summarizing	**10** minutes	
	Apply: Summarizing	**15** minutes	
	Prepare to Write a Summary of *Adelita* **LEARNING COACH CHECK-IN**	**15** minutes	
	Practice Words from *Adelita*	**8** minutes	
WRAP-UP	Question About *Adelita*	**2** minutes	

Content Background

Students will complete a spelling activity, review what they've read in *Yeh-Shen: A Cinderella Story from China* retold by Ai-Ling Louie, and read *Adelita: A Mexican Cinderella Story* by Tomie de Paolo. They will then complete activities in which they learn about writing a summary of a story.

A summary is a brief retelling of a text or story. It should include only the most important events and details of a story. Summarizing is an important strategy that good readers use to pick out the most important ideas of a story and distinguish those from less important information. Summarizing is a way to check that students understand what they have read. It also helps them to remember what they have read.

MATERIALS

Supplied
- *Adelita: A Mexican Cinderella Story* by Tomie de Paolo
- *Summit English Language Arts 4 Activity Book*
  - Spelling List 1 Activity Bank
  - Prepare to Write a Summary of *Adelita*

Also Needed
- completed Spelling List 1 Pretest activity page from Cinderella Around the World (A)

Advance Preparation

Gather students' completed Spelling List 1 Pretest activity page from *Cinderella Around the World (A)*. Students will refer to this page during Get Ready: Spelling List 1 Activity Bank.

Adelita Synopsis

This version of the Cinderella story takes place in a Mexican village. After the death of her mother, Adelita is raised by her father and the loyal Esperanza. Her father remarries and dies, leaving Adelita at the mercy of her cruel stepmother and stepsisters. When a neighboring family holds a party for their son, Adelita's stepmother does not allow her to go. There is no fairy godmother. Instead, Adelita attends the party with the help of Esperanza. And, instead of a glass slipper, she wears her mother's beautiful shawl. When the son seeks out the mysterious young woman who ran away from the party, he recognizes her by the beautiful shawl.

Lesson Goals

- Practice all spelling words offline.
- Read *Adelita: A Mexican Cinderella Story* by Tomie de Paolo.
- Examine the important details to include in a summary of *Adelita*.
- Study the vocabulary in *Adelita*.

GET READY

Introduction to Cinderella Around the World (B)

Students will get a glimpse of what they will learn about in the lesson. They will also read the lesson goals and keywords. Have students select each keyword and preview its definition.

Spelling List 1 Activity Bank

Students will practice all spelling words from the workshop by completing Spelling List 1 Activity Bank from *Summit English Language Arts 4 Activity Book*. Make sure students have their completed Spelling List 1 Pretest activity page from Cinderella Around the World (A) to refer to during this activity.

Remind students to pay special attention to the words they spelled incorrectly on the Spelling Pretest.

GET READY
Cinderella Around the World (B)

Spelling List 1 Activity Bank

Circle any words in the box that you did not spell correctly on the pretest. Using your circled words, complete one activity of your choice. Complete as much of the activity as you can in the time given.

If you spelled all words correctly on the pretest, complete your chosen activity with as many spelling words as you can.

album	optimist	system	magnetism	people
establishment	planet	witness	magnetize	rewind
admit	subject	contest	Connecticut	renew
insect	absent	magnet	Wisconsin	replace
object	habitat	magnetic	could	revise

Spelling Activity Choices

Vowel-Free Words

1. In the left column, write only the consonants in each word and put a dot where each vowel should be.
2. Spell each word out loud, stating which vowels should be in the places you wrote dots.
3. In the right column, rewrite the entire spelling word.
4. Correct any spelling errors.

Alphabetizing

1. In the left column, write your words from the spelling word list in alphabetical order.
2. Correct any spelling errors.

Rhymes

1. In the left column, write your words from the spelling word list.
2. In the right column, write a rhyming word for each of your spelling words.
3. Correct any spelling errors.

Uppercase and Lowercase

1. In the left column, write each of your words in all capital letters, or all uppercase.
2. In the right column, write each of your words in all lowercase letters.
3. Correct any spelling errors.

Complete the activity that you chose.

My chosen activity: _____

1. _____
2. _____
3. _____
4. _____
5. _____
6. _____
7. _____
8. _____
9. _____
10. _____

Students should use this page to complete all steps in their chosen activity.

11. _____
12. _____
13. _____
14. _____
15. _____
16. _____
17. _____
18. _____
19. _____
20. _____
21. _____
22. _____
23. _____
24. _____
25. _____

Recall *Yeh-Shen*

Students will answer some questions to review the reading that they have already completed.

Before You Read *Adelita*

Students will be introduced to some key vocabulary words that they will encounter in the upcoming reading and answer questions to help them set a purpose for their reading.

READ

Adelita

Students will read *Adelita: A Mexican Cinderella Story* by Tomie de Paola.

Check-In: *Adelita*

Students will answer questions to demonstrate their understanding of *Adelita*.

LEARN AND TRY IT

LEARN   Summarizing *Adelita*

Students will learn about summarizing and how to determine information that should be included in the summary of a story.

TRY IT   Practice Summarizing

Students will analyze passages and answer questions about information that should be included in a summary of a story.

If students are unsure if a detail should be included in a summary, ask the following question: Would they still understand the story if the information were left out? If they would still understand the story, then the detail in question would not need to be in a summary.

TRY IT Apply: Summarizing

Students will apply to a new work what they've learned about summarizing.

TRY IT Prepare To Write a Summary of *Adelita*

Students will record information that would be important to include in a summary of *Adelita*. Have students complete Prepare to Write a Summary of *Adelita* from *Summit English Language Arts 4 Activity Book*.

This activity page contains open-ended questions, so it's important that you review students' responses. Give students feedback, using the sample answers provided to guide you.

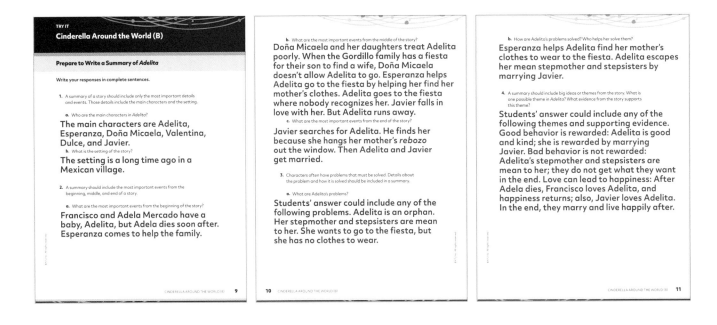

TRY IT Cinderella Around the World (B)

Prepare to Write a Summary of *Adelita*

Write your responses in complete sentences.

1. A summary of a story should include only the most important details and events. Those details include the main characters and the setting.

a. Who are the main characters in *Adelita*?
The main characters are Adelita, Esperanza, Doña Micaela, Valentina, Dulce, and Javier.

b. What is the setting of the story?
The setting is a long time ago in a Mexican village.

2. A summary should include the most important events from the beginning, middle, and end of a story.

a. What are the most important events from the beginning of the story?
Francisco and Adela Mercado have a baby, Adelita, but Adela dies soon after. Esperanza comes to help the family.

b. What are the most important events from the middle of the story?
Doña Micaela and her daughters treat Adelita poorly. When the Gordillo family has a fiesta for their son to find a wife, Doña Micaela doesn't allow Adelita to go. Esperanza helps Adelita go to the fiesta by helping her find her mother's clothes. Adelita goes to the fiesta where nobody recognizes her. Javier falls in love with her. But Adelita runs away.

c. What are the most important events from the end of the story?
Javier searches for Adelita. He finds her because she hangs her mother's *rebozo* out the window. Then Adelita and Javier get married.

3. Characters often have problems that must be solved. Details about the problem and how it is solved should be included in a summary.

a. What are Adelita's problems?
Students' answer could include any of the following problems. Adelita is an orphan. Her stepmother and stepsisters are mean to her. She wants to go to the fiesta, but she has no clothes to wear.

b. How are Adelita's problems solved? Who helps her solve them?
Esperanza helps Adelita find her mother's clothes to wear to the fiesta. Adelita escapes her mean stepmother and stepsisters by marrying Javier.

4. A summary should include big ideas or themes from the story. What is one possible theme in *Adelita*? What evidence from the story supports this theme?
Students' answer could include any of the following themes and supporting evidence. Good behavior is rewarded: Adelita is good and kind; she is rewarded by marrying Javier. Bad behavior is not rewarded: Adelita's stepmother and stepsisters are mean to her; they do not get what they want in the end. Love can lead to happiness: After Adela dies, Francisco loves Adelita, and happiness returns; also, Javier loves Adelita. In the end, they marry and live happily after.

CINDERELLA AROUND THE WORLD (B) 9
10 CINDERELLA AROUND THE WORLD (B)
CINDERELLA AROUND THE WORLD (B) 11

TRY IT Practice Words from *Adelita*

Students will answer questions to demonstrate their understanding of the vocabulary words from the reading.

WRAP-UP

Question About *Adelita*

Students will answer a question to show that they understand the type of information to include in a summary.

Cinderella Around the World (C)

Lesson Overview

ACTIVITY	ACTIVITY TITLE	TIME	ONLINE/OFFLINE
GET READY	Introduction to Cinderella Around the World (C)	**1** minute	
	Spelling List 1 Practice	**10** minutes	
	Recall *Adelita*	**5** minutes	
	Before You Read "Cinderella"	**9** minutes	
READ	"Cinderella"	**30** minutes	
	Check-In: "Cinderella"	**5** minutes	
LEARN AND **TRY IT**	Details Are Key	**10** minutes	
	Key Details in "Cinderella"	**10** minutes	
	Apply: Key Details	**15** minutes	
	Write a Summary of "Cinderella" **LEARNING COACH CHECK-IN**	**15** minutes	
	Practice Words from "Cinderella"	**8** minutes	
WRAP-UP	Question About "Cinderella"	**2** minutes	

Content Background

Students will complete a spelling activity, review *Adelita: A Mexican Cinderella Story* by Tomie de Paolo, and read "Cinderella" in *Expeditions in Reading*. They will then complete activities in which they learn how to distinguish key details, which are the most important details in a story, from minor details, which are less important than key details.

Key details include the main characters, the setting, and the most important events of the plot. Minor details are extra information that help a reader to visualize a scene and gain a better understanding of the key details.

For example, a key detail in "Cinderella" is that the stepmother and stepsisters treat Cinderella badly. Some minor details are that the stepmother and stepsisters yell at Cinderella, and they make her do all the cooking, cleaning, and mending. These minor details help the reader to visualize Cinderella's day-to-day life, and they give the reader a deeper understanding of the key detail that Cinderella is treated badly.

MATERIALS

Supplied
- *Summit English Language Arts 4 Expeditions in Reading*
- *Summit English Language Arts 4 Activity Book*
  - Write a Summary of "Cinderella"

"Cinderella" Synopsis

In this more traditional version of Cinderella, a young maiden is forced to be a servant to her stepmother and stepsisters. Cinderella's father misinterprets her smudged clothes and tears, thus not recognizing how badly she is being treated. When an invitation to a royal ball arrives, Cinderella believes that her hard work will pay off and she will be allowed to attend. But her stepmother and stepsisters prevent her from going. Cinderella's fairy godmother steps in, providing her with a gown, glass slippers, and a carriage to take her to the ball. But the magic wears off at midnight. Cinderella rushes away from the ball leaving behind the prince holding a glass slipper. Once Cinderella is identified as the owner of the glass slipper, she is swept off to the castle to be with her prince.

KEYWORDS

detail – a fact or description that tells more about a topic

summary – a short retelling that includes only the most important ideas or events of a text

Lesson Goals

- Practice all spelling words online.
- Read "Cinderella."
- Examine the key details in, write a summary of, and study the vocabulary in "Cinderella."

GET READY

Introduction to "Cinderella"
Students will get a glimpse of what they will learn about in the lesson. They will also read the lesson goals and keywords. Have students select each keyword and preview its definition.

Spelling List 1 Practice
Students will practice all spelling words from the workshop.

Recall *Adelita*
Students will answer questions to review the reading that they have already completed.

Before You Read "Cinderella"

Students will be introduced to some key vocabulary words that they will encounter in the upcoming reading and answer questions to help them set a purpose for their reading.

READ

"Cinderella"

Students will read "Cinderella" in *Expeditions in Reading*.

Check-In: "Cinderella"

Students will answer several questions to demonstrate their comprehension of "Cinderella."

LEARN AND TRY IT

LEARN   Details Are Key

Students will learn how to identify key details, which are the most important details, as well as the difference between key details and less important or minor details.

TRY IT   Key Details in "Cinderella"

Students will analyze passages and answer questions in which they distinguish between key details and minor details

> **TIP**   Be sure students recognize that key details are used when writing a summary. The key details they identify in this activity could be used in the Write a Summary of "Cinderella" activity, so students may want to jot them down.

TRY IT   Apply: Key Details

Students will read another work and identify key details that would be included in a summary.

TRY IT   Write a Summary of "Cinderella"

Students will complete Write a Summary of "Cinderella" from *Summit English Language Arts 4 Activity Book*.

> **LEARNING COACH CHECK-IN**   This activity page contains an open-ended assignment, so it's important that you review students' responses. Give students feedback, using the sample answers provided to guide you.

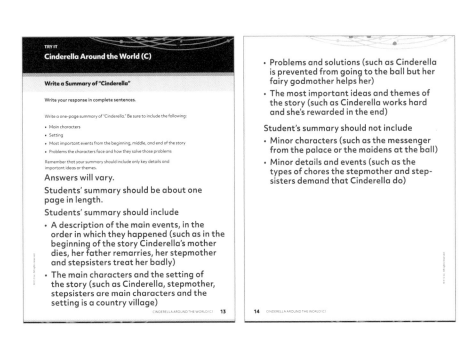

TRY IT **Practice Words from "Cinderella"**

Students will answer questions to demonstrate their understanding of the vocabulary words from the reading.

WRAP-UP

Question About "Cinderella"

Students will answer a question to show that they understand key details in "Cinderella."

Cinderella Around the World (D)

Lesson Overview

ACTIVITY	ACTIVITY TITLE	TIME	ONLINE/OFFLINE
GET READY	Introduction to Cinderella Around the World (D)	**1** minute	🖥️
	Spelling List 1 More Practice	**10** minutes	🖥️
	Recall "Cinderella"	**5** minutes	🖥️
	Before You Read *Glass Slipper, Gold Sandal*	**14** minutes	🖥️
READ	*Glass Slipper, Gold Sandal*	**30** minutes	📄
	Check-In: *Glass Slipper, Gold Sandal*	**5** minutes	🖥️
LEARN AND **TRY IT**	Make Inferences Like a Detective	**10** minutes	🖥️
	Use Clues to Make Inferences	**10** minutes	🖥️
	Apply: Making Inferences	**15** minutes	🖥️
	Write About Inferences **LEARNING COACH CHECK-IN**	**10** minutes	📄
	Practice Words from *Glass Slipper, Gold Sandal*	**8** minutes	🖥️
WRAP-UP	Question About *Glass Slipper, Gold Sandal*	**2** minutes	🖥️

Content Background

Students will complete a spelling activity, review what they've read in "Cinderella," and read *Glass Slipper, Gold Sandal: A Worldwide Cinderella* by Paul Fleischman. They will then complete activities in which they learn about how to make inferences.

Making inferences, or drawing conclusions from a text, is a crucial reading strategy. Not everything in a story is directly stated or spelled out. Readers must notice textual evidence and combine that with what they already know, or their background knowledge, to make sense of text.

Textual evidence: Cinderella's stepmother gives her very little food.

Background knowledge: From other versions of Cinderella, the reader knows that the stepmother favors her own daughters.

Inference: The stepmother is giving most of the food to her own daughters.

MATERIALS

Supplied
- *Glass Slipper, Gold Sandal: A Worldwide Cinderella* by Paul Fleischman
- *Summit English Language Arts 4 Activity Book*
  - Write About Inferences

Glass Slipper, Gold Sandal Synopsis

Glass Slipper, Gold Sandal is truly a worldwide Cinderella story. Paul Fleischman recounts this Cinderella tale by combining details of Cinderella stories from around the globe. A Mexican girl's father marries a widow with two daughters. While an Iraqi girl's stepmother denies her food, Godfather Snake provides an Indian girl with rice. The storyline is familiar, but the details provide a view of each culture's unique take on the Cinderella story.

Lesson Goals

- Practice all spelling words online.
- Read *Glass Slipper, Gold Sandal*.
- Make inferences and study the vocabulary in *Glass Slipper, Gold Sandal*.

GET READY

Introduction to *Glass Slipper, Gold Sandal*

Students will get a glimpse of what they will learn about in the lesson. They will also read the lesson goals and keywords. Have students select each keyword and preview its definition.

Spelling List 1 More Practice

Students will practice all spelling words from the workshop.

Recall "Cinderella"

Students will answer some questions to review the reading that they have already completed.

Before You Read *Glass Slipper, Gold Sandal*

Students will be introduced to some key vocabulary words that they will encounter in the upcoming reading, learn some background related to the reading, and answer questions to help them set a purpose for their reading.

READ

Glass Slipper, Gold Sandal

Students will read *Glass Slipper, Gold Sandal* by Paul Fleischman.

Check-In: *Glass Slipper, Gold Sandal*

Students will answer several questions to demonstrate their comprehension of *Glass Slipper, Gold Sandal*.

LEARN AND TRY IT

LEARN   Make Inferences Like a Detective

Students will learn about making inferences. They will learn how to use information that they already know combined with clues from the text to make an inference.

TRY IT   Use Clues to Make Inferences

Students will analyze passages and answer questions about inferences they can make about those passages.

SUPPORT   For students having difficulty making inferences, help them to recognize that they make inferences on a daily basis. For example, when they see somebody smiling, they can infer that the person is happy. They must put together what they know about happy people with the expression they see on the person's face to make the inference. Reinforce that students' background knowledge is extremely valuable when they read and make inferences.

TRY IT   Apply: Making Inferences

Students will apply to a new work what they've learned about making inferences.

TRY IT   Write About Inferences

Students will complete Write About Inferences from *Summit English Language Arts 4 Activity Book*.

LEARNING COACH CHECK-IN   This activity page contains open-ended questions, so it's important that you review students' responses. Give students feedback, using the sample answers provided to guide you.

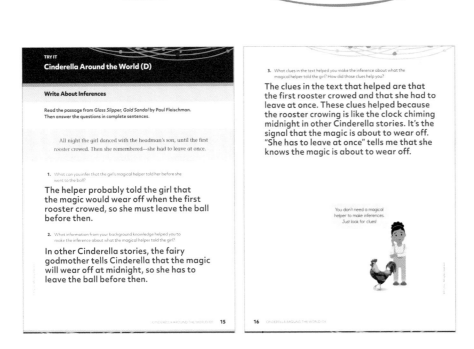

TRY IT
Cinderella Around the World (D)

Write About Inferences

Read the passage from *Glass Slipper, Gold Sandal* by Paul Fleischman. Then answer the questions in complete sentences.

All night the girl danced with the headman's son, until the first rooster crowed. Then she remembered—she had to leave at once.

1. What can you infer that the girl's magical helper told her before she went to the ball?

The helper probably told the girl that the magic would wear off when the first rooster crowed, so she must leave the ball before then.

2. What information from your background knowledge helped you to make the inference about what the magical helper told the girl?

In other Cinderella stories, the fairy godmother tells Cinderella that the magic will wear off at midnight, so she has to leave the ball before then.

3. What clues in the text helped you make the inference about what the magical helper told the girl? How did those clues help you?

The clues in the text that helped are that the first rooster crowed and that she had to leave at once. These clues helped because the rooster crowing is like the clock chiming midnight in other Cinderella stories. It's the signal that the magic is about to wear off. "She has to leave at once" tells me that she knows the magic is about to wear off.

You don't need a magical helper to make inferences. Just look for clues!

TRY IT Practice Words from *Glass Slipper, Gold Sandal*

Students will answer questions to demonstrate their understanding of the vocabulary words from the reading.

WRAP-UP

Question About *Glass Slipper, Gold Sandal*

Students will answer a question to show that they understand how to make inferences.

Cinderella Around the World (E)

Lesson Overview

ACTIVITY	ACTIVITY TITLE	TIME	ONLINE/OFFLINE
GET READY	Introduction to Cinderella Around the World (E)	**1** minute	
	Spelling List 1 Review Game	**10** minutes	
	Recall *Glass Slipper, Gold Sandal*	**5** minutes	
	Before You Read: Comparing Cinderella Stories	**14** minutes	
READ	Comparing Passages from Cinderella Stories	**30** minutes	
LEARN AND **TRY IT**	Comparing Events and Details in Cinderella	**15** minutes	
	What's the Same in Cinderella Stories	**10** minutes	
	Apply: Describing Characters	**15** minutes	
	Compare Cinderella Stories LEARNING COACH CHECK-IN	**18** minutes	
WRAP-UP	Question About Comparing Cinderella Stories	**2** minutes	

Content Background

Students will complete a spelling activity, review *Glass Slipper, Gold Sandal*, and read passages from different versions of Cinderella stories they've read. They will then complete activities in which they learn how to compare events and details from different stories.

Comparing and its opposite, contrasting, are important higher-level thinking skills. These are functional skills that are used in a variety of academic and real-life situations. They help students organize new and familiar information, and they are particularly helpful when students write, giving them a way to organize their thinking.

Lesson Goals

- Practice all spelling words online.

- Compare the details, characters, settings, events, and themes in Cinderella stories from different cultures.

MATERIALS

Supplied
- *Yeh-Shen: A Cinderella Story from China* retold by Ai-Ling Louie
- *Adelita: A Mexican Cinderella Story* by Tomie de Paolo
- *Summit English Language Arts 4 Expeditions in Reading*
- *Summit English Language Arts 4 Activity Book*
  - Compare Cinderella Stories

GET READY

Introduction to Cinderella Around the World (E)

Students will get a glimpse of what they will learn about in the lesson. They will also read the lesson goals and keywords. Have students select each keyword and preview its definition.

Spelling List 1 Review Game

Students will practice all spelling words from the workshop.

Recall *Glass Slipper, Gold Sandal*

Students will answer some questions to review the reading that they have already completed.

Before You Read: Comparing Cinderella Stories

Students will learn what it means to compare and why good readers compare stories. They will also learn about what they should focus on as they compare Cinderella stories from around the world.

READ

Comparing Passages from Cinderella Stories

Students will read and compare passages from *Adelita: A Mexican Cinderella Story* retold by Ai-Ling Louie, *Yeh-Shen: A Cinderella Story from China* by Tomie de Paolo, and "Cinderella" in *Expeditions in Reading*.

As students read the following passages, the following questions should guide their reading: How does the Cinderella character end up with a stepmother? How does the stepmother treat the Cinderella character, and why does the stepmother treat her that way?

- *Adelita*: Read from the beginning to the paragraph that ends "Worst of all, Valentina and Dulce were mean and hateful to her."

- *Yeh-Shen*: Read from the beginning to the paragraph that ends "So in her displeasure she gave poor Yeh-Shen the heaviest and most unpleasant chores."

- "Cinderella": Read from the beginning to the paragraph that ends "They made her do all the chores and wait on them like a servant."

As students read the next passages, the following questions should guide their reading: What is the special event that the Cinderella character wishes to attend? Why is the event so important to Cinderella and her stepsisters?

- *Adelita:* Read from the paragraph that begins "'Mis hijas–my daughters,' Doña Micaela said one morning…" to the paragraph that ends "And each would do anything to get him."

- *Yeh-Shen*: Read just the paragraph that begins "So the time passed and spring came."

- "Cinderella": Read from the paragraph that begins "Then one evening there was a visitor at the door" to the paragraph that ends "'You must not fail me!' the stepmother explained."

TIP Suggest that students begin to fill out the comparison chart Compare Cinderella Stories from *Summit English Language Arts 4 Activity Book* as they complete this activity. Students will find information for the comparison chart as they complete Comparing Events and Details in Cinderella and What's the Same in Cinderella Stories.

LEARN AND TRY IT

LEARN   Comparing Events and Details in Cinderella

Students will learn how to compare stories by looking for similar events and common ideas. They will also explore how differences in details help them learn what is unique to each culture the Cinderella stories come from.

TRY IT   What's the Same in Cinderella Stories

Students will compare passages from three versions of Cinderella and answer questions in which they determine what is similar in passages from the stories.

TRY IT   Apply: Describing Characters

Students will read other works and apply what they've learned.

TRY IT   Compare Cinderella Stories

Students will record information from three versions of Cinderella to complete Compare Cinderella Stories from *Summit English Language Arts 4 Activity Book*.

LEARNING COACH CHECK-IN Once completed, this activity page will contain information that students will refer to for a future writing activity, so it's important that you review students' responses. Give students feedback, using the sample answers provided to guide you.

NOTE Have students keep their completed activity page in a safe place so they can refer to it later.

TRY IT
Cinderella Around the World (E)

Compare Cinderella Stories

Complete the comparison chart with details from each of the Cinderella stories listed.

Title	Yeh-Shen	Adelita	"Cinderella"
Main Characters			
What is the Cinderella character like?	See below.		
Setting			
How does Cinderella end up with a stepmother?			

Title	Yeh-Shen	Adelita	"Cinderella"
Who helps Cinderella? What special items does Cinderella get?			
What is the special event? What is the reason for the special event?	See below and right.		
How is Cinderella's identity revealed?			
How does the story end?			
What is one theme (big idea) of the story?			

Additional answers

Title	Yeh-Shen	Adelita	"Cinderella"
Main Characters	Yeh-Shen Stepmother Stepsister	Adelita Esperanza Doña Micaela Valentina Dulce	Cinderella Stepmother Stepsisters Fairy Godmother
What is the Cinderella character like?	Bright, lovely, and generous	Beautiful, helpful, sweet	Lovely, gentle, kindhearted, hard working
Setting	In the dim past in China	A long time ago in a village in Mexico	A country village
How does Cinderella end up with a stepmother?	Her mother and father died.	Her mother died and her father remarried. Then her father died.	Her mother died, and her father remarried.
Who helps Cinderella? What special items does Cinderella get?	Magic fish bones A gown, a cloak, and gold shoes	Esperanza Her mother's dress and shawl	Fairy godmother A gown and glass slippers
What is the special event? What is the reason for the special event?	Spring festival so young men and women can meet future partners	Fiesta to celebrate homecoming of Javier	A ball for prince to find future bride

Additional answers, continued

Title	Yeh-Shen	Adelita	"Cinderella"
How is Cinderella's identity revealed?	She puts on golden shoes, and her rags are transformed into a cloak and gown.	She hangs the shawl outside her window. Javier sees it.	She shows the other glass slipper to the guest.
How does the story end?	Yeh-Shen marries the king. Her stepmother and stepsister are crushed by stones.	Adelita marries Javier. Esperanza goes to live with them.	Cinderella and her father go to palace. Her stepmother and stepsisters are left behind. Cinderella marries prince.
What is one theme (big idea) of the story?	**Possible answers:** Kindness is rewarded; bad behavior is punished.	**Possible answers:** Good behavior is rewarded; those who love you will be there to help you.	**Possible answers:** Hard work is rewarded.

WRAP-UP

Question About Comparing Cinderella Stories

Students will answer a question to show that they understand how to compare passages from different stories.

Cinderella Around the World Wrap-Up

Lesson Overview

ACTIVITY	ACTIVITY TITLE	TIME	ONLINE/OFFLINE
GET READY	Introduction to Cinderella Around the World Wrap-Up	**1** minute	
TRY IT	Write About Cinderella Stories **LEARNING COACH CHECK-IN**	**30** minutes	
	Read and Record	**10** minutes	
	Review Cinderella Around the World	**20** minutes	
QUIZ	Cinderella Around the World	**30** minutes	
	Spelling List 1	**10** minutes	
WRAP-UP	More Language Arts Practice	**19** minutes	

Advance Preparation

Gather students' completed Compare Cinderella Stories activity page from Cinderella Around the World (E). Students will refer to this page during Try It: Write About Cinderella Stories.

Lesson Goals

- Review *Yeh-Shen*, *Adelita*, "Cinderella," and *Glass Slipper, Gold Sandal*.
- Take a spelling test.
- Take a quiz on *Yeh-Shen*, *Adelita*, "Cinderella," and *Glass Slipper, Gold Sandal*.

MATERIALS

Supplied
- *Yeh-Shen: A Cinderella Story from China* retold by Ai-Ling Louie
- *Adelita: A Mexican Cinderella Story* by Tomie de Paolo
- *Summit English Language Arts 4 Expeditions in Reading*
- *Summit English Language Arts 4 Activity Book*
  - Write About Cinderella Stories

Also Needed
- completed Compare Cinderella Stories activity page from Cinderella Around the World (E)

GET READY

Introduction to Cinderella Around the World Wrap-Up

Students will read the lesson goals.

Write About Cinderella Stories

Students will complete Write About Cinderella Stories from *Summit English Language Arts 4 Activity Book*. Make sure students have their Compare Cinderella Stories activity page from Cinderella Around the World (E) to refer to during this activity.

LEARNING COACH CHECK-IN This activity page contains open-ended questions, so it's important that you review students' responses. Give students feedback, using the sample answers provided to guide you.

TRY IT
Cinderella Around the World Wrap-Up

Write About Cinderella Stories

Possible answers are given if student chooses to compare *Yeh-Shen* and *Adelita*. Refer to the answer key for Compare Cinderella Stories for the details of "Cinderella."

1. Setting: How are the time and place in which the stories are set the same and different?

The settings of *Yeh-Shen* and *Adelita* are alike because both take place a long time ago. But they are different because *Yeh-Shen* takes place in China and *Adelita* takes place in a village in Mexico.

2. Characters: Who are the main characters in each story and what are they like?

The main characters in *Yeh-Shen* are Yeh-Shen, her stepmother, and her stepsister. The characters in *Adelita* are Adelita, Esperanza, the stepmother, and the stepsisters. Yeh-Shen and Adelita are both beautiful and kind. Yeh-Shen gives food to her fish even when she doesn't have much. Adelita helps Esperanza in the kitchen. In both stories, the stepmother and stepsisters are mean and jealous. They make Yeh-Shen and Adelita do all the work.

CINDERELLA AROUND THE WORLD WRAP-UP **19**

3. Events: How are the events of the two stories alike, and how are they different? Be sure to describe each story's ending.

See below.

4. Theme: What is a big idea from each story? How do the events and ending support those themes?

Both stories have a similar theme: good behavior or kindness is rewarded. Yeh-Shen is kind to her fish. She is rewarded in the end when she marries the king. Adelita is good. She helps Esperanza and does what her stepmother and stepsisters tell her to do. She is rewarded in the end when she marries Javier.

20 CINDERELLA AROUND THE WORLD WRAP-UP

Additional answers

3. The stories are alike because a young woman is treated badly by her stepmother and stepsisters. She wants to go to a special event, but her stepmother stops her from going. Someone special helps her attend the event. She meets a young man there who doesn't know who she is. She runs away, so he searches for her. In both stories, he finds her and they get married.

The stories are different because in *Yeh-Shen,* it's fish bones that help. They give Yeh-Shen a special cloak and gold shoes. The king identifies Yeh-Shen because the gold shoes fit her. In *Adelita*, it's a person that helps, and Adelita gets a dress and shawl. Javier identifies Adelita because she hangs the shawl from her window. The stories have different endings, too. In *Yeh-Shen*, the stepmother and stepsister are crushed by rocks. In *Adelita*, the stepmother and stepsisters go to the wedding.

Read and Record

Good readers read quickly, smoothly, and with expression. This is called *fluency*. Students will record themselves reading aloud. They will listen to their recording and think about how quick, smooth, and expressive they sound.

Review Cinderella Around the World

Students will answer questions to review what they have learned about determining themes, summarizing, key details, making inferences, and comparing stories.

QUIZ

Cinderella Around the World

Students will complete the Cinderella Around the World quiz.

Spelling List 1

Students will complete the Spelling List 1 quiz.

WRAP-UP

More Language Arts Practice

Students will practice skills according to their individual needs.

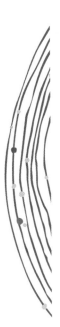

Narrative Writing Skills (A)

Lesson Overview

ACTIVITY	ACTIVITY TITLE	TIME	ONLINE/OFFLINE
GET READY	Introduction to Narrative Writing Skills (A)	**1** minute	🛜
	Spelling List 2 Pretest **LEARNING COACH CHECK-IN**	**10** minutes	🛜 and 📄
	Look Back at Simple Sentences	**5** minutes	🛜
LEARN AND **TRY IT**	Write Complete Sentences	**15** minutes	🛜
	Practice Writing Complete Sentences	**15** minutes	🛜
	Explore the Writing in *Yeh-Shen*	**15** minutes	🛜
	Analyze the Writing in *Adelita*	**15** minutes	🛜
	The Story of an Object **LEARNING COACH CHECK-IN**	**20** minutes	📄
WRAP-UP	Questions About Introductions and Complete Sentences	**4** minutes	🛜
	Go Read!	**20** minutes	🛜 or 📄

Content Background

A *narrative* is a story—it can be either fiction or nonfiction. Students will analyze how authors write narratives and then apply those skills to their own narrative writing. In this lesson, students will focus on the introduction and organization of a narrative.

The introduction refers to the beginning of a narrative, but not necessarily just the first paragraph. A strong beginning to a narrative introduces the main characters and the narrator. It also clarifies the situation—really, the point!—of the story, as well as the setting.

In terms of organization, students will to think of a narrative as having three parts, a beginning (or introduction), middle, and end. In the middle of the story, the writer introduces and develops a problem or series of problems. That problem may be partially solved in the middle of the story. In the end, the writer resolves the problem.

Grammar, Usage, and Mechanics   Students will learn that a sentence tells a complete thought. Additionally, a sentence has a subject and a predicate.

MATERIALS

Supplied
- *Summit English Language Arts 4 Activity Book*
  - Spelling List 2 Pretest
  - The Story of an Object

Also Needed
- reading material for Go Read!

In the following example, the subject is underlined once, and the predicate is underlined twice.

Complete sentence: <u>My sister</u> <u><u>told a joke today</u></u>.

If a word group is missing a subject, a predicate, or both, it is not a sentence. In the following example, the word group has a subject but no predicate.

Incomplete sentence: <u>No one in the room</u>.

A word group may have both a subject and a predicate, but it may not be a complete thought. In the following example, the word group is a dependent clause that cannot stand alone.

Incomplete sentence: After <u>she</u> <u><u>told another joke</u></u>.

Advance Preparation

During the Go Read! activity, students will have the option of using the digital library. Allow extra time for students to make their reading selection, or have students make a selection before beginning the lesson.

Lesson Goals

- Take a spelling pretest.
- Analyze how an author organizes a narrative and introduces the narrator, characters, and setting.
- Start your own narrative: a short story.
- Read for pleasure.

KEYWORDS

character – a person or animal in a story

complex sentence – a sentence that has one independent part and at least one dependent part

compound sentence – a sentence that has at least two independent parts

narrative – a kind of writing that tells a story

narrator – the teller of a story

predicate – the verb or verb phrase in a sentence

sentence – a group of words that tells a complete thought

setting – where and when a literary work takes place

simple sentence – a sentence that is one independent clause

subject – a word or words that tell whom or what the sentence is about

GET READY

Introduction to Narrative Writing Skills (A)
Students will get a glimpse of what they will learn about in the lesson. They will also read the lesson goals and keywords. Have students select each keyword and preview its definition.

Spelling List 2 Pretest
Students will take a spelling pretest.

LEARNING COACH CHECK-IN Have students turn to Spelling List 2 Pretest in *Summit English Language Arts 4 Activity Book* and open the online Spelling Pretest activity. Online, students will listen to the spelling word, type the word in the space indicated, and then check their answer. In the activity book, students will write the correct spelling of the word in the tables provided and

indicate with a ✓ or an ✗ if they spelled the word correctly or incorrectly online. Students will repeat this process with the remaining words.

As needed, help students with the interaction between the online activity and the activity book page until they become comfortable with what they need to do. As students practice their spelling words throughout the workshop, they should pay special attention to words they spelled incorrectly on the pretest.

This is the complete list of words students will be tested on.

Suffix –ed, –er, and –ing	Base create	Prefix un–	Heart Words
blender	create	unlucky	Kansas
fixing	creation	unplug	Ohio
jammed	creativity	uncommon	
slugger		unknown	
smashed		unaware	
splitting			
stepped			

NOTE Have students keep their completed activity page in a safe place so they can refer to it later.

GET READY
Narrative Writing Skills (A)

Spelling List 2 Pretest

1. Open the Spelling Pretest activity online. Listen to the first spelling word. Type the word. Check your answer.

2. Write the correct spelling of the word in the Word column of the Spelling Pretest table on the next page.

Word	✓	✗
1 blindfold		

3. Put a check mark in the ✓ column if you spelled the word correctly online.

Word	✓	✗
1 blindfold	✓	

Put an X in the ✗ column if you spelled the word incorrectly online.

Word	✓	✗
1 blindfold		X

4. Repeat Steps 1–3 for the remaining words in the Spelling Pretest.

NARRATIVE WRITING SKILLS (A)   **21**

Narrative Writing Skills (A)

Spelling List 2 Pretest

Write each spelling word in the Word column, making sure to spell it correctly.

Word	✓	✗		Word	✓	✗
1 blender				10 creativity		
2 fixing				11 Kansas		
3 jammed				12 Ohio		
4 slugger				13 unlucky		
5 smashed				14 unplug		
6 splitting				15 unaware		
7 stepped				16 uncommon		
8 create				17 unknown		
9 creation						

Students should use the ✓ and X columns to indicate whether they spelled each word correctly or incorrectly online.

22   NARRATIVE WRITING SKILLS (A)

Look Back at Simple Sentences

Students will practice the prerequisite skill of constructing simple sentences.

LEARN AND TRY IT

LEARN   Write Complete Sentences

Students will learn how to identify and construct complete sentences.

TRY IT   Practice Writing Complete Sentences

Students will practice identifying and constructing complete sentences. They will receive feedback on their answers.

LEARN   Explore the Writing in *Yeh-Shen*

Students will learn how a writer introduces a narrator and characters and establishes a situation in a narrative. They will also explore how a narrative is organized.

LEARN   Analyze the Writing in *Adelita*

Students will answer questions about how a writer introduces a narrator and characters, establishes a situation, and organizes a narrative. They will receive feedback on their answers.

TRY IT   The Story of an Object

Students will complete The Story of an Object in *Summit English Language Arts 4 Activity Book*.

LEARNING COACH CHECK-IN   This activity page contains open-ended questions, so it's important that you review students' responses. Give students feedback, using the sample answers provided to guide you.

NOTE   Have students keep their completed activity page in a safe place so they can refer to it later.

TRY IT
Narrative Writing Skills (A)

The Story of an Object

Use the story prompt to answer the questions.

Story prompt: Write a story narrated by . . . an object! Have the object describe an experience it had. For example, a coin might describe its journey from a piggy bank to the drawer of a cash register.
Example answers are shown.

1. Think about your story.

   a. Who will narrate the story?
   A left sneaker will narrate the story.

   b. Good writers think about audience. Who do you imagine reading the story?
   I imagine my friends reading the story.

   c. What other characters will be in the story? Describe at least one character.
   The right sneaker will also be in the story. The left and right sneaker always bicker, but they are best friends.

   d. Where is the story set? Give some details about the time and place of the story.
   The story is set in the present time. It is set in my apartment and in a nearby park. In the park, the ground is wet and muddy.

NARRATIVE WRITING SKILLS (A)   **23**

---

24   NARRATIVE WRITING SKILLS (A)

2. Write an introduction to your story. You should introduce the narrator, the setting, and the situation (or point). If you choose, introduce other characters. Imagine that you're writing to your audience.

As a sneaker, I have one fear: puddles. When I see a puddle, I try to wiggle my laces loose so that Jace, my owner, will stop and notice that evil little lake. So when Jace told his mom that he wanted to go hiking the day after a rainstorm, I looked in horror at Righty through all of my eyes.

Now I am starting to feel bad about tossing my sweatshirt into a pile of dirty laundry....

---

3. What happens next? Complete the diagram to describe how your story will be organized. (**Do not write the whole story now. Just describe what will happen.**)

Beginning
A left sneaker hears it is going on a hike, and it becomes nervous that it will have to step in a puddle.

↓

Middle
On the hike, the sneaker is dragged through a muddy puddle. It then has to go through the washing machine, where one of its laces comes loose. But, it also meets a friend in the washing machine.

↓

End
The sneaker realizes it liked the adventure, and it tries to get its owner to go outside in the rain again.

NARRATIVE WRITING SKILLS (A)   **25**

Questions About Introductions and Complete Sentences

Students will answer questions to show that they understand the elements of an introduction to a narrative and how to form a complete sentence.

Go Read!

Students will read for pleasure. They should choose a book or a magazine that interests them, or they may choose a selection from the digital library, linked in the online lesson.

Students should read for the entire time. Have students select something to read ahead of time to help them stay focused.

Narrative Writing Skills (B)

Lesson Overview

ACTIVITY	ACTIVITY TITLE	TIME	ONLINE/OFFLINE
GET READY	Introduction to Narrative Writing Skills (B)	**1** minute	🛜
	Spelling List 2 Activity Bank	**10** minutes	📄
LEARN AND **TRY IT**	Revise Fragments	**10** minutes	🖥
	Practice Revising Fragments	**10** minutes	🖥
	Transitions and Concrete Words in *Yeh-Shen*	**15** minutes	🛜
	Transitions and Concrete Words in *Adelita*	**15** minutes	🛜
	Use Your Best Words **LEARNING COACH CHECK-IN**	**30** minutes	📄
WRAP-UP	Questions About Transitions and Fragments	**4** minutes	🛜
	Go Read!	**25** minutes	🛜 or 📄

Content Background

Students will learn about word choice in narratives, including transitions, concrete language, and sensory language.

Transitions, such as *first*, *after that*, and *suddenly*, connect ideas in text. Narrative writers use transitions to show the order of events. They also use transition to show that one event caused another event.

Concrete and sensory language are related. *Concrete language* refers to something tangible, or real or physical.

> **Concrete:** Her mother hugged her tightly and stroked her hair.

> **Not concrete:** Her mother loved her.

Concrete language often includes *sensory language*, or words that relate to the five senses. Students will learn that good narrative writers show instead of tell. That is, narrative writers use concrete and sensory language to help readers imagine the events in a story and draw clear conclusions about what is happening.

MATERIALS

Supplied
- *Summit English Language Arts 4 Activity Book*
  - Spelling List 2 Activity Bank
  - Use Your Best Words

Also Needed
- completed Spelling List 2 Pretest activity page from Narrative Writing Skills (A)
- completed The Story of an Object activity page from Narrative Writing Skills (A)
- reading material for Go Read!

Grammar, Usage, and Mechanics   Students will learn how to revise a sentence fragment. A fragment is a group of words that is treated like a sentence but is missing a subject, a predicate, or both. Students will learn that to revise a fragment, they must add the missing element or elements.

Fragment: <u>Hid in the laundry basket.</u>

Sentence: <u>The cat</u> <u>hid in the laundry basket.</u>

Advance Preparation

Gather students' completed Spelling List 2 Pretest activity page from Narrative Writing Skills (A). Students will refer to this page during Get Ready: Spelling List 2 Activity Bank.

Gather students' completed The Story of an Object activity page from Narrative Writing Skills (A). Students will refer to this page during Try It: Use Your Best Words.

During the Go Read! activity, students will have the option of using the digital library. Allow extra time for students to make their reading selection, or have students make a selection before beginning the lesson.

Lesson Goals

- Practice all spelling words offline.
- Revise a sentence fragment.
- Explore sensory language and transitions in a personal narrative.
- Continue your short story.
- Read for pleasure.

GET READY

Introduction to Narrative Writing Skills (B)

Students will get a glimpse of what they will learn about in the lesson. They will also read the lesson goals and keywords. Have students select each keyword and preview its definition.

Spelling List 2 Activity Bank

Students will practice all spelling words from the workshop by completing Spelling List 2 Activity Bank from *Summit English Language Arts 4 Activity Book*. Make sure students have their completed Spelling List 2 Pretest activity page from Narrative Writing Skills (A) to refer to during this activity.

KEYWORDS

concrete – real or physical; able to be perceived by the senses

fragment – an incomplete sentence that begins with a capital letter and ends with a punctuation mark

narrative – a kind of writing that tells a story

predicate – the verb or verb phrase in a sentence

sensory language – language that appeals to the five senses

sentence – a group of words that tells a complete thought

subject – a word or words that tell whom or what the sentence is about

transition – a word, phrase, or clause that connects ideas

Spelling List 2 Activity Bank

Circle any words in the box that you did not spell correctly on the pretest. Using your circled words, complete one activity of your choice. Complete as much of the activity as you can in the time given.

If you spelled all words correctly on the pretest, complete your chosen activity with as many spelling words as you can.

blender	smashed	creation	Ohio	unaware
fixing	splitting	creativity	unlucky	uncommon
jammed	stepped	Kansas	unplug	unknown
slugger	create			

Spelling Activity Choices

Silly Sentences

1. Write a silly sentence using your words from the spelling word list.
2. Underline the spelling word in each sentence.
   Example: The dog was driving a car.
3. Correct any spelling errors.

Spelling Story

1. Write a very short story using your words from the spelling word list.
2. Underline the spelling words in the story.
3. Correct any spelling errors.

Riddle Me This

1. Write a riddle for your words from the spelling word list.
   Example: "I have a trunk, but it's not on my car."
2. Write the answer, which is your word, for each riddle.
   Example: Answer: elephant
3. Correct any spelling errors.

RunOnWord

1. Gather some crayons, colored pencils, or markers. Write each of your words, using a different color for each word, end to end as one long word.
   Example: dogcatbirdfishturtle
2. Rewrite the words correctly and with proper spacing.

Complete the activity that you chose.
My chosen activity:

Students should use this page to complete all steps in their chosen activity.

LEARN AND TRY IT

LEARN   Revise Fragments

Students will learn how to revise fragments into complete sentences.

TRY IT   Practice Revising Fragments

Students will practicing revising fragments. They will receive feedback on their answers.

LEARN   Transitions and Concrete Words in *Yeh-Shen*

Students will look closer at the words writers use in narratives. They will learn how a writer uses transitional words and phrases to show the order of events. They will also examine concrete and sensory language.

TRY IT   Transitions and Concrete Words in *Adelita*

Students will answer questions about how a writer uses transitional, concrete, and sensory language.

TRY IT   Use Your Best Words

Students will complete Use Your Best Words in *Summit English Language Arts 4 Activity Book*. Make sure students have their completed The Story of an Object activity page from Narrative Writing Skills (A) to refer to during this activity.

LEARNING COACH CHECK-IN   This activity page contains open-ended questions, so it's important that you review students' responses. Give students feedback, using the sample answers provided to guide you.

NOTE   Have students keep their completed activity page in a safe place so they can refer to it later.

Additional answers

1. I told Righty to run, but he ignored me. That's when I knew I was in trouble.

   We arrived at the park. The trail was wet, very wet. With every step, <u>I felt a squish</u>. And then I saw it in front of me—<u>a big puddle</u>. I screamed to Jace not to step in it, but he ignored me like he always does. I closed all of my eyes as I went into the <u>cold, muddy water</u>.

   "Mom!" Jace yelled. "My left shoe is soaked! My foot is freezing!" Of course, Righty wasn't wet at all. Humph.

   Jace continued to complain. I did, too. We went home, and Jace's mom tossed me and Jace's left sock into the washing machine. I was terrified. Then she grabbed a few more things to toss in. Jace's teddy bear landed on me with a plop. I grabbed onto the bear's foot. "Help me!" I said to the bear.

3a. The phrase "felt a squish" helps readers hear and feel what the narrator heard and felt. The phrase "cold, muddy water" describes the temperature, look, and texture of the puddle.

WRAP-UP

Questions About Transitions and Fragments

Students will answer questions to show that they understand how to effectively use transitions and how to revise fragments.

Go Read!

Students will read for pleasure. They should choose a book or a magazine that interests them, or they may choose a selection from the digital library, linked in the online lesson.

Students should read for the entire time. Have students select something to read ahead of time to help them stay focused.

Narrative Writing Skills (C)

Lesson Overview

ACTIVITY	ACTIVITY TITLE	TIME	ONLINE/OFFLINE
GET READY	Introduction to Narrative Writing Skills (C)	**1** minute	🖥️
	Spelling List 2 Review Game	**10** minutes	🖥️
LEARN AND **TRY IT**	Revise Run-Ons	**10** minutes	🖥️
	Practice Revising Run-Ons	**10** minutes	🖥️
	Dialogue, Description, and Conclusions in *Yeh-Shen*	**15** minutes	🖥️
	Dialogue, Description, and Conclusions in *Adelita*	**15** minutes	🖥️
	Finish Your Story **LEARNING COACH CHECK-IN**	**30** minutes	📄
WRAP-UP	Questions About Conclusions and Run-Ons	**4** minutes	🖥️
	Go Read!	**25** minutes	🖥️ or 📄

Content Background

Students will continue learning about narrative writing by analyzing how authors write narratives and then applying those skills to their own writing. In this lesson, they will focus on using dialogue and description to develop characters and events. They'll also learn how to write an effective conclusion to a narrative.

Students are likely familiar with dialogue and description. This lesson focuses on how writers use dialogue and description purposefully. Instead of simply including dialogue in writing, students should think about how dialogue can show a character's reaction or further the events in a story.

A conclusion is the end of a narrative. It's not necessarily a single paragraph. A strong conclusion to a narrative makes sense, or follows naturally from events or characters' actions in the narrative. A conclusion may include a surprise, but the surprise must be logical. There should be clues throughout the narrative that lead to that surprise.

Grammar, Usage, and Mechanics   Students will learn how to revise a run-on sentence. A run-on is two or more sentences written incorrectly as one sentence. The sentences in a run-on may be joined with no punctuation, just a comma, or just a coordinating conjunction.

MATERIALS

Supplied
- *Summit English Language Arts 4 Activity Book*
  - Finish Your Story

Also Needed
- completed The Story of an Object activity page from Narrative Writing Skills (A)
- completed Use Your Best Words activity page from Narrative Writing Skills (B)
- reading material for Go Read!

Run-On Examples:

No punctuation: Carl was exhausted he fell asleep in a plate of pasta.

Comma only: Carl was exhausted, he fell asleep in a plate of pasta.

Coordinating conjunction only: Carl was exhausted and he fell asleep in a plate of pasta.

Students will learn two ways to fix a run-on sentence:

- Join the sentences with a comma and a coordinating conjunction.
- Separate the sentences with a period.

Sentence Examples:

Comma and coordinating conjunction: Carl was exhausted, so he fell asleep in a plate of pasta.

Period: Carl was exhausted. He fell asleep in a plate of pasta.

Advance Preparation

Gather students' completed The Story of an Object activity page from Narrative Writing Skills (A) and completed Use Your Best Words activity page from Narrative Writing Skills (B). Students will refer to these pages during Try It: Finish Your Story.

During the Go Read! activity, students will have the option of using the digital library. Allow extra time for students to make their reading selection, or have students make a selection before beginning the lesson.

Lesson Goals

- Practice all spelling words online.
- Revise a run-on sentence.
- Analyze dialogue and description and explore the conclusion of a narrative.
- Write the conclusion of your short story.
- Read for pleasure.

conclusion – the final paragraph of a written work

coordinating conjunction – one of seven words—*and, but, for, nor, or, so, yet*—that connects words, phrases, or independent clauses

description – writing that uses words that show how something looks, sounds, feels, tastes, or smells

dialogue – the words that characters say in a written work

narrative – a kind of writing that tells a story

run-on – two or more sentences that have been joined without a conjunction or proper punctuation

sentence – a group of words that tells a complete thought

Introduction to Narrative Writing Skills (C)

Students will get a glimpse of what they will learn about in the lesson. They will also read the lesson goals and keywords. Have students select each keyword and preview its definition.

Spelling List 2 Review Game

Students will practice all spelling words from the workshop.

LEARN AND TRY IT

LEARN Revise Run-Ons

Students will learn how to revise run-ons to make them complete sentences. They will learn two methods: joining sentences with a comma and a coordinating conjunction, and rewriting the run-on as two sentences.

NOTE A semicolon may be used to correctly revise a run-on, but students will not learn how to use a semicolon in this lesson.

TRY IT Practice Revising Run-Ons

Students will practicing revising run-ons. They will receive feedback on their answers.

LEARN Dialogue, Description, and Conclusions in *Yeh-Shen*

Students will answer questions about how a writer uses dialogue and description in a narrative. They will also answer a question about the conclusion of a narrative.

TRY IT Dialogue, Description, and Conclusions in *Adelita*

Students will answer questions about how a writer uses transitional, concrete, and sensory language.

TRY IT Finish Your Story

Students will complete Finish Your Story from *Summit English Language Arts 4 Activity Book*. Make sure students have their completed The Story of an Object activity page from Narrative Writing Skills (A) and Use Your Best Words activity page from Narrative Writing Skills (B) to refer to during this activity.

LEARNING COACH CHECK-IN This activity page contains open-ended questions, so it's important that you review students' responses. Give students feedback, using the sample answers provided to guide you.

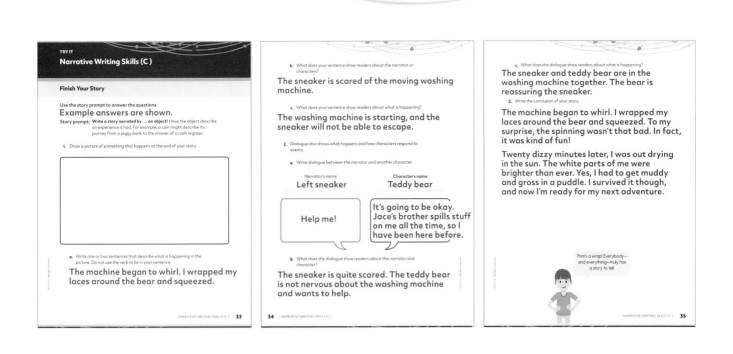

WRAP-UP

Questions About Conclusions and Run-Ons

Students will answer questions to show that they understand the elements of a narrative conclusion and how to revise run-ons.

Go Read!

Students will read for pleasure. They should choose a book or a magazine that interests them, or they may choose a selection from the digital library, linked in the online lesson.

Students should read for the entire time. Have students select something to read ahead of time to help them stay focused.

Narrative Writing Skills Wrap-Up

Lesson Overview

ACTIVITY	ACTIVITY TITLE	TIME	ONLINE/OFFLINE
GET READY	Introduction to Narrative Writing Skills Wrap-Up	**1** minute	
TRY IT	Use Narrative Writing Skills LEARNING COACH CHECK-IN	**35** minutes	📄
	Review Complete Sentences	**20** minutes	📶
QUIZ	Complete Sentences and Narrative Writing Skills	**30** minutes	🖥
	Spelling List 2	**10** minutes	🖥
WRAP-UP	More Language Arts Practice	**9** minutes	🖥
	Go Read!	**15** minutes	🖥 or 📄

Lesson Goals

- Review complete sentences and narrative writing skills.
- Take a quiz on complete sentences and narrative writing skills.
- Take a spelling quiz.

MATERIALS

Supplied
- *Summit English Language Arts 4 Activity Book*
  - Use Narrative Writing Skills

GET READY

Introduction to Narrative Writing Skills Wrap-Up

Students will read the lesson goals.

TRY IT

Use Narrative Writing Skills

Students will complete Use Narrative Writing Skills in *Summit English Language Arts 4 Activity Book* to review the writing objectives that will be assessed on the quiz.

LEARNING COACH CHECK-IN   This activity page contains open-ended questions, so it's important that you review students' responses. Give students feedback, using the sample answers provided to guide you.

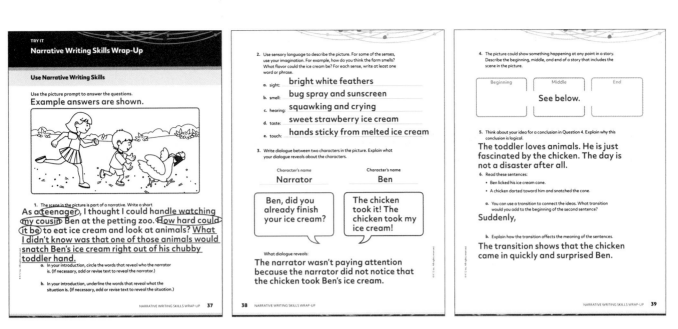

Additional answers

4. **Beginning box:** The narrator and her toddler cousin have a nice visit with animals at the petting zoo.
   Middle box: The narrator buys the toddler ice cream. A chicken steals the toddler's ice cream and runs off.
   End box: The toddler winds up laughing and says it was the best trip to the farm ever.

Review Complete Sentences

Students will answer questions to review what they have learned about forming complete sentences, revising fragments, and revising run-ons.

QUIZ

Complete Sentences and Narrative Writing Skills

Students will complete the Complete Sentences and Narrative Writing Skills quiz.

Spelling List 2

Students will complete the Spelling List 2 quiz.

WRAP-UP

More Language Arts Practice

Students will practice skills according to their individual needs.

Go Read!

Students will read for pleasure. They should choose a book or a magazine that interests them, or they may choose a selection from the digital library, linked in the online lesson.

Students should read for the entire time. Have students select something to read ahead of time to help them stay focused.

Word Relationships

Lesson Overview

ACTIVITY	ACTIVITY TITLE	TIME	ONLINE/OFFLINE
GET READY	Introduction to Word Relationships	**1** minute	
	Look Back at Context and Antonyms	**4** minutes	
LEARN AND **TRY IT**	Word Relationships and Context Clues	**10** minutes	
	Practice Using Word Relationships and Context Clues	**10** minutes	
	Apply: Word Relationships LEARNING COACH CHECK-IN	**15** minutes	
	Go Write!	**15** minutes	
	Review Word Relationships	**15** minutes	
QUIZ	Word Relationships	**15** minutes	
WRAP-UP	More Language Arts Practice	**20** minutes	
	Go Read!	**15** minutes	

Content Background

Students will learn several words that they will typically encounter in testing situations. They will learn how to use context clues to help them define unknown words. They will learn how words are related through synonyms, words with the same or similar meanings, and antonyms, words with opposite meanings. Students will learn that synonyms and antonyms are a type of context clue that can help them to unlock the meanings of unknown words.

For example, in the following sentence *combine* is a synonym for *integrate*, which can help students determine the meaning of *integrate*.

> **Example:** He asked us to integrate, or combine, our ideas.

Advance Preparation

During the Go Read! activity, students will have the option of using the digital library. Allow extra time for students to make their reading selection, or have students make a selection before beginning the lesson.

> **MATERIALS**
>
> **Supplied**
> - *Summit English Language Arts 4 Activity Book*
>   - Apply: Word Relationships
>
> **Also Needed**
> - reading material for Go Read!
> - dictionary
> - thesaurus

Lesson Goals

- Use context clues, synonyms, and antonyms to determine meaning of unknown words.

- Use words that are commonly found on assessments.

- Read and write for pleasure.

Introduction to Word Relationships

Students will get a glimpse of what they will learn about in the lesson. They will also read the lesson goals.

Look Back at Context and Antonyms

Students will revisit content related to context and antonyms to prepare them for Word Relationships.

LEARN AND TRY IT

LEARN   Word Relationships and Context Clues

Students will learn the definitions of several words that they will encounter in testing situations. Students will then watch a video that demonstrates how the words and sentences around an unknown word can provide context clues. These context clues can help to unlock the meaning of a new word.

Finally, students will watch a video in which they learn about synonyms and antonyms. Knowing how words are related, including whether they have similar or opposite meanings, can help them understand new words.

TRY IT   Practice Using Word Relationships and Context Clues

Students will answer questions to practice using word relationships and context clues to determine the meanings of words.

TRY IT   Apply: Word Relationships

Students will complete Apply: Word Relationships from *Summit English Language Arts 4 Activity Book*.

LEARNING COACH CHECK-IN   This activity page contains questions with answers that will depend on the students' dictionary or thesaurus, so it's important that you review students' responses. You may also need to provide students assistance with using the dictionary or thesaurus. Give students feedback, using the sample answers provided to guide you.

TRY IT
Word Relationships

Apply: Word Relationships

Use a dictionary or thesaurus to find synonyms and/or antonyms for each vocabulary word.
Possible answers are shown.

1. **infer**
   synonyms: guess, conclude, judge

2. **integrate**
   synonyms: combine, join, blend
   antonyms: divide, separate, split

3. **interpret**
   synonyms: explain, clarify

4. **paraphrase**
   synonyms: reword, restate
   antonyms: quote

5. **summarize**
   synonyms: recap, sum up
   antonyms: extend, expand

6. **evidence**
   synonyms: proof, confirmation

WORD RELATIONSHIPS   **41**

TRY IT   Review Word Relationships

Students will answer questions to review what they have learned about using context clues, synonyms, and antonyms to determine meanings of words.

QUIZ

Word Relationships

Students will complete the Word Relationships quiz.

WRAP-UP

More Language Arts Practice

Students will practice skills according to their individual needs.

Go Read!

Students will read for pleasure. They should choose a book or a magazine that interests them, or they may choose a selection from the digital library, linked in the online lesson.

Students should read for the entire time. Have students select something to read ahead of time to help them stay focused.

Big Ideas: Mini-Project

Lesson Overview

Big Ideas lessons provide students the opportunity to further apply the knowledge and skills acquired throughout the unit workshops. Each Big Ideas lesson consists of three parts:

1. **Cumulative Review:** Students keep their skills fresh by reviewing prior content.

2. **Preview:** Students practice answering the types of questions they will commonly find on standardized tests.

3. **Synthesis:** Students complete an assignment that allows them to interweave and apply what they've learned. These synthesis assignments will vary throughout the course.

   In the Synthesis portion of this Big Ideas lesson, students will complete a small, creative project designed to tie together concepts and skills that students have encountered across workshops. These small projects are designed to deepen students' understanding of those concepts and skills.

   LEARNING COACH CHECK-IN   Make sure students complete, review, and submit the assignment to their teacher.

All materials needed for this lesson are linked online and not provided in the Activity Book.

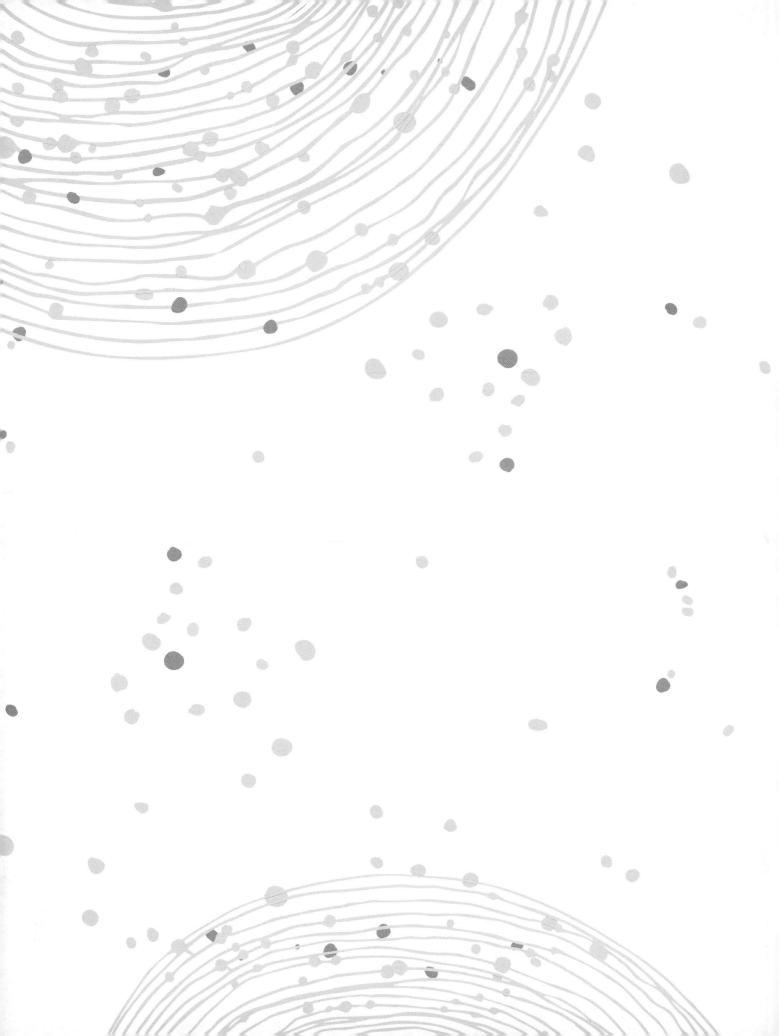

Emoji and Pisa and Birds, Oh My!

"From Cave Paintings to Emoji"

Lesson Overview

ACTIVITY	ACTIVITY TITLE	TIME	ONLINE/OFFLINE
GET READY	*Emoji and Pisa and Birds, Oh My!* Unit Overview	**1** minute	🖥️
	Introduction to "From Cave Paintings to Emoji"	**1** minute	🖥️
	Spelling List 3 Pretest **LEARNING COACH CHECK-IN**	**10** minutes	🖥️ and 📄
	Interesting Magazines in 60 Seconds	**1** minute	🖥️
	Look Back at Nonfiction Text Features	**4** minutes	🖥️
	Before You Read "From Cave Paintings to Emoji"	**10** minutes	🖥️
READ	"From Cave Paintings to Emoji"	**20** minutes	📄
	Check-In: "From Cave Paintings to Emoji"	**5** minutes	🖥️
LEARN AND **TRY IT**	Explore Main Idea and Details	**8** minutes	🖥️
	Examine Main Idea and Details	**10** minutes	🖥️
	Text Structures and Features of Informational Texts	**10** minutes	🖥️
	Analyze Structures and Features of Informational Text	**10** minutes	🖥️
	Apply: Identify Information	**10** minutes	🖥️
	Paraphrase Using a Time Line **LEARNING COACH CHECK-IN**	**10** minutes	📄
	Practice Words from "From Cave Paintings to Emoji"	**8** minutes	🖥️
WRAP-UP	Question About "From Cave Paintings to Emoji"	**2** minutes	🖥️

Content Background

Students will use the time-order (sequential) organizational structure to better understand the text. This organizational structure means that the information is presented in the order in which things happened. For example, "From Cave Paintings to Emoji" begins with ancient communication and ends with smartphones and emoji. It takes the reader on a journey through time to explore the development of human communication. Students will also examine common text structures, such as paragraphs and topic sentences.

MATERIALS

Supplied
- *K12 World: Emoji and Pisa and Birds, Oh My!*
- *Summit English Language Arts 4 Activity Book*
  - Spelling List 3 Pretest
  - Paraphrase Using a Time Line

In addition, authors also use text features to provide clues and to help the reader locate key information. This article uses a time line to visually show how communication has changed over time. It also includes headings before each section to indicate what the section will be about.

"From Cave Paintings to Emoji" Synopsis

The magazine article describes the history of human communication. The article begins with defining **communication** (to share information with others) and discusses the first known form of human communication, cave paintings. Pictures eventually led to using letters and words. With the invention of the printing press, the first real books and newspapers were introduced to the world. Oral communication was hindered by distance, but new inventions, like the telegraph and the telephone, allowed humans to connect despite the distance. As time continued, more inventions, such as the radio and the television, were created. They allowed for more people to be informed and entertained. The inventions of computers and the Internet allowed for faster human connection. This led to mobile phones and smartphones. Finally, in Japan, emoji were invented. Emoji are pictures that describe a feeling or reaction to something. The article concludes with a lingering thought for the reader: human communication began with pictures like today's emoji.

Lesson Goals

- Complete the Spelling List 3 Pretest.
- Read "From Cave Paintings to Emoji."
- Identify conclusions in an informational text.
- Identify how information is organized in a nonfiction text, and explain how organization aids comprehension.
- Use nonfiction text features to locate information and aid comprehension.
- Determine main ideas, supporting details, and meanings of unfamiliar words in the reading.
- Paraphrase key events in an informational text.

Emoji and Pisa and Birds, Oh My! Unit Overview

Students will read a summary of what they will learn in the *Emoji and Pisa and Birds, Oh My!* unit.

Introduction to "From Cave Paintings and Emoji"

Students will get a glimpse of what they will learn about in the lesson. They will also read the lesson goals and keywords. Have students select each keyword and preview its definition.

Spelling List 3 Pretest

Students will take a spelling pretest.

LEARNING COACH CHECK-IN   Have students turn to Spelling List 3 Pretest in *Summit English Language Arts 4 Activity Book* and open the online Spelling Pretest activity. Online, students will listen to the spelling word, type the word in the space indicated, and then check their answer. In the activity book, students will write the correct spelling of the word in the tables provided and indicate with a ✓ or an ✗ if they spelled the word correctly or incorrectly online. Students will repeat this process with the remaining words.

As needed, help students with the interaction between the online activity and the activity book page until they become comfortable with what they need to do. As students practice their spelling words throughout the workshop, they should pay special attention to words they spelled incorrectly on the pretest.

This is the complete list of words students will be tested on.

Adding *s* or *es* to Short Vowel Base Words	Base Word *act*	Heart Words	Prefix *dis–*
buzzes	interact	Arkansas	disagree
connects	react	New Hampshire	disappear
crunches		enough	
diminishes		rough	
glasses			
infants			
invents			
mixes			
recommends			

NOTE   Have students keep their completed activity page in a safe place so they can refer to it later.

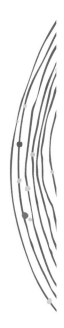

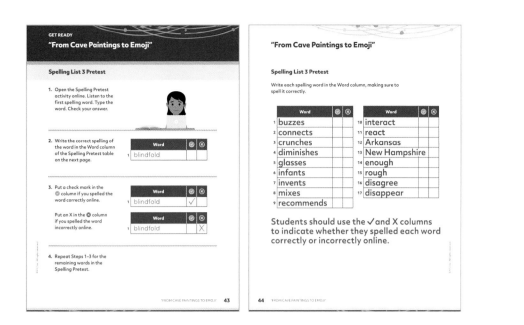

Interesting Magazines in 60 Seconds

Students will watch a short video designed to spark their interest in upcoming topics.

Look Back at Nonfiction Text Features

Students will practice the prerequisite skill of identifying nonfiction text features and how they aid readers in navigating and understanding nonfiction texts.

Before You Read "From Cave Paintings to Emoji"

Students will be introduced to some key vocabulary words that they will encounter in the upcoming reading and answer a question to help them set a purpose for their reading.

NOTE   Students will make a prediction before reading the article.

READ

"From Cave Paintings to Emoji"

Students will read "From Cave Paintings to Emoji" in *Emoji and Pisa and Birds, Oh My!*

Check-In: "From Cave Paintings to Emoji"

Students will answer several questions to demonstrate their comprehension of "From Cave Paintings to Emoji."

NOTE   Students will confirm or modify their prediction after reading the article.

LEARN   Explore Main Idea and Details

Students will learn how to determine the main idea and how key details support the main idea.

TRY IT   Examine Main Idea and Details

Students will examine the main idea and key details in an informational text.

LEARN   Analyze Text Structures and Features of Informational Texts

Students will learn about an organizational structure and nonfiction text features that help the reader comprehend a text. Students will learn how to paraphrase text to show that they understand what they've read.

TRY IT   Investigating Structures and Features of Informational Text

Students will explore common examples of organizational structures used in a text. Also, students will identify and explain the purpose of text structures and features. Finally, students will identify the best example of a paraphrased passage.

TRY IT   Apply: Identify Information

Students will apply their knowledge of informational text structures to identify the main idea and details of a new text.

TRY IT   Paraphrase Using a Time Line

Students will complete Paraphrase Using a Time Line from *Summit English Language Arts 4 Activity Book*. Students will practice paraphrasing information about events on the time line from 1969 to 2015.

TIP   Remind students that paraphrasing requires that information to be stated using one's own words. It is helpful to practice this skill aloud before writing.

LEARNING COACH CHECK-IN   This activity page contains open-ended questions, so it's important that you review students' responses. Give students feedback, using the sample answers provided to guide you.

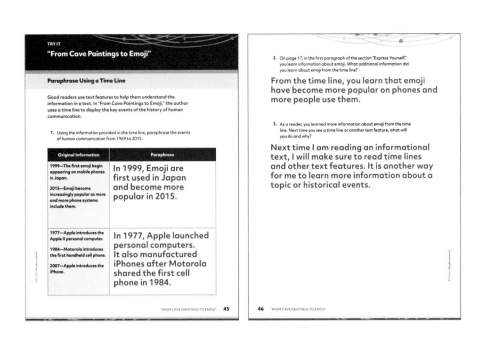

TRY IT   Practice Words from "From Cave Paintings to Emoji"

Students will answer questions to demonstrate their understanding of the vocabulary words from the reading.

WRAP-UP

Question About "From Cave Paintings to Emoji"

Students will answer a question to show that they understand "From Cave Paintings to Emoji."

"From Cave Paintings to Emoji" Wrap-Up

Lesson Overview

ACTIVITY	ACTIVITY TITLE	TIME	ONLINE/OFFLINE
GET READY	Introduction to "From Cave Paintings to Emoji" Wrap-Up	**1** minute	
	Spelling List 3 Activity Bank	**10** minutes	
TRY IT	Paraphrasing Modern Human Communication **LEARNING COACH CHECK-IN**	**30** minutes	
	Read and Record	**10** minutes	
	Review "From Cave Paintings to Emoji"	**20** minutes	
QUIZ	"From Cave Paintings to Emoji"	**30** minutes	
WRAP-UP	More Language Arts Practice	**19** minutes	

Advance Preparation

Gather students' completed Spelling List 3 Pretest activity page from "From Cave Paintings from Emoji." Students will refer to this page during Get Ready: Spelling List 3 Activity Bank.

Lesson Goals

- Practice all spelling words.

- Paraphrase information in a nonfiction text.

- Practice reading aloud to develop fluency.

- Review and take a quiz on main idea, supporting details, conclusions, text structures, and nonfiction text features in informational texts.

MATERIALS

Supplied
- *K12 World: Emoji and Pisa and Birds, Oh My!*
- *Summit English Language Arts 4 Activity Book*
  - Spelling List 3 Activity Bank
  - Paraphrasing Modern Human Communication

Also Needed
- completed Spelling List 3 Pretest activity page from "From Cave Paintings to Emoji"

Introduction to "From Cave Paintings to Emoji" Wrap-Up

Students will read the lesson goals.

Spelling List 3 Activity Bank

Students will practice all spelling words from the workshop by completing Spelling List 3 Activity Bank from *Summit English Language Arts 4 Activity Book*. Make sure students have their completed Spelling List 3 Pretest activity page from "From Cave Paintings to Emoji" to refer to during this activity.

Remind students to pay special attention to words they spelled incorrectly on the Spelling Pretest.

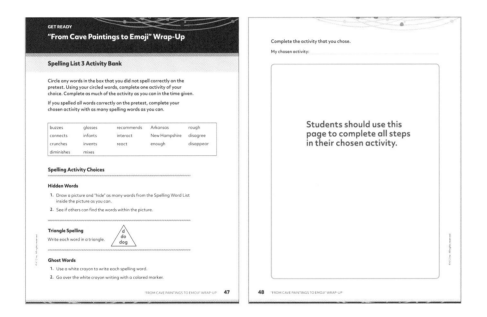

Paraphrasing Modern Human Communication

Students will complete Paraphrasing Modern Human Communication from *Summit English Language Arts 4 Activity Book*.

LEARNING COACH CHECK-IN   This activity page contains open-ended questions, so it's important that you review students' responses. Give students feedback, using the sample answers provided to guide you.

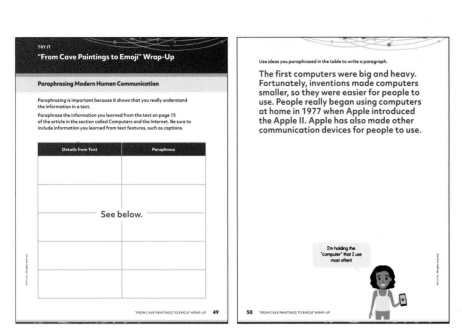

Additional answers

Details from Text	Paraphrase
The earliest computers were gigantic. One weighed 1,000 pounds.	The first computers were big and heavy.
Tiny transistors replaced big vacuum tubes, and microchips helped computers shrink even more.	Inventions made the computer smaller.
Twenty years later, computers became smaller and smarter to be useful to an ordinary person.	Smaller computers meant anyone could use them.
Personal computing began in 1977 with the introduction of the Apple II.	Apple II was introduced in 1977 and allowed people to start using computers.
Since then, the company has introduced the world to many useful communication devices.	Apple has made a lot of communication devices.

Read and Record

Good readers read quickly, smoothly, and with expression. This is called *fluency*. Students will record themselves reading aloud. They will listen to their recording and think about how quick, smooth, and expressive they sound.

TIP Encourage students to rerecord as needed.

Review "From Cave Paintings to Emoji"

Students will answer questions to review what they have learned in "From Cave Paintings to Emoji."

"From Cave Paintings to Emoji"

Students will complete the "From Cave Paintings to Emoji" quiz.

WRAP-UP

More Language Arts Practice

Students will practice skills according to their individual needs.

"Counterfeit Money: Then and Now"

Lesson Overview

ACTIVITY	ACTIVITY TITLE	TIME	ONLINE/OFFLINE
GET READY	Introduction to "Counterfeit Money: Then and Now"	**1** minute	🖥️
	Spelling List 3 Review Game	**10** minutes	🖥️
	Before You Read "Counterfeit Money: Then and Now"	**14** minutes	🖥️
READ	"Counterfeit Money: Then and Now"	**20** minutes	📄
	Check-In: "Counterfeit Money: Then and Now"	**5** minutes	🖥️
LEARN AND **TRY IT**	Identify Informational Structures and Features	**10** minutes	🖥️
	Analyze Informational Structures and Features	**10** minutes	🖥️
	Identify Facts	**7** minutes	🖥️
	Fact Check	**8** minutes	🖥️
	Apply: Informational Texts and Facts	**15** minutes	🖥️
	Compare and Contrast **LEARNING COACH CHECK-IN**	**10** minutes	📄
	Practice Words from "Counterfeit Money: Then and Now"	**8** minutes	🖥️
WRAP-UP	Question About "Counterfeit Money: Then and Now"	**2** minutes	🖥️

Content Background

Students will explore compare-and-contrast organizational structure by looking at similarities and differences in counterfeit money from the past and present. Students will use text features such as a time line and graphics to examine facts, locate information, and further develop their comprehension.

MATERIALS

Supplied
- *K12 World: Emoji and Pisa and Birds, Oh My!*
- *Summit English Language Arts 4 Activity Book*
  - Compare and Contrast

"Counterfeit Money: Then and Now" Synopsis

The magazine article describes the origin of counterfeiting money. It begins by explaining where real money is made and that people have been making fake money almost as long as real money has been made. The article explains how fake money can be detected now as compared to in the past. The article ends with text features that explain steps to follow to determine if a bill is real.

Lesson Goals

- Practice all spelling words.

- Read "Counterfeit Money: Then and Now."

- Identify and explain compare-and-contrast organizational structure in informational text.

- Use text features to locate information and add to understanding of informational text.

- Explain how to verify accurate facts.

- Compare and contrast details in two nonfiction texts.

- Determine meanings of unfamiliar words in the reading.

GET READY

Introduction to "Counterfeit Money: Then and Now"

Students will get a glimpse of what they will learn about in the lesson. They will also read the lesson goals and keywords. Have students select each keyword and preview its definition.

Spelling List 3 Review Game

Students will practice all spelling words from the workshop.

Before You Read "Counterfeit Money: Then and Now"

Students will be introduced to some key vocabulary words that they will encounter in the upcoming reading and answer a question to help them set a purpose for their reading.

NOTE   Students will make a prediction before reading the article.

READ

"Counterfeit Money: Then and Now"

Students will read "Counterfeit Money: Then and Now" in *Emoji and Pisa and Birds, Oh My!*

Check-In: "Counterfeit Money: Then and Now"

Students will answer several questions to demonstrate their comprehension of "Counterfeit Money: Then and Now."

NOTE Students will confirm or modify their prediction after reading the article.

LEARN AND TRY IT

LEARN Identify Informational Structures and Features

Students will learn how to identify compare-and-contrast organizational structure in an informational text. In addition, students will learn how visual text features add additional information to a nonfiction text.

TRY IT Analyze Informational Structures and Features

Students will answer questions about the organizational structure and text features of the article "Counterfeit Money: Then and Now."

LEARN Identify Facts

Students will learn how to identify if a detail is a fact.

TIP Remind students that authors often insert their opinions (personal beliefs) among facts (proven true statements) presented in an article. It is important to be able to distinguish between fact and opinion.

TRY IT Fact Check

Students will explore the accuracy of facts in a text.

TRY IT Apply: Informational Texts and Facts

Students will apply to a new work what they've learned about informational text structures and identifying the accuracy of facts.

TRY IT Compare and Contrast

Students will complete Compare and Contrast from *Summit English Language Arts 4 Activity Book*. Students will practice comparing the similarities and noting the differences in texts by examining the time lines in two articles.

LEARNING COACH CHECK-IN This activity page contains open-ended questions, so it's important that you review students' responses. Give students feedback, using the sample answers provided to guide you.

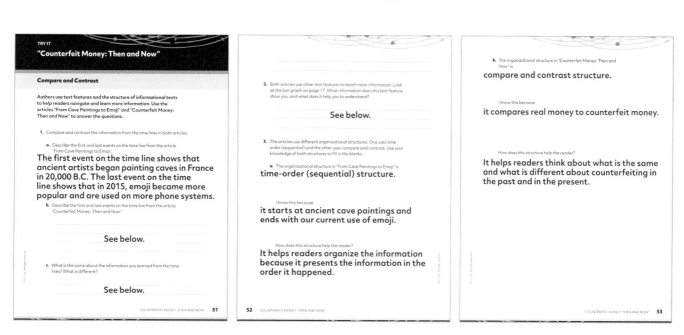

Additional answers

1b. The first event on the time line shows the counterfeiting of money (wampum) by changing the colors of shells in the early 1600s. The last event on the time line shows that money was redesigned with more security features between 2003 and 2008.

1c. Both time lines start a long time ago and give a history of the topic. Both time lines end in the present day. The time lines are different because they cover different topics. One has a lot of events with fewer details, and one has fewer events with more details.

2. The bar graph shows the number of times certain emoji were used on one particular day. It helps us understand which emoji are the most popular.

TRY IT   Practice Words from "Counterfeit Money: Then and Now"

Students will answer questions to demonstrate their understanding of the vocabulary words from the reading.

WRAP-UP

Question About "Counterfeit Money: Then and Now"

Students will answer a question to show they understand how to use text features to locate information.

"Counterfeit Money: Then and Now" Wrap-Up

Lesson Overview

ACTIVITY	ACTIVITY TITLE	TIME	ONLINE/OFFLINE
GET READY	Introduction to "Counterfeit Money: Then and Now" Wrap-Up	**1** minute	
TRY IT	Compare and Contrast Information **LEARNING COACH CHECK-IN**	**30** minutes	
	Read and Record	**10** minutes	
	Review "Counterfeit Money: Then and Now"	**20** minutes	
QUIZ	"Counterfeit Money: Then and Now"	**30** minutes	
	Spelling List 3	**10** minutes	
WRAP-UP	More Language Arts Practice	**19** minutes	

Lesson Goals

- Compare and contrast information in nonfiction texts.

- Practice reading aloud to develop fluency.

- Review and take a quiz on compare-and-contrast organizational structure, text features, and verifying accurate facts.

- Take a spelling quiz.

MATERIALS

Supplied
- *K12 World: Emoji and Pisa and Birds, Oh My!*
- *Summit English Language Arts 4 Activity Book*
  - Compare and Contrast Information

GET READY

Introduction to "Counterfeit Money: Then and Now" Wrap-Up

Students will read the lesson goals.

TRY IT

Compare and Contrast Information

Students will complete Compare and Contrast Information in *Summit English Language Arts 4 Activity Book*.

This activity page contains open-ended questions, so it's important that you review students' responses. Give students feedback, using the sample answers provided to guide you.

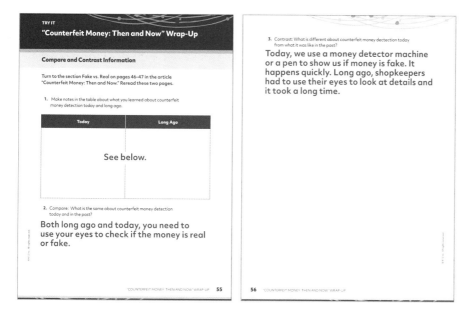

Additional answers

1.

Today	Long Ago
- Look carefully at details of bill - Put bill in money-detector machines (use technology to show if real or fake) - Happens quickly - Color bill with counterfeit detector pen (nothing happens on real bills)	- Shopkeepers used eyes - Compare details of bill with a real bill - Slow process - Humans make mistakes

Read and Record

Good readers read quickly, smoothly, and with expression. This is called *fluency*. Students will record themselves reading aloud. They will listen to their recording and think about how quick, smooth, and expressive they sound.

TIP Encourage students to rerecord as needed.

Review "Counterfeit Money: Then and Now"

Students will answer questions to review what they have learned about "Counterfeit Money: Then and Now."

"Counterfeit Money: Then and Now"

Students will complete the "Counterfeit Money: Then and Now" quiz.

Spelling List 3

Students will complete the Spelling List 3 quiz.

WRAP-UP

More Language Arts Practice

Students will practice skills according to their individual needs.

Narrative Writing: Prewriting (A)

Lesson Overview

ACTIVITY	ACTIVITY TITLE	TIME	ONLINE/OFFLINE
GET READY	Introduction to Narrative Writing: Prewriting (A)	**2** minutes	🖥
	Spelling List 4 Pretest **LEARNING COACH CHECK-IN**	**10** minutes	🖥 and 📄
	Look Back at Punctuating Dialogue	**10** minutes	🖥
LEARN AND **TRY IT**	Use Direct Quotations	**15** minutes	🖥
	Practice Using Direct Quotations	**15** minutes	🖥
	Explore a Student's Personal Narrative	**20** minutes	🖥
	Brainstorming for a Personal Narrative	**15** minutes	🖥
	Brainstorm for Your Personal Narrative **LEARNING COACH CHECK-IN**	**30** minutes	📄
WRAP-UP	Questions About Brainstorming and Dialogue	**3** minutes	🖥

Content Background

Students will begin working on a **personal narrative** about a meaningful moment in their lives. They will complete this assignment over the course of several lessons by following the writing process. Students will begin by prewriting.

Writing Process

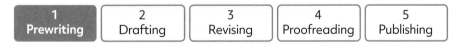

| 1 Prewriting | 2 Drafting | 3 Revising | 4 Proofreading | 5 Publishing |

During **prewriting**, writers choose a topic and create a plan for their writing assignment. In this lesson, students will complete the first part of prewriting, choosing a topic. To do that, they'll **brainstorm** by listing and evaluating several different topics.

Grammar, Usage, and Mechanics Students will learn how to correctly write a direct quotation. A **direct quotation** is a person's exact words. To punctuate a direct quotation, enclose it in quotation marks, and separate it from the sentence with commas.

MATERIALS

Supplied
- *Summit English Language Arts 4 Activity Book*
- Spelling List 4 Pretest
- Brainstorm for Your Personal Narrative
- Personal Narrative Instructions (printout)

Also Needed
- folder for organizing personal narrative writing assignment pages

Examples:

Aaron asked**,** **"**Does this shirt look good?**"**
The coach had clearly said**,** **"**Wear your uniform to the game.**"**
"I better change**,"** thought Aaron with a sigh.

Note that the first word of a direct quotation begins with a capital letter even if the direct quotation is not at the beginning of a sentence. In the examples, the words *Does* and *Wear* correctly begin with capital letters.

Advance Preparation

Gather a folder that students can use to keep all notes and activity pages related to their personal narrative.

Lesson Goals

- Take a spelling pretest.

- Write a direct quotation correctly.

- Identify the steps in the writing process.

- Analyze how an author brainstorms.

- Brainstorm topics for your personal narrative.

GET READY

Introduction to Narrative Writing: Prewriting (A)

Students will get a glimpse of what they will learn about in the lesson. They will also read the lesson goals and keywords. Have students select each keyword and preview its definition.

Spelling List 4 Pretest

Students will take a spelling pretest.

LEARNING COACH CHECK-IN   Have students turn to Spelling List 4 Pretest in *Summit English Language Arts 4 Activity Book* and open the online Spelling Pretest activity. Online, students will listen to the spelling word, type the word in the space indicated, and then check their answer. In the activity book, students will write the correct spelling of the word in the tables provided and indicate with a ✓ or an ✗ if they spelled the word correctly or incorrectly online. Students will repeat this process with the remaining words.

As needed, help students with the interaction between the online activity and the activity book page until they become comfortable with what they need to do. As students practice their spelling words throughout the workshop, they should pay special attention to words they spelled incorrectly on the pretest.

This is the complete list of words students will be tested on.

Long *a* Spelled *a, ai, ay, a–e*	Base Word *port*	Heart Words	Prefix *pre–*
bacon	portable	Delaware	precaution
danger	transport	Maine	prehistoric
erase			preview
essay			
exhale			
fragrant			
layer			
scale			
sustain			
waiting			

NOTE   Have students keep their completed activity page in a safe place so they can refer to it later.

Look Back at Punctuating Dialogue

Students will practice the prerequisite skill of punctuating simple dialogue.

LEARN   Use Direct Quotations

Students will learn how to correctly punctuate and capitalize direct quotations. They will learn the basic rules of enclosing a direct quotation in quotation marks, setting it off from the rest of the sentence with commas, and capitalizing the first letter.

TIP   There are exceptions to the rules for punctuating and capitalizing direct quotations. This lesson will focus on mastery of the rules, not on the exceptions.

TRY IT   Practice Using Direct Quotations

Students will answer questions about punctuating and capitalizing direct quotations. They will receive feedback on their answers.

LEARN   Explore a Student's Personal Narrative

To help them better understand their writing assignment, students will read a model personal narrative and explore the elements that make it successful.

LEARN   Brainstorming for a Personal Narrative

Students will learn about the writing process in general. Then they will closely investigate brainstorming, which is the first part of the prewriting step.

There are many ways to brainstorm. This activity introduces students to one effective brainstorming technique: making a list of ideas and systematically evaluating those ideas.

TIP   Discuss times that you have brainstormed. Maybe you brainstormed ideas for a dinner menu, or maybe you brainstormed solutions for creating a study space in cramped living quarters. How did you come up with and evaluate ideas?

TRY IT   Brainstorm for Your Personal Narrative

Students will complete Brainstorm for Your Personal Narrative from *Summit English Language Arts 4 Activity Book*.

LEARNING COACH CHECK-IN   Review students' responses. Ensure that students have selected a topic for their personal narrative that meets the criteria listed in Question 3 of the activity page. When students have completed the page, they should store it in a folder so that they can refer to it throughout the writing process.

NOTE   In addition to the brainstorming activity, this activity page contains the instructions for the personal narrative. Students should read the instructions carefully, but in this lesson, they should complete the brainstorming activity only (not the entire assignment). If you or students wish, you can download and print another copy of the Personal Narrative Instructions online.

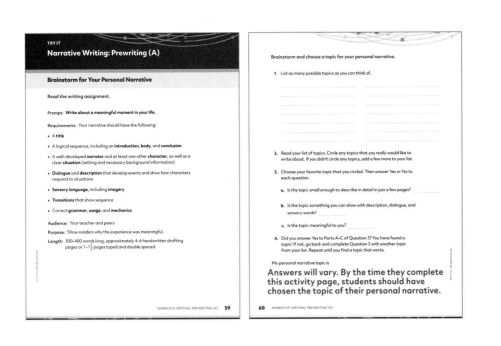

WRAP-UP

Questions About Brainstorming and Dialogue

Students will answer questions to show that they understand how to brainstorm a topic for a narrative and how to correctly write a direct quotation.

Narrative Writing: Prewriting (B)

Lesson Overview

ACTIVITY	ACTIVITY TITLE	TIME	ONLINE/OFFLINE
GET READY	Introduction to Narrative Writing: Prewriting (B)	**2** minutes	🖥
	Spelling List 4 Activity Bank	**10** minutes	📄
LEARN AND **TRY IT**	Order Adjectives	**10** minutes	🖥
	Practice Ordering Adjectives	**10** minutes	🖥
	Prewriting for a Personal Narrative	**15** minutes	🖥
	Prewrite for Your Personal Narrative **LEARNING COACH CHECK-IN**	**40** minutes	📄
WRAP-UP	Questions About Prewriting and Adjectives	**3** minutes	🖥
	Go Read!	**30** minutes	🖥 or 📄

Content Background

Students will continue working on their **personal narrative** about a meaningful moment in their lives. They will complete this assignment over the course of several lessons by following the writing process. In this lesson, students will complete the prewriting step.

Writing Process

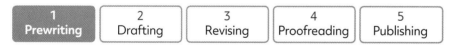

| 1 Prewriting | 2 Drafting | 3 Revising | 4 Proofreading | 5 Publishing |

In this part of **prewriting**, students will plan key elements of their narrative. They'll use a graphic organizer to plan the order in which they'll present the events of their narrative. Students will plan the beginning (introduction), the middle (which includes a problem that escalates and is resolved), and the end.

After they determine the order of events, they will determine what key details readers need to know about the narrator, main characters, and situation in the introduction. Finally, they will plan ways they can use dialogue and description to convey important information to readers.

MATERIALS

Supplied
- *Summit English Language Arts 4 Activity Book*
  - Spelling List 4 Activity Bank
  - Prewrite for Your Personal Narrative
- Personal Narrative Instructions (printout)

Also Needed
- completed Spelling List 4 Pretest activity page from Narrative Writing: Prewriting (A)
- folder in which students are storing personal narrative writing assignment pages
- reading material for Go Read!

Grammar, Usage, and Mechanics Students will learn how to logically order adjectives that come before the same noun or pronoun. In general, order adjectives before a noun as follows:

1. opinion (e.g., *cute*, *kind*, *silly*)
2. size (e.g., *tiny*, *tall*)
3. color

Examples:
The **large orange** mouse sat on the chair.
An **ugly small blue** snake slithered up the chair leg.

While there are additional categories of adjectives, such as adjectives that describe shape and age, students will focus on ordering adjectives that describe opinion, size, and color.

Advance Preparation

Gather students' completed Spelling List 4 Pretest activity page from Narrative Writing: Prewriting (A). Students will refer to this page during Get Ready: Spelling List 4 Activity Bank.

Gather the folder that students are using to store the activity pages related to their personal narrative. The folder should contain the following:

- Students' completed Brainstorm for Your Personal Narrative activity page from Narrative Writing: Prewriting (A)

During the Go Read! activity, students will have the option of using the digital library. Allow extra time for students to make their reading selection, or have students make a selection before beginning the lesson.

Lesson Goals

- Practice spelling words offline.
- Order adjectives correctly in a sentence.
- Analyze how an author plans a personal narrative.
- Plan your personal narrative.
- Read for pleasure.

GET READY

Introduction to Narrative Writing: Prewriting (B)
Students will get a glimpse of what they will learn about in the lesson. They will also read the lesson goals and keywords. Have students select each keyword and preview its definition.

Spelling List 4 Activity Bank

Students will practice all spelling words from the workshop by completing Spelling List 4 Activity Bank from *Summit English Language Arts 4 Activity Book*. Make sure students have their completed Spelling List 4 Pretest activity page from Narrative Writing: Prewriting (A) to refer to during this activity.

Remind students to pay special attention to words they spelled incorrectly on the Spelling Pretest.

LEARN AND TRY IT

LEARN   Order Adjectives

Students will learn how to logically order adjectives that come before a noun or a pronoun.

> **TIP**   An adjective that comes before a noun or pronoun is called a *coordinate adjective*. An adjective that comes after a linking verb (e.g., *kind* in the sentence, "He is kind.") is called a *predicate adjective*.

TRY IT   Practice Ordering Adjectives

Students will answer questions about logically ordering adjectives that come before a noun or a pronoun. They will receive feedback on their answers.

LEARN   Prewriting for a Personal Narrative

Students will explore how to prewrite for a personal narrative.

> **TIP**   Students may wish to jot notes on their Prewrite for Your Personal Narrative activity page as they work through this activity.

TRY IT   Prewrite for Your Personal Narrative

Students will complete Prewrite for Your Personal Narrative from *Summit English Language Arts 4 Activity Book*. Make sure students have their completed Brainstorm for Your Personal Narrative activity page from Narrative Writing: Prewriting (A) to refer to during this activity.

LEARNING COACH CHECK-IN   Review students' responses. Ensure that the narrative students are planning is in line with the assignment criteria outlined on the Brainstorm for Your Personal Narrative activity page. When students have completed the activity page, they should store it in the folder they are using to organize their writing assignment pages.

SUPPORT   Students may have difficultly planning a time line that they can cover in a 400-word narrative. To help students shorten a too-long time line, have them choose a new Beginning from the Middle section of their graphic organizer.

NOTE   If you or students wish, you can download and print another copy of the Personal Narrative Instructions online.

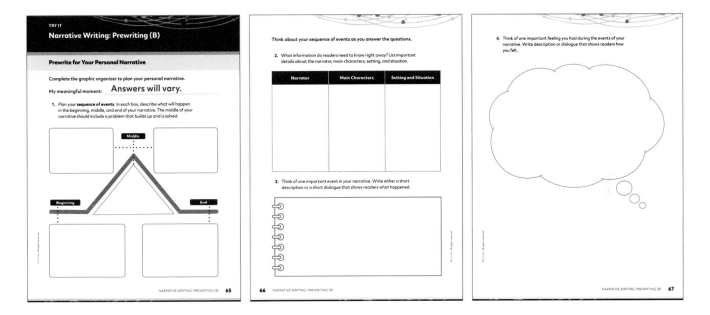

WRAP-UP

Questions About Prewriting and Adjectives

Students will answer questions to show that they understand how to prewrite for a narrative and how to logically order adjectives.

Go Read!

Students will read for pleasure. They should choose a book or a magazine that interests them, or they may choose a selection from the digital library, linked in the online lesson.

Students should read for the entire time. Have students select something to read ahead of time to help them stay focused.

Narrative Writing: Drafting (A)

Lesson Overview

ACTIVITY	ACTIVITY TITLE	TIME	ONLINE/OFFLINE
GET READY	Introduction to Narrative Writing: Drafting (A)	**2** minutes	🖥️
	Spelling List 4 Review Game	**10** minutes	🖥️
	Tap Dancing	**10** minutes	🖥️
LEARN AND **TRY IT**	Drafting a Personal Narrative	**15** minutes	🖥️
	Draft Your Personal Narrative **LEARNING COACH CHECK-IN**	**60** minutes	📄
WRAP-UP	Question About Drafting	**3** minutes	🖥️
	Go Read!	**20** minutes	🖥️ or 📄

Content Background

Students will continue working on their **personal narrative** about a meaningful moment in their lives. They will complete this assignment over the course of several lessons by following the writing process. In this lesson, students will begin drafting their narrative.

Writing Process

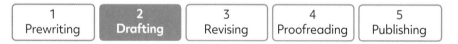

1 Prewriting	2 Drafting	3 Revising	4 Proofreading	5 Publishing

During **drafting**, students will use their prewriting as a guide as they write a rough draft of their personal narrative. A rough draft is a complete first version of a piece of writing. Writers create rough drafts to get all their ideas fleshed out and in order, from beginning to end. In other words, a rough draft is a starting point, or a first attempt, at a complete narrative. During revision and proofreading, writers refine their ideas and fix any errors.

Students are expected to write about half of their rough draft in this lesson (although they may write more if they wish). They will have time to finish and submit their draft in Narrative Writing: Drafting (B).

Advance Preparation

Gather the folder that students are using to store the activity pages related to their personal narrative. The folder should contain the following:

- Students' completed Brainstorm for Your Personal Narrative activity page from Narrative Writing: Prewriting (A)

- Students' completed Prewrite for Your Personal Narrative activity page from Narrative Writing: Prewriting (B)

During the Go Read! activity, students will have the option of using the digital library. Allow extra time for students to make their reading selection, or have students make a selection before beginning the lesson.

Lesson Goals

- Practice spelling words online.

- Practice grammar skills by editing a passage.

- Analyze how an author writes a rough draft.

- Start the rough draft of your personal narrative.

- Read for pleasure.

GET READY

Introduction to Narrative Writing: Drafting (A)

Students will get a glimpse of what they will learn about in the lesson. They will also read the lesson goals and keywords. Have students select each keyword and preview its definition.

Spelling List 4 Review Game

Students will practice all spelling words from the workshop.

Tap Dancing

Students will edit a short passage to practice applying grammar skills. This passage contains errors and questions related to direct quotations, order of adjectives, subject-verb agreement, and complete sentences.

LEARN   Drafting a Personal Narrative

Students will explore how to use work completed during prewriting to draft a personal narrative.

TIP   Emphasize that rough drafts are not perfect. Even expert writers make many revisions to their rough drafts.

TRY IT   Draft Your Personal Narrative

Students will complete half of their rough draft using Draft Your Personal Narrative in *Summit English Language Arts 4 Activity Book*. If students wish, they may complete more than half of their draft.

Make sure students have their completed Brainstorm for Your Personal Narrative activity page from Narrative Writing: Prewriting (A) and Prewrite for Your Personal Narrative activity page from Narrative Writing: Prewriting (B) to refer to during this activity.

LEARNING COACH CHECK-IN   Review students' responses. Ensure that students' draft is in line with the assignment criteria outlined on the Brainstorm for Your Personal Narrative activity page. Students should store their draft in the folder they are using to organize their writing assignment pages.

NOTE   If you or students wish, you can download and print another copy of the Personal Narrative Instructions online. Additional sheets of Drafting Paper are also available online.

TRY IT
Narrative Writing: Drafting (A)

Draft Your Personal Narrative

Write the first draft of your personal narrative. Write only on the white rows. You will use the purple rows for revisions later.

Title

start here ▶

Students should write their draft in the white rows only.

keep writing ▶

Draft Page 1

NARRATIVE WRITING: DRAFTING (A)   **69**

---

70   NARRATIVE WRITING: DRAFTING (A)

keep writing ▶

Draft Page 2

---

keep writing ▶

Draft Page 3

NARRATIVE WRITING: DRAFTING (A)   **71**

Draft Page 4

keep writing ►

Draft Page 5

keep writing ►

Draft Page 6

WRAP-UP

Question About Drafting

Students will answer a question to show that they understand how to draft a narrative.

Go Read!

Students will read for pleasure. They should choose a book or a magazine that interests them, or they may choose a selection from the digital library, linked in the online lesson.

Students should read for the entire time. Have students select something to read ahead of time to help them stay focused.

Narrative Writing: Drafting (B)

Lesson Overview

ACTIVITY	ACTIVITY TITLE	TIME	ONLINE/OFFLINE
GET READY	Introduction to Narrative Writing: Drafting (B)	**1** minute	
TRY IT	Review Direct Quotations and Order of Adjectives	**10** minutes	
QUIZ	Direct Quotations and Order of Adjectives	**20** minutes	
	Spelling List 4	**10** minutes	
TRY IT	Finish Drafting Your Personal Narrative **LEARNING COACH CHECK-IN**	**60** minutes	
WRAP-UP	Turn In Your Personal Narrative Draft	**1** minute	
	More Language Arts Practice	**8** minutes	
	Go Read!	**10** minutes	

Content Background

Students will continue working on their **personal narrative** about a meaningful moment in their lives. In this lesson, students will finish and submit their rough draft. In later lessons, students will revise, proofread, and publish their personal narrative.

Writing Process

1 Prewriting	2 Drafting	3 Revising	4 Proofreading	5 Publishing

Advance Preparation

Gather the folder that students are using to store the activity pages related to their personal narrative. The folder should contain the following:

- Students' completed Brainstorm for Your Personal Narrative activity page from Narrative Writing: Prewriting (A)

- Students' completed Prewrite for Your Personal Narrative activity page from Narrative Writing: Prewriting (B)

- Students' in-progress Draft Your Personal Narrative activity page from Narrative Writing: Drafting (A)

MATERIALS

Supplied
- *Summit English Language Arts 4 Activity Book*
  - Draft Your Personal Narrative
- Personal Narrative Instructions (printout)
- Drafting Paper (printout)

Also Needed
- folder in which students are storing personal narrative writing assignment pages

Lesson Goals

- Review how to write a direct quotation and logically order adjectives.
- Take a quiz on direct quotations and ordering adjectives.
- Take a spelling quiz.
- Finish and submit the rough draft of your personal narrative.

GET READY

Introduction to Narrative Writing: Drafting (B)

Students will read the lesson goals.

TRY IT

Review Direct Quotations and Order of Adjectives

Students will answer questions to review what they have learned about writing direct quotations and logically ordering adjectives that come before a noun or pronoun.

QUIZ

Direct Quotations and Order of Adjectives

Students will complete the Direct Quotations and Order of Adjectives quiz.

Spelling List 4

Students will complete the Spelling List 4 quiz.

TRY IT

Finish Drafting Your Personal Narrative

Students will complete the rough draft of their personal narrative. Students should gather the Draft Your Personal Narrative activity page that they started in Narrative Writing: Drafting (A) and complete it.

Make sure students also have their completed Brainstorm for Your Personal Narrative activity page from Narrative Writing: Prewriting (A) and Prewrite for Your Personal Narrative activity page from Narrative Writing: Prewriting (B) to refer to during this activity.

LEARNING COACH CHECK-IN   Review students' draft. Ensure that students' draft is in line with the assignment criteria outlined on the Brainstorm for Your Personal Narrative activity page. If necessary, remind students not to focus on perfection at this stage of the writing process.

NOTE   If you or students wish, you can download and print another copy of the Personal Narrative Instructions online. Additional sheets of Drafting Paper are also available online.

Narrative Writing: Drafting (A)

Draft Your Personal Narrative

Write the first draft of your personal narrative. Write only on the white rows. You will use the purple rows for revisions later.

Title

start here ►

Students should write their draft in the white rows only.

keep writing ►

Draft Page 1

keep writing ►

Draft Page 2

keep writing ►

Draft Page 3

keep writing ►

Draft Page 4

keep writing ►

Draft Page 5

Draft Page 6

WRAP-UP

Turn In Your Personal Narrative Draft

Students will submit their completed rough draft to their teacher.

More Language Arts Practice

Students will practice skills according to their individual needs.

Go Read!

Students will read for pleasure. They should choose a book or a magazine that interests them, or they may choose a selection from the digital library, linked in the online lesson.

Students should read for the entire time. Have students select something to read ahead of time to help them stay focused.

Nuance

Lesson Overview

ACTIVITY	ACTIVITY TITLE	TIME	ONLINE/OFFLINE
GET READY	Introduction to Nuance	**1** minute	🖥️
LEARN AND **TRY IT**	Look Back at Shades of Meaning	**4** minutes	🖥️
	What's the Difference?	**10** minutes	🖥️
	Which Works Best?	**10** minutes	🖥️
	Apply: Nuance **LEARNING COACH CHECK-IN**	**15** minutes	📄
	Go Write!	**15** minutes	📄
	Review Nuance	**15** minutes	🖥️
QUIZ	Nuance	**15** minutes	🖥️
WRAP-UP	More Language Arts Practice	**25** minutes	🖥️
	Go Read!	**10** minutes	🖥️ or 📄

Content Background

Students will learn several words whose meanings are similar but subtly different. These subtle differences in meaning are called *nuances*. Students will use context clues to help them figure out which word among those with similar meanings is the best word in a situation. For example, the words *tropical* and *hot* have similar meanings. Because of the nuance between the two words, you would use *tropical* to describe weather but not soup.

Advance Preparation

During the Go Read! activity, students will have the option of using the digital library. Allow extra time for students to make their reading selection, or have students make a selection before beginning the lesson.

MATERIALS

Supplied
- *Summit English Language Arts 4 Activity Book*
  - Apply: Nuance

Also Needed
- reading material for Go Read!

KEYWORDS

context clue – a word or phrase in a text that helps you figure out the meaning of an unknown word

nuance – a very small difference in meaning

Lesson Goals

- Use context clues to help determine the meaning of unknown words.
- Recognize subtle differences in the meanings of words.
- Use words correctly.
- Read and write for pleasure.

GET READY

Introduction to Nuance

Students will get a glimpse of what they will learn about in the lesson. They will also read the lesson goals and keywords. Have students select each keyword and preview its definition.

Look Back at Shades of Meaning

Students will practice the prerequisite skill of distinguishing between words that have similar, but not identical, meanings.

LEARN AND TRY IT

LEARN What's the Difference?

Students will be introduced to the vocabulary words for the lesson. Then they will learn that choosing between words with subtle differences in meaning can help writers convey clearer, more exact messages. Students will also learn that context clues can help them determine which of two words with similar meanings best completes a sentence.

TRY IT Which Works Best?

Students will practice recognizing nuance and choosing between words with subtly different meanings.

TRY IT Apply: Nuance

Students will complete Apply: Nuance from *Summit English Language Arts 4 Activity Book*.

LEARNING COACH CHECK-IN   In the second part of this activity page, students will ask you to complete sentences they write. During the activity, give students feedback using the suggestions provided to guide you.

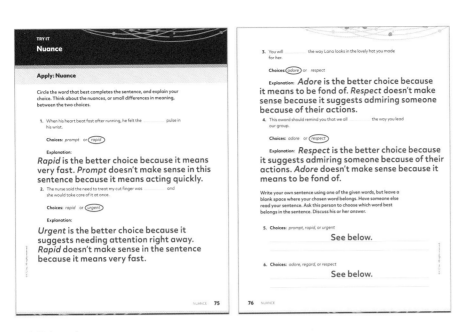

Additional answers

5. Answers will vary. Encourage students to point out the context clues in their sentence that make one word a more appropriate choice to complete the sentence than the other two.

6. Answers will vary. Encourage students to point out the context clues in their sentence that make one word a more appropriate choice to complete the sentence than the other two.

TRY IT   Go Write!

Students will write independently for pleasure. As they write, they should consider the nuances of words they use. They should choose words that are right for the message they want their writing to convey.

TRY IT   Review Nuance

Students will answer questions to review what they have learned about nuance.

QUIZ

Nuance

Students will complete the Nuance quiz.

More Language Arts Practice

Students will practice skills according to their individual needs.

Go Read!

Students will read for pleasure. They should choose a book or a magazine that interests them, or they may choose a selection from the digital library, linked in the online lesson.

Students should read for the entire time. Have students select something to read ahead of time to help them stay focused.

"Still Standing: The Leaning Tower of Pisa"

Lesson Overview

ACTIVITY	ACTIVITY TITLE	TIME	ONLINE/OFFLINE
GET READY	Introduction to "Still Standing: The Leaning Tower of Pisa"	**1** minute	🖥️
	Spelling List 5 Pretest **LEARNING COACH CHECK-IN**	**10** minutes	🖥️ and 📄
	Before You Read "Still Standing: The Leaning Tower of Pisa"	**10** minutes	🖥️
READ	"Still Standing: The Leaning Tower of Pisa"	**20** minutes	📄
	Check-In: "Still Standing: The Leaning Tower of Pisa"	**4** minutes	🖥️
LEARN AND **TRY IT**	Explaining Information from Text Structure and Graphics	**10** minutes	🖥️
	Interpreting Information from Text Structure and Graphics	**10** minutes	🖥️
	Skim and Scan to Identify Author's Points	**10** minutes	🖥️
	Skim and Scan to Explain Author's Points	**10** minutes	🖥️
	Apply: Main Idea	**15** minutes	🖥️
	Supporting Author's Points **LEARNING COACH CHECK-IN**	**10** minutes	📄
	Practice Words from "Still Standing: The Leaning Tower of Pisa"	**8** minutes	🖥️
WRAP-UP	Question About "Still Standing: The Leaning Tower of Pisa"	**2** minutes	🖥️

Content Background

Students will continue exploring organizational structures of informational text, specifically the problem-and-solution structure. In this case, the problem is the tower continues to lean, and the author presents a few ways to solve the problem. This article also includes many diagrams, particularly a section on explaining objects and their center of gravity. It is critical to focus on the specific details included in the diagrams.

In another part of the lesson, students will use skimming and scanning techniques to locate information. Skimming involves a quick glance to get a general overview of a text, while scanning involves focusing on parts of a text to locate specific information.

MATERIALS

Supplied
- *K12 World: Emoji and Pisa and Birds, Oh My!*
- *Summit English Language Arts 4 Activity Book*
  - Spelling List 5 Pretest
  - Supporting Author's Points

"Still Standing: The Leaning Tower of Pisa" Synopsis

The magazine article describes the Learning Tower of Pisa, a bell tower standing in Pisa, Italy. The tower was built on soft soil that was unable to support the weight of the tower. As each level was added, the tower tilted more and more. The builders attempted to solve this problem but were unable to stop the shifting. As time went on, the tower continued to lean farther and farther. In 1911, scientists began to measure and record the tower's movement. They were able to predict that the tower would fall over once it tilted 5.44 degrees. The engineers attempted to stop the tilting, but again they were unsuccessful. As predicted, the tower reached 5.44 degrees, but surprisingly, it did not collapse. The article explains how the tower is still standing, providing the reader with background information on the concept of center of gravity. The Leaning Tower of Pisa has not fallen over because the line through its center of gravity has always intersected the base of the tower. The article concludes with another attempt by scientists and engineers to solve this problem, which was successful.

KEYWORDS

diagram – a drawing or design that shows how pieces of information are related

graphic – a picture, photograph, map, diagram, or other image

problem-solution structure – organizational pattern in which a problem is described, followed by descriptions of its solution or possible solutions

Lesson Goals

- Take a spelling pretest.
- Read "Still Standing: The Learning Tower of Pisa."
- Identify and describe problem-and-solution organizational structure in a nonfiction text.
- Interpret information presented in graphics in the text.
- Apply skimming and scanning techniques to locate information.
- Explain how an author uses reasons or evidence to support points in a text.
- Determine meanings of unfamiliar words in the reading.

GET READY

Introduction to "Still Standing: The Learning Tower of Pisa"

Students will get a glimpse of what they will learn about in the lesson. They will also read the lesson goals and keywords. Have students select each keyword and preview its definition.

Spelling List 5 Pretest

Students will take a spelling pretest.

LEARNING COACH CHECK-IN   Have students turn to Spelling List 5 Pretest in *Summit English Language Arts 4 Activity Book* and open the online Spelling Pretest activity. Online, students will listen to the spelling word, type the word in the space indicated, and then check their answer. In the activity book, students will write the correct spelling of the word in the tables provided and indicate with a ✓ or an ✗ if they spelled the word correctly or incorrectly online. Students will repeat this process with the remaining words.

As needed, help students with the interaction between the online activity and the activity book page until they become comfortable with what they need to do. As students practice their spelling words throughout the workshop, they should pay special attention to words they spelled incorrectly on the pretest.

This is the complete list of words students will be tested on.

Long *a* Spelled *eigh*	Long *a* Spelled *ey*	Long *a* Spelled *ea*	Heart Words	Prefix *sub-*
eighty	convey	breaking	Pennsylvania	submarine
freighter	obey	steakhouse	Texas	substandard
neighborly	survey	great		subtitle
weighing				subway
eighteen				

NOTE   Have students keep their completed activity page in a safe place so they can refer to it later.

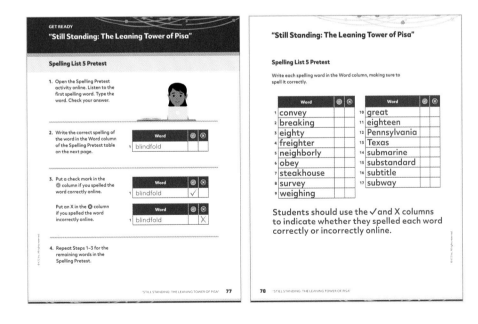

Before You Read "Still Standing: The Leaning Tower of Pisa"

Students will be introduced to some key vocabulary words that they will encounter in the upcoming reading and answer a question to help them set a purpose for their reading.

NOTE Students will make a prediction before reading the article.

READ

"Still Standing: The Leaning Tower of Pisa"

Students will read "Still Standing: The Leaning Tower of Pisa" in *Emoji and Pisa and Birds, Oh My!*

Check-In: "Still Standing: The Leaning Tower of Pisa"

Students will answer several questions to demonstrate their comprehension of "Still Standing: The Leaning Tower of Pisa."

NOTE Students will confirm or modify their prediction after reading the article.

LEARN AND TRY IT

LEARN   Explaining Information from Text and Graphics

Students will learn how to identify problem-and-solution text structure and how graphics provide visual information to help explain concepts in a text.

TRY IT   Interpreting Information from Text and Graphics

Students will answer questions in which they identify the organizational structure of the text and interpret information from both the text and graphics presented in the article.

LEARN   Skim and Scan to Identify Author's Points

Students will learn about skimming and scanning techniques to locate the author's specific points in an informational text.

TIP   Skimming and scanning are actions a reader takes to quickly locate valuable information.

TRY IT   Skim and Scan to Explain Author's Points

Students will apply skimming and scanning techniques to locate an author's points. Also, students will explain how an author uses reasons or evidence to support these points.

TRY IT   Apply: Main Idea

Students will apply to a new work what they've learned.

TRY IT Supporting Author's Points

Students will complete Supporting Author's Points from *Summit English Language Arts 4 Activity Book.*

LEARNING COACH CHECK-IN This activity page contains open-ended questions, so it's important that you review students' responses. Give students feedback, using the sample answers provided to guide you.

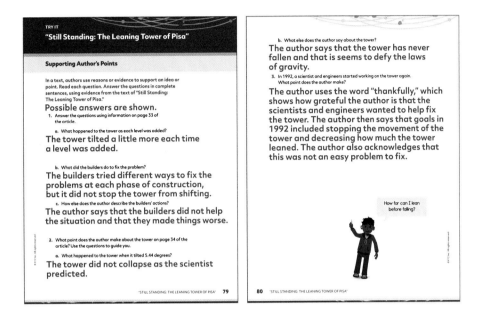

TRY IT Practice Words from "Still Standing: The Leaning Tower of Pisa"

Students will answer questions to demonstrate their understanding of the vocabulary words from the reading.

WRAP-UP

Question About "Still Standing: The Learning Tower of Pisa"

Students will answer a question to show that they understand how to identify an author's point in an informational text.

"Still Standing: The Leaning Tower of Pisa" Wrap-Up

Lesson Overview

ACTIVITY	ACTIVITY TITLE	TIME	ONLINE/OFFLINE
GET READY	Introduction to "Still Standing: The Leaning Tower of Pisa" Wrap-Up	**1** minute	🖥
	Spelling List 5 Activity Bank	**10** minutes	📄
TRY IT	Explain the Leaning Tower of Pisa **LEARNING COACH CHECK-IN**	**30** minutes	📄
	Read and Record	**10** minutes	🖥
	Review "Still Standing: The Leaning Tower of Pisa"	**20** minutes	🖥
QUIZ	"Still Standing: The Leaning Tower of Pisa"	**30** minutes	🖥
WRAP-UP	More Language Arts Practice	**19** minutes	🖥

Advance Preparation

Gather students' completed Spelling List 5 Pretest activity page from "Still Standing: The Leaning Tower of Pisa." Students will refer to this page during Get Ready: Spelling List 5 Activity Bank.

Lesson Goals

- Practice all spelling words.
- Explain concepts in "Still Standing: The Leaning Tower of Pisa" based on specific text information.
- Practice reading aloud to develop fluency.
- Review and take a quiz on problem-and-solution organizational structure, graphics, skimming and scanning, main idea and supporting details, and evidence that supports an author's points.

GET READY

Introduction to "Still Standing: The Leaning Tower of Pisa" Wrap-Up
Students will read the lesson goals.

Spelling List 5 Activity Bank

Students will practice all spelling words from the workshop by completing Spelling List 5 Activity Bank from *Summit English Language Arts 4 Activity Book*. Make sure students have their completed Spelling List 5 Pretest activity page from *Still Standing: The Leaning Tower of Pisa* to refer to during this activity.

Remind students to pay special attention to words they spelled incorrectly on the Spelling Pretest.

TRY IT

Explain the Leaning Tower of Pisa

Students will complete Explain the Leaning Tower of Pisa from *Summit English Language Arts 4 Activity Book*.

TIP   Remind students to include information they learned from the diagrams in their response.

LEARNING COACH CHECK-IN   This activity page contains open-ended questions, so it's important that you review students' responses. Give students feedback, using the sample answer provided to guide you.

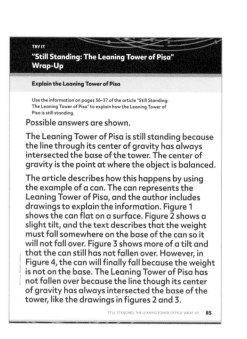

Read and Record

Good readers read quickly, smoothly, and with expression. This is called *fluency*. Students will record themselves reading aloud. They will listen to their recording and think about how quick, smooth, and expressive they sound.

TIP   Encourage students to rerecord as needed.

Review "Still Standing: The Leaning Tower of Pisa"

Students will answer questions to review what they have learned about "Still Standing: The Leaning Tower of Pisa."

QUIZ

"Still Standing: The Leaning Tower of Pisa"

Students will complete the "Still Standing: The Leaning Tower of Pisa" quiz.

WRAP-UP

More Language Arts Practice

Students will practice skills according to their individual needs.

"The Many Colors of Birds"

Lesson Overview

ACTIVITY	ACTIVITY TITLE	TIME	ONLINE/OFFLINE
GET READY	Introduction to "The Many Colors of Birds"	**1** minute	
	Spelling List 5 Review Game	**10** minutes	
	Before You Read "The Many Colors of Birds"	**10** minutes	
READ	"The Many Colors of Birds"	**20** minutes	
	Check-In: "The Many Colors of Birds"	**4** minutes	
LEARN AND **TRY IT**	Information Organized by Cause and Effect	**10** minutes	
	Identify Cause-and-Effect Relationships	**10** minutes	
	Use Text Features	**10** minutes	
	Categorize, Organize, Summarize	**10** minutes	
	Apply: Details to Support the Main Idea	**15** minutes	
	Write Notes for a Summary **LEARNING COACH CHECK-IN**	**10** minutes	
	Practice Words from "The Many Colors of Birds"	**8** minutes	
WRAP-UP	Question About "The Many Colors of Birds"	**2** minutes	

Content Background

Students will continue working with organizational structures of informational texts. This text is written with a cause-and-effect organizational structure, in which one event leads to, or causes, another. Students will continue to use text features to learn more from an article. This text has extensive information in the captions included with each photograph.

MATERIALS

Supplied
- *K12 World: Emoji and Pisa and Birds, Oh My!*
- *Summit English Language Arts 4 Activity Book*
  - Write Notes for a Summary

"The Many Colors of Birds" Synopsis

"The Many Colors of Birds" is an informational magazine article written in a cause-and-effect organizational structure. The text explains how we see color and provides specific information on how the colors of birds are produced. For example, blacks and browns are the results of pigments produced in the cells of a bird's body. Other colors are the results of pigments from a bird's diet or the result of the structure of a bird's feathers.

Lesson Goals

- Practice all spelling words.
- Read "The Many Colors of Birds."
- Describe the organizational structure of a text and how the structure aids comprehension.
- Explain concepts in a scientific text and relationships among those concepts.
- Organize and categorize information in a nonfiction text.
- Identify what makes an effective summary.
- Write a summary of information from a text.
- Determine meanings of unfamiliar words in the reading.

GET READY

Introduction to "The Many Colors of Birds"

Students will get a glimpse of what they will learn about in the lesson. They will also read the lesson goals and keywords. Have students select each keyword and preview its definition.

Spelling List 5 Review Game

Students will practice all spelling words from the workshop.

Before You Read "The Many Colors of Birds"

Students will be introduced to some key vocabulary words that they will encounter in the upcoming reading and answer a question to help them set a purpose for their reading.

NOTE   Students will make a prediction before reading the article.

"The Many Colors of Birds"

Students will read "The Many Colors of Birds" from *Emoji and Pisa and Birds, Oh My!*

Check-In: "The Many Colors of Birds"

Students will answer several questions to demonstrate their comprehension of "The Many Colors of Birds."

NOTE Students will confirm or modify their prediction after reading the article.

LEARN AND TRY IT

LEARN   Information Organized by Cause and Effect

Students will learn about the cause-and-effect text structure used to organize information in the article "The Many Colors of Birds." They will also learn about sidebars and diagrams, nonfiction text features that provide extra information beyond the main body of a text.

TRY IT   Identify Cause-and-Effect Relationships

Students will analyze passages to determine cause-and-effect relationships and identify how cause-and-effect text structure aids comprehension.

LEARN   Organize and Summarize Information

Students will learn how information can be categorized and organized in an informational text. They will also learn how to create an effective summary that demonstrates understanding of text.

TRY IT   Categorize, Organize, Summarize

Students will answer questions to demonstrate their knowledge of effective summaries and their ability to organize information into categories.

TRY IT   Apply: Details to Support the Main Idea

Students will explain how key details support the main idea(s) in a given text.

SUPPORT For students having difficulty recognizing key details, suggest that students categorize the information as interesting or important.

TRY IT   Write Notes for a Summary

Students will complete Write Notes for a Summary from *Summit English Language Arts 4 Activity Book*.

LEARNING COACH CHECK-IN Students will refer to the information they gather in this activity to complete another writing activity, so it's important that you review students' responses. Give students feedback, using the sample answers provided to guide you.

TRY IT
"The Many Colors of Birds"

Write Notes for a Summary

Record notes about the important information on pages 22–23 of "The Many Colors of Birds" in preparation to write a summary. Make sure to include information from the text features, such as the captions and sidebars.

Location	Notes
page 22 Pigmentation	
pages 22–23 Blacks and Browns	See below.
page 23 caption	
page 23 sidebar	

"THE MANY COLORS OF BIRDS" **87**

Additional answers

Location	Notes
page 22 Pigmentation	• chemicals that give living things their color • absorbs certain colors from light, others reflected • eyes, skin, and hair color in people • pigments make colors of bird feathers
page 22–23 Blacks and Browns	• melanin makes feathers look brown or black • color reflected depends on how much melanin is produced • brown and black feathers are important to white birds • feathers with melanin don't break down as easily
page 23 caption	• melanin makes a seagull's dark feathers stronger than the white ones
page 23 sidebar	• white can be seen because it reflects all colors of light • white crows don't have melanin • white crows are not common

TRY IT Practice Words from "The Many Colors of Birds"

Students will answer questions to demonstrate their understanding of the vocabulary words from the reading.

WRAP-UP

Question About "The Many Colors of Birds"

Students will answer a question to show that they can explain ideas included in nonficiton text features.

"The Many Colors of Birds" Wrap-Up

Lesson Overview

ACTIVITY	ACTIVITY TITLE	TIME	ONLINE/OFFLINE
GET READY	Introduction to "The Many Colors of Birds" Wrap-Up	**1** minute	🖥️
TRY IT	Write About Pigmentation LEARNING COACH CHECK-IN	**30** minutes	📄
	Read and Record	**10** minutes	🖥️
	Review "The Many Colors of Birds"	**20** minutes	🖥️
QUIZ	"The Many Colors of Birds"	**30** minutes	🖥️
	Spelling List 5	**10** minutes	🖥️
WRAP-UP	More Language Arts Practice	**19** minutes	🖥️

Advance Preparation

Gather students' completed Write Notes for a Summary activity page from "The Many Colors of Birds." Students will refer to this page during the Try It: Write About Pigmentation activity.

Lesson Goals

- Summarize ideas in an informational text.
- Practice reading aloud to develop fluency.
- Review and take a quiz on text structure, text features, and effective summaries.
- Take a spelling quiz.

GET READY

Introduction to "The Many Colors of Birds" Wrap-Up

Students will read the lesson goals.

Write About Pigmentation

Students will complete Write About Pigmentation from *Summit English Language Arts 4 Activity Book*.

LEARNING COACH CHECK-IN This activity page contains open-ended questions, so it's important that you review students' responses. Give students feedback, using the sample answers provided to guide you.

TRY IT

"The Many Colors of Birds" Wrap-Up

Write About Pigmentation

Use the text and your completed Notes for a Summary activity page from "The Many Colors of Birds." Write a summary that includes all the important information from the text and the text features.

See right.

"THE MANY COLORS OF BIRDS" WRAP-UP **89**

Additional answers

Possible answers are shown.

Pigments are chemicals that give living things their color. Certain pigments absorb colors from light and cause other colors to be reflected. For example, our eyes, skin, and hair are the colors they are because of pigments. Pigments are also the reason that bird feathers are so many different colors.

Sparrows make pigments in their body. Their feathers get color from a pigment called melanin. Melanin makes bird feathers look brown or black. The color that is reflected depends on how much melanin is made. For example, crows and eagles are black, so they have a lot of melanin. One rare bird is the white crow. It's white, so it does not make melanin.

Brown or black feathers, which have melanin, are important to white birds. Feathers with melanin do not break down as quickly or as easily as feathers without melanin. In the seagull, the dark feathers are on the wings. Seagulls need stronger feathers to use for flying.

Pigments are chemicals that give living things their color. Melanin is a kind of pigment that makes some feathers brown or black in birds.

Read and Record

Good readers read quickly, smoothly, and with expression. This is called *fluency*. Students will record themselves reading aloud. They will listen to their recording and think about how quick, smooth, and expressive they sound.

TIP Encourage students to rerecord as needed.

Review "The Many Colors of Birds."

Students will answer questions to review what they have learned about "The Many Colors of Birds."

"The Many Colors of Birds"

Students will complete the "The Many Colors of Birds" quiz.

Spelling List 5

Students will complete the Spelling List 5 quiz.

More Language Arts Practice

Students will practice skills according to their individual needs.

Big Ideas: Critical Skills Assignment

Lesson Overview

Big Ideas lessons provide students the opportunity to further apply the knowledge acquired and skills learned throughout the unit workshops. Each Big Ideas lesson consists of these parts:

1. **Cumulative Review:** Students keep their skills fresh by reviewing prior content.

2. **Preview:** Students practice answering the types of questions they will commonly find on standardized tests.

3. **Synthesis:** Students complete an assignment that allows them to connect and apply what they have learned. Synthesis assignments vary throughout the course.

   In the Synthesis portion of this Big Ideas lesson, students will read new selections. They will answer literal and inferential comprehension questions and complete writing questions that ask for short responses about the reading selections. Students should refer to the selections while answering the questions, because the questions emphasize using textual evidence. The questions call for students to demonstrate critical thinking, reading, and writing skills.

   LEARNING COACH CHECK-IN   This is a graded assessment. Make sure students complete, review, and submit the assignment to their teacher.

All materials needed for this lesson are linked online and not provided in the Activity Book.

Mystery!

Narrative Writing: Revising

Lesson Overview

ACTIVITY	ACTIVITY TITLE	TIME	ONLINE/OFFLINE
GET READY	Mystery! Unit Overview	**1** minute	📶
	Introduction to Narrative Writing: Revising	**1** minute	📶
	Look Back at Narrative Writing Skills	**15** minutes	📶
LEARN AND **TRY IT**	Revising a Personal Narrative	**20** minutes	📶
	Revise Your Personal Narrative **LEARNING COACH CHECK-IN**	**60** minutes	📄
WRAP-UP	Question About Revising	**3** minutes	📶
	Go Read!	**20** minutes	📶 or 📄

Content Background

Students will continue working on their **personal narrative** about a meaningful moment in their lives. In this lesson, students will **revise** their rough draft.

Writing Process

| 1 Prewriting | 2 Drafting | 3 Revising | 4 Proofreading | 5 Publishing |

To revise their narratives, students will use a checklist. The checklist focuses on organization (*Are any ideas in the wrong place?*) and content (*Are there details I can show instead of tell?*). At the end of this lesson, students will be ready to proofread their narratives for grammar, usage, and mechanics.

Students may not understand the difference between revising and proofreading. When revising, writers focus on large issues, such as the order or ideas or the amount of dialogue. When proofreading, writers fix errors in grammar, usage, and mechanics, such as spelling or punctuation mistakes. Encourage students to focus on revision during this lesson. In the next lesson, students will proofread their narratives.

MATERIALS

Supplied
- *Summit English Language Arts 4 Activity Book*
  - Revise Your Personal Narrative
- Personal Narrative: Revision Feedback Sheet (printout)
- Personal Narrative Instructions (printout)

Also Needed
- folder in which students are storing personal narrative writing assignment pages
- reading material for Go Read!

Advance Preparation

Gather the folder that students are using to store the activity pages related to their personal narrative. The folder should contain the following:

- Students' completed Brainstorm for Your Personal Narrative activity page from Narrative Writing: Prewriting (A)

- Students' completed Prewrite for Your Personal Narrative activity page from Narrative Writing: Prewriting (B)

- Students' completed rough draft from Narrative Writing: Drafting (B)

Prior to the Revise Your Personal Narrative activity in this lesson, read students' rough draft and complete Personal Narrative: Revision Feedback Sheet.

During the Go Read! activity, students will have the option of using the digital library. Allow extra time for students to make their reading selection, or have students make a selection before beginning the lesson.

Lesson Goals

- Use a checklist to revise your narrative.

- Read for pleasure.

KEYWORDS

personal narrative – an essay about a personal experience of the writer

revising – the stage or step of the writing process in which the writer rereads and edits the draft, correcting errors and making changes in content or organization that improve the piece

GET READY

Mystery! Unit Overview

Students will read a summary of what they will learn in the Mystery! unit.

Introduction to Narrative Writing: Revising

Students will get a glimpse of what they will learn about in the lesson. They will also read the lesson goals and keywords. Have students select each keyword and preview its definition.

Look Back at Narrative Writing Skills

Students will answer questions to review how a writer begins a narrative and sequences ideas.

LEARN   Revising a Personal Narrative

Students will learn about revising, including how to use a revision checklist. Through a guided activity, they will explore how to revise a sample student narrative.

TRY IT   Revise Your Personal Narrative

Students will complete Revise Your Personal Narrative in *Summit English Language Arts 4 Activity Book*. They will need their completed rough draft from Narrative Writing: Drafting (B). They should have their folder containing all of their work related to their narrative available in case they need to refer to the assignment instructions or their prewriting.

LEARNING COACH CHECK-IN   Guide students through the revision process.

1. Use the Personal Narrative: Revision Feedback Sheet that you filled out to guide a discussion with students.

   - Tell students the strengths of their narrative. Provide positive comments about the ideas, language, detail, or other elements of the narrative that you enjoyed.

   - Walk through your feedback with students.

   - As you discuss your feedback, encourage students to actively revise their draft in response. Reassure students that it's okay to remove or move around ideas and sentences. Students should revise their draft directly on the page, using the lines they left blank.

2. Have students review their draft once more, using the Revise Your Personal Narrative activity page.

   - For students having difficulty recognizing areas they should revise, suggest a revision, and think aloud to model your revising. For example, *This detail doesn't sound right here. It really goes with the ideas in the second paragraph. Let's move it there, or else the reader might get confused. Can you find any other details that are out of place?*

3. Make sure students store their revised draft in the folder they are using to organize their writing assignment pages.

   TIP   Remind students to focus on the checklist questions. Emphasize that they should not worry about spelling, punctuation, grammar, and so on.

   NOTE   If you or students wish, you can download and print another copy of the Personal Narrative Instructions online.

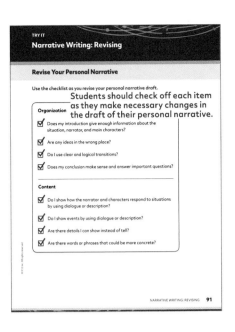

WRAP-UP

Question About Revising

Students will answer a question to show that they understand a key revision skill.

Go Read!

Students will read for pleasure. They should choose a book or a magazine that interests them, or they may choose a selection from the digital library, linked in the online lesson.

Students should read for the entire time. Have students select something to read ahead of time to help them stay focused.

Narrative Writing: Proofreading

Lesson Overview

ACTIVITY	ACTIVITY TITLE	TIME	ONLINE/OFFLINE
GET READY	Introduction to Narrative Writing: Proofreading	**2** minutes	🖥️
	Look Back at Writing Complete Sentences	**15** minutes	🖥️
LEARN AND **TRY IT**	Proofreading a Personal Narrative	**20** minutes	🖥️
	Proofread Your Personal Narrative **LEARNING COACH CHECK-IN**	**60** minutes	📄
WRAP-UP	Question About Proofreading	**3** minutes	🖥️
	Go Read!	**20** minutes	🖥️ or 📄

Content Background

Students will continue working on their **personal narrative** about a meaningful moment in their lives. In this lesson, students will **proofread** their revised rough draft.

Writing Process

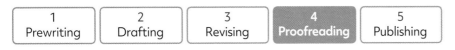

| 1 Prewriting | 2 Drafting | 3 Revising | **4 Proofreading** | 5 Publishing |

To proofread their narrative, students will use a checklist. The checklist focuses on grammar (*Are all sentences complete and correct?*), usage (*Are adjectives ordered correctly in a sentence?*), and mechanics (*Is every word spelled correctly?*). After completing this lesson, students will be ready to prepare a clean copy of their narrative.

Proofreading is sometimes called *editing*.

Advance Preparation

Gather the folder that students are using to store the activity pages related to their personal narrative. The folder should contain the following:

- Students' completed Brainstorm for Your Personal Narrative activity page from Narrative Writing: Prewriting (A)

MATERIALS

Supplied

- *Summit English Language Arts 4 Activity Book*
  - Proofread Your Personal Narrative
  - Personal Narrative: Proofreading Feedback Sheet (printout)
  - Personal Narrative Instructions (printout)

Also Needed

- folder in which students are storing personal narrative writing assignment pages
- reading material for Go Read!

- Students' completed Prewrite for Your Personal Narrative activity page from Narrative Writing: Prewriting (B)

- Students' revised rough draft from Narrative Writing: Revising

Prior to the Proofread Your Personal Narrative activity in this lesson, read students' revised draft. As you read, complete Personal Narrative: Proofreading Feedback Sheet.

During the Go Read! activity, students will have the option of using the digital library. Allow extra time for students to make their reading selection, or have students make a selection before beginning the lesson.

Lesson Goals

- Use a checklist to proofread your narrative.

- Read for pleasure.

GET READY

Introduction to Narrative Writing: Proofreading

Students will get a glimpse of what they will learn about in the lesson. They will also read the lesson goals and keywords. Have students select each keyword and preview its definition.

Look Back at Writing Complete Sentences

Students will practice fixing sentence errors. This is a key skill that they'll use as they proofread their own narrative.

LEARN AND TRY IT

LEARN   Proofreading a Personal Narrative

Students will learn about proofreading, including how to use a proofreading checklist. Through a guided activity, they will explore how to proofread a sample student narrative.

TRY IT   Proofread Your Personal Narrative

Students will complete Proofread Your Personal Narrative in *Summit English Language Arts 4 Activity Book*. They will need their revised rough draft from Narrative Writing: Revising.

LEARNING COACH CHECK-IN   Guide students through the proofreading process.

1. Have students read their draft aloud, listening for errors such as missing words, incomplete sentences, and agreement errors. As students catch errors, have them fix the errors.

   - For students having difficultly noticing errors as they read aloud, model the process. Slowly read a sentence aloud. Pause and model your thinking when you encounter an error. For example, *"Opened the door." This sentence sounds wrong. Who opened the door? The subject is missing. Since Joe opened the door, I'll write "Joe" at the beginning of the sentence and lowercase the word "Opened."*

2. Have students review their draft once more, using the Proofread Your Personal Narrative activity page.

3. Review with students your comments on the Personal Narrative: Proofreading Feedback Sheet. Praise students for the errors that they caught, and guide students to recognize any errors that they have not yet fixed.

4. Have students store their edited draft in the folder they are using to organize their writing assignment pages.

OPTIONAL   Have students exchange revised narratives with a peer and use the Proofread Your Personal Narrative activity page to proofread each other's narratives.

NOTE   If you or students wish, you can download and print another copy of the Personal Narrative Instructions online.

TRY IT
Narrative Writing: Proofreading

Proofread Your Personal Narrative

Use the checklist as you proofread your personal narrative draft.

Grammar and Usage

☑ Are all sentences complete and correct?

☑ Are there any missing or extra words?

☑ Are all verbs in the appropriate tense?

☑ Are adjectives ordered correctly in each sentence?

☑ Are there other grammatical or usage errors?

Students should check off each item as they make necessary changes in the draft of their personal narrative.

Mechanics

☑ Is every word spelled correctly, including frequently confused words?

☑ Does every sentence begin with a capital letter and end with the appropriate punctuation?

☑ Is dialogue punctuated correctly?

☑ Are there other punctuation or capitalization errors?

NARRATIVE WRITING: PROOFREADING   **93**

Question About Proofreading

Students will answer a question to show that they understand a key proofreading skill.

Go Read!

Students will read for pleasure. They should choose a book or a magazine that interests them, or they may choose a selection from the digital library, linked in the online lesson.

Students should read for the entire time. Have students select something to read ahead of time to help them stay focused.

Narrative Writing: Publishing

Lesson Overview

ACTIVITY	ACTIVITY TITLE	TIME	ONLINE/OFFLINE
GET READY	Introduction to Narrative Writing: Publishing	**2** minutes	📶
LEARN AND **TRY IT**	Publishing a Personal Narrative	**15** minutes	📶
	Publish Your Personal Narrative	**60** minutes	📶
WRAP-UP	Turn In Your Personal Narrative	**1** minute	📶
	More Language Arts Practice	**42** minutes	📶

Content Background

Students will continue working on their **personal narrative** about a meaningful moment in their lives. In this lesson, students will **publish** their narrative. Then they will submit their completed narrative to their teacher.

Writing Process

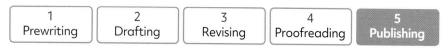

1 Prewriting 2 Drafting 3 Revising 4 Proofreading 5 Publishing

Students will need to type their narrative using a word-processing program. They will complete an activity to review basic word-processing skills, such as using a keyboard and saving a document.

Advance Preparation

Gather the folder that students are using to store the activity pages related to their personal narrative. The folder should contain the following:

- Students' completed Brainstorm for Your Personal Narrative activity page from Narrative Writing: Prewriting (A)

- Students' completed Prewrite for Your Personal Narrative activity page from Narrative Writing: Prewriting (B)

- Students' revised and edited rough draft from Narrative Writing: Proof-reading

---

MATERIALS

Supplied
- Personal Narrative Instructions (printout)

Also Needed
- folder in which students are storing personal narrative writing assignment pages

KEYWORDS

personal narrative – an essay about a personal experience of the writer

publishing – the stage or step of the writing process in which the writer makes a clean copy of the piece and shares it

Lesson Goals

- Type your personal narrative.
- Submit your narrative to your teacher.

GET READY

Introduction to Narrative Writing: Publishing

Students will get a glimpse of what they will learn about in the lesson. They will also read the lesson goals and keywords. Have students select each keyword and preview its definition.

LEARN AND TRY IT

LEARN   Publishing a Personal Narrative

Students will learn about word-processing skills in preparation for typing their personal narrative.

TRY IT   Publish Your Personal Narrative

Students will type a final copy of their personal narrative. Students should gather their revised and proofread draft, and they should type it using a word-processing program.

NOTE   If you or students wish, you can download and print another copy of the Personal Narrative Instructions online.

WRAP-UP

Turn In Your Personal Narrative

Students will submit their writing assignment to their teacher.

More Language Arts Practice

Students will practice skills according to their individual needs.

Precise Words

Lesson Overview

ACTIVITY	ACTIVITY TITLE	TIME	ONLINE/OFFLINE
GET READY	Introduction to Precise Words	**1** minute	🖥️
	Look Back at Nuance	**4** minutes	🖥️
LEARN AND **TRY IT**	Say Exactly What You Mean	**10** minutes	🖥️
	Which Is the Precise Word?	**10** minutes	🖥️
	Apply: Precise Words LEARNING COACH CHECK-IN	**15** minutes	📄
	Go Write!	**15** minutes	📄
	Review Precise Words	**15** minutes	🖥️
QUIZ	Precise Words	**15** minutes	🖥️
WRAP-UP	More Language Arts Practice	**20** minutes	🖥️
	Go Read!	**15** minutes	🖥️ or 📄

Content Background

Students will learn why it's important to use precise words in their writing. They will explore using context clues, nuance, and reference materials to choose precise words.

Advance Preparation

During the Go Read! activity, students will have the option of using the digital library. Allow extra time for students to make their reading selection, or have students make a selection before beginning the lesson.

MATERIALS

Supplied
- *Summit English Language Arts 4 Activity Book*
  - Apply: Precise Words

Also Needed
- reading material for Go Read!

Lesson Goals

- Use context clues to help determine the meaning of unknown words.
- Use reference materials, synonyms, and antonyms to better understand the meaning of words.
- Recognize subtle differences in the meanings of words.
- Read and write for pleasure.

GET READY

Introduction to Precise Words

Students will get a glimpse of what they will learn about in the lesson. They will also read the lesson goals and keywords. Have students select each keyword and preview its definition.

LEARN Look Back at Nuance

Students will revisit content related to the idea that words can have similar, but not identical, meanings to prepare them for Precise Words.

LEARN AND TRY IT

LEARN Say Exactly What You Mean

Students will be introduced to the vocabulary words for the lesson. Then they will learn that choosing precise words can help writers convey clearer, more exact messages.

TRY IT Which Is the Precise Word?

Students will practice choosing the precise word to complete a sentence.

TRY IT Apply: Precise Words

Students will complete Apply: Precise Words from *Summit English Language Arts 4 Activity Book*.

TIP Remind students to look for context clues to determine the best word to complete the sentences and to use a dictionary if they need help with the meaning of any of the words.

LEARNING COACH CHECK-IN This activity page contains open-ended questions, so it's important that you review students' responses. Give students feedback, using the sample answers provided to guide you.

TRY IT
Precise Words

Apply: Precise Words

Circle the word that best completes the sentence, and explain your choice. Think about which choice is the precise word to create the clearest writing.

1. Martin felt nervous as he looked out at the large crowd. He took a deep breath and stepped up to the microphone. He had practiced his speech a million times, but now he couldn't remember a single word. He began to _____. No matter how hard he tried to speak clearly and smoothly, he couldn't say a complete sentence without stopping and starting.

   Choices: stammer or whisper

   See right.

2. The bird flew up to _____ on a small branch near the top of the tree. It seemed to balance easily, even as the wind blew the leaves and branches back and forth. The bird never wobbled or became unsteady as the tree swayed in the breeze.

   Choices: perch or squawk

   See right.

PRECISE WORDS **95**

Additional answers

1. **Stammer** is the better choice because it means "to speak with frequent stops and starts." The context clues tell us Martin is nervous and can't speak clearly or smoothly. Also, the phrase "couldn't say a complete sentence without stopping and starting" includes part of the definition of **stammer**. **Whisper** is not the best choice to complete the sentence. Although someone who is nervous may speak in a whisper, none of the details in the passage support that Martin spoke in a quiet voice.

2. **Perch** is the better choice because it means "to rest on" and is usually used to describe someone or something sitting high up or on something unstable. Although **squawk** makes sense in the passage, it is not the best choice to complete the sentence. The bird may squawk while sitting in the tree, but the details in the passage do not describe any noise the bird makes.

TRY IT   Go Write!

Students will write independently for pleasure. As they write, they should think about choosing the precise words to say exactly what they mean.

TRY IT   Review Precise Words

Students will answer questions to review what they have learned about precise words.

QUIZ

Precise Words

Students will complete the Precise Words quiz.

WRAP-UP

More Language Arts Practice

Students will practice skills according to their individual needs.

Go Read!

Students will read for pleasure. They should choose a book or a magazine that interests them, or they may choose a selection from the digital library, linked in the online lesson.

Students should read for the entire time. Have students select something to read ahead of time to help them stay focused.

On the Case (A)

Lesson Overview

ACTIVITY	ACTIVITY TITLE	TIME	ONLINE/OFFLINE
GET READY	Introduction to On the Case (A)	**1** minute	
	Spelling List 6 Pretest **LEARNING COACH CHECK-IN**	**10** minutes	
	The Missing Sneaker in 60 seconds	**1** minute	
	Look Back at Narrative Point of View	**4** minutes	
	Before You Read "The Mystery of the Missing Hamburger"	**14** minutes	
READ	"The Mystery of the Missing Hamburger"	**30** minutes	
	Check-In: "The Mystery of the Missing Hamburger"	**5** minutes	
LEARN AND **TRY IT**	First-Person Narrator in "The Mystery of the Missing Hamburger"	**10** minutes	
	Explore First-Person Narrator in "Missing Hamburger"	**10** minutes	
	Apply: First-Person Narrator	**15** minutes	
	What Do You Know About Juan? **LEARNING COACH CHECK-IN**	**10** minutes	
	Practice Words from "The Mystery of the Missing Hamburger"	**8** minutes	
WRAP-UP	Questions About First-Person Narrator	**2** minutes	

Content Background

Students will complete a spelling activity and read "The Mystery of the Missing Hamburger" in *Expeditions in Reading*. They will then complete activities in which they learn about first-person narrators. A first-person narrator is a character in a story who tells the story from his or her point of view, using pronouns such as *I*, *me*, and *we*.

MATERIALS

Supplied

- *Summit English Language Arts 4 Expeditions in Reading*
- *Summit English Language Arts 4 Activity Book*
  - Spelling List 6 Pretest
  - What Do You Know About Juan?

"The Mystery of the Missing Hamburger" Synopsis

Juan is a detective who lives with his mother. Early one morning, he receives a phone call from Veronica asking for his help finding her missing hamburger. Juan agrees to help and heads off to solve the case. At Veronica's house, Juan meets her brother, Vinnie, and her bird, Squawk. After examining the clues and questioning Veronica and Vinnie, Juan determines that Squawk is the culprit.

Lesson Goals

- Take a spelling pretest.

- Read and answer questions about "The Mystery of the Missing Hamburger."

- Examine the narrator's point of view in "The Mystery of the Missing Hamburger."

- Understand the vocabulary in the reading.

GET READY

Introduction to On the Case (A)

Students will get a glimpse of what they will learn about in the lesson. They will also read the lesson goals and keywords. Have students select each keyword and preview its definition.

Spelling List 6 Pretest

Students will take a spelling pretest.

LEARNING COACH CHECK-IN   Have students turn to Spelling List 6 Pretest in *Summit English Language Arts 4 Activity Book* and open the online Spelling Pretest activity. Online, students will listen to the spelling word, type the word in the space indicated, and then check their answer. In the activity book, students will write the correct spelling of the word in the tables provided and indicate with a ✓ or an ✗ if they spelled the word correctly or incorrectly online. Students will repeat this process with the remaining words.

As needed, help students with the interaction between the online activity and the activity book page until they become comfortable with what they need to do. As students practice their spelling words throughout the workshop, they should pay special attention to words they missed on the pretest.

This is the complete list of words students will be tested on.

Long e Sound	Root *struct*	Heart Words
breathe	construction	Alabama
chimpanzee	instruct	Tennessee
determine	obstruction	answer
eager	structure	listen
evening		
extreme		
speed		
plead		
remain		

NOTE Have students keep their completed activity page in a safe place so they can refer to it later.

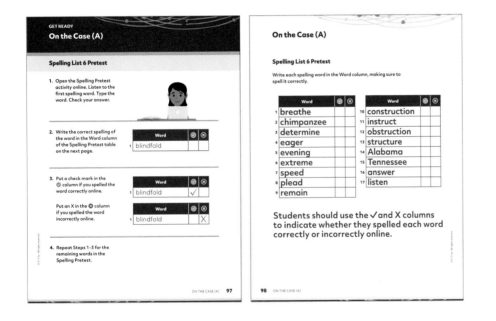

The Missing Sneaker in 60 Seconds
Students will watch a short video designed to spark their interest in upcoming topics.

Look Back at Narrative Point of View
Students will practice identifying the narrator and point of view of a text.

Before You Read "The Mystery of the Missing Hamburger"

Students will be introduced to some key vocabulary words that they will encounter in the upcoming reading, learn some important background related to the reading, and answer questions to help them set a purpose for their reading.

READ

"The Mystery of the Missing Hamburger"

Students will read "The Mystery of the Missing Hamburger" in *Expeditions in Reading*.

Check-In: "The Mystery of the Missing Hamburger"

Students will answer several questions to demonstrate their comprehension of "The Mystery of the Missing Hamburger."

LEARN AND TRY IT

LEARN   First-Person Narrator in "The Mystery of the Missing Hamburger"

Students will learn about the first-person narrator in the story.

TRY IT   Explore First-Person Narrator in "The Mystery of the Missing Hamburger"

Students will analyze several passages and answer questions related to the story's first-person point of view.

TRY IT   Apply: First-Person Narrator

Students will apply to a new work what they've learned about first-person point of view.

TRY IT   What Do You Know About Juan?

Students will complete What Do You Know About Juan? from *Summit English Language Arts 4 Activity Book*.

LEARNING COACH CHECK-IN   This activity page contains an open-ended question, so it's important that you review students' responses. Give students feedback, using the sample answer provided to guide you.

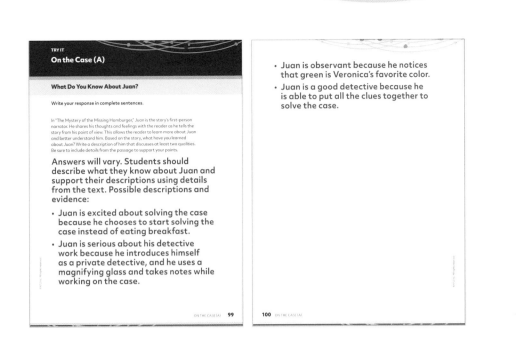

TRY IT   Practice Words from "The Mystery of the Missing Hamburger"

Students will answer questions to demonstrate their understanding of the vocabulary words in this lesson's reading.

WRAP-UP

Questions About First-Person Narrator

Students will answer questions to show that they understand the characteristics of a first-person narrator.

On the Case (B)

Lesson Overview

ACTIVITY	ACTIVITY TITLE	TIME	ONLINE/OFFLINE
GET READY	Introduction to On the Case (B)	**1** minute	🖥️
	Spelling List 6 Activity Bank	**10** minutes	📄
	Recall "The Mystery of the Missing Hamburger"	**5** minutes	🖥️
	Before You Read "The Mystery of the Topaz Heart"	**9** minutes	🖥️
READ	"The Mystery of the Topaz Heart"	**30** minutes	📄
	Check-In: "The Mystery of the Topaz Heart"	**5** minutes	🖥️
LEARN AND **TRY IT**	Third-Person Narrator in "The Mystery of the Topaz Heart"	**10** minutes	🖥️
	Explore Third-Person Narrator in "Topaz Heart"	**10** minutes	🖥️
	Apply: Third-Person Narrator	**15** minutes	🖥️
	Write a Summary of "The Mystery of the Topaz Heart" **LEARNING COACH CHECK-IN**	**15** minutes	📄
	Practice Words from "The Mystery of the Topaz Heart"	**8** minutes	🖥️
WRAP-UP	Questions About Third-Person Narrator	**2** minutes	🖥️

Content Background

Students will read "The Mystery of the Topaz Heart" and learn about third-person narrators. A third-person narrator is not a character in the story. This type of narrator tells the story as an observer watching from outside the action and uses words such as *she*, *he*, and *they* while telling the story.

Advance Preparation

Gather students' completed Spelling List 6 Pretest activity page from On the Case (A). Students will refer to this page during Get Ready: Spelling List 6 Activity Bank.

MATERIALS

Supplied
- *Summit English Language Arts 4 Expeditions in Reading*
- *Summit English Language Arts 4 Activity Book*
  - Spelling List 6 Activity Bank
  - Write a Summary of "The Mystery of the Topaz Heart"

Also Needed
- completed Spelling List 6 Pretest activity Page from On the Case (A)

"The Mystery of the Topaz Heart" Synopsis

Edgerton is a small, quiet town. It doesn't have many people or much excitement, but it does have the topaz heart. The topaz heart is a 28-pound gem, said to be the largest cut topaz in the world. One day, William Bell, owner of the gallery where the topaz heart is displayed, reports the jewel stolen. Paula Cortez, an Edgerton resident and investigative journalist for the local newspaper, interviews Bell and begins her search for answers. She follows the clues to determine that William Bell is responsible for the gem's disappearance.

Lesson Goals

- Practice all spelling words offline.
- Read and answer questions about "The Mystery of the Topaz Heart."
- Examine the narrator's point of view in "The Mystery of the Topaz Heart."
- Understand the vocabulary in the reading.

GET READY

Introduction to On the Case (B)

Students will get a glimpse of what they will learn about in the lesson. They will also read the lesson goals and keywords. Have students select each keyword and preview its definition.

Spelling List 6 Activity Bank

Students will practice all spelling words from the workshop by completing Spelling List 6 Activity Bank from *Summit English Language Arts 4 Activity Book*. Make sure students have their completed Spelling List 6 Pretest activity page from On the Case (A) to refer to during this activity.

Remind students to pay special attention to words they spelled incorrectly on the Spelling Pretest.

Spelling List 6 Activity Bank

Circle any words in the box that you did not spell correctly on the pretest. Using your circled words, complete one activity of your choice. Complete as much of the activity as you can in the time given.

If you spelled all words correctly on the pretest, complete your chosen activity with as many spelling words as you can.

breathe	evening	remain	obstruction	Tennessee
chimpanzee	extreme	construction	structure	answer
determine	speed	instruct	Alabama	listen
eager	plead			

Spelling Activity Choices

Silly Sentences
1. Write a silly sentence using your words from the spelling word list.
2. Underline the spelling word in each sentence.
   Example: The dog was _driving_ a car.
3. Correct any spelling errors.

Spelling Story
1. Write a very short story using your words from the spelling word list.
2. Underline the spelling words in the story.
3. Correct any spelling errors.

Riddle Me This
1. Write a riddle for your words from the spelling word list.
   Example: "I have a trunk, but it's not on my car."
2. Write the answer, which is your word, for each riddle.
   Example: Answer: elephant
3. Correct any spelling errors.

RunOnWord
1. Gather some crayons, colored pencils, or markers. Write each of your words, using a different color for each word, end to end as one long word.
   Example: dogcatbirdfishturtle
2. Rewrite the words correctly and with proper spacing.

Complete the activity that you chose.

My chosen activity:

Students should use this page to complete all steps in their chosen activity.

Recall "The Mystery of the Topaz Heart"
Students will answer some questions to review the reading that they have already completed.

Before You Read "The Mystery of the Topaz Heart"
Students will be introduced to some key vocabulary words that they will encounter in the upcoming reading.

READ

"The Mystery of the Topaz Heart"
Students will read "The Mystery of the Topaz Heart" in _Expeditions in Reading_.

Check-In: "The Mystery of the Topaz Heart"
Students will answer several questions to demonstrate their comprehension of "The Mystery of the Topaz Heart."

LEARN AND TRY IT

LEARN   Third-Person Narrator in "The Mystery of the Topaz Heart"
Students will learn about the third-person narrator in the story.

TRY IT   Explore Third-Person Narrator in "The Mystery of the Topaz Heart"
Students will analyze several passages and answer questions related to the story's third-person point of view.

TRY IT Apply: Third-Person Narrator

Students will apply to a new work what they've learned about third-person point of view.

TRY IT Write a Summary of "The Mystery of the Topaz Heart"

Students will complete Write a Summary of "The Mystery of the Topaz Heart" from *Summit English Language Arts 4 Activity Book*.

LEARNING COACH CHECK-IN This activity page contains open-ended questions, so it's important that you review students' responses. Give students feedback, using the sample answers provided to guide you.

TRY IT
On the Case (B)

Write a Summary of "The Mystery of the Topaz Heart"

Write your response in complete sentences.

Write a one-page summary of "The Mystery of the Topaz Heart." Be sure to include the following:

- Main characters
- Setting
- Most important events from the beginning, middle, and end of the story

Remember that your summary should include only key details.

Students' summary should include the following:

- **The main characters of the story (Paula Cortez and William Bell)**
- **The setting (the Bell Gallery)**
- **A description of the main events, in the order in which they happen (such as the topaz heart is stolen, Paula Cortez interviews William Bell and investigates the robbery, Paula solves the case by figuring out William Bell is the thief)**

ON THE CASE (B) **105**

Students' summary should not include the following:
- **Minor characters (such as Arthur Bell or Molly Foster)**
- **Minor details and events (such as reporters from all over the country travel to Edgerton to interview William Bell or Paula passes news vans after leaving the Bell Gallery)**

Writing a summary is a good way to focus on important ideas.

106 ON THE CASE (B)

TRY IT Practice Words from "The Mystery of the Topaz Heart"

Students will answer questions to demonstrate their understanding of the vocabulary words in this lesson's reading.

WRAP-UP

Questions About Third-Person Narrator

Students will answer questions to show that they understand the characteristics of a third-person narrator.

On the Case (C)

Lesson Overview

ACTIVITY	ACTIVITY TITLE	TIME	ONLINE/OFFLINE
GET READY	Introduction to On the Case (C)	**1** minute	📶
	Spelling List 6 Review Game	**10** minutes	📶
	Recall "The Mystery of the Topaz Heart"	**5** minutes	📶
	Before You Read: Comparing Mysteries	**14** minutes	📶
READ	Comparing Mysteries	**30** minutes	📄
LEARN AND TRY IT	Compare First-Person and Third-Person Narrators	**10** minutes	📶
	Compare Narrators	**15** minutes	📶
	Apply: Comparing Narrative Point of View	**15** minutes	📶
	Compare the Mysteries **LEARNING COACH CHECK-IN**	**10** minutes	📄
	Practice Words from Mysteries	**8** minutes	📶
WRAP-UP	Questions About Narrative Point of View	**2** minutes	📶

Content Background

Students will compare narrative points of view. Narrative point of view refers to the perspective from which a story is told. Stories told from the first-person point of view have narrators who are characters in the text. They reveal their own private thoughts and feelings, but they do not know what other characters privately think or feel. Stories told from the third-person point of view have narrators who are not characters in the text. They do not reveal their own private thoughts and feelings, but they may know what other characters privately think or feel.

> ### MATERIALS
>
> **Supplied**
> - *Summit English Language Arts 4 Activity Book*
>   - Compare the Mysteries

Lesson Goals

- Practice all spelling words online.

- Compare first-person and third-person narrators.

- Use details or examples from "The Mystery of the Missing Hamburger" and "The Mystery of the Topaz Heart" to explain the stories.

GET READY

Introduction to On the Case (C)

Students will get a glimpse of what they will learn about in the lesson. They will also read the lesson goals and keywords. Have students select each keyword and preview its definition.

Spelling List 6 Review Game

Students will practice all spelling words from the workshop.

Recall "The Mystery of the Topaz Heart"

Students will answer some questions to review the reading that they have already completed.

Before You Read: Comparing Mysteries

Students will review characteristics of first-person and third-person narrators.

READ

Comparing Mysteries

Students will review the two mystery stories they have already read, "The Mystery of the Missing Hamburger" and "The Mystery of the Topaz Heart" in *Expeditions in Reading*.

LEARN AND TRY IT

LEARN   Compare First-Person and Third-Person Narrators

Students will explore the similarities and differences between first-person and third-person narrators.

TRY IT   Compare Narrators

Students will compare the narrators of "The Mystery of the Missing Hamburger" and "The Mystery of the Topaz Heart."

TRY IT   Apply: Comparing Narrative Point of View

Students will apply to new works what they've learned about analyzing narrative points of view.

TRY IT   Compare the Mysteries

Students will complete Compare the Mysteries from *Summit English Language Arts 4 Activity Book*.

LEARNING COACH CHECK-IN   This activity page contains open-ended questions, so it's important that you review students' responses. Give students feedback, using the sample answers provided to guide you.

KEYWORDS

first-person narrator – a narrator who tells a story from the first-person point of view

first-person point of view – the telling of a story by a character in that story, using pronouns such as *I*, *me*, and *we*

third-person narrator – a narrator who tells the story from the third-person point of view

third-person point of view – the telling of a story by someone outside of the action, using the third-person pronouns *he*, *she*, and *they*

On the Case (C)

Compare the Mysteries

Answer the following questions to compare "The Mystery of the Missing Hamburger" and "The Mystery of the Topaz Heart." Be sure to include details from both stories to support your points.

Title	Setting: Where and when does each story take place, and how are these stories' settings the same and different?
"The Mystery of the Missing Hamburger"	takes place mostly in an apartment
"The Mystery of the Topaz Heart"	takes place mostly in a gallery
Both	take place in the present day

Title	Characters: Who are the main characters in each story, and how are they alike and different?
"The Mystery of the Missing Hamburger"	
"The Mystery of the Topaz Heart"	See below.
Both	

Title	Events: How are the events of the two stories alike, and how are they different?
"The Mystery of the Missing Hamburger"	
"The Mystery of the Topaz Heart"	See below.
Both	

Title	Theme: In both stories, one of the big ideas is that paying attention to small details can lead to big discoveries. What details from the texts support this theme?
"The Mystery of the Missing Hamburger"	
"The Mystery of the Topaz Heart"	See below.

Additional answers

Title	Characters: Who are the main characters in each story, and how are they alike and different?
"The Mystery of the Missing Hamburger"	Juan Lopez and Veronica Weiss Juan is also the narrator of the story.
"The Mystery of the Topaz Heart"	Paula Cortez and William Bell William Bell is dishonest because he actually stole the item he reports missing.
Both	Juan and Paula are both observant and both solve mysteries. Veronica and William both have something that belongs to them go missing.

Title	Events: How are the events of the two stories alike, and how are they different?
"The Mystery of the Missing Hamburger"	The hamburger truly is missing, and Juan figures out what happened to it.
"The Mystery of the Topaz Heart"	The topaz is only hidden, and Paula figures out who hid it.
Both	Veronica and William both ask for help. Juan and Paula investigate and solve the mystery by interviewing and following clues.

Title	Theme: In both stories, one of the big ideas is that paying attention to small details can lead to big discoveries. What details from the texts support this theme?
"The Mystery of the Missing Hamburger"	Juan notices that the sesame seeds at the bottom of Squawk's cage don't match the seeds in his feed. This observation leads Juan to determine that Squawk ate the missing burger.
"The Mystery of the Topaz Heart"	Paula notices glass on the ground in front of the Bell Gallery. This observation leads her to determine that the window must have been broken from the inside by William Bell rather than from the outside by someone trying to break into the gallery.

126 ENGLISH LANGUAGE ARTS 4

TRY IT Practice Words from Mysteries

Students will complete an online activity in which they answer questions to practice the vocabulary words from the reading.

Questions About Narrative Point of View

Students will answer questions to show that they understand first-person and third-person points of view.

On the Case Wrap-Up

Lesson Overview

ACTIVITY	ACTIVITY TITLE	TIME	ONLINE/OFFLINE
GET READY	Introduction to On the Case Wrap-Up	**1** minute	
TRY IT	Change the Point of View **LEARNING COACH CHECK-IN**	**30** minutes	
	Read and Record	**10** minutes	
	Review First-Person and Third-Person Narrator	**20** minutes	
QUIZ	First-Person and Third-Person Narrator	**30** minutes	
	Spelling List 6	**10** minutes	
WRAP-UP	More Language Arts Practice	**19** minutes	

Lesson Goals

- Determine the theme of a story based on details in the story.
- Explain the differences between first-person and third-person narrators.
- Describe first-person and third-person points of view.
- Compare the narrator's point of view in two stories.
- Take a spelling quiz.

MATERIALS

Supplied
- *Summit English Language Arts 4 Activity Book*
  - Change the Point of View

GET READY

Introduction to On the Case Wrap-Up

Students will read the lesson goals.

TRY IT

Change the Point of View

Students will complete Change the Point of View from *Summit English Language Arts 4 Activity Book*.

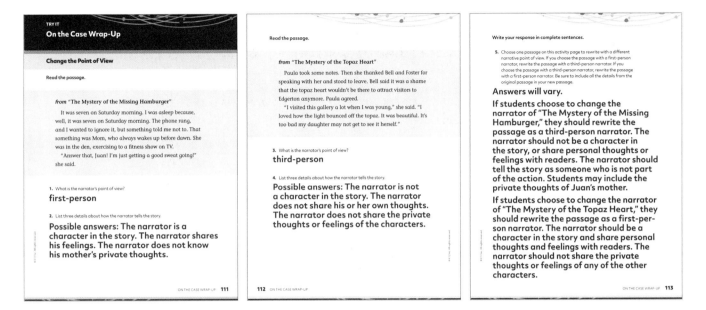

Read and Record

Good readers read quickly, smoothly, and with expression. This is called *fluency*. Students will record themselves reading aloud. They will listen to their recording and think about how quick, smooth, and expressive they sound.

TIP   Encourage students to rerecord as needed.

Review First-Person and Third-Person Narrator

Students will answer questions to review what they have learned about first-person and third-person narrators.

QUIZ

First-Person and Third-Person Narrator

Students will complete the First-Person and Third-Person Narrator quiz.

Spelling List 6

Students will complete the Spelling List 6 quiz.

WRAP-UP

More Language Arts Practice

Students will practice skills according to their individual needs.

Big Ideas: Respond to a Prompt

Lesson Overview

Big Ideas lessons provide students the opportunity to further apply the knowledge and skills acquired throughout the unit workshops. Each Big Ideas lesson consists of three parts:

1. **Cumulative Review:** Students keep their skills fresh by reviewing prior content.

2. **Preview:** Students practice answering the types of questions they will commonly find on standardized tests.

3. **Synthesis:** Students complete an assignment that allows them to interweave and apply what they've learned. These synthesis assignments will vary throughout the course.

In the Synthesis portion of this Big Ideas lesson, students will respond to an essay prompt based on reading selections. To respond meaningfully, students will need to use their own ideas as well as examples from the readings. Students' writing will be assessed in four categories: purpose and content; structure and organization; language and word choice; and grammar, ussage, and mechanics.

LEARNING COACH CHECK-IN   This is a graded assessment. Make sure students complete, review, and submit the assignment to their teacher.

All materials needed for this lesson are linked online. The materials are not provided in this Lesson Guide or in the Activity Book.

Frontiers
of Flight

Space Flight (A)

Lesson Overview

ACTIVITY	ACTIVITY TITLE	TIME	ONLINE/OFFLINE
GET READY	Frontiers of Flight Unit Overview	**1** minute	🖥️
	Introduction to Space Flight (A)	**1** minute	🖥️
	Spelling List 7 Pretest **LEARNING COACH CHECK-IN**	**10** minutes	🖥️ and 📄
	Pioneers of Flight in 60 Seconds	**1** minute	🖥️
	Look Back at Key Details	**4** minutes	🖥️
	Before You Read "Go, John Glenn!"	**14** minutes	🖥️
READ	"Go, John Glenn!"	**30** minutes	📄
	Check-In: "Go, John Glenn!"	**5** minutes	🖥️
LEARN AND **TRY IT**	What's the Main Idea?	**9** minutes	🖥️
	Find the Main Idea	**10** minutes	🖥️
	Apply: Main Idea and Supporting Details	**15** minutes	🖥️
	Write About the Main Idea **LEARNING COACH CHECK-IN**	**10** minutes	📄
	Practice Words from "Go, John Glenn!"	**8** minutes	🖥️
WRAP-UP	Question About "Go, John Glenn!"	**2** minutes	🖥️

Content Background

Students will read "Go, John Glenn!" by Brian Floca in *Expeditions in Reading*. They will learn about main ideas and supporting details.

Main ideas are the most important points that authors make in a text. A text can have an overall main idea and main ideas within passages of the text. Supporting details are the details that lead to a main idea. Main ideas can be directly stated, but sometimes a reader must infer the main idea from the supporting details.

MATERIALS

Supplied
- *Summit English Language Arts 4 Expeditions in Reading*
- *Summit English Language Arts 4 Activity Book*
  - Spelling List 7 Pretest
  - Write About the Main Idea

"Go, John Glenn!" Synopsis

"Go, John Glenn!" takes us to an exciting period in American history when the United States is competing with the Soviet Union in a space race. John Glenn is one of the first American astronauts and the first American to attempt to orbit the earth. The eyes of the world are on Glenn as he is launched into orbit and then faces the potentially deadly failure of his capsule's heat shield.

KEYWORDS

infer – to use clues and what you already know to make a guess

inference – a guess that readers make using the clues that authors give them in a piece of writing

main idea – the most important point

supporting detail – a detail that gives more information about a main idea

Lesson Goals

- Take a spelling pretest.
- Determine a purpose for reading "Go, John Glenn!"
- Read "Go, John Glenn!"
- Determine main ideas, supporting details, and meanings of unfamiliar words in the reading.

GET READY

Frontiers of Flight Unit Overview
Students will read a summary of what they will learn in the Frontiers of Flight unit.

Introduction to Space Flight (A)
Students will get a glimpse of what they will learn about in the lesson. They will also read the lesson goals and keywords. Have students select each keyword and preview its defisnition.

Spelling List 7 Pretest
Students will take a spelling pretest.

LEARNING COACH CHECK-IN   Have students turn to Spelling List 7 Pretest in *Summit English Language Arts 4 Activity Book* and open the online Spelling Pretest activity. Online, students will listen to the spelling word, type the word in the space indicated, and then check their answer. In the activity book, students will write the correct spelling of the word in the tables provided and indicate with with a ✓ or an ✗ if they spelled the word correctly or incorrectly online. Students will repeat this process with the remaining words.

As needed, help students with the interaction between the online activity and the activity book page until they become comfortable with what they need

to do. As students practice their spelling words throughout the workshop, they should pay special attention to words they spelled incorrectly on the pretest.

This is the complete list of words students will be tested on.

Word with Long e Sound	Root *scribe*	Heart Words
achieve	scribe	Kentucky
believe	prescribe	New Jersey
ceiling	scribble	calendar
receive		grammar
thief		
agency		
attorney		
chimney		
fantasy		
greedy		

NOTE   Have students keep their completed activity page in a safe place so they can refer to it later.

Pioneers of Flight in 60 Seconds

Students will watch a short video designed to spark their interest in upcoming topics.

Look Back at Key Details

Students will practice the prerequisite skill of explaining key details.

Before You Read "Go, John Glenn!"

Students will be introduced to some key vocabulary words that they will encounter in the upcoming reading, learn some important historical background related to the reading, and answer questions to help them set a purpose for their reading.

READ

"Go, John Glenn!"

Students will read "Go, John Glenn!" by Brian Floca in *Expeditions in Reading*.

Check-In: "Go, John Glenn!"

Students will answer several questions to demonstrate their comprehension of "Go, John Glenn!."

LEARN AND TRY IT

LEARN What's the Main Idea?

Students will learn about main ideas and how to use supporting details to determine main ideas.

TRY IT Find the Main Idea

Students will analyze passages and answer questions about the main ideas and supporting details in the reading.

SUPPORT   For students having difficulty determining the main idea of a passage, explain that they can test their thinking in this way: (1) State what they believe is the main idea. (2) Read each sentence in the passage. (3) If most of the sentences are related to their stated main idea, then they are probably correct. (4) If most of the sentences are not related to their stated main idea, then they are not correct. (5) If they are not correct, they should repeat these steps with a new statement of the main idea.

TRY IT Apply: Main Idea and Supporting Details

Students will apply to a new work what they've learned about determining main ideas and supporting details.

TRY IT Write About the Main Idea

Students will complete Write About the Main Idea from *Summit English Language Arts 4 Activity Book*.

LEARNING COACH CHECK-IN This activity page contains open-ended questions, so it's important that you review students' responses. Give students feedback, using the sample answers provided to guide you.

TRY IT
Space Flight (A)

Write About the Main Idea

Read the passage. Then answer the questions in complete sentences.

Now the *Friendship 7* capsule was speeding smoothly in orbit. "Capsule is turning around," Glenn reported. And then, "Oh, that view is tremendous!"

Below rolled the wide, blue Earth. Rivers and continents spread out like pages in an atlas. Lightning flickered through storms on the Atlantic. Moonlight silvered the clouds over Africa. On darkened Australia, city lights glowed brightly, turned on as a beacon for the astronaut far overhead.

Over the Pacific, water droplets from the capsule froze into ice particles. They caught the sunlight and floated around *Friendship 7*, looking like fireflies dancing in space.

What is the main idea of this passage? What supporting details led you to this main idea?

The main idea of this passage is that the view from John Glenn's capsule is tremendous. The supporting details that lead to this main idea are the descriptions of what Glenn sees from the capsule.

SPACE FLIGHT (A) **117**

118 SPACE FLIGHT (A)

TRY IT Practice Words from "Go, John Glenn!"

Students will answer questions to demonstrate their understanding of the vocabulary words from the reading.

WRAP-UP

Question About "Go, John Glenn!"

Students will answer a question to show that they understand how to determine a main idea in "Go, John Glenn!"

Space Flight (B)

Lesson Overview

ACTIVITY	ACTIVITY TITLE	TIME	ONLINE/OFFLINE
GET READY	Introduction to Space Flight (B)	**1** minute	🖥️
	Spelling List 7 Activity Bank	**10** minutes	📄
	Recall "Go, John Glenn!"	**5** minutes	🖥️
	Before You Read About John Glenn	**10** minutes	🖥️
READ	About John Glenn	**30** minutes	📄
	Check-In: About John Glenn	**5** minutes	🖥️
LEARN AND TRY IT	Features of Firsthand and Secondhand Accounts	**10** minutes	🖥️
	Is It Firsthand or Secondhand?	**10** minutes	🖥️
	Apply: Firsthand and Secondhand Accounts	**15** minutes	🖥️
	Prepare to Write a Firsthand Account **LEARNING COACH CHECK-IN**	**15** minutes	📄
	Practice Words from About John Glenn	**7** minutes	🖥️
WRAP-UP	Question About John Glenn	**2** minutes	🖥️

Content Background

Students will read two accounts of the same event, John Glenn's historic orbit of the earth. One is a firsthand account while the other is secondhand.

A firsthand account is a text based on the direct personal experience of the author. Examples of firsthand accounts include autobiographies, diaries, and interviews.

A secondhand account is a text based on an author's research, not personal experience. Examples of secondhand accounts include newspaper articles, biographies, and encyclopedia entries.

Advance Preparation

Gather students' completed Spelling List 7 Pretest activity page from Space Flight (A). Students will refer to this page during Get Ready: Spelling List 7 Activity Bank.

MATERIALS

Supplied
- *Summit English Language Arts 4 Expeditions in Reading*
- *Summit English Language Arts 4 Activity Book*
  - Spelling List 7 Activity Bank
  - Prepare to Write a Firsthand Account

Also Needed
- completed Spelling List 7 Pretest activity page from Space Flight (A)

About John Glenn Synopsis

In "Project Mercury's 50th Anniversary: Interview with John Glenn," Glenn gives a firsthand account of his rocket's launch, the confidence he felt that day, and the historic backdrop of the Cold War during which his flight in *Friendship 7* took place.

In "John Glenn and *Friendship 7*" we read about the same event, Glenn's attempt to become the first American to orbit the earth. This secondhand account presents facts about the problems that arose during Glenn's flight that could have spelled disaster.

Lesson Goals

- Practice all spelling words offline.
- Read firsthand and secondhand accounts of John Glenn's mission to orbit the earth.
- Determine characteristics of and differences between firsthand and secondhand accounts of the same event.
- Determine meanings of unfamiliar words in the readings.

GET READY

Introduction to Space Flight (B)

Students will get a glimpse of what they will learn about in the lesson. They will also read the lesson goals and keywords. Have students select each keyword and preview its definition.

Spelling List 7 Activity Bank

Students will practice all spelling words from the workshop by completing Spelling List 7 Activity Bank from *Summit English Language Arts 4 Activity Book*. Make sure students have their completed Spelling List 7 Pretest activity page from Space Flight (A) to refer to during this activity.

Remind students to pay special attention to words they spelled incorrectly on the Spelling Pretest.

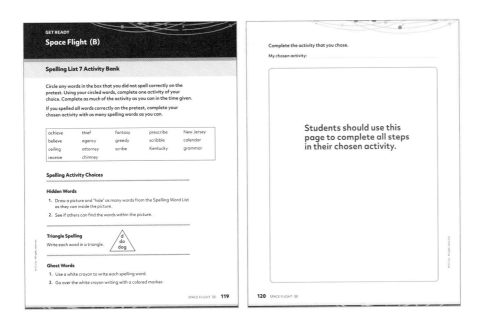

Recall "Go, John Glenn!"

Students will answer questions to review the reading that they have already completed.

Before You Read About John Glenn

Students will be introduced to some key vocabulary words that they will encounter in the upcoming readings and learn some important historical background related to the readings.

About John Glenn

Students will listen to and read "Project Mercury's 50th Anniversary: Interview with John Glenn" in *Expeditions in Reading*, in which he discusses his experience becoming the first American to orbit the earth. They will then read "John Glenn and *Friendship 7*," a secondhand account of the same event, in the reader.

Check-In: About John Glenn

Students will answer questions to demonstrate their comprehension of the readings.

LEARN   Features of Firsthand and Secondhand Accounts

Students will learn about the features of firsthand and secondhand accounts. They will learn how to tell the difference between a firsthand and secondhand account about the same event.

TRY IT Is It Firsthand or Secondhand?

Students will analyze passages and answer questions about whether a passage is a firsthand or secondhand account.

TIP Remind students to focus on who wrote the account. Is the author of the account talking about himself or herself? If so, then this is a firsthand account. Is the author talking about other people and not something that he or she experienced personally? If so, then this is a secondhand account.

TRY IT Apply: Firsthand and Secondhand Accounts

Students will apply to a new work what they've learned about determining whether a text is a firsthand or secondhand account.

TRY IT Prepare to Write a Firsthand Account

Students will complete Prepare to Write a Firsthand Account from *Summit English Language Arts 4 Activity Book*.

LEARNING COACH CHECK-IN This activity page contains open-ended questions, so it's important that you review students' responses. Give students feedback, using the sample answers provided to guide you.

NOTE Have students keep their completed activity page in a safe place so they can refer to it later.

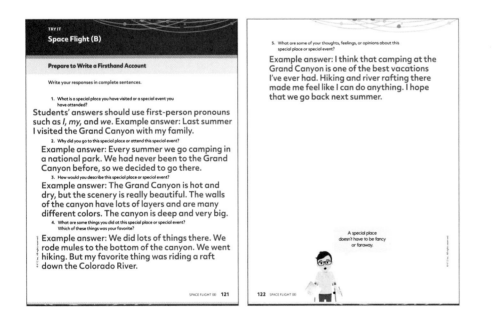

TRY IT Practice Words from About John Glenn

Students will answer questions to demonstrate their understanding of the vocabulary from the reading.

Question About John Glenn

Students will answer a question to show that they understand how to determine if a text is a firsthand account or secondhand account.

Space Flight (C)

Lesson Overview

ACTIVITY	ACTIVITY TITLE	TIME	ONLINE/OFFLINE
GET READY	Introduction to Space Flight (C)	**1** minute	🖥
	Spelling List 7 Review Game	**10** minutes	🖥
	Recall About John Glenn	**5** minutes	🖥
	Before You Read "Two Views of Project Mercury"	**10** minutes	🖥
READ	"Two Views of Project Mercury"	**30** minutes	📄
	Check-In: "Two Views of Project Mercury"	**5** minutes	🖥
LEARN AND **TRY IT**	One Topic, Two Views	**10** minutes	🖥
	Compare and Contrast Firsthand and Secondhand	**10** minutes	🖥
	Apply: Comparing Accounts	**15** minutes	🖥
	Research for a Secondhand Account **LEARNING COACH CHECK-IN**	**15** minutes	📄
	Practice Words from "Two Views of Project Mercury"	**7** minutes	🖥
WRAP-UP	Question About "Two Views of Project Mercury"	**2** minutes	🖥

Content Background

Students will read a firsthand account and secondhand account of the same topic. They will review the features of firsthand and secondhand accounts. They will compare and contrast the firsthand and secondhand accounts.

A firsthand account is a text based on the direct personal experience of the author. A secondhand account is a text based on an author's research, not personal experience.

To compare means to explain how things are alike. When comparing texts, a reader should explain how the content of the texts is the same. Contrasting texts involves a reader explaining how the content of the texts is different.

MATERIALS

Supplied
- *Summit English Language Arts 4 Expeditions in Reading*
- *Summit English Language Arts 4 Activity Book*
  - Research for a Secondhand Account

"Two Views of Project Mercury" Synopsis

The first American astronauts were the face of Project Mercury. But the American space program never would have gotten off the ground without the work and dedication of a large group of NASA scientists and engineers.

"Two Views of Project Mercury" explores the importance of these people in two ways. The first is through the eyes of the young daughter of a NASA engineer. She watches her dad go off to work every day where he and his colleagues are working to put John Glenn in space. The second view is a secondhand account about the thousands of scientists and engineers that worked tirelessly to develop the technology for space travel.

Lesson Goals

- Practice all spelling words online.
- Read and compare and contrast firsthand and secondhand accounts of the same topic.
- Determine meanings of unfamiliar words in the reading.

GET READY

Introduction to Space Flight (C)
Students will get a glimpse of what they will learn about in the lesson. They will also read the lesson goals and keywords. Have students select each keyword and preview its definition.

Spelling List 7 Review Game
Students will practice all spelling words from the workshop.

Recall About John Glenn
Students will answer questions to review the reading that they have already completed.

Before You Read "Two Views of Project Mercury"
Students will be introduced to key vocabulary words that they will encounter in the upcoming reading and learn some important historical background related to the reading.

"Two Views of Project Mercury"

Students will read "Two Views of Project Mercury" in *Expeditions in Reading*.

Check-In: "Two Views of Project Mercury"

Students will answer questions to demonstrate their comprehension of "Two Views of Project Mercury."

LEARN AND TRY IT

LEARN   One Topic, Two Views

Students will learn about comparing and contrasting firsthand and secondhand accounts of the same topic.

TRY IT   Compare and Contrast Firsthand and Secondhand

Students will analyze passages and answer questions that ask them to compare and contrast firsthand and secondhand accounts of the same topic.

TRY IT   Apply: Comparing Accounts

Students will apply to a new work what they've learned about comparing firsthand and secondhand accounts.

TRY IT   Research for a Secondhand Account

Students will complete Research for a Secondhand Account from *Summit English Language Arts 4 Activity Book*. To complete this activity, students will need to interview a person of their choice.

LEARNING COACH CHECK-IN   This activity page contains open-ended questions, so it's important that you review students' responses. Give students feedback, using the sample answers provided to guide you.

NOTE   Have students keep their completed activity page in a safe place so they can refer to it later.

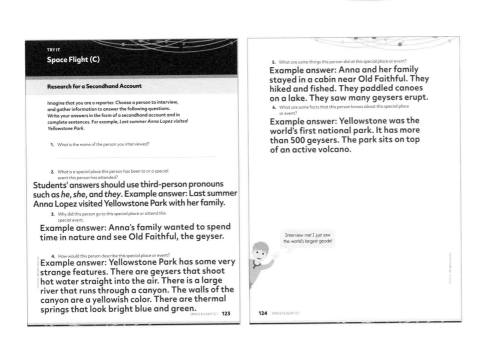

TRY IT Practice Words from "Two Views of Project Mercury"

Students will answer questions to demonstrate their understanding of the vocabulary from the reading.

Question About "Two Views of Project Mercury"

Students will answer a question to show that they understand how to compare and contrast a firsthand and secondhand account of the same topic.

Space Flight Wrap-Up

Lesson Overview

ACTIVITY	ACTIVITY TITLE	TIME	ONLINE/OFFLINE
GET READY	Introduction to Space Flight Wrap-Up	**1** minute	
TRY IT	Write About Firsthand and Secondhand Accounts **LEARNING COACH CHECK-IN**	**30** minutes	
	Read and Record	**20** minutes	
	Review Space Flight	**15** minutes	
QUIZ	Space Flight	**30** minutes	
	Spelling List 7	**10** minutes	
WRAP-UP	More Language Arts Practice	**14** minutes	

Advance Preparation

Gather students' completed Prepare to Write a Firsthand Account activity page from Space Flight (B) and Research for a Secondhand Account activity page from Space Flight (C). Students will refer to these pages during Try It: Write About Firsthand and Secondhand Accounts.

Lesson Goals

- Write about firsthand and secondhand accounts.

- Review firsthand and secondhand accounts about John Glenn and Project Mercury.

- Practice reading aloud to develop fluency.

- Take a quiz on main ideas, details, inferences, and distinguishing firsthand accounts from secondhand accounts.

- Take a spelling quiz.

MATERIALS

Supplied
- *Summit English Language Arts 4 Expeditions in Reading*
- *Summit English Language Arts 4 Activity Book*
  - Write About Firsthand and Secondhand Accounts

Also Needed
- completed Prepare to Write a Firsthand Account activity page from Space Flight (B)
- completed Research for a Secondhand Account activity page from Space Flight (C)

Introduction to Space Flight Wrap-Up

Students will read the lesson goals.

Write About Firsthand and Secondhand Accounts

Students will complete Write About Firsthand and Secondhand Accounts from *Summit English Language Arts 4 Activity Book*. Information students recorded on Prepare to Write a Firsthand Account activity page from Space Flight (B) and Research for a Secondhand Account activity page from Space Flight (C) will be needed for this writing activity.

TIP Remind students that they do not have to write complete firsthand and secondhand accounts. They only need to write 2 or 3 sentences to introduce each account.

LEARNING COACH CHECK-IN This activity page contains open-ended questions, so it's important that you review students' responses. Give students feedback, using the sample answers provided to guide you.

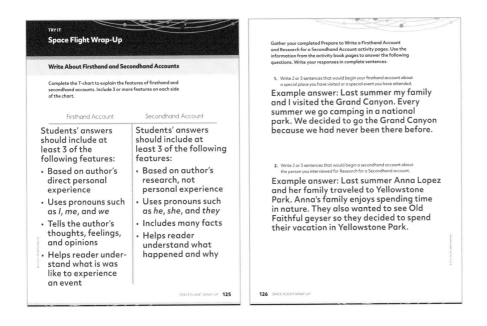

Read and Record

Good readers read quickly, smoothly, and with expression. This is called *fluency*. Students will record themselves reading aloud. They will listen to their recording and think about how quick, smooth, and expressive they sound.

TIP Encourage students to rerecord as needed.

Review Space Flight

Students will answer questions to review what they have learned about firsthand and secondhand accounts.

Space Flight

Students will complete the Space Flight quiz.

Spelling List 7

Students will complete the Spelling List 7 quiz.

More Language Arts Practice

Students will practice skills according to their individual needs.

Air and Space Words

Lesson Overview

ACTIVITY	ACTIVITY TITLE	TIME	ONLINE/OFFLINE
GET READY	Introduction to Air and Space Words	**1** minute	🖥️
	Look Back at Context Clues	**4** minutes	🖥️
LEARN AND **TRY IT**	Context Clues and Air and Space Words	**10** minutes	🖥️
	Practice Using Context Clues	**10** minutes	🖥️
	Apply: Air and Space Words **LEARNING COACH CHECK-IN**	**15** minutes	📄
	Go Write!	**15** minutes	📄
	Review Air and Space Words	**15** minutes	🖥️
QUIZ	Air and Space Words	**15** minutes	🖥️
WRAP-UP	More Language Arts Practice	**15** minutes	🖥️
	Go Read!	**20** minutes	🖥️ or 📄

Content Background

Students will learn several words related to aviation and space exploration. They will learn how to use context clues to help them define unknown words.

Context clues are words and phrases in a text that help you figure out the meaning of an unknown word. For example, in the sentence, "The rocket was launched, or shot into space," the phrase "shot into space" is a context clue. It helps the reader determine that the word *launched* means shot into space.

Advance Preparation

During the Go Read! activity, students will have the option of using the digital library. Allow extra time for students to make their reading selection, or have students make a selection before beginning the lesson.

Lesson Goals

- Use context clues to determine the meaning of unknown words.

- Use words related to the topics of air and space travel.

- Read and write for pleasure.

Introduction to Air and Space Words

Students will get a glimpse of what they will learn about in the lesson. They will also read the lesson goals.

Look Back at Context Clues

Students will answer questions to review using context clues to determine the meanings of unknown words.

LEARN AND **TRY IT**

LEARN   Context Clues and Air and Space Words

Students will learn the definitions of several words and terms related to aviation and space exploration.

They will also learn that the words and sentences around an unknown word can provide context clues. These context clues can help to unlock the meaning of a new word.

TRY IT   Practice Using Context Clues

Students will be guided through the steps of using context clues to determine the meaning of an unknown word. Then they will practice using context clues on their own.

TRY IT   Apply: Air and Space Words

Students will complete Apply: Air and Space Words from *Summit English Language Arts 4 Activity Book*.

LEARNING COACH CHECK-IN   This activity page contains open-ended questions, so it's important that you review students' responses. Give students feedback, using the example answers provided to guide you.

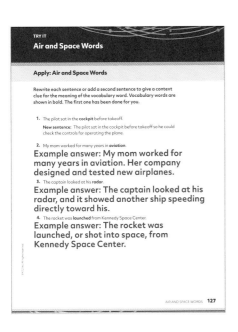

TRY IT
Air and Space Words

Apply: Air and Space Words

Rewrite each sentence or add a second sentence to give a context clue for the meaning of the vocabulary word. Vocabulary words are shown in bold. The first one has been done for you.

1. The pilot sat in the **cockpit** before takeoff.

   New sentence: The pilot sat in the cockpit before takeoff so he could check the controls for operating the plane.

2. My mom worked for many years in **aviation**.

   Example answer: My mom worked for many years in aviation. Her company designed and tested new airplanes.

3. The captain looked at his **radar**.

   Example answer: The captain looked at his radar, and it showed another ship speeding directly toward his.

4. The rocket was **launched** from Kennedy Space Center.

   Example answer: The rocket was launched, or shot into space, from Kennedy Space Center.

AIR AND SPACE WORDS **127**

TRY IT   Go Write!

Students will write independently for pleasure. As they write, they should think about using context clues in their writing.

TRY IT   Review Air and Space Words

Students will answer questions to review the meanings of their vocabulary words and what they have learned about using context clues to help them determine the meanings of words.

QUIZ

Air and Space Words

Students will complete the Air and Space Words quiz.

WRAP-UP

More Language Arts Practice

Students will practice skills according to their individual needs.

Go Read!

Students will read for pleasure. They should choose a book or a magazine that interests them, or they may choose a selection from the digital library, linked in the online lesson.

Students should read for the entire time. Have students select something to read ahead of time to help them stay focused.

First Flights (A)

Lesson Overview

ACTIVITY	ACTIVITY TITLE	TIME	ONLINE/OFFLINE
GET READY	Introduction to First Flights (A)	**1** minute	🖥️
	Spelling List 8 Pretest **LEARNING COACH CHECK-IN**	**10** minutes	🖥️ and 📄
	Look Back at Cause and Effect	**4** minutes	🖥️
	Before You Read "Wilbur and Orville Wright: Men with Wings"	**15** minutes	🖥️
READ	"Wilbur and Orville Wright: Men with Wings"	**30** minutes	📄
	Check-In: "Wilbur and Orville Wright: Men with Wings"	**5** minutes	🖥️
LEARN AND **TRY IT**	What Happened and Why	**10** minutes	🖥️
	Explain the Events	**10** minutes	🖥️
	Apply: Explain Events and Ideas	**15** minutes	🖥️
	Write About "Wilbur and Orville Wright: Men with Wings" **LEARNING COACH CHECK-IN**	**10** minutes	📄
	Practice Words from "Wilbur and Orville Wright"	**8** minutes	🖥️
WRAP-UP	Question About "Wilbur and Orville Wright"	**2** minutes	🖥️

Content Background

Students will read "Wilbur and Orville Wright: Men with Wings" by Dorothy Haas in *Expeditions in Reading*. They will learn about using text information to explain events in a nonfiction text.

A reader can use text information to explain what happened and why in a couple of ways. The reader can locate the information right in the text, which means that the author has directly stated it. Other times, a reader must use text information to make an inference that explains why something happened.

MATERIALS

Supplied
- *Summit English Language Arts 4 Expeditions in Reading*
- *Summit English Language Arts 4 Activity Book*
  - Spelling List 8 Pretest
  - Write About "Wilbur and Orville Wright: Men with Wings"

"Wilbur and Orville Wright" Synopsis

In the early 1900s, many people were attempting to be the first to fly a motor-driven aircraft. Wilbur and Orville Wright were among them, but the Wright brothers' ideas about how to achieve this goal were very different from everybody else's.

"Wilbur and Orville Wright: Men with Wings" follows the Wright brothers from their childhood flying kites and observing birds to the day of December 17, 1903. On that day, Wilbur and Orville completed flights in the airplane they built, which proved they could fly and control a motor-driven aircraft.

Lesson Goals

- Take a spelling pretest.
- Read and summarize the events in "Wilbur and Orville Wright: Men with Wings."
- Determine main ideas, supporting details, and meanings of unfamiliar words in the reading.
- Explain the events that led to the Wright brothers' historic first flight.

GET READY

Introduction to First Flights (A)

Students will get a glimpse of what they will learn about in the lesson. They will also read the lesson goals and keywords. Have students select each keyword and preview its definition.

Spelling List 8 Pretest

Students will take a spelling pretest.

LEARNING COACH CHECK-IN Have students turn to Spelling List 8 Pretest in *Summit English Language Arts 4 Activity Book* and open the online Spelling Pretest activity. Online, students will listen to the spelling word, type the word in the space indicated, and then check their answer. In the activity book, students will write the correct spelling of the word in the tables provided and indicate with a ✓ or an ✗ if they spelled the word correctly or incorrectly online. Students will repeat this process with the remaining words.

As needed, help students with the interaction between the online activity and the activity book page until they become comfortable with what they need to do. As students practice their spelling words throughout the workshop, they should pay special attention to words they spelled incorrectly on the pretest.

This is the complete list of words students will be tested on.

Long *i* Sound	Root *spec*	Prefix *mis–*	Heart Words
analyze	inspect	misjudge	Rhode Island
apologize	spectator	misspell	South Carolina
dynamite			everyone
enlighten			patient
fright			
identify			
license			
recognize			
tiger			

NOTE Have students keep their completed activity page in a safe place so they can refer to it later.

Look Back at Cause and Effect

Students will practice the prerequisite skill of identifying cause-and-effect relationships.

Before You Read "Wilbur and Orville Wright: Men with Wings"

Students will be introduced to some key vocabulary words that they will encounter in the upcoming reading, learn some important historical background related to the reading, and answer questions to help them set a purpose for their reading.

READ

"Wilbur and Orville Wright: Men with Wings"

Students will read "Wilbur and Orville Wright: Men with Wings" by Dorothy Haas in *Expeditions in Reading*.

Check-In: "Wilbur and Orville Wright: Men with Wings"

Students will answer questions to demonstrate their comprehension "Wilbur and Orville Wright: Men with Wings."

LEARN AND TRY IT

LEARN   What Happened and Why

Students will learn about using information in a text to explain what happened and why.

TIP   Make sure that students understand that sometimes a text directly explains why something happened. Other times, they must use information in the text to make an inference to explain why something happened.

TRY IT   Explain the Events

Students will analyze passages and answer questions to explain the events in the reading.

TRY IT   Apply: Explain Events and Ideas

Students will apply to a new work what they've learned about explaining events and ideas.

TRY IT   Write About "Wilbur and Orville Wright: Men with Wings"

Students will complete Write About "Wilbur and Orville Wright: Men with Wings" from *Summit English Language Arts 4 Activity Book*.

LEARNING COACH CHECK-IN   This activity page contains open-ended questions, so it's important that you review students' responses. Give students feedback, using the sample answers provided to guide you.

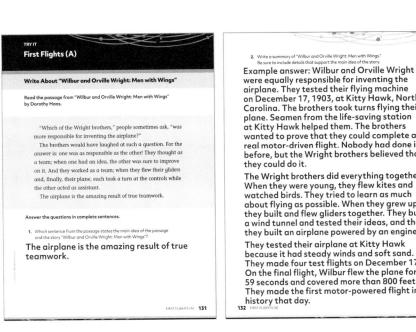

TRY IT

First Flights (A)

Write About "Wilbur and Orville Wright: Men with Wings"

Read the passage from "Wilbur and Orville Wright: Men with Wings" by Dorothy Haas.

"Which of the Wright brothers," people sometimes ask, "was more responsible for inventing the airplane?"

The brothers would have laughed at such a question. For the answer is: one was as responsible as the other! They thought as a team; when one had an idea, the other was sure to improve on it. And they worked as a team; when they flew their gliders and, finally, their plane, each took a turn at the controls while the other acted as assistant.

The airplane is the amazing result of true teamwork.

Answer the questions in complete sentences.

1. Which sentence from the passage states the main idea of the passage and the story "Wilbur and Orville Wright: Men with Wings"?

The airplane is the amazing result of true teamwork.

FIRST FLIGHTS (A) **131**

2. Write a summary of "Wilbur and Orville Wright: Men with Wings." Be sure to include details that support the main idea of the story.

Example answer: Wilbur and Orville Wright were equally responsible for inventing the airplane. They tested their flying machine on December 17, 1903, at Kitty Hawk, North Carolina. The brothers took turns flying their plane. Seamen from the life-saving station at Kitty Hawk helped them. The brothers wanted to prove that they could complete a real motor-driven flight. Nobody had done it before, but the Wright brothers believed that they could do it.

The Wright brothers did everything together. When they were young, they flew kites and watched birds. They tried to learn as much about flying as possible. When they grew up, they built and flew gliders together. They built a wind tunnel and tested their ideas, and then they built an airplane powered by an engine.

They tested their airplane at Kitty Hawk because it had steady winds and soft sand. They made four test flights on December 17. On the final flight, Wilbur flew the plane for 59 seconds and covered more than 800 feet. They made the first motor-powered flight in history that day.

132 FIRST FLIGHTS (A)

TRY IT Practice Words from "Wilbur and Orville Wright"

Students will answer questions to demonstrate their understanding of the vocabulary words from the reading.

WRAP-UP

Question About "Wilbur and Orville Wright"

Students will answer a question to show that they understand how to explain the events described in the reading.

First Flights (B)

Lesson Overview

ACTIVITY	ACTIVITY TITLE	TIME	ONLINE/OFFLINE
GET READY	Introduction to First Flights (B)	**1** minute	
	Spelling List 8 Activity Bank	**10** minutes	
	Recall "Wilbur and Orville Wright: Men with Wings"	**5** minutes	
	Before You Read "The Challenge: Bessie Coleman's Story"	**10** minutes	
READ	"The Challenge: Bessie Coleman's Story"	**30** minutes	
	Check-In: "The Challenge: Bessie Coleman's Story"	**5** minutes	
LEARN AND **TRY IT**	Integrate Ideas from Two Texts	**10** minutes	
	Practice Integrating Ideas	**10** minutes	
	Apply: Integrating Ideas	**15** minutes	
	Write Notes for Integrating Ideas **LEARNING COACH CHECK-IN**	**15** minutes	
	Practice Words from "The Challenge: Bessie Coleman's Story"	**7** minutes	
WRAP-UP	Question About "The Challenge: Bessie Coleman's Story"	**2** minutes	

Content Background

Students will learn about integrating ideas from more than one text. Integrating ideas is an important skill. It allows readers to write and speak knowledgeably about a topic. Gathering information from multiple sources helps a reader gain a full understanding of topics and events. To integrate ideas, a reader must first identify what is the same and what is different in texts on the same topic.

Here is an example of passages from two texts and a paragraph that integrates ideas from both.

Excerpt from "Wilbur and Orville Wright: Men with Wings" by Dorothy Haas

> But nobody had been able to put a motor-powered plane in the air and keep it there.

Wilbur and Orville Wright believed this could be done. They did not listen to people who laughed and said, "If men had been meant to fly, they would have been given wings."

As boys they flew kites. They tried to understand what kept the kites in the air. And they watched the birds. ...

When they grew up they built a glider. They flew that.

Excerpt from "The Challenge: Bessie Coleman's Story"
by Margaret Roberts

She quickly learned that all doors to aviation were closed to her. A black woman wanting to fly airplanes? Unthinkable! But Bessie Coleman refused to take no for an answer.

She introduced herself to Robert S. Abbott. He was the African American owner of the *Chicago Defender*, a respected newspaper in the city. She hoped he would have some ideas for her, and he did.

Integrated Information:

The early pioneers of flight had something in common. They were dedicated to reaching their goals. And they were not going to let anybody's ideas or actions get in their way. When people said humans could not fly, the Wright brothers did not listen. They began to teach themselves about flight when they were young. They flew kites. They watched birds. They built and flew gliders. When Bessie Coleman found her way to flight school blocked, she continued to work toward her goal. She reached out for help from Robert Abbott, the African American owner of a Chicago newspaper.

Advance Preparation

Gather students' completed Spelling List 8 Pretest activity page from First Flights (A). Students will refer to this page during Get Ready: Spelling List 8 Activity Bank.

"The Challenge: Bessie Coleman's Story" Synopsis

Just a few short years after the Wright brothers' success, many people wanted to learn to fly. Bessie Coleman was one. This young African American woman from Texas worked toward her goal from the time she was a teenager. But she had to overcome many barriers to fulfill her dreams. Doors were closed to her not only because she was black, but also because she was a woman. Through hard work and determination, Bessie Coleman was the first black woman to become a licensed pilot.

Lesson Goals

- Practice all spelling words.
- Identify the main idea of and explain the events in "The Challenge: Bessie Coleman's Story."
- Draw on information from more than one text on the same topic to answer questions.
- Determine the meanings of unfamiliar words in the reading.

GET READY

Introduction to First Flights (B)

Students will get a glimpse of what they will learn about in the lesson. They will also read the lesson goals and keywords. Have students select each keyword and preview its definition.

Spelling List 8 Activity Bank

Students will practice all spelling words from the workshop by completing Spelling List 8 Activity Bank from *Summit English Language Arts 4 Activity Book*. Make sure students have their completed Spelling List 8 Pretest activity page from First Flights (A) to refer to during this activity.

Remind students to pay special attention to words they spelled incorrectly on the Spelling Pretest.

Recall "Wilbur and Orville Wright: Men with Wings"

Students will answer questions to review the reading that they have already completed.

Before You Read "The Challenge: Bessie Coleman's Story"

Students will be introduced to some key vocabulary words that they will encounter in the upcoming reading.

READ

"The Challenge: Bessie Coleman's Story"

Students will read "The Challenge: Bessie Coleman's Story" by Margaret Roberts in *Expeditions in Reading*.

Check-In: "The Challenge: Bessie Coleman's Story"

Students will answer questions to demonstrate their comprehension of "The Challenge: Bessie Coleman's Story."

LEARN AND TRY IT

LEARN   Integrate Ideas from Two Texts

Students will learn how to integrate, or combine, ideas from more than one text.

NOTE   This activity will include passages from "Wilbur and Orville Wright: Men with Wings." Students may want to have the story handy for reference.

TRY IT   Practice Integrating Ideas

Students will practice analyzing passages to determine which idea is the same in two passages. They will also practice identifying a paragraph that is the best example of integrating ideas from two passages.

TRY IT   Apply: Integrating Ideas

Students will apply to a new work what they've learned about integrating ideas.

TRY IT   Write Notes for Integrating Ideas

Students will complete Write Notes for Integrating Ideas from *Summit English Language Arts 4 Activity Book*. Students will complete the first part of a chart to prepare for integrating ideas from two stories.

NOTE   Students should fill in only the first column of the chart. They will complete the chart over the course of two lessons. Have students keep their activity page in a safe place so they can refer to it later.

LEARNING COACH CHECK-IN   Students will gather information on this activity page that they will reference for a later writing activity, so it's important that you review students' responses. Give students feedback, using the sample answers provided to guide you.

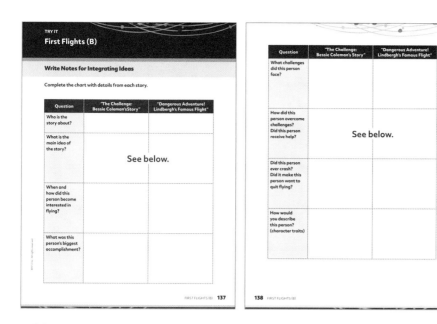

Additional answers

Question	"The Challenge: Bessie Coleman's Story"	"Dangerous Adventure! Lindbergh's Famous Flight"
Who is the story about?	Bessie Coleman	
What is the main idea of the story?	Through hard work and determination, Bessie was the first black woman to become a pilot.	
When and how did this person become interested in flying?	She dreamed of becoming a pilot when she was a teenager.	
What was this person's biggest accomplishment?	She was the first black woman to become a licensed pilot.	
What challenges did this person face?	She couldn't go to high school and had to earn money to pay for flying lessons. Flight schools wouldn't accept her because she was black and a woman.	
How did this person overcome challenges? Did this person receive help?	She did laundry and worked in a barber shop to earn money. She went to France to learn to fly. Robert Abbott helped her by suggesting she go to France. He also arranged her first American show.	
Did this person ever crash? Did it make this person want to quit flying?	Yes. She broke a leg and ribs, but she didn't stop flying.	
How would describe this person? (characer traits)	Determined, confident, a hard worker	

TRY IT Practice Words from "The Challenge: Bessie Coleman's Story"

Students will answer questions to demonstrate their understanding of the vocabulary words from the reading.

Question About "The Challenge: Bessie Coleman's Story"

Students will answer a question to show that they understand how to integrate ideas.

First Flights (C)

Lesson Overview

ACTIVITY	ACTIVITY TITLE	TIME	ONLINE/OFFLINE
GET READY	Introduction to First Flights (C)	**1** minute	
	Spelling List 8 Review Game	**10** minutes	
	Recall "The Challenge: Bessie Coleman's Story"	**5** minutes	
	Before You Read "Dangerous Adventure!"	**10** minutes	
READ	"Dangerous Adventure! Lindbergh's Famous Flight"	**30** minutes	
	Check-In: "Dangerous Adventure! Lindbergh's Famous Flight"	**5** minutes	
LEARN AND **TRY IT**	More About Integrating Ideas	**10** minutes	
	More Practice Integrating Ideas	**10** minutes	
	Apply: Integrating Ideas from Multiple Sources	**15** minutes	
	Finish Writing Notes for Integrating Ideas **LEARNING COACH CHECK-IN**	**15** minutes	
	Practice Words from "Dangerous Adventure!"	**7** minutes	
WRAP-UP	Question About "Dangerous Adventure!"	**2** minutes	

Content Background

Students will continue to learn about integrating ideas from more than one text on the same topic. Integrating ideas is an important skill that allows readers to write and speak knowledgeably about a topic. It also helps readers gain a full understanding of topics and events by gathering information from multiple sources.

Advance Preparation

Gather students' Write Notes for Integrating Ideas activity page from First Flights (B). Students will complete to this page during Try It: Finish Writing Notes for Integrating Ideas.

"Dangerous Adventure!" Synopsis

When Charles Lindbergh was a boy, he imagined he had wings and could fly over fences and houses. By the time he was 21, he had achieved this dream and had his own plane. He moved on to barnstorming, doing dangerous stunts like walking on the plane's wings and parachuting out of it. He then worked flying the mail from city to city. During that time, he decided to pursue a new goal—win a $25,000 prize for being the first person to fly nonstop from New York to Paris. This was not an easy goal. Lindbergh had to overcome many obstacles to make his historic flight. But like other pioneers of aviation, once Lindbergh decided on his goal, he achieved it through hard work and determination.

Lesson Goals

- Practice all spelling words.

- Identify the main idea of and explain the events in "Dangerous Adventure! Lindbergh's Famous Flight."

- Draw on information from more than one text on the same topic to answer questions.

- Determine the meanings of unfamiliar words in the reading.

GET READY

Introduction to First Flights (C)

Students will get a glimpse of what they will learn about in the lesson. They will also read the lesson goals and keywords. Have students select each keyword and preview its definition.

Spelling List 8 Review Game

Students will practice all spelling words from the workshop.

Recall "The Challenge: Bessie Coleman's Story"

Students will answer questions to review the reading that they have already completed.

Before You Read "Dangerous Adventure! Lindbergh's Famous Flight"

Students will be introduced to some key vocabulary words that they will encounter in the upcoming reading.

"Dangerous Adventure! Lindbergh's Famous Flight"

Students will read "Dangerous Adventure! Lindbergh's Famous Flight" by Ruth Belov Gross in *Expeditions in Reading*.

Check-In: "Dangerous Adventure! Lindbergh's Famous Flight"

Students will answer questions to demonstrate their comprehension of "Dangerous Adventure! Lindbergh's Famous Flight."

LEARN AND **TRY IT**

LEARN More About Integrating Ideas

Students will continue to learn about integrating, or combining, ideas from more than one text on the same topic.

NOTE This activity will include passages from "The Challenge: Bessie Coleman's Story." Students may want to have the story handy for reference.

TRY IT More Practice Integrating Ideas

Students will practice analyzing passages to determine which idea is the same in passages from different texts. They will also practice identifying a paragraph that is the best example of integrating ideas from two passages.

TRY IT Apply: Integrating Ideas from Multiple Sources

Students will apply to a new text what they've learned about integrating ideas.

TRY IT Finish Writing Notes for Integrating Ideas

Students will complete Write Notes for Integrating Ideas from *Summit English Language Arts 4 Activity Book*.

LEARNING COACH CHECK-IN Students will gather information on this activity page that they will reference for a later writing activity, so it's important that you review students' responses. Give students feedback, using the sample answers provided to guide you.

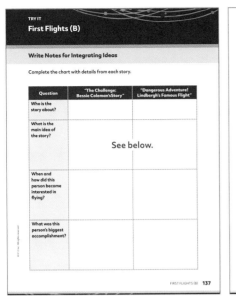

Additional answers

Question	"The Challenge: Bessie Coleman's Story"	"Dangerous Adventure! Lindbergh's Famous Flight"
Who is the story about?	Bessie Coleman	Charles Lindbergh
What is the main idea of the story?	Through hard work and determination, Bessie was the first black woman to become a pilot.	Lindbergh worked hard and took risks, and he made the first nonstop flight from New York to Paris in history.
When and how did this person become interested in flying?	She dreamed of becoming a pilot when she was a teenager.	When he was young, he imagined he had wings and could fly.
What was this person's biggest accomplishment?	She was the first black woman to become a licensed pilot.	He made the first nonstop flight from New York to Paris.
What challenges did this person face?	She couldn't go to high school and had to earn money to pay for flying lessons. Flight schools wouldn't accept her because she was black and a woman.	He did not have enough money for a plane. People who made planes wouldn't sell him one.
How did this person overcome challenges? **Did this person receive help?**	She did laundry and worked in a barber shop to earn money. She went to France to learn to fly. Robert Abbott helped her by suggesting she go to France. He also arranged her first American show.	St. Louis businessmen helped pay for his plane. He found a company in California to build his plane.
Did this person ever crash? **Did it make this person want to quit flying?**	Yes. She broke a leg and ribs, but she didn't stop flying.	Yes. Two times when he was flying to carry the mail, he had to jump out of his plane with a parachute. He did not quit flying.
How would describe this person? (characer traits)	Determined, confident, a hard worker	Determined, brave

TRY IT   Practice Words from "Dangerous Adventure!"

Students will answer questions to demonstrate their understanding of the vocabulary words from the reading.

Question About "Dangerous Adventure!"

Students will answer a question to show that they understand how to integrate ideas from two texts on the same topic.

First Flights Wrap-Up

Lesson Overview

ACTIVITY	ACTIVITY TITLE	TIME	ONLINE/OFFLINE
GET READY	Introduction to First Flights Wrap-Up	**1** minute	📶
TRY IT	Write About Bessie and Charles **LEARNING COACH CHECK·IN**	**30** minutes	📄
	Read and Record	**20** minutes	📶
	Review First Flights	**15** minutes	📶
QUIZ	First Flights	**30** minutes	📶
	Spelling List 8	**10** minutes	📶
WRAP-UP	More Language Arts Practice	**14** minutes	📶

Advance Preparation

Gather students' completed Write Notes for Integrating Ideas activity page from First Flights (B) and (C). Students will refer to this page during Try It: Write About Bessie and Charles.

MATERIALS

Supplied
- *Summit English Language Arts 4 Activity Book*
  - Write About Bessie and Charles

Also Needed
- completed Write Notes for Integrating Ideas activity page from First Flights (B) and (C)

Lesson Goals

- Write about Bessie Coleman and Charles Lindbergh.

- Practice reading aloud.

- Review and take a quiz on using details, identifying the main idea and supporting details, and integrating information from two texts.

- Take a spelling quiz.

GET READY

Introduction to First Flights Wrap-Up

Students will read the lesson goals.

Write About Bessie and Charles

Students will complete Write About Bessie and Charles from *Summit English Language Arts 4 Activity Book*. Students should refer to their completed Write Notes for Integrating Ideas activity page for information to help them complete the writing activity.

SUPPORT For students having difficulty writing a paragraph, provide them an example of a paragraph that integrates information on one thing that the pilots had in common.

Example: Bessie and Charles were both willing to take risks even if crashing was a possibility. Bessie had a crash that broke her leg and several ribs. Charles had to jump out of a plane with a parachute, twice, before his plane crashed. But both pilots kept on flying even after their crashes.

LEARNING COACH CHECK-IN This activity page contains open-ended questions, so it's important that you review students' responses. Give students feedback, using the sample answers provided to guide you.

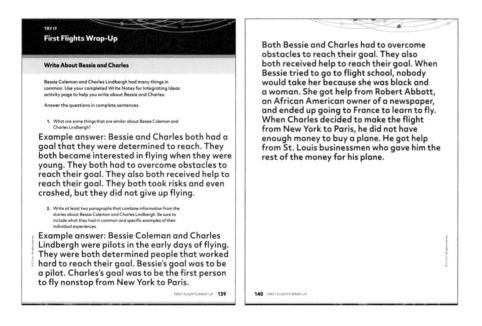

TRY IT
First Flights Wrap-Up

Write About Bessie and Charles

Bessie Coleman and Charles Lindbergh had many things in common. Use your completed Write Notes for Integrating Ideas activity page to help you write about Bessie and Charles.

Answer the questions in complete sentences.

1. What are some things that are similar about Bessie Coleman and Charles Lindbergh?

Example answer: Bessie and Charles both had a goal that they were determined to reach. They both became interested in flying when they were young. They both had to overcome obstacles to reach their goal. They also both received help to reach their goal. They both took risks and even crashed, but they did not give up flying.

2. Write at least two paragraphs that combine information from the stories about Bessie Coleman and Charles Lindbergh. Be sure to include what they had in common and specific examples of their individual experiences.

Example answer: Bessie Coleman and Charles Lindbergh were pilots in the early days of flying. They were both determined people that worked hard to reach their goal. Bessie's goal was to be a pilot. Charles's goal was to be the first person to fly nonstop from New York to Paris.

Both Bessie and Charles had to overcome obstacles to reach their goal. They also both received help to reach their goal. When Bessie tried to go to flight school, nobody would take her because she was black and a woman. She got help from Robert Abbott, an African American owner of a newspaper, and ended up going to France to learn to fly. When Charles decided to make the flight from New York to Paris, he did not have enough money to buy a plane. He got help from St. Louis businessmen who gave him the rest of the money for his plane.

FIRST FLIGHTS WRAP-UP **139**

140 FIRST FLIGHTS WRAP-UP

Read and Record

Good readers read quickly, smoothly, and with expression. This is called *fluency*. Students will record themselves reading aloud. They will listen to their recording and think about how quick, smooth, and expressive they sound.

TIP Encourage students to rerecord as needed.

Review First Flights

Students will answer questions to review what they have learned about explaining events in a historical text, identifying main idea and supporting details, and integrating information from two texts on the same topic.

First Flights

Students will complete the First Flights quiz.

Spelling List 8

Students will complete the Spelling List 8 quiz.

More Language Arts Practice

Students will practice skills according to their individual needs.

Informational Writing Skills (A)

Lesson Overview

ACTIVITY	ACTIVITY TITLE	TIME	ONLINE/OFFLINE
GET READY	Introduction to Informational Writing Skills (A)	**1** minute	🖥️
	Spelling List 9 Pretest **LEARNING COACH CHECK-IN**	**10** minutes	🖥️ and 📄
	Look Back at Verb Tense	**5** minutes	🖥️
LEARN AND **TRY IT**	Use Present Progressive Tense	**15** minutes	🖥️
	Practice Using Present Progressive Tense	**15** minutes	🖥️
	Explore the Writing in "Go, John Glenn!"	**15** minutes	🖥️
	Explore the Writing in "The Challenge: Bessie Coleman's Story"	**15** minutes	🖥️
	Write an Informational Paragraph **LEARNING COACH CHECK-IN**	**20** minutes	📄
WRAP-UP	Questions About Introductions and Present Progressive Tense	**4** minutes	🖥️
	Go Read!	**20** minutes	🖥️ or 📄

Content Background

Informational text is factual text written to share information. Students will analyze how authors write informational text and apply those skills to their own informational writing.

In this lesson, students will learn how writers begin and organize informational text. Writers introduce informational text with a *hook*, something that grabs readers' attention. Writers also clearly introduce the main idea of the text. Writers then group related ideas in support of the main idea.

Students will also explore how writers use graphics, such as pictures and diagrams, to support their main idea. Most important, students will learn that graphics have a purpose beyond decoration and that they should think critically about how they choose graphics to support their own informational writing.

MATERIALS

Supplied
- *Summit English Language Arts 4 Activity Book*
  - Spelling List 9 Pretest
  - Write an Informational Paragraph

Also Needed
- reading material for Go Read!

Grammar, Usage, and Mechanics Students will begin learning about the progressive tenses of verbs, beginning with the present progressive tense. The present progressive tense describes action that is ongoing in the present. It is formed by combining the present tense of "to be" (*am*, *is*, or *are*) with the present participle of the action verb. The present participle is the form of the verb that ends in *-ing*.

Example: The boulder **is rolling** down the hill.

Advance Preparation

During the Go Read! activity, students will have the option of using the digital library. Allow extra time for students to make their reading selection, or have students make a selection before beginning the lesson.

Lesson Goals

- Take a spelling pretest.
- Form and use the present progressive verb tense.
- Explore how to introduce topics and organize ideas in informational writing.
- Begin to write an informational paragraph.
- Read for pleasure.

GET READY

Introduction to Informational Writing Skills (A)

Students will get a glimpse of what they will learn about in the lesson. They will also read the lesson goals and keywords. Have students select each keyword and preview its definition.

Spelling List 9 Pretest

Students will take a spelling pretest.

LEARNING COACH CHECK-IN Have students turn to Spelling List 9 Pretest in *Summit English Language Arts 4 Activity Book* and open the online Spelling Pretest activity. Online, students will listen to the spelling word, type the word in the space indicated, and then check their answer. In the activity book, students will write the correct spelling of the word in the tables provided and indicate with a ✓ or an ✗ if they spelled the word correctly or incorrectly online. Students will repeat this process with the remaining words.

As needed, help students with the interaction between the online activity and the activity book page until they become comfortable with what they need to do. As students practice their spelling words throughout the workshop, they should pay special attention to words they spelled incorrectly on the pretest.

This is the complete list of words students will be tested on.

Long o Sound	Root *val*	Prefix *in–*	Heart Words
approach	evaluate	inadequate	Nevada
boastful	valuable	incomplete	New York
bowling		incorrect	
coastal			
foe			
growth			
oboe			
throat			
thrown			
tomorrow			

NOTE Have students keep their completed activity page in a safe place so they can refer to it later.

Look Back at Verb Tense

Students will practice the prerequisite skill of recognizing and using different verb tenses.

LEARN   Use Present Progressive Tense

Students will learn how to form and use the present progressive tense of a verb.

NOTE   The present progressive tense can also correctly indicate a future action (I **am going** to the beach tomorrow). Students will not learn or be assessed on this use of the present progressive tense.

TRY IT   Practice Using Present Progressive Tense

Students will answer questions about forming and using the present progressive tense. They will receive feedback on their answers.

LEARN   Explore the Writing in "Go, John Glenn!"

Students will examine some of the elements of "Go, John Glenn!," an informational text about the first astronaut to orbit the earth. They will focus on the piece's use of a hook, how it groups related information together, and the role of images in the text.

TRY IT   Explore the Writing in "The Challenge: Bessie Coleman's Story"

Students will answer questions about how a writer grabs the attention of readers, groups related information, and uses images to enhance reader experience and understanding. They will receive feedback on their answers.

TRY IT   Write an Informational Paragraph

Students will complete Write an Informational Paragraph from *Summit English Language Arts 4 Activity Book*.

LEARNING COACH CHECK-IN   This activity page contains open-ended questions, so it's important that you review students' responses. Give students feedback, using the sample answers provided to guide you.

NOTE   Have students keep their completed activity page in a safe place so they can refer to it later.

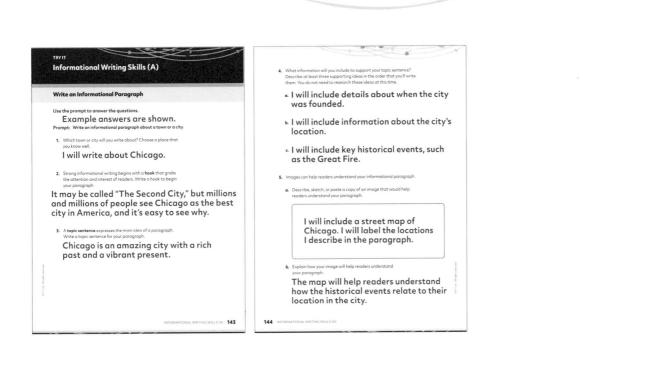

WRAP-UP

Questions About Introductions and Present Progressive Tense

Students will answer questions to show that they understand how to create an effective introduction to a piece of informational writing and how to use the present progressive tense.

Go Read!

Students will read for pleasure. They should choose a book or a magazine that interests them, or they may choose a selection from the digital library, linked in the online lesson.

Students should read for the entire time. Have students select something to read ahead of time to help them stay focused.

Informational Writing Skills (B)

Lesson Overview

ACTIVITY	ACTIVITY TITLE	TIME	ONLINE/OFFLINE
GET READY	Introduction to Informational Writing Skills (B)	**1** minute	🖥️
	Spelling List 9 Activity Bank	**10** minutes	📄
LEARN AND **TRY IT**	Use Past Progressive Tense	**10** minutes	🖥️
	Practice Using Past Progressive Tense	**10** minutes	🖥️
	Support and Links in "Go, John Glenn!"	**17** minutes	🖥️
	Support and Links in "The Challenge: Bessie Coleman's Story"	**15** minutes	🖥️
	Develop Your Topic LEARNING COACH CHECK-IN	**30** minutes	📄
WRAP-UP	Questions About Facts and Past Progressive	**2** minutes	🖥️
	Go Read!	**25** minutes	🖥️ or 📄

Content Background

Students will continue learning about informational writing by analyzing the work of expert writers and then applying those skills to their own writing. In this lesson, they will learn how writers use evidence to develop their ideas and transitions to connect ideas.

Students will learn about the evidence that informational writers use, such as facts, definitions, concrete details, examples, and quotations. They will also learn about transitions that link categories of information. For example, the transition *because* shows reason, and the transition *also* shows similarity. The transition *for example* tells the reader that the upcoming text is an example of the previous text.

Grammar, Usage, and Mechanics   Students will continue learning about the progressive tense of verbs. They will learn that the past progressive tense describes action that was ongoing in the past. It is often used to describe what was happening when some other event occurred. It is formed by combining the past tense of the "to be" verb (*was* or *were*) with the present participle (-ing form) of the action verb.

> **Example:** The skiers **were riding** the lift up the mountain when the storm began.

MATERIALS

Supplied
- *Summit English Language Arts 4 Activity Book*
  - Spelling List 9 Activity Bank
  - Develop Your Topic

Also Needed
- completed Spelling List 9 Pretest activity page from Informational Writing Skills (A)
- completed Write an Informational Paragraph activity page from Informational Writing Skills (A)
- reading material for Go Read!

Advance Preparation

Gather students' completed Spelling List 9 Pretest activity page from Informational Writing Skills (A). Students will refer to this page during Get Ready: Spelling List 9 Activity Bank.

Gather students' completed Write an Informational Paragraph activity page from Informational Writing Skills (A). Students will refer to this page during Try It: Develop Your Topic.

During the Go Read! activity, students will have the option of using the digital library. Allow extra time for students to make their reading selection, or have students make a selection before beginning the lesson.

Lesson Goals

- Practice all spelling words offline.
- Form and use the past progressive tense.
- Explore how to support and connect ideas in informational writing.
- Continue to write an informational paragraph.
- Read for pleasure.

GET READY

Introduction to Informational Writing Skills (B)

Students will get a glimpse of what they will learn about in the lesson. They will also read the lesson goals and keywords. Have students select each keyword and preview its definition.

Spelling List 9 Activity Bank

Students will practice all spelling words from the workshop by completing Spelling List 9 Activity Bank from *Summit English Language Arts 4 Activity Book*. Make sure students have their completed Spelling List 9 Pretest activity page from Informational Writing Skills (A) to refer to during this activity.

Remind students to pay special attention to words they spelled incorrectly on the Spelling Pretest.

LEARN AND TRY IT

LEARN Use Past Progressive Tense

Students will learn how to form and use the past progressive tense of a verb.

TRY IT Practice Using Past Progressive Tense

Students will answer questions about forming and using the past progressive tense. They will receive feedback on their answers.

LEARN Support and Links in "Go, John Glenn!"

Students will continue to examine some of the elements of "Go, John Glenn!," an informational text about the first astronaut to orbit the earth. They will focus on the piece's supporting details, how those details help convey and reinforce main ideas, and the text's use of transitions to link ideas and show the relationships between them.

TRY IT Support and Links in "The Challenge: Bessie Coleman's Story"

Students will answer questions about how a writer uses supporting details to convey and reinforce main ideas, as well as how a writer uses transitions to link ideas and show relationships between them. They will receive feedback on their answers.

TRY IT Develop Your Topic

Students will complete Develop Your Topic from *Summit English Language Arts 4 Activity Book*. Make sure students have their completed Write an Informational Paragraph activity page from Informational Writing Skills (A) to refer to during this activity.

LEARNING COACH CHECK-IN This activity page contains open-ended questions, so it's important that you review students' responses. Give students feedback, using the sample answers provided to guide you.

TIP Students may need to do research to develop their supporting ideas. Work together with students to locate trustworthy websites, such as those run by city and state governments or government organizations, or trustworthy print sources, such as encyclopedias or reputable travel guides. Additionally, students may research by interviewing someone who knows a lot about their topic (maybe that's you!).

NOTE Have students keep their completed activity page in a safe place so they can refer to it later.

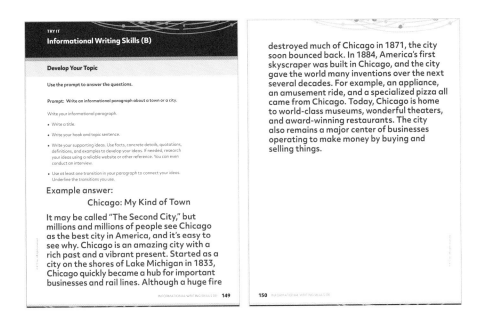

INFORMATIONAL WRITING SKILLS (B) 149

150 INFORMATIONAL WRITING SKILLS (B)

WRAP-UP

Questions About Facts and Past Progressive Tense

Students will answer questions to show that they understand why writers of informational texts include supporting details in their work and how to use the past progressive tense.

Go Read!

Students will read for pleasure. They should choose a book or a magazine that interests them, or they may choose a selection from the digital library, linked in the online lesson.

Students should read for the entire time. Have students select something to read ahead of time to help them stay focused.

Informational Writing Skills (C)

Lesson Overview

ACTIVITY	ACTIVITY TITLE	TIME	ONLINE/OFFLINE
GET READY	Introduction to Informational Writing Skills (C)	**1** minute	🖥️
	Spelling List 9 Review Game	**10** minutes	🖥️
LEARN AND **TRY IT**	Use Future Progressive Tense	**12** minutes	🖥️
	Practice Using Future Progressive Tense	**10** minutes	🖥️
	Words and Endings in "Go, John Glenn!"	**15** minutes	🖥️
	Words and Endings in "The Challenge: Bessie Coleman's Story"	**15** minutes	🖥️
	Finish Your Informational Paragraph **LEARNING COACH CHECK-IN**	**35** minutes	📄
WRAP-UP	Questions About Word Choice and Future Progressive	**2** minutes	🖥️
	Go Read!	**20** minutes	🖥️ or 📄

Content Background

Students will continue learning about informational writing by analyzing how authors write informational texts and then applying those skills to their own writing. In this lesson, they will focus on using precise, formal, and domain-specific language. They'll also learn how to write an effective conclusion to an informational text.

Formal language does not contain contractions, abbreviations, or slang. It follows all of the rules of grammar, usage, and mechanics. It helps establish the knowledge of the writer and the seriousness of a text. The term *precise language* refers to language that clearly and succinctly describes complex content. *Domain-specific language* refers to terms that are related to a particular field or subject. Using domain-specific language is something that also helps establish the authority or expertise of a writer.

A conclusion is the end of a text. It's not necessarily a single paragraph or a single sentence. The length of a conclusion can vary. A strong conclusion to an informational text wraps up the text, stressing the meaning or importance of the subject.

MATERIALS

Supplied
- *Summit English Language Arts 4 Activity Book*
  - Finish Your Informational Paragraph

Also Needed
- completed Write an Informational Paragraph activity page from Informational Writing Skills (A)
- completed Develop Your Topic activity page from Informational Writing Skills (B)
- reading material for Go Read!

Grammar, Usage, and Mechanics   Students will learn about the remaining progressive verb tense, the future progressive. The future progressive tense describes action that will be ongoing in the future. Specifically, this tense is used to describe an action that will be in progress at a given future time or when a future event occurs. It is formed by combining the helping verbs *will be* with the present participle (-ing form) of the action verb.

> **Example:** The guests **will be dining** when you arrive.

Advance Preparation

Gather students' completed Write an Informational Paragraph activity page from Informational Writing Skills (A) and completed Develop Your Topic activity page from Informational Writing Skills (B). Students will refer to these pages during Try It: Finish Your Informational Paragraph.

During the Go Read! activity, students will have the option of using the digital library. Allow extra time for students to make their reading selection, or have students make a selection before beginning the lesson.

Lesson Goals

- Practice all spelling words online.

- Form and use the future progressive tense.

- Explore how to use domain-specific and formal language in informational writing.

- Finish writing an informational paragraph.

- Read for pleasure.

GET READY

Introduction to Informational Writing Skills (C)

Students will get a glimpse of what they will learn about in the lesson. They will also read the lesson goals and keywords. Have students select each keyword and preview its definition.

Spelling List 9 Review Game

Students will practice all spelling words from the workshop.

LEARN Use Future Progressive Tense

Students will learn how to recognize and use the future progressive tense appropriately.

TRY IT Practice Using Future Progressive Tense

Students will answer questions about recognizing and using the future progressive tense. They will receive feedback on their answers.

LEARN Words and Endings in "Go, John Glenn!"

Students will continue examining some of the elements of "Go, John Glenn!," an informational text about the first astronaut to orbit the earth. They will focus on the piece's use of precise, formal, and domain-specific language, as well as how its conclusion wraps up the text and stresses the subject's importance and meaning.

TRY IT Words and Endings in "The Challenge: Bessie Coleman's Story"

Students will answer questions about how a writer uses precise, formal, and domain-specific language in an informational text, as well as how a writer concludes an informational text. They will receive feedback on their answers.

TRY IT Finish Your Informational Paragraph

Students will complete Finish Your Informational Paragraph from *Summit English Language Arts 4 Activity Book*. Make sure students have their completed Write an Informational Paragraph activity page from Informational Writing Skills (A) and Develop Your Topic activity page from Informational Writing Skills (B) to refer to during this activity.

LEARNING COACH CHECK-IN   This activity page contains open-ended questions, so it's important that you review students' responses. Give students feedback, using the sample answers provided to guide you.

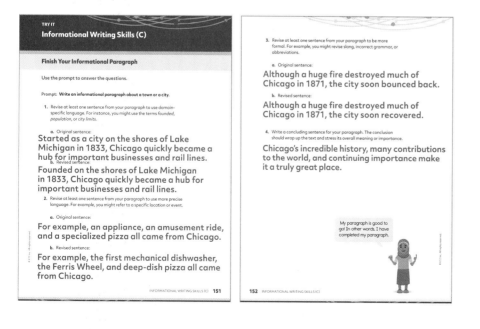

Questions About Word Choice and Future Progressive

Students will answer questions to show that they understand why writers of informational texts use precise, formal, and domain-specific language in their work and how to use the future progressive tense.

Go Read!

Students will read for pleasure. They should choose a book or a magazine that interests them, or they may choose a selection from the digital library, linked in the online lesson.

Students should read for the entire time. Have students select something to read ahead of time to help them stay focused.

Informational Writing Skills Wrap-Up

Lesson Overview

ACTIVITY	ACTIVITY TITLE	TIME	ONLINE/OFFLINE
GET READY	Introduction to Informational Writing Skills Wrap-Up	**1** minute	🖥️
TRY IT	Use Informational Writing Skills **LEARNING COACH CHECK-IN**	**35** minutes	📄
	Review Progressive Tenses	**20** minutes	🖥️
QUIZ	Progressive Tenses and Informational Writing Skills	**30** minutes	🖥️
	Spelling List 9	**10** minutes	🖥️
WRAP-UP	More Language Arts Practice	**9** minutes	🖥️
	Go Read!	**15** minutes	🖥️ or 📄

Lesson Goals

- Review progressive verb tenses and informational writing skills.

- Take a quiz on progressive verb tenses and informational writing skills.

- Take a spelling quiz.

MATERIALS

Supplied
- *Summit English Language Arts 4 Activity Book*
  - Use Informational Writing Skills

GET READY

Introduction to Informational Writing Skills Wrap-Up

Students will read the lesson goals.

TRY IT

Use Informational Writing Skills

Students will complete Use Informational Writing Skills in *Summit English Language Arts 4 Activity Book* to review the writing objectives that will be assessed on the quiz.

LEARNING COACH CHECK-IN   This activity page contains open-ended questions, so it's important that you review students' responses. Give students feedback, using the sample answers provided to guide you.

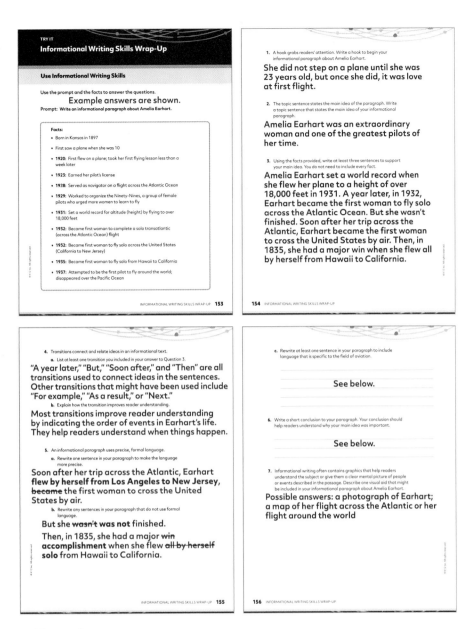

TRY IT

Informational Writing Skills Wrap-Up

Use Informational Writing Skills

Use the prompt and the facts to answer the questions.

Example answers are shown.

Prompt: Write an informational paragraph about Amelia Earhart.

Facts:
- Born in Kansas in 1897
- First saw a plane when she was 10
- **1920:** First flew on a plane; took her first flying lesson less than a week later
- **1923:** Earned her pilot's license
- **1928:** Served as navigator on a flight across the Atlantic Ocean
- **1929:** Worked to organize the Ninety-Nines, a group of female pilots who urged more women to learn to fly
- **1931:** Set a world record for altitude (height) by flying to over 18,000 feet
- **1932:** Became first woman to complete a solo transatlantic (across the Atlantic Ocean) flight
- **1932:** Became first woman to fly solo across the United States (California to New Jersey)
- **1935:** Became first woman to fly solo from Hawaii to California
- **1937:** Attempted to be the first pilot to fly around the world; disappeared over the Pacific Ocean

INFORMATIONAL WRITING SKILLS WRAP-UP **153**

1. A hook grabs readers' attention. Write a hook to begin your informational paragraph about Amelia Earhart.

She did not step on a plane until she was 23 years old, but once she did, it was love at first flight.

2. The topic sentence states the main idea of the paragraph. Write a topic sentence that states the main idea of your informational paragraph.

Amelia Earhart was an extraordinary woman and one of the greatest pilots of her time.

3. Using the facts provided, write at least three sentences to support your main idea. You do not need to include every fact.

Amelia Earhart set a world record when she flew her plane to a height of over 18,000 feet in 1931. A year later, in 1932, Earhart became the first woman to fly solo across the Atlantic Ocean. But she wasn't finished. Soon after her trip across the Atlantic, Earhart became the first woman to cross the United States by air. Then, in 1835, she had a major win when she flew all by herself from Hawaii to California.

154 INFORMATIONAL WRITING SKILLS WRAP-UP

4. Transitions connect and relate ideas in an informational text.

a. List at least one transition you included in your answer to Question 3.

"A year later," "But," "Soon after," and "Then" are all transitions used to connect ideas in the sentences. Other transitions that might have been used include "For example," "As a result," or "Next."

b. Explain how the transition improves reader understanding.

Most transitions improve reader understanding by indicating the order of events in Earhart's life. They help readers understand when things happen.

5. An informational paragraph uses precise, formal language.

a. Rewrite one sentence in your paragraph to make the language more precise.

Soon after her trip across the Atlantic, Earhart **flew by herself from Los Angeles to New Jersey,** ~~became~~ the first woman to cross the United States by air.

b. Rewrite any sentences in your paragraph that do not use formal language.

But she ~~wasn't~~ **was not** finished.

Then, in 1835, she had a major ~~win~~ **accomplishment** when she flew ~~all by herself~~ **solo** from Hawaii to California.

INFORMATIONAL WRITING SKILLS WRAP-UP **155**

c. Rewrite at least one sentence in your paragraph to include language that is specific to the field of aviation.

See below.

6. Write a short conclusion to your paragraph. Your conclusion should help readers understand why your main idea was important.

See below.

7. Informational writing often contains graphics that help readers understand the subject or give them a clear mental picture of people or events described in the passage. Describe one visual aid that might be included in your informational paragraph about Amelia Earhart.

Possible answers: a photograph of Earhart; a map of her flight across the Atlantic or her flight around the world

156 INFORMATIONAL WRITING SKILLS WRAP-UP

Additional answers

5c. Earhart set a world record when she flew her plane to ~~a height~~ **an altitude** of over 18,000 feet in 1931.

A year later, in 1932, Earhart became the first woman to ~~fly solo across the Atlantic Ocean~~ **complete a solo transatlantic flight**.

6. Amelia Earhart attempted to become the first person to fly around the world in 1937, but her plane disappeared over the Pacific Ocean. Nevertheless, her amazing accomplishments and great bravery made Amelia Earhart one of the greatest pilots ever.

Review Progressive Tenses

Students will answer questions to review what they have learned about the present, past, and future progressive tenses.

Progressive Tenses and Informational Writing Skills

Students will complete the Progressive Tenses and Informational Writing Skills quiz.

Spelling List 9

Students will complete the Spelling List 9 quiz.

WRAP-UP

More Language Arts Practice

Students will practice skills according to their individual needs.

Go Read!

Students will read for pleasure. They should choose a book or a magazine that interests them, or they may choose a selection from the digital library, linked in the online lesson.

Students should read for the entire time. Have students select something to read ahead of time to help them stay focused.

Big Ideas: Mini-Project

Lesson Overview

Big Ideas lessons provide students the opportunity to further apply the knowledge and skills acquired throughout the unit workshops. Each Big Ideas lesson consists of three parts:

1. **Cumulative Review:** Students keep their skills fresh by reviewing prior content.

2. **Preview:** Students practice answering the types of questions they will commonly find on standardized tests.

3. **Synthesis:** Students complete an assignment that allows them to interweave and apply what they've learned. These synthesis assignments will vary throughout the course.

   In the Synthesis portion of this Big Ideas lesson, students will complete a small, creative project designed to tie together concepts and skills that students have encountered across workshops. These small projects are designed to deepen students' understanding of those concepts and skills.

   LEARNING COACH CHECK-IN Make sure students complete, review, and submit the assignment to their teacher.

All materials needed for this lesson are linked online and not provided in the Activity Book.

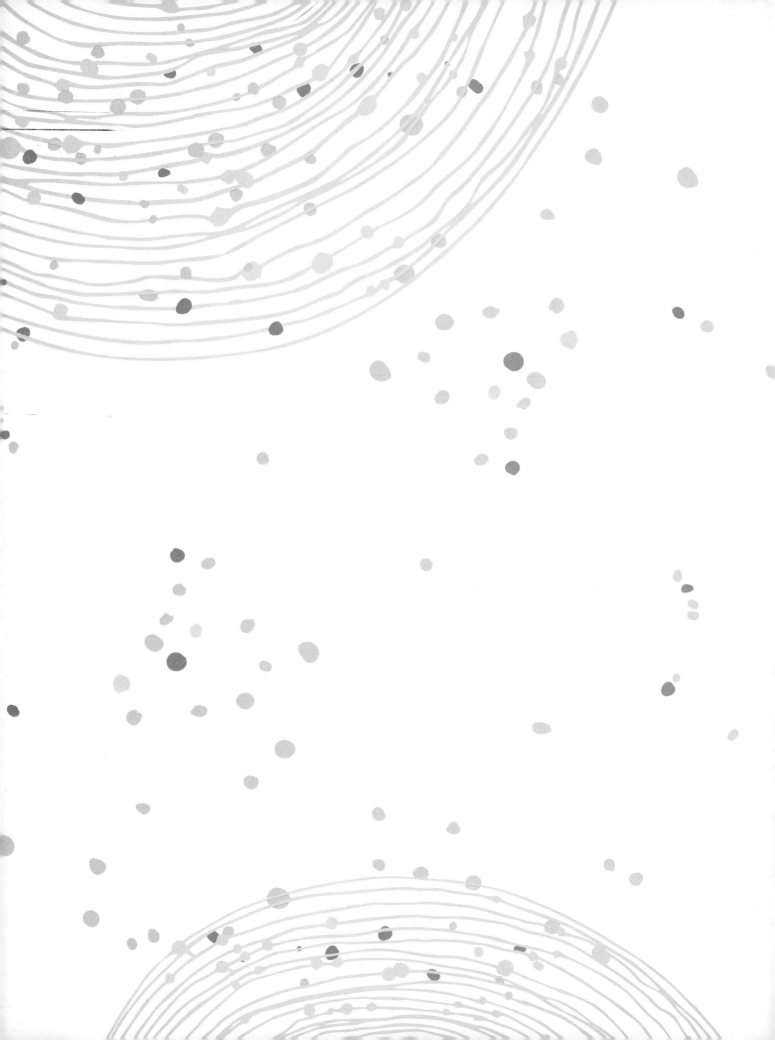

Pax

Pax (A)

Lesson Overview

ACTIVITY	ACTIVITY TITLE	TIME	ONLINE/OFFLINE
GET READY	*Pax* Unit Overview	**1** minute	🖥
	Introduction to *Pax* (A)	**1** minute	🖥
	Spelling List 10 Pretest **LEARNING COACH CHECK-IN**	**10** minutes	🖥 and 📄
	Pax in 60 Seconds	**1** minute	🖥
	Before You Read *Pax*, Chapters 1–3	**14** minutes	🖥
READ	*Pax*, Chapters 1–3	**30** minutes	📄
	Check-In: *Pax*, Chapters 1–3	**5** minutes	🖥
LEARN AND **TRY IT**	Describing Characters	**10** minutes	🖥
	Describe Characters in *Pax*	**10** minutes	🖥
	Apply: Describing Characters	**15** minutes	🖥
	Describe Peter and Pax **LEARNING COACH CHECK-IN**	**13** minutes	📄
	Practice Words from *Pax*, Chapters 1–3	**8** minutes	🖥
WRAP-UP	Question About *Pax*, Chapters 1–3	**2** minutes	🖥

Content Background

Students will begin reading the novel *Pax* by Sara Pennypacker. They will learn about using text details to describe characters.

At times, an author will explicitly state details that describe a character. For example, in *Pax* the text states, "The boy had grown very tall recently." This explicit detail tells the reader that the character of Peter is tall.

Other times, a reader will use text details to make an inference about a character. For example, the author provides the following information about the character of Peter's father: "But gradually his face had hardened into the permanent threat of a scowl, and his hands clenched by his sides as if itching for something to set him off." From these text details, a reader can infer that Peter's father is an angry person.

Pax, Chapters 1–3 Synopsis

Peter and his pet fox, Pax, have been together since Pax was a kit. Now a war is coming and Peter's father enlists to serve in the military. Peter must go live with his grandfather, 300 miles from home, but he cannot bring Pax with him. As a result, Peter's father makes him return his fox to the wild. After arriving at his grandfather's, Peter realizes that he must go back to Pax. Peter decides to set out alone and on foot to return to his loyal fox.

Lesson Goals

- Take a spelling pretest.

- Read Chapters 1–3 of *Pax*.

- Use text details to describe characters.

- Make inferences about characters based on their thoughts, what they say, and what they do.

- Determine meanings of unfamiliar words in the reading.

GET READY

Pax Unit Overview

Students will read a summary of what they will learn in the *Pax* unit.

Introduction to *Pax* (A)

Students will get a glimpse of what they will learn about in the lesson. They will also read the lesson goals and keywords. Have students select each keyword and preview its definition.

Spelling List 10 Pretest

Students will take a spelling pretest.

LEARNING COACH CHECK-IN   Have students turn to Spelling List 10 Pretest in *Summit English Language Arts 4 Activity Book* and open the online Spelling Pretest activity. Online, students will listen to the spelling word, type the word in the space indicated, and then check their answer. In the activity book, students will write the correct spelling of the word in the tables provided and indicate with a ✓ or an ✗ if they spelled the word correctly or incorrectly online. Students will repeat this process with the remaining words.

As needed, help students with the interaction between the online activity and the activity book page until they become comfortable with what they need to do. As students practice their spelling words throughout the workshop, they should pay special attention to words they spelled incorrectly on the pretest.

This is the complete list of words students will be tested on.

Long *i* Sound	Root *rupt*	Prefix *bi–*	Heart Words
global	disrupt	biannual	New Mexico
soldier	erupt	bicycle	Oklahoma
buffalo	interrupt	bimonthly	
earlobe	rupture	biweekly	
doughnut			
though			
motivate			
telescope			
trombone			
decompose			
diagnose			

NOTE Have students keep their completed activity page in a safe place so they can refer to it later.

GET READY
Pax (A)

Spelling List 10 Pretest

1. Open the Spelling Pretest activity online. Listen to the first spelling word. Type the word. Check your answer.

2. Write the correct spelling of the word in the Word column of the Spelling Pretest table on the next page.

Word		
1 blindfold		

3. Put a check mark in the ⊙ column if you spelled the word correctly online.

Word		
1 blindfold	✓	

Put an X in the ⊗ column if you spelled the word incorrectly online.

Word		
1 blindfold		X

4. Repeat Steps 1–3 for the remaining words in the Spelling Pretest.

Pax (A)

Spelling List 10 Pretest

Write each spelling word in the Word column, making sure to spell it correctly.

Word				Word		
1 global				12 disrupt		
2 soldier				13 erupt		
3 buffalo				14 interrupt		
4 earlobe				15 rupture		
5 doughnut				16 New Mexico		
6 though				17 Oklahoma		
7 motivate				18 biannual		
8 telescope				19 bicycle		
9 trombone				20 bimonthly		
10 decompose				21 biweekly		
11 diagnose						

Students should use the ✓ and X columns to indicate whether they spelled each word correctly or incorrectly online.

Pax in 60 Seconds

Students will watch a short video designed to spark their interest in upcoming topics.

Before You Read *Pax*, Chapters 1–3

Students will be introduced to some key vocabulary words that they will encounter in the upcoming reading, learn some important background related to the reading, and answer questions to help them set a purpose for their reading.

READ

Pax, Chapters 1–3

Students will read Chapters 1–3 of *Pax* by Sara Pennypacker.

Check-In: *Pax*, Chapters 1–3

Students will answer questions to demonstrate their comprehension of Chapters 1–3 of *Pax*.

LEARN AND TRY IT

LEARN   Describing Characters

Students will learn about using text details to describe characters.

TIP   Make sure that students understand that sometimes a text will directly state details that describe a character. Other times, they must use text details to make inferences about what a character is like.

TRY IT   Describe Characters in *Pax*

Students will analyze passages and answer questions to describe characters in the reading.

TRY IT   Apply: Describing Characters

Students will apply to a new work what they've learned about using text details to describe characters.

TRY IT   Describe Peter and Pax

Students will complete Describe Peter and Pax from *Summit English Language Arts 4 Activity Book*.

LEARNING COACH CHECK-IN   This activity page contains open-ended questions, so it's important that you review students' responses. Give students feedback, using the sample answers provided to guide you.

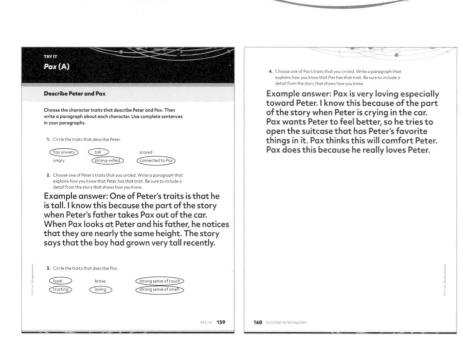

TRY IT   Practice Words from *Pax*, Chapters 1–3

Students will answer questions to demonstrate their understanding of the vocabulary words from the reading.

WRAP-UP

Question About *Pax*, Chapters 1–3

Students will answer a question to show that they understand how to use text details to describe a character.

Pax (B)

Lesson Overview

ACTIVITY	ACTIVITY TITLE	TIME	ONLINE/OFFLINE
GET READY	Introduction to *Pax* (B)	**1** minute	🖥️
	Spelling List 10 Activity Bank	**10** minutes	📄
	Recall *Pax*, Chapters 1–3	**5** minutes	🖥️
	Before You Read *Pax*, Chapters 4–6	**9** minutes	🖥️
READ	*Pax*, Chapters 4–6	**30** minutes	📄
	Check-In: *Pax*, Chapters 4–6	**5** minutes	🖥️
LEARN AND TRY IT	Describing Setting	**10** minutes	🖥️
	What's the Setting?	**10** minutes	🖥️
	Apply: Describing Setting	**15** minutes	🖥️
	Write About Setting **LEARNING COACH CHECK-IN**	**15** minutes	📄
	Practice Words from *Pax*, Chapters 4–6	**8** minutes	🖥️
WRAP-UP	Question About *Pax*, Chapters 4–6	**2** minutes	🖥️

Content Background

Students will continue to read *Pax* by Sara Pennypacker. They will learn about using text details to describe the setting and how the setting can affect the story.

The setting is where and when the story takes place. The author may provide explicit details that tell a reader about the setting. For example, in Chapter 6 of *Pax*, the author provides details of the small town Peter is walking through. It has a town square, a hardware store, a library, a bus station, and a diner.

At times, though, the reader must use text details to make inferences about the setting. The author of *Pax* is very vague about the time period of the novel. But we can infer that the story is happening in modern times because people drive cars.

MATERIALS

Supplied
- *Pax* by Sara Pennypacker
- *Summit English Language Arts 4 Activity Book*
  - Spelling List 10 Activity Bank
  - Write About Setting

Also Needed
- completed Spelling List 10 Pretest activity page from *Pax* (A)

Advance Preparation

Gather students' completed Spelling List 10 Pretest activity page from *Pax* (A). Students will refer to this page during Get Ready: Spelling List 10 Activity Bank.

Pax, Chapters 4–6 Synopsis

Peter sets out on his journey to return to Pax. He tries to stay in the forest, but must pass through a small town where people eye him suspiciously. As Peter watches the local baseball team practice, he thinks back to when his mother died in a car accident. Peter sets off again, only to find that he can't reach a shortcut he'd planned on taking. In addition, he learns that traveling on foot in a wooded area can be dangerous. Meanwhile, Pax has his first encounter with wild foxes.

Lesson Goals

- Practice all spelling words.

- Read Chapters 4–6 of *Pax*.

- Use text details to describe and make inferences about the setting.

- Determine the meanings of unfamiliar words in the reading.

GET READY

Introduction to *Pax* (B)

Students will get a glimpse of what they will learn about in the lesson. They will also read the lesson goals and keywords. Have students select each keyword and preview its definition.

Spelling List 10 Activity Bank

Students will practice all spelling words from the workshop by completing Spelling List 10 Activity Bank from *Summit English Language Arts 4 Activity Book*. Make sure students have their completed Spelling List 10 Pretest activity page from *Pax* (A) to refer to during this activity.

Remind students to pay special attention to words they spelled incorrectly on the Spelling Pretest.

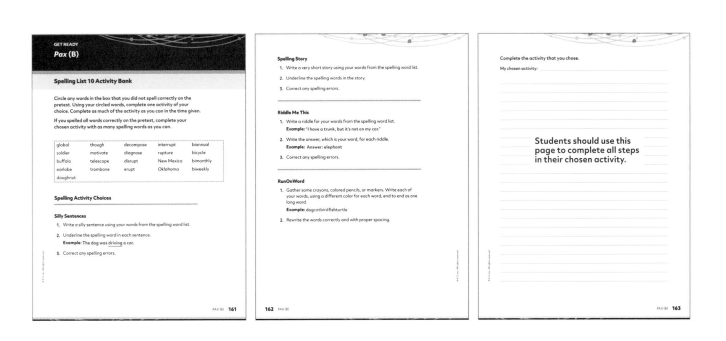

Recall *Pax*, Chapters 1–3

Students will answer questions to review the reading that they have already completed.

Before You Read *Pax*, Chapters 4–6

Students will be introduced to some key vocabulary words that they will encounter in the upcoming reading and learn some important background related to the reading.

READ

Pax, Chapters 4–6

Students will read Chapters 4–6 of *Pax* by Sara Pennypacker.

Check-In: *Pax*, Chapters 4–6

Students will answer questions to demonstrate their comprehension Chapters 4–6 of *Pax*.

LEARN AND TRY IT

LEARN   Describing Setting

Students will learn about how text details give information about the setting of a story.

TRY IT   What's the Setting?

Students will analyze passages and answer questions about the setting of the story.

TRY IT   Apply: Describing Setting

Students will apply to a new work what they've learned about using text details to describe a setting.

TRY IT   Write About Setting

Students will complete Write About Setting from *Summit English Language Arts 4 Activity Book*.

TIP   Make sure students understand that they are making up things about the setting to add to information the author has provided. The paragraphs students write should include details from the text and details from their imagination.

LEARNING COACH CHECK-IN   This activity page contains open-ended questions, so it's important that you review students' responses. Give students feedback, using the sample answers provided to guide you.

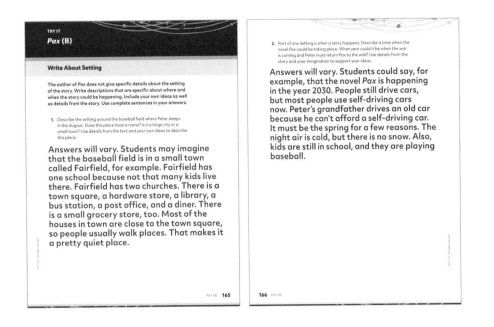

TRY IT   Practice Words from *Pax*, Chapters 4–6

Students will answer questions to demonstrate their understanding of the vocabulary words from the reading.

WRAP-UP

Question About *Pax*, Chapters 4–6

Students will answer a question to show that they understand the setting in the reading.

Pax (C)

Lesson Overview

ACTIVITY	ACTIVITY TITLE	TIME	ONLINE/OFFLINE
GET READY	Introduction to *Pax* (C)	**1** minute	📶
	Spelling List 10 Practice	**9** minutes	📶
	Recall *Pax*, Chapters 4–6	**5** minutes	📶
	Before You Read *Pax*, Chapters 7–9	**10** minutes	📶
READ	*Pax*, Chapters 7–9	**30** minutes	📄
	Check-In: *Pax*, Chapters 7–9	**5** minutes	📶
LEARN AND **TRY IT**	Describing Events	**10** minutes	📶
	Describe Events in *Pax*	**10** minutes	📶
	Apply: Describing Events	**15** minutes	📶
	Write About What's Happened So Far **LEARNING COACH CHECK-IN**	**15** minutes	📄
	Practice Words from *Pax*, Chapters 7–9	**8** minutes	📶
WRAP-UP	Question About *Pax*, Chapters 7–9	**2** minutes	📶

Content Background

Students will continue to read *Pax* by Sara Pennypacker. They will learn about using text details to describe the events of the plot.

The plot is what happens in a story. It is the sequence of events. The author may give explicit details that explain what happened. For example, the text directly states how Peter catches his foot on a root and breaks his foot.

Sometimes the reader must use text details to make inferences about the story's events. For example, when Peter meets a new character, Vola, the text tells us that Vola was a medic, and she has a wooden leg. We can infer that she was injured in a previous war.

MATERIALS

Supplied
- *Pax* by Sara Pennypacker
- *Summit English Language Arts 4 Activity Book*
  - Write About What's Happened So Far

KEYWORDS

plot – what happens in a story; the sequence of events

summarize – to tell in order the most important ideas or events of a text

Pax, Chapters 7–9 Synopsis

Pax is with a group of foxes now. He meets Gray, the leader of the foxes. Gray tells Pax about war and the devastating effect it has on the land and animals. Gray calls it a human sickness. Pax decides that he will travel south in the hope of finding Peter back at his home. Gray plans to travel with Pax. He wants to search for a new home for his family before the war arrives. After breaking his foot, Peter finds shelter in a barn on a farm. Vola, the owner of the farm, is angry at finding Peter there. She makes him crutches and insists that he leave.

Lesson Goals

- Practice all spelling words.
- Read Chapters 7–9 of of *Pax*.
- Describe and summarize important events of a story's plot.
- Determine the meanings of unfamiliar words in the reading.

GET READY

Introduction to *Pax* (C)

Students will get a glimpse of what they will learn about in the lesson. They will also read the lesson goals and keywords. Have students select each keyword and preview its definition.

Spelling List 10 Practice

Students will practice all spelling words from the workshop.

Recall *Pax*, Chapters 4–6

Students will answer questions to review the reading that they have already completed.

Before You Read *Pax*, Chapters 7–9

Students will be introduced to some key vocabulary words that they will encounter in the upcoming reading and learn some important background related to the reading.

NOTE This activity contains information on the concept of war to help students better understand the story's events. The information given is age-appropriate for fourth graders. Be sure to read the information prior to the lesson so you are prepared to answer questions students may have.

READ

Pax, Chapters 7–9

Students will read Chapters 7–9 of *Pax* by Sara Pennypacker.

Check-In: *Pax*, Chapters 7–9

Students will answer questions to demonstrate their comprehension of Chapters 7–9 of *Pax*.

LEARN AND TRY IT

LEARN   Describing Events

Students will learn how to use text details to describe the events of a story's plot.

TRY IT   Describe Events in *Pax*

Students will analyze passages and answer questions about the events of the plot.

TRY IT   Apply: Describing Events

Students will apply to a new work what they've learned about using text details to describe a story's events.

TRY IT   Write About What's Happened So Far

Students will complete Write About What's Happened So Far from *Summit English Language Arts 4 Activity Book*. In this activity, students will write a summary of the most important events of the story so far.

LEARNING COACH CHECK-IN   This activity page contains open-ended questions, so it's important that you review students' responses. Give students feedback, using the sample answers provided to guide you.

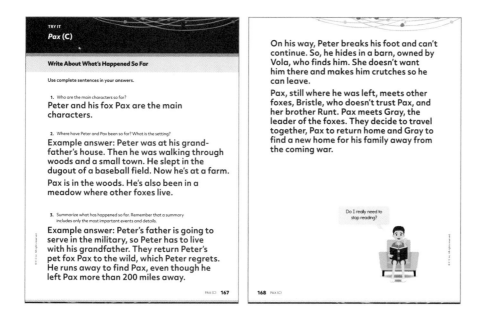

TRY IT Practice Words from *Pax*, Chapters 7–9

Students will answer questions to demonstrate their understanding of the vocabulary words from the reading.

Question About *Pax*, Chapters 7–9

Students will answer a question to show that they understand how to use text details to make inferences about a story's events.

Pax (D)

Lesson Overview

ACTIVITY	ACTIVITY TITLE	TIME	ONLINE/OFFLINE
GET READY	Introduction to *Pax* (D)	**1** minute	🖥️
	Spelling List 10 Review Game	**10** minutes	🖥️
	Recall *Pax*, Chapters 7–9	**5** minutes	🖥️
	Before You Read *Pax*, Chapters 10–13	**9** minutes	🖥️
READ	*Pax*, Chapters 10–13	**30** minutes	📄
	Check-In: *Pax*, Chapters 10–13	**5** minutes	🖥️
LEARN AND **TRY IT**	How Characters Affect Plot	**10** minutes	🖥️
	Characters Make Things Happen	**10** minutes	🖥️
	Apply: Characters and Plot	**15** minutes	🖥️
	Write About Characters and Plot **LEARNING COACH CHECK-IN**	**15** minutes	📄
	Practice Words from *Pax*, Chapters 10–13	**8** minutes	🖥️
WRAP-UP	Question About *Pax*, Chapters 10–13	**2** minutes	🖥️

Content Background

Students will continue to read *Pax* by Sara Pennypacker. They will learn about how characters affect the plot of a story.

The plot is the events that happen in a story. Understanding cause and effect provides a foundation for understanding how a character can affect the plot.

A cause is something that happens. The effect is the result of the cause.

> **Example:** I water a seed (the cause). A sprout grows (the effect).

A character's actions often cause other things to happen. Thus, the character affects the plot. For example, in *Pax*, Peter's father signs up to serve in the military (the cause). As a result, Peter must go live with his grandfather (the effect). The characters' actions shape the story. If Peter's father had not signed up to serve in the military, Peter would not have had to go to his grandfather's. The events of the story would have been different.

MATERIALS

Supplied
- *Pax* by Sara Pennypacker
- *Summit English Language Arts 4 Activity Book*
  - Write About Characters and Plot

Pax, Chapters 10–13 Synopsis

Peter heads out from Vola's farm on his new crutches, but he quickly changes his mind. He returns to the barn and asks Vola for help. She agrees to help him, and Peter begins to learn more about Vola's background and her life on the farm.

Bristle tells Pax the heartbreaking story of what happened to her parents. He now understands her hatred of humans. Pax is very weak because he hasn't eaten in several days. He recognizes that death is a possibility. Luckily, Runt recognizes Pax's dangerous situation and brings him food.

KEYWORDS

cause and effect – a situation in which one condition or fact, the cause, results in another, the effect

plot – what happens in a story; the sequence of events

Lesson Goals

- Practice all spelling words.
- Read *Pax*, Chapters 10–13.
- Determine cause-and-effect relationships and how characters affect a story's events.
- Determine meanings of unfamiliar words in the reading.

GET READY

Introduction to *Pax* (D)

Students will get a glimpse of what they will learn about in the lesson. They will also read the lesson goals and keywords. Have students select each keyword and preview its definition.

Spelling List 10 Review Game

Students will practice all spelling words from the workshop.

Recall *Pax*, Chapters 7–9

Students will answer questions to review the reading that they have already completed.

Before You Read *Pax*, Chapters 10–13

Students will be introduced to some key vocabulary words that they will encounter in the upcoming reading and learn some important background related to the reading.

READ

Pax, Chapters 10–13

Students will read Chapters 10–13 of *Pax* by Sara Pennypacker.

Check-In: *Pax*, Chapters 10–13

Students will answer questions to demonstrate their comprehension of Chapters 10–13 of *Pax*.

LEARN AND TRY IT

LEARN   How Characters Affect Plot

Students will learn how a character can affect the events of the plot.

SUPPORT   For students having difficulty recognizing cause-and-effect relationships, provide several real-life examples such as the following:

The sidewalk was icy (cause). The man fell (effect).

The girl forgot to put on sunblock at the beach (cause). She got sunburned (effect).

The boy studied hard (cause). He got an A on his math test (effect).

TRY IT   Characters Make Things Happen

Students will analyze passages and answer questions about how characters can affect the events of the plot.

TRY IT   Apply: Characters and Plot

Students will apply to a new work what they've learned about how characters affect the events of the plot.

TRY IT   Write About Characters and Plot

Students will complete Write About Characters and Plot from *Summit English Language Arts 4 Activity Book*.

LEARNING COACH CHECK-IN   This activity page contains open-ended questions, so it's important that you review students' responses. Give students feedback, using the sample answers provided to guide you.

TRY IT   Practice Words from *Pax*, Chapters 10–13

Students will answer questions to demonstrate their understanding of the vocabulary words from the reading.

WRAP-UP

Question About *Pax*, Chapters 10–13

Students will answer a question to show that they understand how characters affect the events of the plot.

Pax (E)

Lesson Overview

ACTIVITY	ACTIVITY TITLE	TIME	ONLINE/OFFLINE
GET READY	Introduction to *Pax* (E)	**1** minute	🖥️
	Recall *Pax*, Chapters 10–13	**5** minutes	🖥️
	Before You Read *Pax*, Chapters 14–15	**9** minutes	🖥️
READ	*Pax*, Chapters 14–15	**30** minutes	📄
	Check-In: *Pax*, Chapters 14–15	**5** minutes	🖥️
LEARN AND **TRY IT**	How Setting Affects Plot	**10** minutes	🖥️
	Setting Affects the Plot	**10** minutes	🖥️
	Apply: Setting and Plot	**15** minutes	🖥️
	Change the Setting **LEARNING COACH CHECK-IN**	**15** minutes	📄
	Practice Words from *Pax*, Chapters 14–15	**8** minutes	🖥️
QUIZ	Spelling List 10	**10** minutes	🖥️
WRAP-UP	Question About *Pax*, Chapters 14–15	**2** minutes	🖥️

Content Background

Students will continue to read *Pax* by Sara Pennypacker. They will learn about how the setting affects the plot of a story.

The setting is where and when a story takes place. In *Pax*, when the story happens is vague. But we do know that it is taking place in modern times because of references to modern items such as cars and electricity.

The plot is the events that happen in a story. Understanding cause and effect provides a foundation for understanding how the setting can affect the plot.

A cause is a certain condition or something that happens. The effect is the result of the cause. For example, the setting of a room is small and crowded (the cause). A person in the room feels uncomfortable due to the small crowded space (the effect).

> ### MATERIALS
>
> **Supplied**
> - *Pax* by Sara Pennypacker
> - *Summit English Language Arts 4 Activity Book*
>   - Change the Setting

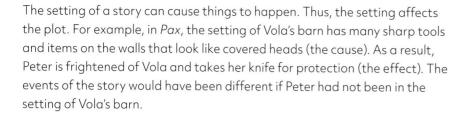

The setting of a story can cause things to happen. Thus, the setting affects the plot. For example, in *Pax*, the setting of Vola's barn has many sharp tools and items on the walls that look like covered heads (the cause). As a result, Peter is frightened of Vola and takes her knife for protection (the effect). The events of the story would have been different if Peter had not been in the setting of Vola's barn.

Pax, Chapters 14–15 Synopsis

Peter and Vola get to know each other better. Peter opens up to Vola about what the charm bracelet he carries meant to his mother. Vola tells a story about what happened to her after her military service. The story explains why she's living on the farm.

As Pax and Gray journey south, they come to the territory of the fox that is challenging Gray. The challenger wounds Gray, but Pax is able to fight off the other fox due to his strong instinct to protect Gray. Pax and Gray continue on and come across a camp full of soldiers.

Lesson Goals

- Read *Pax*, Chapters 14–15.
- Determine cause-and-effect relationships and how the setting affects the plot.
- Determine meanings of unfamiliar words in the reading.
- Take a spelling quiz.

GET READY

Introduction to *Pax* (E)

Students will get a glimpse of what they will learn about in the lesson. They will also read the lesson goals and keywords. Have students select each keyword and preview its definition.

Recall *Pax*, Chapters 10–13

Students will answer questions to review the reading that they have already completed.

Before You Read *Pax*, **Chapters 14–15**

Students will be introduced to some key vocabulary words that they will encounter in the upcoming reading and learn some important background related to the reading.

READ

***Pax*, Chapters 14–15**

Students will read Chapters 14–15 of *Pax* by Sara Pennypacker.

Check-In: *Pax*, **Chapters 14–15**

Students will answer questions to demonstrate their comprehension of Chapters 14–15 of *Pax*.

LEARN AND TRY IT

LEARN   How Setting Affects Plot

Students will learn how the setting can affect the events of the plot.

> **SUPPORT**   For students having difficulty recognizing how the setting affects a story's events, provide an example from a familiar story such as the fairy tale "Rapunzel." The setting of Rapunzel's tower affects the story's events. Because there are no stairs to enter the tower, the witch and the prince must enter by using Rapunzel's hair as a rope. If the setting of the tower were different, the events of the story would be different.

TRY IT   Setting Affects the Plot

Students will analyze passages and answer questions about how the setting affects the plot.

TRY IT   Apply: Setting and Plot

Students will apply to a new work what they've learned about how the setting affects the plot of the story.

TRY IT   Change the Setting

Students will complete Change the Setting from *Summit English Language Arts 4 Activity Book*.

> **SUPPORT**   For students who don't have a favorite story to write about, explain that the story they choose does not have to be a favorite. Instead, it can be a story with which they are very familiar. If they still cannot decide on a story, offer them two to three choices of stories that they are probably familiar with and that have a setting that's easy to determine. Examples could be "Rapunzel" or "The Three Little Pigs."

This activity page contains open-ended questions, so it's important that you review students' responses. Give students feedback, using what you know about how the setting can influence a story's events.

TRY IT   Practice Words from *Pax*, Chapters 14–15

Students will answer questions to demonstrate their understanding of the vocabulary words from the reading.

QUIZ

Spelling List 10

Students will complete the Spelling List 10 quiz.

WRAP-UP

Question About *Pax*, Chapters 14–15

Students will answer a question to show that they understand how the setting of a story affects the plot.

Pax (F)

Lesson Overview

ACTIVITY	ACTIVITY TITLE	TIME	ONLINE/OFFLINE
GET READY	Introduction to *Pax* (F)	**1** minute	🖥️
	Spelling List 11 Pretest **LEARNING COACH CHECK-IN**	**10** minutes	🖥️ and 📄
	Recall *Pax*, Chapters 14–15	**5** minutes	🖥️
	Before You Read *Pax*, Chapters 16–18	**9** minutes	🖥️
READ	*Pax*, Chapters 16–18	**30** minutes	📄
	Check-In: *Pax*, Chapters 16–18	**5** minutes	🖥️
LEARN AND **TRY IT**	How Events Affect Plot	**10** minutes	🖥️
	Events Affect the Plot	**10** minutes	🖥️
	Apply: Events and Plot	**15** minutes	🖥️
	Summarize Events **LEARNING COACH CHECK-IN**	**15** minutes	📄
	Practice Words from *Pax*, Chapters 16–18	**8** minutes	🖥️
WRAP-UP	Question About *Pax*, Chapters 16–18	**2** minutes	🖥️

Content Background

Students will continue to read *Pax* by Sara Pennypacker. They will learn how events affect other events in the plot of a story.

The plot is the events that happen in a story. Understanding cause and effect provides a foundation for understanding how one event can affect other events in the plot.

A cause is a certain condition or something that happens. The effect is the result of the cause. For example, in *Pax* the event of the coming war causes other events to happen. It causes Peter's father to sign up for the military. It leads to Peter having to live with his grandfather. And, it causes Peter's father to make Peter put Pax back in the wild. The events of the story would have been different if there were no war coming.

MATERIALS

Supplied
- *Pax* by Sara Pennypacker
- *Summit English Language Arts 4 Activity Book*
  - Spelling List 11 Pretest
  - Summarize Events

Pax, Chapter 16–18 Synopsis

Vola tells Peter that she killed someone in the war. She found *The Seven Voyages of Sinbad* on the man's body. So she decides to tell a story from the book that was important to the man she'd killed. Vola uses marionettes that she made with heads she carved out of wood. She wants Peter to learn how to operate the marionettes so she can see what the story looks like. Peter is reluctant because it doesn't get him closer to finding Pax. Also, he struggles with controlling the marionettes.

Pax and Gray are across the river from the soldiers' camp. Gray is not recovering from his wound. Pax watches the soldiers. He learns their routine so he can sneak into the food tent and steal food. He also sees the humans laying out wires and burying mines by the river. Gray sets off one of the mines, which explodes and causes his death. Pax returns to the meadow to tell the other foxes of Gray's death.

Lesson Goals

- Take a spelling pretest.
- Read *Pax*, Chapters 16–18.
- Determine cause-and-effect relationships and how a story's events affect other events of the plot.
- Determine meanings of unfamiliar words in the reading.

GET READY

Introduction to *Pax* (F)

Students will get a glimpse of what they will learn about in the lesson. They will also read the lesson goals and keywords. Have students select each keyword and preview its definition.

Spelling List 11 Pretest

Students will take a spelling pretest.

LEARNING COACH CHECK-IN   Have students turn to Spelling List 11 Pretest in *Summit English Language Arts 4 Activity Book* and open the online Spelling Pretest activity. Online, students will listen to the spelling word, type the word in the space indicated, and then check their answer. In the activity book, students will write the correct spelling of the word in the tables provided and indicate with a ✓ or an ✗ if they spelled the word correctly or incorrectly online. Students will repeat this process with the remaining words.

As needed, help students with the interaction between the online activity and the activity book page until they become comfortable with what they need to do. As students practice their spelling words throughout the workshop, they should pay special attention to words they spelled incorrectly on the pretest.

This is the complete list of words students will be tested on.

Long *u* Sound	Root *dict*	Prefix *semi–*	Heart Words
issue	dictator	semicircle	Georgia
community	dictionary	semifinal	Virginia
commute	predict	semipro	against
cue		semiformal	restaurant
execute			
pupil			
refugee			
uniform			
union			
university			

NOTE Have students keep their completed activity page in a safe place so they can refer to it later.

Recall *Pax*, Chapters 14–15

Students will answer questions to review the reading that they have already completed.

Before You Read *Pax*, Chapters 16–18

Students will be introduced to some key vocabulary words that they will encounter in the upcoming reading and learn some important background related to the reading.

READ

Pax, Chapters 16–18

Students will read Chapters 16–18 of *Pax* by Sara Pennypacker.

NOTE Chapters 16–18 of *Pax* deal with death and grief.

Check-In: *Pax*, Chapters 16–18

Students will answer questions to demonstrate their comprehension of Chapters 16–18 of *Pax*.

LEARN AND TRY IT

LEARN How Events Affect Plot

Students will learn how events can affect other events of a story's plot.

TRY IT Events Affect the Plot

Students will analyze passages and answer questions about how a story's events can cause other events to happen.

TRY IT Apply: Events and Plot

Students will apply to a new work what they've learned about how events affect other events of a plot.

TRY IT Summarize Events

Students will complete Summarize Events from *Summit English Language Arts 4 Activity Book*.

LEARNING COACH CHECK-IN This activity page contains open-ended questions, so it's important that you review students' responses. Give students feedback, using the sample answers provided to guide you.

Additional answers

1. Peter's key details for a summary: In Chapter 10, Vola decides to help Peter because she is impressed by his commitment to Pax. In Chapter 12, Vola sets three conditions for helping Peter: he must check in with his grandfather, answer a question about the bracelet he carries that belonged to his mother, and help Vola with something. Peter learns about Vola's losing her leg in a war. Vola shares with Peter her return from the war and how she felt then, as well as her war experiences, including having killed someone. They share a meal and are getting to know each other. In Chapter 14, Vola uses marionettes to tell a story that was important to the man she killed. Peter tells Vola about his mother's phoenix charm and what it meant to her. They talk more about what they've learned about each other so far, about Peter's search for Pax and Vola's solitary life. In Chapter 16, Vola wants Peter to learn to use the marionettes, her third condition for helping him, so that she can see the story herself. In Chapter 18, Peter learns about Vola's woodworking, including the marionettes' heads. Peter asks her to teach him how to carve a fox.

TRY IT   Practice Words from *Pax*, Chapters 16–18

Students will answer questions to demonstrate their understanding of the vocabulary words from the reading.

WRAP-UP

Question About *Pax*, Chapters 16–18

Students will answer a question to show that they understand how the events of a story can affect the other events of the plot.

Pax (G)

Lesson Overview

ACTIVITY	ACTIVITY TITLE	TIME	ONLINE/OFFLINE
GET READY	Introduction to *Pax* (G)	**1** minute	🖥️
	Spelling List 11 Activity Bank	**10** minutes	📄
	Recall *Pax*, Chapters 16–18	**5** minutes	🖥️
	Before You Read *Pax*, Chapters 19–22	**9** minutes	🖥️
READ	*Pax*, Chapters 19–22 (G)	**30** minutes	📄
	Check-In: *Pax*, Chapters 19–22	**5** minutes	🖥️
LEARN **AND** **TRY IT**	Events Affect Plot	**10** minutes	🖥️
	Events Cause Other Events	**10** minutes	🖥️
	Apply: Events Affect Plot	**15** minutes	🖥️
	They Live in a Cauldron? **LEARNING COACH CHECK-IN**	**15** minutes	📄
	Practice Words from *Pax*, Chapters 19–22	**8** minutes	🖥️
WRAP-UP	Question About *Pax*, Chapters 19–22	**2** minutes	🖥️

Content Background

Students will continue to read *Pax* by Sara Pennypacker. They will review how events affect other events in the plot of a story.

The plot is the events that happen in a story. Understanding cause and effect provides a foundation for understanding how one event can affect other events in the plot.

An example of an event affecting the plot in *Pax* is Peter's breaking his foot. The effect of that event is that Peter takes shelter in Vola's barn and meets Vola. The story would have been different if the event of Peter breaking his foot had not happened.

Advance Preparation

Gather students' completed Spelling List 11 Pretest activity page from *Pax* (F). Students will refer to this page during Get Ready: Spelling List 11 Activity Bank.

> **MATERIALS**
>
> **Supplied**
> - *Pax* by Sara Pennypacker
> - *Summit English Language Arts 4 Activity Book*
>   - Spelling List 11 Activity Bank
>   - They Live In a Cauldron?
>
> **Also Needed**
> - completed Spelling List 11 Pretest activity page from *Pax* (F)

Pax, Chapter 19–22 Synopsis

Pax returns to the soldiers' camp with the intention of chewing through the land mine wires to disable them. He believes that Peter could go to the area because his father is there and then be injured by an explosion. Bristle follows Pax and tries to stop him from chewing through the wires. In the middle of their fight, Runt arrives and sets off a land mine. He is seriously injured. As Bristle and Pax care for the wounded Runt, Pax comes to understand that Peter left him in the woods on purpose.

Peter and Vola have a serious conversation about Peter's strong connection to Pax and why Vola continues to shut herself away from the world after 20 years of living alone. Peter is anxious to perform the puppet show so he can continue on his search for Pax. When he performs the show though, he catches Vola off-guard and changes it into a story about her. His hope is to convince her that she's a good person and shouldn't isolate herself. After the show, Peter sees a newspaper article that says armed forces are preparing for battle very close to where he left Pax. He decides he must leave immediately to find Pax.

KEYWORDS

cause and effect – a situation in which one condition or fact, the cause, results in another, the effect

plot – what happens in a story; the sequence of events

Lesson Goals

- Practice all spelling words.
- Read *Pax*, Chapters 19–22.
- Determine cause-and-effect relationships and how a story's events affect other events of the plot.
- Determine meanings of unfamiliar words in the reading.

GET READY

Introduction to *Pax* (G)

Students will get a glimpse of what they will learn about in the lesson. They will also read the lesson goals and keywords. Have students select each keyword and preview its definition.

Spelling List 11 Activity Bank

Students will practice all spelling words from the workshop by completing Spelling List 11 Activity Bank from *Summit English Language Arts 4 Activity Book*. Make sure students have their completed Spelling List 11 Pretest activity page from *Pax* (F) to refer to during this activity.

Remind students to pay special attention to words they spelled incorrectly on the Spelling Pretest.

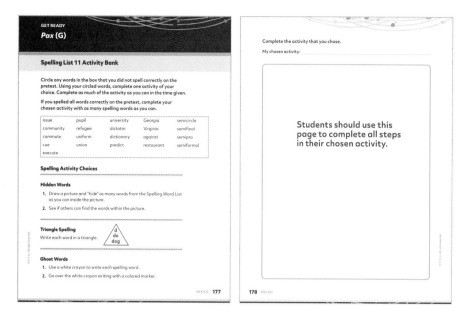

Recall *Pax*, Chapters 16–18

Students will answer questions to review the reading that they have already completed.

Before You Read *Pax*, Chapters 19–22

Students will be introduced to some key vocabulary words that they will encounter in the upcoming reading and learn some important background related to the reading.

READ

Pax, Chapters 19–22

Students will read Chapters 19–22 of *Pax* by Sara Pennypacker.

Check-In: *Pax*, Chapters 19–22

Students will answer questions to demonstrate their comprehension of Chapters 19–22 of *Pax*.

LEARN AND TRY IT

LEARN   Events Affect Plot

Students will review how a story's events can affect other events of the plot.

TRY IT   Events Cause Other Events

Students will analyze passages and answer questions about how a story's events can cause other events to happen.

SUPPORT   For students having difficulty recognizing how one event can affect the plot, have them reflect on how the story would be different if a certain event had not happened. For example, how would the story be different if Gray had not set off a land mine? Help students recognize that Gray might still be alive if he had not set off the land mine. This may help students to understand that one event, such as Gray setting off the land mine, causes another event, Gray's death.

TRY IT   Apply: Events Affect Plot

Students will apply to a new work what they've learned about how events affect other events of a plot.

TRY IT   They Live in a Cauldron?

Students will complete They Live in a Cauldron? from *Summit English Language Arts 4 Activity Book*.

LEARNING COACH CHECK-IN   This activity page contains an open-ended question, so it's important that you review students' responses. Give students feedback, using the example answer provided to guide you.

TRY IT   Practice Words from *Pax*, Chapters 19–22

Students will answer questions to demonstrate their understanding of the vocabulary words from the reading.

WRAP-UP

Question About *Pax*, Chapters 19–22

Students will answer a question to show that they understand how a story's events can affect other events of the plot.

Pax (H)

Lesson Overview

ACTIVITY	ACTIVITY TITLE	TIME	ONLINE/OFFLINE
GET READY	Introduction to *Pax* (H)	**1** minute	
	Spelling List 11 Practice	**10** minutes	
	Recall *Pax*, Chapters 19–22	**5** minutes	
	Before You Read *Pax*, Chapters 23–26	**9** minutes	
READ	*Pax*, Chapters 23–26	**30** minutes	
	Check-In: *Pax*, Chapters 23–26	**5** minutes	
LEARN AND **TRY IT**	Connect to a Story	**10** minutes	
	Visual and Oral Presentations	**10** minutes	
	Apply: Connect to a Story	**15** minutes	
	How a Picture Makes You Feel **LEARNING COACH CHECK-IN**	**15** minutes	
	Practice Words from *Pax*, Chapters 23–26	**8** minutes	
WRAP-UP	Question About *Pax*, Chapters 23–26	**2** minutes	

Content Background

Students will learn how a visual or oral presentation of a text can help them better understand a story. It can also help them connect to the story. They will learn that pictures can convey the mood of a story. Pictures also provide details not found in the text. Hearing a story read aloud can help students determine the feelings of the characters. It can also help them make an emotional connection to the story.

For the novel *Pax*, the term *visual* refers to the illustrations. The stark, black-and-white pictures convey the mood of the story. The term *mood* means the emotions or feelings conveyed in a story. For example, the illustration on pages 164–165 of *Pax* conveys a dark mood. The isolation of the setting shown in the picture reflects how Vola has isolated herself from the world.

An oral presentation of a text means that the text is read aloud. Voices convey emotions. So hearing a character's voice can help students connect to the feelings conveyed in the story. It is easier to remember something that is

MATERIALS

Supplied
- *Pax* by Sara Pennypacker
- *Summit English Language Arts 4 Activity Book*
  - How a Picture Makes You Feel

KEYWORDS

mood – the emotions or feelings conveyed in a literary work

visual – a graphic, picture, or photograph

tied to strong emotions. So connecting to the feelings conveyed by a story not only helps students understand the story, but also helps them to remember it.

Pax, Chapter 23–26 Synopsis

Pax returns to the soldiers' camp to find more food. While he's in the food tent, he has another encounter with Peter's father. Pax and Bristle watch over the injured Runt and help him adjust to walking on three legs. When a deer sets off another land mine, the foxes realize that they must leave the area. After getting Runt settled in an abandoned den, Bristle teaches Pax to hunt. As Pax celebrates his first successful hunt, he scents something new and dangerous nearby.

As Peter prepares to leave Vola's, he discovers that she is wearing her prosthetic leg, his first condition. His other conditions are that she donate the marionettes to the town library and teach the town's children how to use them. When Peter sees the date of a newspaper article, he realizes that his father knew there would be a battle near the spot they left Pax. Vola helps Peter come to terms with the anger caused by this realization. As Peter climbs on the bus to leave, Vola tells him that she considers him family. After getting off the bus, Peter walks through abandoned towns and finally arrives at the spot where he left Pax.

Lesson Goals

- Practice all spelling words.
- Read *Pax*, Chapters 23–26.
- Make connections to a story.
- Compare pictures and text read aloud to the words of a story.
- Determine meanings of unfamiliar words in the reading.

GET READY

Introduction to *Pax* (H)
Students will get a glimpse of what they will learn about in the lesson. They will also read the lesson goals and keywords. Have students select each keyword and preview its definition.

Spelling List 11 Practice
Students will practice all spelling words from the workshop.

Recall *Pax*, Chapters 19–22

Students will answer questions to review the reading that they have already completed.

Before You Read *Pax*, Chapters 23–26

Students will be introduced to some key vocabulary words that they will encounter in the upcoming reading.

NOTE   This lesson's assigned reading is longer than usual. To allow enough time for students to read, the Before You Read activity is shorter than usual. This should allow students enough time to complete the reading.

READ

Pax, Chapters 23–26

Students will read Chapters 23–26 of *Pax* by Sara Pennypacker.

Check-In: *Pax*, Chapters 23–26

Students will answer questions to demonstrate their comprehension of Chapters 23–26 of *Pax*.

LEARN AND TRY IT

LEARN   Connect to a Story

Students will learn how seeing illustrations and hearing a story read aloud can help them connect to the story and better understand it.

TRY IT   Visual and Oral Presentations

Students will analyze passages and answer questions about information conveyed by a story's illustrations and information conveyed by an oral presentation of a story.

TRY IT   Apply: Connect to a Story

Students will apply to a new work what they've learned about a story's illustrations and an oral presentation of a story.

TRY IT   How a Picture Makes You Feel

Students will complete How a Picture Makes You Feel from *Summit English Language Arts 4 Activity Book*.

LEARNING COACH CHECK-IN   This activity page contains open-ended questions, so it's important that you review students' responses. Give students feedback, using the sample answers provided to guide you.

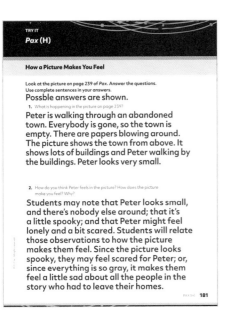

TRY IT   Practice Words from *Pax*, Chapters 23–26

Students will answer questions to demonstrate their understanding of the vocabulary words from the reading.

WRAP-UP

Question About *Pax*, Chapters 23–26

Students will answer a question to show that they understand how an illustration compares to the text of a story.

Pax (I)

Lesson Overview

ACTIVITY	ACTIVITY TITLE	TIME	ONLINE/OFFLINE
GET READY	Introduction to *Pax* (I)	**1** minute	🖥️
	Spelling List 11 Review Game	**10** minutes	🖥️
	Recall *Pax*, Chapters 23–26	**5** minutes	🖥️
	Before You Read *Pax*, Chapters 27–34	**9** minutes	🖥️
READ	*Pax*, Chapters 27–34	**30** minutes	📄
	Check-In: *Pax*, Chapters 27–34	**5** minutes	🖥️
LEARN AND **TRY IT**	A Theme Is a Lesson	**10** minutes	🖥️
	Think About Theme	**10** minutes	🖥️
	Apply: Think About Theme	**15** minutes	🖥️
	Write About Theme in *Pax* **LEARNING COACH CHECK-IN**	**15** minutes	📄
	Practice Words from *Pax*, Chapters 27–34	**8** minutes	🖥️
WRAP-UP	Question About *Pax*, Chapters 27–34	**2** minutes	🖥️

Content Background

Students will finish reading the novel *Pax*. They will explore the themes in the novel. They will learn that the characters' actions and experiences can help a reader determine themes and that the story's details support the themes.

A theme is a message the author conveys in a story. A story may have more than one theme. An example of a theme in *Pax* is that the costs of war are too high. This theme is supported by details that explain how war has affected the story's characters. Vola and Runt have both lost legs due to war. Peter and Pax have been separated. In addition, families have had to evacuate and abandon their homes and towns.

MATERIALS

Supplied
- *Pax* by Sara Pennypacker
- *Summit English Language Arts 4 Activity Book*
  - Write About Theme in *Pax*

KEYWORDS

theme – the author's message or big idea

Pax, Chapters 27–34 Synopsis

As Peter approaches the area where he left Pax, Pax senses that Peter is near. Peter pushes himself hard to reach Pax, travelling over muddy ground and climbing rock walls, all while dealing with his crutches. While he travels, Peter reflects on the steep costs of war.

Runt has recovered enough to play. But while the foxes are playing, a coyote that has followed Runt's trail threatens them. Meanwhile, Peter reaches the abandoned mill and sees the devastation caused by the soldiers. He finds the remains of Runt's leg and Pax's toy soldier, which leads him to believe that Pax is dead.

While Pax and Bristle are fending off coyotes, Pax hears Peter's voice. Pax races to where he can see the soldiers' camp and sees Peter. But he isn't sure if it's Peter because he seems different. Peter realizes that his father has lied to him about his involvement in the war and that the soldiers are using land mines.

Peter finally hears Pax bark when he calls his name. He follows Pax who leads him to the clearing where the coyotes have Bristle treed. Peter chases off the coyotes and has an emotional reunion with Pax. But Peter realizes that he and Pax can't stay together because Pax now has a new family with Bristle and Runt.

Lesson Goals

- Practice all spelling words.
- Read *Pax,* Chapters 27–34.
- Examine theme in *Pax.*
- Determine meanings of unfamiliar words in the reading.

GET READY

Introduction to *Pax* (I)
Students will get a glimpse of what they will learn about in the lesson. They will also read the lesson goals and keywords. Have students select each keyword and preview its definition.

Spelling List 11 Review Game
Students will practice all spelling words from the workshop.

Recall *Pax*, Chapters 23–26
Students will answer questions to review the reading that they have already completed.

Before You Read *Pax*, Chapters 27–34
Students will be introduced to some key vocabulary words that they will encounter in the upcoming reading.

READ

Pax, Chapters 27–34
Students will read Chapters 27–34 of *Pax* by Sara Pennypacker.

Check-In: *Pax*, Chapters 27–34
Students will answer questions to demonstrate their comprehension of Chapters 27–34 of *Pax*.

LEARN AND TRY IT

LEARN   A Theme Is a Lesson
Students will learn how characters' actions and experiences in a story develop the story's themes.

TIP   Remind students that a topic and a theme are not the same. A topic is stated in one or two words while a theme is stated in a complete sentence. But a topic can help you determine a theme. For example, war is a topic of *Pax*, but the story's theme related to war is that the costs of war are too high.

TRY IT   Think About Theme
Students will analyze passages and answer questions about the story's themes.

TRY IT   Apply: Think About Theme
Students will apply to a new work what they've learned about theme.

TRY IT   Write About Theme in *Pax*
Students will complete Write About Theme in *Pax* from *Summit English Language Arts 4 Activity Book.*

LEARNING COACH CHECK-IN   This activity page contains open-ended questions, so it's important that you review students' responses. Give students feedback, using the sample answers provided to guide you.

Additional answers

1. Possible themes include the following: You can choose the kind of person you want to be and follow your own path; just like the phoenix, we can change and renew ourselves; there are no separations because everything is connected.

   Example answer: One theme of *Pax* is that we can change and renew ourselves. Many of the characters experience change and renewal.

2. Vola changes when she starts to wear her prosthetic leg. Just like the phoenix burns and rises from the ashes, Vola seems to rise from the ashes when she burns her wooden leg. Vola begins to rejoin the world after isolating herself for so long. She brings the marionettes to the library to teach the children how to use them.

   Pax changes and renews himself. At the end of the story, Pax is not just a tame fox anymore. He has learned to survive in the wild. When he catches his first mouse, he sees the world differently and realizes that he can take care of himself.

   Peter changes and renews himself. He physically changes. Vola helps him become stronger. He holds his shoulders back and doesn't hang his head. He stands up to his father, something Pax has never seen Peter do.

TRY IT   Practice Words from *Pax*, Chapters 27–34

Students will answer questions to demonstrate their understanding of the vocabulary words from the reading.

WRAP-UP

Question About *Pax*, Chapters 27–34

Students will answer a question to show that they understand how to determine the theme of a story.

Pax Wrap-Up

Lesson Overview

ACTIVITY	ACTIVITY TITLE	TIME	ONLINE/OFFLINE
GET READY	Introduction to *Pax* Wrap-Up	**1** minute	🖥
TRY IT	Write a Summary of *Pax* **LEARNING COACH CHECK-IN**	**30** minutes	📄
	Read and Record	**10** minutes	🖥
	Review *Pax*	**20** minutes	🖥
QUIZ	*Pax*	**30** minutes	🖥
	Spelling List 11	**10** minutes	🖥
WRAP-UP	More Language Arts Practice	**19** minutes	🖥

Lesson Goals

- Write a summary of *Pax*, including information on theme.
- Practice reading aloud to develop fluency.
- Review the novel *Pax*.
- Take a quiz on characters, setting, plot, and theme.
- Take a spelling quiz.

MATERIALS

Supplied
- *Summit English Language Arts 4 Activity Book*
  - Write a Summary of *Pax*

GET READY

Introduction to *Pax* Wrap-Up

Students will read the lesson goals.

TRY IT

Write a Summary of *Pax*

Students will complete Write a Summary of *Pax* from *Summit English Language Arts 4 Activity Book*.

For students having difficulty summarizing the story, suggest that they divide their summary into what happened in the beginning, middle, and end of the story.

This activity page contains an open-ended question, so it's important that you review students' responses. Give students feedback, using the sample answer provided to guide you.

TRY IT
Pax Wrap-Up

Write a Summary of *Pax*

Remember: A good summary includes the most important events, characters, and key details in a story. Events in a summary should be described in the order they happen in the story.

Write a 1- to 2-page summary of *Pax*. Write your response in complete sentences.

See below.

PAX WRAP-UP **185**

186 PAX WRAP-UP

Additional answers

Answers will vary.

Example summary: At the beginning of *Pax*, a boy, Peter, and his father take Peter's pet fox, Pax, and leave him in the woods. A war is coming, Peter's father is going to be a soldier, and Peter goes to live with his grandfather. Peter decides to return for Pax, no matter the distance. On his way hiking, Peter falls and breaks his foot. Meanwhile, Pax meets other foxes and joins them in the meadow where they live. One of the foxes, Bristle, doesn't trust Pax because he smells like humans.

In the middle of the story, Peter meets Vola when she finds him hiding in her barn. She was a medic and lost a leg in a war. She wears a wooden leg to punish herself for things she did in the war. Vola decides to help Peter. She tends to his injury, makes him crutches, and helps him heal with food and exercise so he can be strong enough to go find Pax. Peter and Vola get to know each other, and Peter helps her see herself better by way of of her storytelling marionettes. Meanwhile, Pax travels south with Gray, the leader of the foxes. Gray is looking for a new home for his family because the war is coming. They reach a spot where men are preparing for battle by burying land mines. Pax sees Peter's father among the soldiers there. Gray is killed by a land mine. Pax returns to the meadow to tell the others about Gray. When Pax goes back to the soldiers' camp to find Peter, Bristle follows him.

Peter sees an old newspaper article about men preparing for a battle right near where he left Pax. He seems angry but claims not to be because he does not want to be like his father. He decides he has to leave Vola's. But first, he persuades Vola to wear her prosthetic leg and give her marionettes to the library where she can teach kids how to use them. She is beginning to change and renew herself, which is one of the themes of the story. Near the soldiers' camp, Pax tries to chew through the land

mine wires. Bristle tries to stop him. Then Bristle's brother, Runt, shows up and sets off a land mine and loses a leg. Bristle and Pax take care of Runt while he heals.

At the end of the story, Peter reaches the place where the soldiers are burying land mines. He finds his father there and realizes that his father lied to him about what he is doing in the war. Peter realizes that he will never be like his father. Peter and Pax are finally reunited. Peter realizes that Pax has also changed and renewed himself. Pax now has a family with Bristle and Runt, and Peter has grown up enough to know and accept that Pax needs to stay in the wild as a fox with other foxes.

Read and Record

Good readers read quickly, smoothly, and with expression. This is called *fluency*. Students will record themselves reading aloud. They will listen to their recording and think about how quick, smooth, and expressive they sound.

TIP   Encourage students to rerecord as needed.

Review *Pax*

Students will answer questions to review what they have learned about characters, setting, plot, and theme.

QUIZ

Pax

Students will complete the *Pax* quiz.

Spelling List 11

Students will complete the Spelling List 11 quiz.

WRAP-UP

More Language Arts Practice

Students will practice skills according to their individual needs.

Similes

Lesson Overview

ACTIVITY	ACTIVITY TITLE	TIME	ONLINE/OFFLINE
GET READY	Introduction to Similes	**1** minute	📶
	Look Back at Literal and Nonliteral Meanings	**4** minutes	📶
LEARN AND **TRY IT**	Similes Are Descriptive	**10** minutes	🖥
	Practice Using Similes	**10** minutes	🖥
	Apply: Similes **LEARNING COACH CHECK-IN**	**15** minutes	📄
	Go Write!	**15** minutes	📄
	Review Similes	**15** minutes	📶
QUIZ	Similes	**15** minutes	🖥
WRAP-UP	More Language Arts Practice	**15** minutes	📶
	Go Read!	**20** minutes	📶 or 📄

Content Background

Students will learn about a form of figurative language called *simile*. They will learn how to identify similes and how to determine the meanings of similes.

A simile is a type of figurative language that makes a comparison using the words *like* or *as*. An example of a simile is the phrase *busy as a bee* in the sentence *He is working on so many things at once that he is busy as a bee.* Similes help create a vivid image in a reader's mind and make writing more interesting.

Advance Preparation

During the Go Read! activity, students will have the option of using the digital library. Allow extra time for students to make their reading selection, or have students make a selection before beginning the lesson.

MATERIALS

Supplied
- *Summit English Language Arts 4 Activity Book*
  - Apply: Similes

Also Needed
- reading material for Go Read!

Lesson Goals

- Define *simile*.
- Identify similes in text.
- Explain the meaning of similes.
- Use context clues to determine the meaning of similes.
- Read and write for pleasure.

Introduction to Similes

Students will get a glimpse of what they will learn about in the lesson. They will also read the lesson goals.

Look Back at Literal and Nonliteral Meanings

Students will review phrases that have a literal, or exact, meaning and a nonliteral meaning.

> **NOTE**   An example of a phrase with a nonliteral meaning is *get cold feet*. These types of phrases are also known as *idioms*; however, this term has not been introduced to students. A review of phrases with nonliteral meanings will provide a connection to the concept of similes since similes also have nonliteral meanings.

LEARN AND **TRY IT**

LEARN   Similes Are Descriptive

Students will learn the definition of several similes that use the words *like* or *as* to make comparisons. They will also learn how to identify similes and how the words and phrases around a simile can help them determine what the simile means.

TRY IT   Practice Using Similes

Students will practice identifying similes, identifying the meaning of similes, and creating text clues that clarify the meanings of similes.

TRY IT   Apply: Similes

Students will complete Apply: Similes from *Summit English Language Arts 4 Activity Book*.

> **LEARNING COACH CHECK-IN**   This activity page contains open-ended questions, so it's important that you review students' responses. Give students feedback, using the sample answers provided to guide you.

TRY IT Go Write!

Students will write independently for pleasure. As they write, they should think about using similes in their writing.

TRY IT Review Similes

Students will answer questions to review what they have learned about similes.

Similes

Students will complete the Similes quiz.

More Language Arts Practice

Students will practice skills according to their individual needs.

Go Read!

Students will read for pleasure. They should choose a book or a magazine that interests them, or they may choose a selection from the digital library, linked in the online lesson.

Students should read for the entire time. Have students select something to read ahead of time to help them stay focused.

Informational Writing: Prewriting (A)

Lesson Overview

ACTIVITY	ACTIVITY TITLE	TIME	ONLINE/OFFLINE
GET READY	Introduction to Informational Writing: Prewriting (A)	**2** minutes	🖥️
	Spelling List 12 Pretest **LEARNING COACH CHECK-IN**	**10** minutes	🖥️ and 📄
	Look Back at Nouns and Adjectives	**10** minutes	🖥️
LEARN AND **TRY IT**	Capitalize Proper Nouns and Adjectives	**15** minutes	🖥️
	Practice Capitalizing Proper Nouns and Adjectives	**15** minutes	🖥️
	Explore a Student's History Report	**15** minutes	🖥️
	Brainstorming for a History Report	**15** minutes	🖥️
	Brainstorm for Your History Report **LEARNING COACH CHECK-IN**	**30** minutes	📄
WRAP-UP	Questions About Brainstorming and Capitalization	**8** minutes	🖥️

Content Background

Students will begin working on an **informational essay**, specifically a history report about a subject of their choice. They will complete this assignment over the course of several lessons by following the writing process. Students will begin by prewriting.

Writing Process

1 Prewriting	2 Drafting	3 Revising	4 Proofreading	5 Publishing

During **prewriting**, writers choose a topic, conduct research, and create a plan for their writing assignment. In this lesson, students will complete the first part of prewriting, choosing a topic. To do that, they'll **brainstorm** by creating an idea web and evaluating several different topics.

Grammar, Usage, and Mechanics   Students will learn how to recognize and capitalize proper nouns and adjectives. A proper noun names a particular person, place, or thing. A proper adjective is formed from a proper noun. Proper nouns and adjectives should always be capitalized, no matter where they appear in a sentence.

MATERIALS

Supplied
- *Summit English Language Arts 4 Activity Book*
  - Spelling List 12 Pretest
  - Brainstorm for Your History Report
- History Report Instructions (printout)

Also Needed
- folder for organizing informational writing assignment pages

Examples: Proper Nouns: Hercules, China, France, February, Tuesday
Proper Adjectives: Herculean, Chinese, French

Advance Preparation

Gather a folder that students can use to keep all notes and activity pages related to their history report.

Lesson Goals

- Take a spelling pretest.

- Learn to capitalize proper nouns and adjectives.

- Explore a model informational essay.

- Analyze how an author brainstorms.

- Brainstorm topics for your history report.

GET READY

Introduction to Informational Writing: Prewriting (A)

Students will get a glimpse of what they will learn about in the lesson. They will also read the lesson goals and keywords. Have students select each keyword and preview its definition.

Spelling List 12 Pretest

Students will take a spelling pretest.

LEARNING COACH CHECK-IN   Have students turn to Spelling List 12 Pretest in *Summit English Language Arts 4 Activity Book* and open the online Spelling Pretest activity. Online, students will listen to the spelling word, type the word in the space indicated, and then check their answer. In the activity book, students will write the correct spelling of the word in the tables provided and indicate with a ✓ or an ✗ if they spelled the word correctly or incorrectly online. Students will repeat this process with the remaining words.

As needed, help students with the interaction between the online activity and the activity book page until they become comfortable with what they need to do. As students practice their spelling words throughout the workshop, they should pay special attention to words they spelled incorrectly on the pretest.

This is the complete list of words students will be tested on.

Long Double o Sound	Root *tract*	Prefix *mid–*	Heart Words
baboon	distract	midmorning	Illinois
droop	subtract	midriff	Wyoming
exclude	traction	midweek	
fluent	tractor	midtown	
acoustic	retract		
inconclusive			
mushroom			
raccoon			
rude			
mousse			

NOTE   Have students keep their completed activity page in a safe place so they can refer to it later.

GET READY
Informational Writing: Prewriting (A)

Spelling List 12 Pretest

1. Open the Spelling Pretest activity online. Listen to the first spelling word. Type the word. Check your answer.

2. Write the correct spelling of the word in the Word column of the Spelling Pretest table on the next page.

Word	✓	✗
1 blindfold		

3. Put a check mark in the ✓ column if you spelled the word correctly online.

Word	✓	✗
1 blindfold	✓	

Put an X in the ✗ column if you spelled the word incorrectly online.

Word	✓	✗
1 blindfold		X

4. Repeat Steps 1–3 for the remaining words in the Spelling Pretest.

Informational Writing: Prewriting (A)

Spelling List 12 Pretest

Write each spelling word in the Word column, making sure to spell it correctly.

Word	✓	✗		Word	✓	✗
1 baboon				12 subtract		
2 droop				13 traction		
3 exclude				14 tractor		
4 fluent				15 retract		
5 acoustic				16 Illinois		
6 inconclusive				17 Wyoming		
7 mushroom				18 midmorning		
8 raccoon				19 midriff		
9 rude				20 midweek		
10 mousse				21 midtown		
11 distract						

Students should use the ✓ and X columns to indicate whether they spelled each word correctly or incorrectly online.

Look Back at Nouns and Adjectives

Students will practice the prerequisite skill of identifying nouns and adjectives in sentences.

LEARN   Capitalize Proper Nouns and Adjectives

Students will learn how to recognize and correctly capitalize proper nouns and proper adjectives.

TRY IT   Practice Capitalizing Proper Nouns and Adjectives

Students will answer questions about recognizing and capitalizing proper nouns and adjectives. They will receive feedback on their answers.

LEARN   Explore a Student's History Report

To help them better understand their writing assignment, students will read a model history report and explore the elements that make it successful.

LEARN   Brainstorming for a History Report

Students will closely investigate brainstorming, which is the first part of the prewriting step of the writing process.

TRY IT   Brainstorm for Your History Report

Students will complete Brainstorm for Your History Report from *Summit English Language Arts 4 Activity Book*.

LEARNING COACH CHECK-IN   Review students' responses. Ensure that students have selected a topic for their history report that meets the criteria listed in Question 5 of the activity page. When students have completed the page, they should store it in a folder so that they can refer to it throughout the writing process.

NOTE   In addition to the brainstorming activity, this activity page contains the instructions for the history report. Students should read the instructions carefully, but in this lesson, they should complete the brainstorming activity only (not the entire assignment). If you or students wish, you can download and print another copy of the History Report Instructions online.

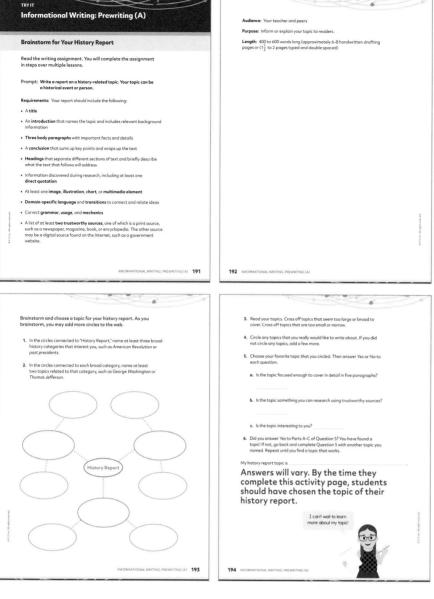

TRY IT
Informational Writing: Prewriting (A)

Brainstorm for Your History Report

Read the writing assignment. You will complete the assignment in steps over multiple lessons.

Prompt: Write a report on a history-related topic. Your topic can be a historical event or person.

Requirements: Your report should include the following:

- A **title**
- An **introduction** that names the topic and includes relevant background information
- **Three body paragraphs** with important facts and details
- A **conclusion** that sums up key points and wraps up the text
- **Headings** that separate different sections of text and briefly describe what the text that follows will address
- Information discovered during research, including at least one **direct quotation**
- At least one **image, illustration, chart,** or **multimedia element**
- **Domain-specific language** and **transitions** to connect and relate ideas
- Correct **grammar, usage,** and **mechanics**
- A list of at least **two trustworthy sources,** one of which is a print source, such as a newspaper, magazine, book, or encyclopedia. The other source may be a digital source found on the Internet, such as a government website.

INFORMATIONAL WRITING: PREWRITING (A) **191**

192 INFORMATIONAL WRITING: PREWRITING (A)

Audience: Your teacher and peers

Purpose: Inform or explain your topic to readers.

Length: 400 to 600 words long (approximately 6–8 handwritten drafting pages or (1½ to 2 pages typed and double spaced)

Brainstorm and choose a topic for your history report. As you brainstorm, you may add more circles to the web.

1. In the circles connected to "History Report," name at least three broad history categories that interest you, such as *American Revolution* or *past presidents.*

2. In the circles connected to each broad category, name at least two topics related to that category, such as *George Washington* or *Thomas Jefferson.*

History Report

INFORMATIONAL WRITING: PREWRITING (A) **193**

3. Read your topics. Cross off topics that seem too large or broad to cover. Cross off topics that are too small or narrow.

4. Circle any topics that you really would like to write about. If you did not circle any topics, add a few more.

5. Choose your favorite topic that you circled. Then answer Yes or No to each question.

   a. Is the topic focused enough to cover in detail in five paragraphs?

   b. Is the topic something you can research using trustworthy sources?

   c. Is the topic interesting to you?

6. Did you answer Yes to Parts A–C of Question 5? You have found a topic! If not, go back and complete Question 5 with another topic you named. Repeat until you find a topic that works.

My history report topic is

Answers will vary. By the time they complete this activity page, students should have chosen the topic of their history report.

I can't wait to learn more about my topic!

194 INFORMATIONAL WRITING: PREWRITING (A)

WRAP-UP

Questions About Brainstorming and Capitalization

Students will answer questions to show that they understand how to brainstorm a topic for a history report and how to recognize and capitalize proper nouns and adjectives.

Informational Writing: Prewriting (B)

Lesson Overview

ACTIVITY	ACTIVITY TITLE	TIME	ONLINE/OFFLINE
GET READY	Introduction to Informational Writing: Prewriting (B)	**2** minutes	online
	Spelling List 12 Activity Bank	**10** minutes	offline
LEARN AND **TRY IT**	Capitalize the Correct Words in Titles	**10** minutes	online
	Practice Capitalizing the Correct Words in Titles	**10** minutes	online
	Conduct Research for a History Report	**15** minutes	online
	Conduct Research for Your History Report — **LEARNING COACH CHECK-IN**	**50** minutes	offline
WRAP-UP	Questions About Research and Capitalization	**3** minutes	online
	Go Read!	**20** minutes	online or offline

Content Background

Students will continue to work on their **history report**, an assignment that they will complete over the course of several lessons by following the writing process.

Writing Process

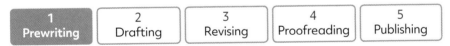

| 1 Prewriting | 2 Drafting | 3 Revising | 4 Proofreading | 5 Publishing |

During **prewriting**, writers choose a topic, conduct research, and create a plan for their writing assignment. In this lesson, students will complete the second part of prewriting: conducting research.

First, students will create a **research question**, a question that will guide and focus their research and that their report will answer. Then they will find trustworthy print and digital sources with information about their topic. They will take notes on their topic, using at least two sources. They will also find at least one direct quotation to include in their report.

MATERIALS

Supplied
- *Summit English Language Arts 4 Activity Book*
  - Spelling List 12 Activity Bank
  - Conduct Research for Your History Report
- History Report Instructions (printout)
- Research Notes (printout)

Also Needed
- completed Spelling List 12 Pretest activity page from Informational Writing: Prewriting (A)
- folder for organizing informational writing assignment pages
- reading material for Go Read!

Grammar, Usage, and Mechanics   Students will learn to capitalize the correct words in titles according to these rules:

1. Capitalize first and last words.

2. Lowercase the following, unless they are the first or last words:

- *the*, *a*, or *an*

- coordinating conjunctions, such as *and* and *or*

- prepositions that have four or fewer letters

3. Capitalize all other words.

> **Examples: Short story:** "Goldilocks and the Three Bears"
>
> **Book:** *The Tale of Peter Rabbit*
>
> **Song:** "The Farmer in the Dell"

For this lesson, proper formatting (quotation marks, italicizing, and underlining) is not addressed.

Advance Preparation

Gather students' completed Spelling List 12 Pretest activity page from Informational Writing: Prewriting (A). Students will refer to this page during Get Ready: Spelling List 12 Activity Bank.

Gather the folder that students are using to store the activity pages related to their history report. The folder should contain the following:

- Completed Brainstorm for Your History Report activity page from Informational Writing: Prewriting (A)

During the Go Read! activity, students will have the option of using the digital library. Allow extra time for students to make their reading selection, or have students make a selection before beginning the lesson.

Lesson Goals

- Practice spelling words offline.

- Learn how to capitalize the correct words in titles.

- Learn how to conduct research.

- Research the topic of your history report.

- Read for pleasure.

Introduction to Informational Writing: Prewriting (B)

Students will get a glimpse of what they will learn about in the lesson. They will also read the lesson goals and keywords. Have students select each keyword and preview its definition.

Spelling List 12 Activity Bank

Students will practice all spelling words from the workshop by completing Spelling List 12 Activity Bank from *Summit English Language Arts 4 Activity Book*. Make sure students have their completed Spelling List 12 Pretest activity page Informational Writing: Prewriting (A) to refer to during this activity.

Remind students to pay special attention to words they spelled incorrectly on the Spelling Pretest.

LEARN Capitalize the Correct Words in Titles

Students will learn to capitalize the correct words in titles.

TRY IT Practice Capitalizing the Correct Words in Titles

Students will answer questions about capitalizing the correct words in titles. They will receive feedback on their answers.

LEARN   Researching a History Report

Students will learn about creating an effective research question and about conducting research, which is the second part of the prewriting step. They will focus on how to choose trustworthy sources and how to take notes.

TIP   Tell students that major newspapers, such as the *New York Times*, the *Washington Post*, and the *Chicago Tribune* are all trustworthy sources. Likewise, government websites, such as those run by the Library of Congress and other agencies, contain reliable and useful information. Print reference books, such as *Encyclopedia Britannica* and the *World Book Encyclopedia*, are also credible sources of information.

TRY IT   Conduct Research for Your History Report

Students will complete Conduct Research for Your History Report from *Summit English Language Arts 4 Activity Book*.

LEARNING COACH CHECK-IN   Review students' responses. Ensure that students have created an effective research question that meets the criteria on the activity page. Then ensure that students have found and taken notes from two appropriate and trustworthy sources, one of which should be a print source. Their notes should also include at least one direct quotation from one of their sources. When students have completed the pages with their notes, they should store them in a folder so that they can refer to them throughout the writing process.

NOTE   If you or your students wish, you can download and print another copy of the History Report Instructions online. Additional sheets for Research Notes are also available online.

WRAP-UP

Questions About Research and Capitalization

Students will answer questions to show that they understand how to conduct research and how to capitalize the correct words in titles.

Go Read!

Students will read for pleasure. They should choose a book or a magazine that interests them, or they may choose a selection from the digital library, linked in the online lesson.

Students should read for the entire time. Have students select something to read ahead of time to help them stay focused.

Informational Writing: Prewriting (C)

Lesson Overview

ACTIVITY	ACTIVITY TITLE	TIME	ONLINE/OFFLINE
GET READY	Introduction to Informational Writing: Prewriting (C)	**2** minutes	🖥️
	Spelling List 12 Practice	**10** minutes	🖥️
	Mammoth Cave	**10** minutes	🖥️
LEARN AND **TRY IT**	Prewriting a History Report	**15** minutes	🖥️
	Prewriting Your History Report **LEARNING COACH CHECK-IN**	**60** minutes	📄
WRAP-UP	Question About Prewriting	**3** minutes	🖥️
	Go Read!	**20** minutes	🖥️ or 📄

Content Background

Students will continue to work on their **history report**, an assignment that they will complete over the course of several lessons by following the writing process.

Writing Process

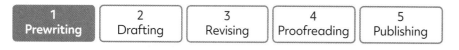

During **prewriting**, writers choose a topic, conduct research, and create a plan for their writing assignment. In this lesson, students will complete the third part of prewriting: creating a plan. To create their plan, they will complete a graphic organizer.

First, students will gather the notes they took during research. Then they will use these notes to help them create a plan for their history report by completing a graphic organizer provided to them in their activity book. The graphic organizer will allow them to organize information in the same order that they will present it in their report. The graphic organizer will also help students group together related information.

Remind students that it is not necessary to write in complete sentences when completing a graphic organizer.

MATERIALS

Supplied

- *Summit English Language Arts 4 Activity Book*
  - Prewriting Your History Report
- History Report Instructions (printout)

Also Needed

- folder for organizing informational writing assignment pages

Advance Preparation

Gather the folder that students are using to keep all notes and activity pages related to their history report. The folder should contain the following:

- Students' completed Brainstorm for Your History Report activity page from Informational Writing: Prewriting (A)

- Students' completed research notes from Informational Writing: Prewriting (B)

During the Go Read! activity, students will have the option of using the digital library. Allow extra time for students to make their reading selection, or have students make a selection before beginning the lesson.

Lesson Goals

- Practice spelling words online.

- Practice grammar skills by editing a passage.

- Learn how to organize a history report.

- Complete a graphic organizer for your history report.

- Read for pleasure.

KEYWORDS

graphic organizer – visual device, such as a diagram or chart, that helps a writer plan a piece of writing

hook – a surprising idea or group of words used to grab the reader's attention, usually at the beginning of a work

informational text – text written to explain and give information on a topic

prewriting – the stage or step of writing in which a writer chooses a topic, gathers ideas, and plans what to write

thesis statement – the sentence that states the main idea of an essay

GET READY

Introduction to Informational Writing: Prewriting (C)

Students will get a glimpse of what they will learn about in the lesson. They will also read the lesson goals and keywords. Have students select each keyword and preview its definition.

Spelling List 12 Practice

Students will practice all spelling words from the workshop.

Mammoth Cave

Students will edit a short passage to practice applying grammar skills. This passage contains errors and opportunities to improve the writing related to capitalization, incomplete sentences, and pronoun-antecedent agreement.

LEARN   Prewriting a History Report

Students will learn about creating a plan, which is the third part of the prewriting step in the writing process. The activity focuses on how to group related ideas discovered during research by using a graphic organizer.

TRY IT   Prewriting Your History Report

Students will complete Prewriting Your History Report from *Summit English Language Arts 4 Activity Book*. Make sure students have their completed research notes to refer to during this activity.

LEARNING COACH CHECK-IN   Review students' responses. Ensure that students have completed the graphic organizer in a way that meets the criteria on the activity page. That means making certain that they have completed the graphic organizer by using notes taken during research; the information in the graphic organizer follows the appropriate order for a five-paragraph essay; and related information is grouped together within the graphic organizer. When students have completed their graphic organizer, they should store it in the folder they are using to organize their writing assignment pages.

NOTE   If you or students wish, you can download and print another copy of the History Report Instructions online.

TRY IT
Informational Writing: Prewriting (C)

Prewriting Your History Report

Use your research notes to complete a graphic organizer for your history report. You do not need to use complete sentences in your graphic organizer.

Note: Your report must include at least one direct quotation and one piece of media, such as a picture, chart, or video clip. So, you only need to fill in one blank labeled "Direct Quotation" and one blank labeled "Possible Use of Media" in your graphic organizer.

Report Title _____

Introduction
Hook: _____
Background: _____
Thesis Statement: _____

INFORMATIONAL WRITING: PREWRITING (C) **203**

Body Paragraph 1
Subtopic: _____
Related Information/Details: _____
Direct Quotation (if appropriate): _____
Image or Media (if appropriate): _____

Body Paragraph 2
Subtopic: _____
Related Information/Details: _____
Direct Quotation (if appropriate): _____
Image or Media (if appropriate): _____

204 INFORMATIONAL WRITING: PREWRITING (C)

Body Paragraph 3
Subtopic: _____
Related Information/Details: _____
Direct Quotation (if appropriate): _____
Image or Media (if appropriate): _____

Conclusion
Brief Restatement of Thesis: _____
Short Summary of Key Points: _____

INFORMATIONAL WRITING: PREWRITING (C) **205**

Question About Prewriting

Students will answer a question to show that they understand how to complete a graphic organizer.

Go Read!

Students will read for pleasure. They should choose a book or a magazine that interests them, or they may choose a selection from the digital library, linked in the online lesson.

Students should read for the entire time. Have students select something to read ahead of time to help them stay focused.

Informational Writing: Drafting (A)

Lesson Overview

ACTIVITY	ACTIVITY TITLE	TIME	ONLINE/OFFLINE
GET READY	Introduction to Informational Writing: Drafting (A)	**2** minutes	🖥️
	Spelling List 12 Review Game	**10** minutes	🖥️
	Flying High	**10** minutes	🖥️
LEARN AND **TRY IT**	Drafting a History Report	**15** minutes	🖥️
	Draft Your History Report **LEARNING COACH CHECK-IN**	**60** minutes	📄
WRAP-UP	Question About Drafting	**3** minutes	🖥️
	Go Read!	**20** minutes	🖥️ or 📄

Content Background

Students will continue working on their **history report**. They will complete this assignment over the course of several lessons by following the writing process. In this lesson, students will begin drafting their report.

Writing Process

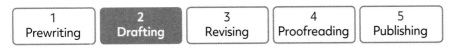

1 Prewriting	2 Drafting	3 Revising	4 Proofreading	5 Publishing

During **drafting**, students will use their notes and their completed graphic organizers as guides as they write a rough draft of their history report. Students are expected to write about half of their rough draft in this lesson (although they may write more if they wish). They will have time to finish and submit their draft in Informational Writing: Drafting (B).

Advance Preparation

Gather the folder that students are using to store the activity pages related to their history report. The folder should contain the following:

- Students' completed Brainstorm for Your History Report activity page from Informational Writing: Prewriting (A)

- Students' completed research notes from Informational Writing: Prewriting (B)

MATERIALS

Supplied
- *Summit English Language Arts 4 Activity Book*
  - Draft Your History Report
- History Report Instructions (printout)
- Drafting Paper (printout)

Also Needed
- folder in which students are storing history report writing assignment pages
- reading material for Go Read!

- Students' completed Prewriting Your History Report activity page from Informational Writing: Prewriting (C)

During the Go Read! activity, students will have the option of using the digital library. Allow extra time for students to make their reading selection, or have students make a selection before beginning the lesson.

KEYWORDS

draft – an early effort at a piece of writing, not the finished work

heading – title within the body of a text that tells the reader something important about a section of the text

informational text – text written to explain and give information on a topic

topic sentence – the sentence that expresses the main idea of a paragraph

Lesson Goals

- Practice all spelling words online.
- Practice grammar skills by editing a passage.
- Explore how to draft a history report.
- Begin to draft your history report.
- Read for pleasure.

GET READY

Introduction to Informational Writing: Drafting (A)
Students will get a glimpse of what they will learn about in the lesson. They will also read the lesson goals and keywords. Have students select each keyword and preview its definition.

Spelling List 12 Review Game
Students will practice all spelling words from the workshop.

Flying High
Students will edit a short passage to practice applying grammar skills. This passage contains errors and opportunities to improve the writing related to capitalization, incomplete sentences, and pronoun-antecedent agreement.

LEARN AND TRY IT

LEARN   Drafting a History Report
Students will explore how a student drafts a history report using her graphic organizer and her notes to guide her.

TRY IT   Draft Your History Report
Students will complete half of their first draft using Draft Your History Report in *Summit English Language Arts 4 Activity Book*. If students wish, they may complete more than half of their draft.

Make sure students have their completed Brainstorm for Your History Report activity page from Informational Writing: Prewriting (A), their research notes from Informational Writing: Prewriting (B), and their Prewriting Your History Report activity page from Informational Writing: Prewriting (C) to refer to during this activity.

LEARNING COACH CHECK-IN Review students' responses. Ensure that students' draft is in line with the assignment criteria outlined on the Brainstorm for Your History Report activity page. If necessary, remind students not to focus on perfection at this stage of the writing process. Students should store their draft in the folder they are using to organize their writing assignment pages.

NOTE If you or students wish, you can download and print another copy of the History Report Instructions online. Additional sheets of Drafting Paper are also available online.

TRY IT
Informational Writing: Drafting (A)

Draft Your History Report

Using your notes and your graphic organizer to guide you, write the first draft of your history report. Write only on the white rows. You will use the purple rows for revisions later.

Title

start here ►

Students should write their draft in the white rows only.

keep writing ►

Draft Page 1

INFORMATIONAL WRITING: DRAFTING (A) **207**

keep writing ►

208 INFORMATIONAL WRITING: DRAFTING (A)

Draft Page 2

keep writing ►

Draft Page 3

INFORMATIONAL WRITING: DRAFTING (A) **209**

keep writing ►

Draft Page 4

210 INFORMATIONAL WRITING: DRAFTING (A)

keep writing ►

Draft Page 5

INFORMATIONAL WRITING: DRAFTING (A) **211**

Draft Page 6

212 INFORMATIONAL WRITING: DRAFTING (A)

Question About Drafting

Students will answer a question to show that they understand how to draft a history report.

Go Read!

Students will read for pleasure. They should choose a book or a magazine that interests them, or they may choose a selection from the digital library, linked in the online lesson.

Students should read for the entire time. Have students select something to read ahead of time to help them stay focused.

Informational Writing: Drafting (B)

Lesson Overview

ACTIVITY	ACTIVITY TITLE	TIME	ONLINE/OFFLINE
GET READY	Introduction to Informational Writing: Drafting (B)	**1** minute	📶
TRY IT	Review Correct Capitalization	**10** minutes	📶
QUIZ	Capitalization	**20** minutes	📶
	Spelling List 12	**10** minutes	📶
TRY IT	Finish Drafting Your History Report **LEARNING COACH CHECK-IN**	**60** minutes	📄
WRAP-UP	Turn In Your History Report Draft	**1** minute	📶
	More Language Arts Practice	**8** minutes	📶
	Go Read!	**10** minutes	📶 or 📄

Content Background

Students will continue working on their **history report**. In this lesson, students will finish and submit their rough draft. They will revise, proofread, and publish their report in a future workshop.

Writing Process

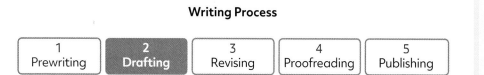

| 1 Prewriting | 2 Drafting | 3 Revising | 4 Proofreading | 5 Publishing |

Advance Preparation

Gather the folder that students are using to store the activity pages related to their history report. The folder should contain the following:

- Students' completed Brainstorm for Your History Report activity page from Informational Writing: Prewriting (A)

- Students' completed research notes from Informational Writing: Prewriting (B)

- Students' completed Prewriting Your History Report activity page from Informational Writing: Prewriting (C)

- Students' in-progress Draft Your History Report activity page from Informational Writing: Drafting (A)

Lesson Goals

- Review correct capitalization of proper nouns, proper adjectives, and titles of works.
- Take a quiz on capitalization.
- Take a spelling quiz.
- Finish and submit the rough draft of your history report.

GET READY

Introduction to Informational Writing: Drafting (B)
Students will read the lesson goals.

TRY IT

Review Correct Capitalization
Students will answer questions to review what they have learned about correctly capitalizing proper nouns, adjectives, and titles of works.

QUIZ

Capitalization
Students will complete the Capitalization quiz.

Spelling List 12
Students will complete the Spelling List 12 quiz.

TRY IT

Finish Drafting Your History Report
Students will complete the rough draft of their history report. They should gather the Draft Your History Report activity page that they started in Informational Writing: Drafting (A) and complete it.

Make sure students also have their completed Brainstorm for Your History Report activity page from Informational Writing: Prewriting (A), their research notes activity page from Informational Writing: Prewriting (B), and their Prewriting Your History Report activity page from Informational Writing: Prewriting (C) to refer to during this activity.

TRY IT

Informational Writing: Drafting (A)

Draft Your History Report

Using your notes and your graphic organizer to guide you, write the first draft of your history report. Write only on the white rows. You will use the purple rows for revisions later.

Title

start here ▶

Students should write their draft in the white rows only.

keep writing ▶

Draft Page 1

INFORMATIONAL WRITING: DRAFTING (A) **207**

208 INFORMATIONAL WRITING DRAFTING (A)

Draft Page 2

keep writing ▶

Draft Page 3

keep writing ▶

INFORMATIONAL WRITING DRAFTING (A) **209**

210 INFORMATIONAL WRITING DRAFTING (A)

Draft Page 4

keep writing ▶

Draft Page 5

keep writing ▶

INFORMATIONAL WRITING DRAFTING (A) **211**

212 INFORMATIONAL WRITING DRAFTING (A)

Draft Page 6

Turn In Your History Report Draft

Students will submit their writing assignment to their teacher.

More Language Arts Practice

Students will practice skills according to their individual needs.

Go Read!

Students will read for pleasure. They should choose a book or a magazine that interests them, or they may choose a selection from the digital library, linked in the online lesson.

Students should read for the entire time. Have students select something to read ahead of time to help them stay focused.

Big Ideas: Critical Skills Assignment

Lesson Overview

Big Ideas lessons provide students the opportunity to further apply the knowledge acquired and skills learned throughout the unit workshops. Each Big Ideas lesson consists of these parts:

1. **Cumulative Review:** Students keep their skills fresh by reviewing prior content.

2. **Preview:** Students practice answering the types of questions they will commonly find on standardized tests.

3. **Synthesis:** Students complete an assignment that allows them to connect and apply what they have learned. Synthesis assignments vary throughout the course.

   In the Synthesis portion of this Big Ideas lesson, students will read new selections. They will answer literal and inferential comprehension questions and complete writing questions that ask for short responses about the reading selections. Students should refer to the selections while answering the questions, because the questions emphasize using textual evidence. The questions call for students to demonstrate critical thinking, reading, and writing skills.

   LEARNING COACH CHECK-IN   This is a graded assessment. Make sure students complete, review, and submit the assignment to their teacher.

All materials needed for this lesson are linked online and not provided in the Activity Book.

Childhood
Classics

Metaphors

Lesson Overview

ACTIVITY	ACTIVITY TITLE	TIME	ONLINE/OFFLINE
GET READY	Childhood Classics Unit Overview	**1** minute	🖥️
	Introduction to Metaphors	**1** minute	🖥️
	Look Back at Figurative Language	**4** minutes	🖥️
LEARN **AND** **TRY IT**	Metaphors Compare	**10** minutes	🖥️
	Practice Using Metaphors	**10** minutes	🖥️
	Apply: Metaphors **LEARNING COACH CHECK-IN**	**15** minutes	📄
	Go Write!	**15** minutes	📄
	Review Metaphors	**15** minutes	🖥️
QUIZ	Metaphors	**15** minutes	🖥️
WRAP-UP	More Language Arts Practice	**19** minutes	🖥️
	Go Read!	**15** minutes	🖥️ or 📄

Content Background

Students will learn about metaphor, a form of figurative language. They will learn how to identify metaphors and how to determine the meanings of metaphors.

A metaphor compares two things that are not alike at all. It compares by saying one thing is another thing. An example of a metaphor is the phrase *two peas in a pod* in the sentence *My brothers are two peas in a pod.* This sentence compares two unlike things, the brothers and peas in a pod. The metaphor is a descriptive way of saying that the brothers are very similar.

Advance Preparation

During the Go Read! activity, students will have the option of using the digital library. Allow extra time for students to make their reading selection, or have students make a selection before beginning the lesson.

Lesson Goals

- Define *metaphor*.
- Identify and describe the meaning of metaphors in text.
- Use context clues to determine the meaning of metaphors
- Read and write for pleasure.

Childhood Classics Unit Overview

Students will read a summary of what they will learn in the Childhood Classics unit.

Introduction to Metaphors

Students will get a glimpse of what they will learn about in the lesson. They will also read the lesson goals.

Look Back at Figurative Language

Students will review what it means for a phrase to have a nonliteral meaning. They will also review similes, a form of figurative language that compares.

NOTE An example of a phrase with a nonliteral meaning is "to drop the ball." The nonliteral meaning is "to make a mistake or to fail at something." Similes compare using the words *like* or *as*. Similes also have nonliteral meanings. For example, the simile "busy as a bee" describes somebody that is very busy or works very hard. Phrases with nonliteral meanings and similes will provide a connection to the concept of metaphor. Metaphors also have nonliteral meanings, and they compare.

LEARN AND TRY IT

LEARN   Metaphors Compare

Students will learn the definitions of several metaphors. They will learn how to identify metaphors and how to use context clues to help them determine what a metaphor means.

TRY IT   Practice Using Metaphors

Students will analyze passages and answer questions about metaphors.

TRY IT   Apply: Metaphors

Students will complete Apply: Metaphors from *Summit English Language Arts 4 Activity Book*.

This activity page contains open-ended questions, so it's important that you review students' responses. Give students feedback, using the example answers provided to guide you.

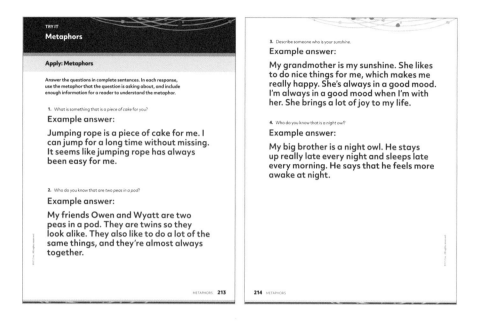

TRY IT
Metaphors

Apply: Metaphors

Answer the questions in complete sentences. In each response, use the metaphor that the question is asking about, and include enough information for a reader to understand the metaphor.

1. What is something that is a *piece of cake* for you?
Example answer:

Jumping rope is a piece of cake for me. I can jump for a long time without missing. It seems like jumping rope has always been easy for me.

2. Who do you know that are *two peas in a pod?*
Example answer:

My friends Owen and Wyatt are two peas in a pod. They are twins so they look alike. They also like to do a lot of the same things, and they're almost always together.

METAPHORS **213**

3. Describe someone who is your *sunshine*.
Example answer:

My grandmother is my sunshine. She likes to do nice things for me, which makes me really happy. She's always in a good mood. I'm always in a good mood when I'm with her. She brings a lot of joy to my life.

4. Who do you know that is a *night owl?*
Example answer:

My big brother is a night owl. He stays up really late every night and sleeps late every morning. He says that he feels more awake at night.

214 METAPHORS

TRY IT Go Write!

Students will write independently for pleasure. As they write, they should think about using metaphors in their writing.

TRY IT Review Metaphors

Students will answer questions to review what they have learned about metaphors.

QUIZ

Metaphors

Students will complete the Metaphors quiz.

WRAP-UP

More Language Arts Practice

Students will practice skills according to their individual needs.

Go Read!

Students will read for pleasure. They should choose a book or a magazine that interests them, or they may choose a selection from the digital library, linked in the online lesson.

Students should read for the entire time. Have students select something to read ahead of time to help them stay focused.

Poetry (A)

Lesson Overview

ACTIVITY	ACTIVITY TITLE	TIME	ONLINE/OFFLINE
GET READY	Introduction to Poetry (A)	**1** minute	🖥️
	Spelling List 13 Pretest **LEARNING COACH CHECK-IN**	**10** minutes	🖥️ and 📄
	Poetry in 60 Seconds	**1** minute	🖥️
	Look Back at Poetry	**5** minutes	🛜
	Before You Read "The Ecchoing Green" and "Try, Try Again"	**13** minutes	🖥️
READ	"The Ecchoing Green" and "Try, Try Again"	**10** minutes	📄
	Check-In: "The Ecchoing Green" and "Try, Try Again"	**5** minutes	🖥️
LEARN AND **TRY IT**	Common Elements	**10** minutes	🖥️
	Common Elements of "Try, Try Again"	**10** minutes	🖥️
	Structural Elements	**10** minutes	🖥️
	Structural Elements of "Try, Try Again"	**10** minutes	🖥️
	Apply: Poetry	**15** minutes	🖥️
	Write a Summary of a Poem **LEARNING COACH CHECK-IN**	**10** minutes	📄
	Practice Words from Poetry	**8** minutes	🖥️
WRAP-UP	Question About Poetry	**2** minutes	🖥️

Content Background

Students will read two poems, "The Ecchoing Green" by William Blake and "Try, Try Again" by T.H. Palmer. Students will learn about the structural elements of poetry: what makes a piece of writing a poem rather than a story or a play. They will also learn how to identify the speaker of a poem, the reason why a poet wrote a poem, and a poem's theme.

In many ways, elements of poetry are similar to elements of stories. For example, the speaker of a poem is often like the narrator of a story. In "The Ecchoing Green," the speaker in the poem is a child. Also, the reason a poet writes a poem is similar to the author's purpose for writing a story. A poem has a theme, just as a story has a theme or message. For example, one theme in "The Ecchoing Green" is that life repeats itself as children grow up and have children of their own.

Structural elements students will learn include stanza, verse, rhythm, and meter. The words *stanza* and *verse* both name a group of lines in a poem. The rhythm of a poem is the beat of the poem that gives it a musical quality when read aloud. The rhythm is established with stressed and unstressed syllables. The meter of a poem is the pattern of stressed and unstressed syllables.

"The Ecchoing Green" and "Try, Try Again" Synopses

"The Ecchoing Green" by William Blake describes a day at the beginning of spring on a village green. Children play as older people watch and reminisce about the days when they were young and played on the green.

"Try, Try Again" by T.H. Palmer is an inspirational poem that encourages the reader not to give up when things are difficult. Perseverance and patience are traits than can lead to success.

Lesson Goals

- Take a spelling pretest.
- Read a poem, and identify the speaker, purpose, and theme, as well as the meaning of unfamiliar words.
- Identify structural elements of a poem.
- Write a summary of a poem.

KEYWORDS

line – a row of words in a poem

meter – the arrangement of words in poetry based on rhythm, accents, and the number of syllables in a line

repetition – repeating words or phrases

rhyme – the use of words that end with the same sounds; for example, *cat* and *hat* rhyme

rhyme scheme – the patterns of rhymes made by the last sounds in the lines of a poem, shown by a different letter of the alphabet to represent each rhyme

rhythm – a regular pattern of sound within a poem

speaker – the imaginary person who speaks the words of a poem; not the poet

stanza – a group of lines in a poem

theme – the author's message or big idea

GET READY

Introduction to Poetry (A)

Students will get a glimpse of what they will learn about in the lesson. They will also read the lesson goals and keywords. Have students select each keyword and preview its definition.

Spelling List 13 Pretest

Students will take a spelling pretest.

LEARNING COACH CHECK-IN   Have students turn to Spelling List 13 Pretest in *Summit English Language Arts 4 Activity Book* and open the online Spelling Pretest activity. Online, students will listen to the spelling word, type the word in the space indicated, and then check their answer. In the activity book, students will write the correct spelling of the word in the tables provided and indicate with a ✓ or an ✗ if they spelled the word correctly or incorrectly online. Students will repeat this process with the remaining words.

As needed, help students with the interaction between the online activity and the activity book page until they become comfortable with what they need to do. As students practice their spelling words throughout the workshop, they should pay special attention to words they spelled incorrectly on the pretest.

This is the complete list of words students will be tested on.

Words with *r*-controlled vowels	Heart Words
absurd	Alaska
concern	Vermont
disturb	
firm	
shirt	
misery	
observe	
pearl	
figure	
survive	
thirsty	
research	
mockingbird	
unlearn	
earning	

NOTE   Have students keep their completed activity page in a safe place so they can refer to it later.

Poetry in 60 Seconds

Students will watch a short video designed to spark their interest in upcoming topics.

Look Back at Poetry

Students will practice the prerequisite skill of identifying structural elements of poetry.

Before You Read "The Ecchoing Green" and "Try, Try Again"

Students will be introduced to some key vocabulary words that they will encounter in the upcoming reading and review important background related to the reading. They will also review elements of stories to help them see the similarities among story and poetry elements.

READ

"The Ecchoing Green" and "Try, Try Again"

Students will read "The Ecchoing Green" by William Blake and "Try, Try Again" by T.H. Palmer in *Expeditions in Reading*.

Check-In: "The Ecchoing Green" and "Try, Try Again"

Students will answer several questions to demonstrate their comprehension of "The Ecchoing Green" and "Try, Try Again."

LEARN   Common Elements

Students will learn about the poetic elements of speaker, purpose, and theme.

TRY IT   Common Elements in "Try, Try Again"

Students will analyze a poem and answer questions about the speaker, the reason the poet wrote the poem, and the theme.

LEARN   Structural Elements

Students will learn about the structural elements of a poem, including stanza, verse, rhythm, and meter.

TIP   If students have difficulty determining the rhythm of a poem, have them try clapping the rhythm of simple nursery rhymes such as "Jack and Jill" or "Little Bo Peep." Then help them clap the rhythm of "The Ecchoing Green."

TRY IT   Structural Elements in "Try, Try Again"

Students will analyze a poem and answer questions about the poem's structural elements.

TRY IT   Apply: Poetry

Students will read more poetry and apply what they've learned about a poem's elements, including structural elements.

TRY IT   Write a Summary of a Poem

Students will complete Write a Summary of a Poem from *Summit English Language Arts 4 Activity Book*.

LEARNING COACH CHECK-IN   This activity page contains an open-ended question, so it's important that you review students' responses. Give students feedback, using the sample answer provided to guide you.

Write a Summary of a Poem

Write your response in complete sentences.

Write a summary of the poem "The Ecchoing Green." Be sure to include the most important information from each stanza. Also include the theme of the poem.

Example answer:

In the first stanza of "The Ecchoing Green," the day is beginning. The birds are singing and bells are ringing. Children are playing on the village green.

In the second stanza, the old folks are watching the children play. They are remembering when they were children and used to play on the village green.

In the third stanza, the day is ending. The children are all tired. They have stopped playing, and they're gathering around their mothers.

The theme of the poem is that life repeats itself as children grow up and have children of their own.

TRY IT Practice Words from Poetry

Students will answer questions to demonstrate their understanding of the vocabulary words from the reading.

WRAP-UP

Question About Poetry

Students will answer a question to show that they understand terminology for structural elements of poems.

Poetry (B)

Lesson Overview

ACTIVITY	ACTIVITY TITLE	TIME	ONLINE/OFFLINE
GET READY	Introduction to Poetry (B)	**1** minute	
	Spelling List 13 Activity Bank	**10** minutes	
	Recall "The Ecchoing Green"	**5** minutes	
	Before You Read "Wynken, Blynken, and Nod"	**10** minutes	
READ	"Wynken, Blynken, and Nod"	**10** minutes	
	Check-In: "Wynken, Blynken, and Nod"	**5** minutes	
LEARN AND **TRY IT**	More on Structural Elements	**10** minutes	
	Structural Elements in "Bed in Summer"	**10** minutes	
	Poetry vs. Prose	**10** minutes	
	Poetry vs. Prose with "Bed in Summer"	**10** minutes	
	Apply: Poetry vs. Prose	**15** minutes	
	Write Poetry into Prose **LEARNING COACH CHECK-IN**	**15** minutes	
	Practice Words from Poetry	**7** minutes	
WRAP-UP	Question About Prose and Poetry	**2** minutes	

Content Background

Students will read two poems in *Expeditions in Reading*, "Wynken, Blynken, and Nod" by Eugene Field and "Bed in Summer" by Robert Louis Stevenson. Students will take the figurative language and structural elements they learned in previous lessons and use this basic foundation to analyze poems at a much deeper level. Instead of merely identifying the examples of these elements, they will use their understanding of them to better understand how poets use them to fulfill their overall purpose.

Students will also learn about two elements of figurative language used when analyzing poems: simile and personification. They also will look for imagery and descriptive details, theme, and tone to help them better understand the content of the poems.

MATERIALS

Supplied
- *Summit English Language Arts 4 Expeditions in Reading*
- *Summit English Language Arts 4 Activity Book*
  - Spelling List 13 Activity Bank
  - Write Poetry into Prose

Also Needed
- completed Spelling List 13 Pretest activity page from Poetry (A)

Knowing different elements that poets use will assist students in comparing poetry to other genres, like prose. When students understand the similarities and differences among poetry and prose texts, they will better understand the reasons writers use these specific elements and the overall effects of them on text in any genre.

Advance Preparation

Gather students' completed Spelling List 13 Pretest activity page from Poetry (A). Students will refer to this page during Get Ready: Spelling List Activity Bank.

"Wynken, Blynken, and Nod" and "Bed in Summer" Synopses

"Wynken, Blynken, and Nod" by Eugene Field is a narrative poem and an extended metaphor for a child's dreams and imagination. The poet compares the features of a sleeping child to three characters—Wynken, Blynken, and Nod. In the poem—a child's dream—Wynken, Blynken, and Nod journey off in a sailing ship (a wooden shoe) to catch herring-fish (the stars) and speak to the moon.

"Bed in Summer" by Robert Louis Stevenson gives voice to a young speaker's experience with the changing seasons. As winter gives way to summer, the speaker struggles with going to bed while there is still daylight and activities that continue without him.

Lesson Goals

- Practice all spelling words offline.
- Explore the theme, tone, figurative language, and structural elements of a poem.
- Compare the elements of poetry and prose.
- Write a poem version of a prose text.
- Determine meanings of unfamiliar words in the reading.

KEYWORDS

dialogue – the words that characters say in a written work

figurative language – words that describe something by comparing it to something completely different

imagery – language that helps readers imagine how something looks, sounds, smells, feels, or tastes

metaphor – a figure of speech that compares two unlike things, without using the word like or as; example: The cat's eyes were emeralds shining in the night.

meter – the arrangement of words in poetry based on rhythm, accents, and the number of syllables in a line

narrative – a kind of writing that tells a story

narrator – the teller of a story

personification – giving human qualities to something that is not human

poem – a piece of poetry

prose – the form of written language without the rhyme, rhythm, and meter that the language of poetry has

rhyme scheme – the pattern of rhymes made by the last sounds in the lines of a poem, shown by a different letter of the alphabet to represent each rhyme

rhythm – a regular pattern of sound within a poem

simile – a comparison between two things using the words *like* or *as*

speaker – the imaginary person who speaks the words of a poem; not the poet

stanza – a group of lines in a poem

theme – the author's message or big idea

tone – the author's feelings toward the subject and characters of a text

Introduction to Poetry (B)

Students will get a glimpse of what they will learn about in the lesson. They will also read the lesson goals and keywords. Have students select each keyword and preview its definition.

Spelling List 13 Activity Bank

Students will practice all spelling words from the workshop by completing Spelling List 13 Activity Bank from *Summit English Language Arts 4 Activity Book*. Make sure students have their completed Spelling List 13 Pretest activity page from Poetry (A) to refer to during this activity.

Remind students to pay special attention to words they spelled incorrectly on the Spelling Pretest.

Recall "The Ecchoing Green"

Students will answer some questions to review the reading that they have already completed.

Before You Read "Wynken, Blynken, and Nod"

Students will be introduced to some key vocabulary words that they will encounter in the upcoming reading, learn some important historical background related to the reading, and answer questions to help them set a purpose for their reading.

"Wynken, Blynken, and Nod"

Students will read "Wynken, Blynken, and Nod" by Eugene Field in *Expeditions in Reading*.

Check-In: "Wynken, Blynken, and Nod"

Students will answer several questions to demonstrate their comprehension of "Wynken, Blynken, and Nod."

LEARN AND TRY IT

LEARN   More on Structural Elements

Students will apply the figurative and structural elements they learned in previous lessons to more deeply analyze the events of "Wynken, Blynken, and Nod" by Eugene Field. In addition, students will identify the poet's use of imagery, theme, and tone while reading.

TRY IT   Structural Elements in "Bed in Summer"

Students will analyze a poem and answer questions about the different structural and figurative elements in the poem.

LEARN   Poetry vs. Prose

Students will learn about the similarities and differences between poetry and prose. They will focus primarily on the use of language, structure, and form.

TRY IT   Poetry vs. Prose with "Bed in Summer"

Students will look at examples of poetry and prose and answer questions about their similarities and differences.

TRY IT   Apply: Poetry vs. Prose

Students will apply to new works what they have learned about the similarities and differences in poetry and prose.

TRY IT   Write Poetry into Prose

Students will complete Write Poetry into Prose in *Summit English Language Arts 4 Activity Book*. For this activity, students will need to refer to the poem "Bed in Summer" by Robert Louis Stevenson in *Expeditions in Reading*.

LEARNING COACH CHECK-IN   This activity page contains an open-ended question, so it's important that you review students' responses. Give students feedback, using the sample answer provided to guide you. If students are struggling, be sure to review Poetry vs. Prose with "Bed in Summer."

TRY IT
Poetry (B)

Write Poetry into Prose

Write your response in complete sentences.

Write a prose version of the poem "Bed in Summer."

Example prose:

    In the winter, I get up when it is still nighttime. As I am getting dressed, I need candlelight, since it is hard to see anything. When it's the end of the day, I go to sleep when it is dark. In the summer, the sun sets later than in the winter. This means I have to go to sleep when it is still sunny outside.

    I have to go to bed even though I can see that the birds in the trees are still awake. People are still walking on the street outside my window.

    Don't you think it is hard to have to go to sleep so early in the summer? I would rather play outside under a clear blue sky than go to bed when it is still light out.

POETRY (B) **223**

In northern Alaska, it stays light nearly 24 hours a day in the summer.

224 POETRY (B)

TRY IT   Practice Words from Poetry

Students will answer questions to demonstrate their understanding of the vocabulary words from the reading.

WRAP-UP

Question About Poetry

Students will answer a question to show that they understand terminology for structural elements of poems.

Poetry (C)

Lesson Overview

ACTIVITY	ACTIVITY TITLE	TIME	ONLINE/OFFLINE
GET READY	Introduction to Poetry (C)	**1** minute	🖥️
	Spelling List 13 Review Game	**10** minutes	🖥️
	Before You Write a Narrative Poem	**10** minutes	🖥️
LEARN AND **TRY IT**	Writing a Found Narrative Poem	**15** minutes	🖥️
	Write a Found Narrative Poem **LEARNING COACH CHECK-IN**	**82** minutes	📄
WRAP-UP	Question About Narrative Poetry	**2** minutes	🖥️

Content Background

Students will learn how to write their own narrative poems. They will focus on learning about the form of and different elements found in narrative poems. Then they will write their own narrative poem.

Students will use "Wynken, Blynken, and Nod" to identify and discuss different examples of narrative poetry. They will then explore how the story "Cinderella" can be turned into a found poem.

When students create their own found poems, they should include examples of figurative language (such as similes, metaphors, and personification), key elements of a story (beginning, middle, end, dialogue, setting, characters), and elements of poetry (stanza, rhyme scheme, meter, rhythm, and imagery).

Advance Preparation

For Write a Found Narrative Poem, students need a narrative, or story. Students may choose a narrative they read in the course, a narrative they wrote, or another narrative to which they have access. It's important that students have access to the full text of the narrative for this activity.

MATERIALS

Supplied
- *Summit English Language Arts 4 Expeditions in Reading*
- *Summit English Language Arts 4 Activity Book*
  - Write a Found Narrative Poem

Lesson Goals

- Review all spelling words.
- Identify the elements of a narrative poem.
- Learn the steps of creating a found poem.
- Write a found narrative poem.

KEYWORDS

dialogue – the words that characters say in a written work

figurative language – words that describe something by comparing it to something completely different

imagery – language that helps readers imagine how something looks, sounds, smells, feels, or tastes

meter – the arrangement of words in poetry based on rhythm, accents, and the number of syllables in a line

narrative – a kind of writing that tells a story

narrator – the teller of a story

problem – an issue a character must solve in a story

rhyme scheme – the pattern of rhymes made by the last sounds in the lines of a poem, shown by a different letter of the alphabet to represent each rhyme

rhythm – a regular pattern of sound within a poem

speaker – the imaginary person who speaks the words of a poem; not the poet

stanza – a group of lines in a poem

theme – the author's message or big idea

tone – the author's feelings toward the subject and characters of a text

GET READY

Introduction to Poetry (C)

Students will get a glimpse of what they will learn about in this lesson. They will also read the lesson goals and keywords. Have students select each keyword and preview its definition.

Spelling List 13 Review Game

Students will practice all spelling words from the workshop.

Before You Write a Narrative Poem

Students will be introduced to elements of narrative poems to prepare for writing their own. They will use "Wynken, Blynken, and Nod" as the model for identifying and analyzing these elements.

LEARN AND TRY IT

LEARN   Writing a Found Narrative Poem

Students will learn the different steps for creating their own narrative found poem. The narrative story "Cinderella" will be used as a model to help students identify and apply these steps to their own writing.

TRY IT   Write a Found Narrative Poem

Students will complete Write a Found Narrative Poem from *Summit English Language Arts 4 Activity Book*.

LEARNING COACH CHECK-IN   Students are going to be writing their own found narrative poem. Check in with students at each step of the writing process. First, students will use the provided graphic organizer to plan and organize the details of their poem. They will then use those details to write at least one stanza for each section of the narrative (beginning, middle, and end). After students write their poem, they should read it aloud to you.

OPTIONAL   Have students exchange their poems with peers.

Poetry (C)

Write a Found Narrative Poem

Write your own found narrative poem.

Answers will vary.

1. Choose a narrative story. It can be a narrative that you have written or one that you have read. Write your story's title:

2. Use the graphic organizer to plan your poem.
   a. Write one sentence each to describe the beginning, the middle, and the end of the narrative.
   b. Record words and phrases from the narrative that show the beginning, the middle, and the end. You can also add your own details.

> Beginning

↓

> Middle

↓

> End

3. Write your found narrative poem. Make sure your poem
   - Is at least three stanzas long
   - Tells a narrative with a beginning, middle, and end
   - Includes sensory details and figurative language
   - Has at least two structural elements, such as rhyme, rhythm, and meter

start here ►

keep writing ►

Draft Page 1

4. Read your poem aloud. Use the items in Question 3 as a checklist to revise your poem.

5. Write a final copy of your poem.

WRAP-UP

Question About Narrative Poetry

Students will answer a question to show they understand the different elements of narrative poetry.

Poetry Wrap-Up

Lesson Overview

ACTIVITY	ACTIVITY TITLE	TIME	ONLINE/OFFLINE
GET READY	Introduction to Poetry Wrap-Up	**1** minute	
TRY IT	Write About Your Favorite Poem **LEARNING COACH CHECK-IN**	**30** minutes	
	Read and Record	**15** minutes	
	Review Poetry	**15** minutes	
QUIZ	Poetry	**30** minutes	
	Spelling List 13	**10** minutes	
WRAP-UP	More Language Arts Practice	**19** minutes	

Lesson Goals

- Reflect on one of the poems read.
- Practice reading aloud to develop fluency.
- Review poetry.
- Take a poetry quiz.
- Take a spelling quiz.

MATERIALS

Supplied
- *Summit English Language Arts 4 Activity Book*
  - Write About Your Favorite Poem

GET READY

Introduction to Poetry Wrap-Up

Students will read the lesson goals.

TRY IT

Write About Your Favorite Poem

Students will complete Write About Your Favorite Poem from *Summit English Language Arts 4 Activity Book*.

LEARNING COACH CHECK-IN   This activity page contains an open-ended prompt, so it's important that you review students' responses. Give students feedback, making sure they are using examples from the poem of their choice to support their response.

TRY IT
Poetry Wrap-Up

Write About Your Favorite Poem

Poems may make us think about things we have experienced or books we have read. They may make us think about the world around us.

Which poem did **you** connect with the most? Why?

- "The Ecchoing Green" by William Blake
- "Try, Try Again" by William Edward Hickson
- "Wynken, Blyken, and Nod" by Eugene Field
- "Bed in Summer" by Robert Louis Stevenson

Answers will vary.

POETRY WRAP-UP **229**

230 POETRY WRAP-UP

Read and Record

Good readers read quickly, smoothly, and with expression. This is called *fluency*. Students will record themselves reading aloud. They will listen to their recording and think about how quick, smooth, and expressive they sound.

TIP   Encourage students to rerecord as needed.

Review Poetry

Students will answer questions to review what they have learned about poetry.

QUIZ

Poetry

Students will complete the Poetry quiz.

Spelling List 13

Students will complete the Spelling List 13 quiz.

WRAP-UP

More Language Arts Practice

Students will practice skills according to their individual needs.

Informational Writing: Revising

Lesson Overview

ACTIVITY	ACTIVITY TITLE	TIME	ONLINE/OFFLINE
GET READY	Introduction to Informational Writing: Revising	**2** minutes	📶
	Look Back at Informational Writing Skills	**10** minutes	📶
LEARN AND **TRY IT**	Revising a History Report	**20** minutes	📶
	Revise Your History Report **LEARNING COACH CHECK-IN**	**60** minutes	📄
WRAP-UP	Question About Revising a Report	**5** minutes	📶
	Go Read!	**23** minutes	📶 or 📄

Content Background

Students will continue working on their **history report** about a history topic that fascinates them. In this lesson, students will **revise** their rough draft.

Writing Process

| 1 Prewriting | 2 Drafting | **3 Revising** | 4 Proofreading | 5 Publishing |

To revise their history report, students will use a checklist. The checklist focuses on organization (*Does my introduction clearly state the topic?*) and content (*Is my report factual and well researched, showing that I understand the topic?*). At the end of this lesson, students will be ready to proofread their history report for grammar, usage, and mechanics.

Students may not understand the difference between revising and proofreading. When revising, writers focus on large issues, such as the order of ideas, whether each idea is well supported with research, and if the language is precise and domain-specific. When proofreading, writers fix errors in grammar, usage, and mechanics, such as spelling or punctuation mistakes. Encourage students to focus on revision during this lesson. In the next lesson, students will proofread their history report.

MATERIALS

Supplied
- *Summit English Language Arts 4 Activity Book*
  - Revise Your History Report
- History Report Instructions (printout)
- History Report: Revision Feedback Sheet (printout)

Also Needed
- folder in which students are storing history report writing assignment pages
- reading material for Go Read!

Advance Preparation

Gather the folder that students are using to store the activity pages related to their history report. The folder should contain the following:

- Students' completed Brainstorm for Your History report activity page from Informational Writing: Prewriting (A)

- Students' completed research notes from Informational Writing: Prewriting (B)

- Students' completed Prewriting Your History Report activity page from Informational Writing: Prewriting (C)

- Students' completed rough draft from Informational Writing: Drafting (B)

Prior to the Revise Your History Report activity in this lesson, read students' rough draft and complete History Report: Revision Feedback Sheet.

During the Go Read! activity, students will have the option of using the digital library. Allow extra time for students to make their reading selection, or have students make a selection before beginning the lesson.

Lesson Goals

- Use a checklist to revise your history report.
- Read for pleasure.

GET READY

Introduction to Informational Writing: Revising

Students will get a glimpse of what they will learn about in the lesson. They will read the lesson goals and keywords. Have students select each keyword and preview its definition.

Look Back at Informational Writing Skills

Students will review how to organize informational writing, including how to write a clear and effective introduction.

> **KEYWORDS**
>
> **informational text** – text written to explain and give information on a topic
>
> **revising** – the stage or step of the writing process in which the writer goes back, rereads the piece, and makes changes in content or organization

LEARN   Revising a History Report

Students will learn about revising, including how to use a revision checklist. Through a guided activity, they will explore how to revise a sample student history report.

TRY IT   Revise Your History Report

Students will complete Revise Your History Report in *Summit English Language Arts 4 Activity Book*. They will need their completed rough draft from Informational Writing: Drafting (B).

LEARNING COACH CHECK-IN   Guide students through the revision process.

1. Gather and use the History Report: Revision Feedback Sheet that you filled out to guide a discussion with students.

    • Tell students the strengths of their history report. Provide positive comments about the ideas, language, detail, or other elements of the report that you enjoyed.

    • Share your constructive feedback with students.

    • As you discuss your feedback, encourage students to actively revise their draft in response. Reassure students that it's okay to remove or move around ideas and sentences. Students should revise their draft directly on the page, using the lines they left blank.

2. Have students review their draft once more, using the Revise Your History Report activity page.

    • For students having difficulty recognizing areas they should revise, suggest a revision, and think aloud to model your revising. For example, *This detail doesn't sound right here. It really goes with the ideas in the second paragraph. Let's move it there, or else the reader might get confused. Can you find any other details that are out of place?*

3. Make sure students store their revised draft in the folder they are using to organize their writing assignment pages.

TIP   Remind students to focus on the checklist questions. Emphasize that they should not worry about spelling, punctuation, grammar, and so on.

NOTE   If you need a copy of the History Report Instructions, you can download and print one online.

WRAP-UP

Question About Revising a Report

Students will answer a question to show that they understand what makes a strong thesis statement.

Go Read!

Students will read for pleasure. They should choose a book or a magazine that interests them, or they may choose a selection from the digital library, linked in the online lesson.

Students should read for the entire time. Have students select something to read ahead of time to help them stay focused.

Informational Writing: Proofreading

Lesson Overview

ACTIVITY	ACTIVITY TITLE	TIME	ONLINE/OFFLINE
GET READY	Introduction to Informational Writing: Proofreading	**2** minutes	🖥
	Look Back at Capitalization and the Progressive Tense	**10** minutes	🖥
LEARN AND **TRY IT**	Proofreading a History Report	**20** minutes	🖥
	Proofread Your History Report **LEARNING COACH CHECK-IN**	**60** minutes	📄
WRAP-UP	Question About Proofreading a Report	**5** minutes	🖥
	Go Read!	**23** minutes	🖥 or 📄

Content Background

Students will continue working on their **history report** about a history topic that fascinates them. In this lesson, students will **revise** their rough draft.

Writing Process

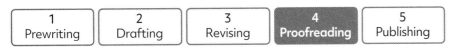

1 Prewriting	2 Drafting	3 Revising	4 Proofreading	5 Publishing

To proofread their history reports, students will use a checklist. The checklist focuses on grammar, usage, and mechanics (*Are there any missing or extra words? Are titles of works capitalized correctly?*). After completing this lesson, students will be ready to prepare a clean copy of their history report.

Proofreading is sometimes called *editing*.

Advance Preparation

Gather the folder that students are using to store the activity pages related to their history report. The folder should contain the following:

- Students' completed Brainstorm for Your History report activity page from Informational Writing: Prewriting (A)

- Students' completed research notes from Informational Writing: Prewriting (B)

- Students' completed Prewriting Your History Report activity page from Informational Writing: Prewriting (C)

- Students' revised rough draft from Informational Writing: Revising

Prior to the Proofread Your History Report activity in this lesson, read students' revised rough draft and complete History Report: Proofreading Feedback Sheet.

During the Go Read! activity, students will have the option of using the digital library. Allow extra time for students to make their reading selection, or have students make a selection before beginning the lesson.

KEYWORDS

informational text – text written to explain and give information on a topic

proofreading – the stage or step of the writing process in which the writer checks for errors in grammar, punctuation, capitalization, and spelling

Lesson Goals

- Use a checklist to proofread your history report.

- Read for pleasure.

GET READY

Introduction to Informational Writing: Proofreading

Students will get a glimpse of what they will learn about in the lesson. They will read the lesson goals and keywords. Have students select each keyword and preview its definition.

Look Back at Capitalization and the Progressive Tense

Students will practice some of the skills that they will use to proofread their report.

LEARN AND TRY IT

LEARN   Proofread a History Report

Students will learn about proofreading, including how to use a proofreading checklist. Through a guided activity, they will explore how to proofread a sample student history report.

TRY IT   Proofread Your History Report

Students will complete Proofread Your History Report in *Summit English Language Arts 4 Activity Book*. They will need their revised rough draft from Informational Writing: Drafting (B).

Guide students through the proofreading process.

1. Have students read their draft aloud, listening for errors such as missing words, incomplete sentences, and verb-tense errors. As students catch errors, have them fix the errors.

   - For students having difficultly noticing errors as they read aloud, model the process. Slowly read a sentence aloud. Pause and model your thinking when you encounter an error. For example, *"Opened the door." This sentence sounds wrong. Who opened the door? The subject is missing. Since Joe opened the door, I'll write "Joe" at the beginning of the sentence and lowercase the word "Opened."*

2. Have students review their draft once more, using the Proofread Your History Report activity page. Students should fix any additional errors that they find.

3. Review with students your comments on the History Report: Proofreading Feedback Sheet. Praise students for the errors that they caught, and guide students to recognize any errors that they have not yet fixed.

4. Have students store their edited draft in the folder they are using to organize their writing assignment pages.

OPTIONAL Have students exchange revised reports with a peer and use the Proofread Your History Report activity page to proofread each other's reports.

NOTE If you need a copy of the History Report Instructions, you can download and print one online.

TRY IT
Informational Writing: Proofreading

Proofread Your History Report

Use the checklist as you proofread your history report draft.

Grammar and Usage

☑ Are all sentences complete and correct?

☑ Are there any missing or extra words?

☑ Are all verbs in the appropriate tense?

☑ Are there other grammatical or usage errors?

Mechanics

☑ Is every word spelled correctly, including frequently confused words?

☑ Does every sentence begin with a capital letter and end with the appropriate punctuation?

☑ Are proper nouns and adjectives capitalized?

☑ Are direct quotations punctuated correctly?

☑ Are titles of works capitalized correctly?

☑ Are there other punctuation or capitalization errors?

Students should check off each item as they make necessary changes in the revised draft of their history report.

INFORMATIONAL WRITING: PROOFREADING **233**

Question About Proofreading

Students will answer a question to show that they understand a key proofreading skill.

Go Read!

Students will read for pleasure. They should choose a book or a magazine that interests them, or they may choose a selection from the digital library, linked in the online lesson.

Students should read for the entire time. Have students select something to read ahead of time to help them stay focused.

Informational Writing: Publishing

Lesson Overview

ACTIVITY	ACTIVITY TITLE	TIME	ONLINE/OFFLINE
GET READY	Introduction to Informational Writing: Publishing	**2** minutes	🖥️
LEARN AND **TRY IT**	Publishing a History Report	**15** minutes	🖥️
	Publish Your History Report	**60** minutes	🖥️
WRAP-UP	Turn In Your History Report	**1** minute	🖥️
	More Language Arts Practice	**22** minutes	🖥️
	Go Read!	**20** minutes	🖥️ or 📄

Content Background

Students will continue working on their **history report** about a historical topic they find fascinating. In this lesson, students will **publish** their report. Then they will submit their completed report to their teacher.

Writing Process

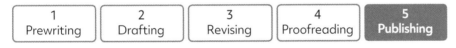

| 1 Prewriting | 2 Drafting | 3 Revising | 4 Proofreading | 5 Publishing |

Students will need to type their history report using a word-processing program. They will complete an activity to review basic word-processing skills, such as using a keyboard and saving a document.

Advance Preparation

Gather the folder that students are using to store the activity pages related to their history report. The folder should contain the following:

- Students' completed Brainstorm for Your History Report activity page from Informational Writing: Prewriting (A)

- Students' completed research notes from Informational Writing: Prewriting (B)

- Students' completed Prewriting Your History Report activity page from Informational Writing: Prewriting (C)

- Students' revised and edited rough draft from Informational Writing: Proofreading

During the Go Read! activity, students will have the option of using the digital library. Allow extra time for students to make their reading selection, or have students make a selection before beginning the lesson.

Lesson Goals

- Type your history report.
- Submit your report to your teacher.
- Read for pleasure.

GET READY

Introduction to Informational Writing: Publishing

Students will read the lesson goals and keywords. Have students select each keyword and preview its definition.

LEARN AND TRY IT

LEARN   Publishing a History Report

Students will learn about word-processing skills in preparation for typing their history report.

TRY IT   Publish Your History Report

Students will type a final copy of their history report. Students should gather their revised and proofread draft, and they should type it using a word-processing program.

NOTE   If you need a copy of the History Report Instructions, you can download and print one online.

WRAP-UP

Turn In Your History Report

Students will submit their writing assignment to their teacher.

More Language Arts Practice

Students will practice skills according to their individual needs.

Go Read!

Students will read for pleasure. They should choose a book or a magazine that interests them, or they may choose a selection from the digital library, linked in the online lesson.

Students should read for the entire time. Have students select something to read ahead of time to help them stay focused.

"Rikki-Tikki-Tavi" (A)

Lesson Overview

ACTIVITY	ACTIVITY TITLE	TIME	ONLINE/OFFLINE
GET READY	Introduction to "Rikki-Tikki-Tavi" (A)	**1** minute	
	Spelling List 14 Pretest **LEARNING COACH CHECK-IN**	**10** minutes	and
	Before You Read "Rikki-Tikki-Tavi," Chapter 1	**10** minutes	
READ	"Rikki-Tikki-Tavi," Chapter 1	**30** minutes	
	Check-In: "Rikki-Tikki-Tavi," Chapter 1	**5** minutes	
LEARN AND **TRY IT**	Making Inferences	**15** minutes	
	Use Details to Support Inferences	**15** minutes	
	Apply: Making Inferences	**15** minutes	
	Write About a True Mongoose **LEARNING COACH CHECK-IN**	**10** minutes	
	Practice Words from "Rikki-Tikki-Tavi," Chapter 1	**7** minutes	
WRAP-UP	Questions About "Rikki-Tikki-Tavi," Chapter 1	**2** minutes	

Content Background

Students will complete a spelling pretest and read "Rikki-Tikki-Tavi," Chapter 1 by Rudyard Kipling. They will then complete activities in which they learn how to support inferences with details from the story.

Making inferences, or drawing conclusions from a text, is an important reading strategy. Readers must support inferences with evidence from the text. Students should combine details from the text with background knowledge to make an inference.

Textual evidence: "It is the hardest thing in the world to frighten a mongoose."

Background knowledge: It is difficult to frighten someone who is brave.

Inference: The mongoose Rikki-tikki is brave.

MATERIALS

Supplied
- *Summit English Language Arts 4 Expeditions in Reading*
- *Summit English Language Arts 4 Activity Book*
  - Spelling List 14 Pretest
  - Write About a True Mongoose

KEYWORDS

inference – a guess that readers make using the clues that an author gives them in a piece of writing

"Rikki-Tikki-Tavi," Chapter 1 Synopsis

"Rikki-Tikki-Tavi" is a story from *The Jungle Book* by Rudyard Kipling. "Rikki-Tikki-Tavi" is a fable in which the main characters are animals. In Chapter 1, the mongoose Rikki-tikki is taken in by the human family of Teddy and his mother and father. Rikki-tikki meets the Darzee the Tailorbird and his wife as well as the wicked cobras, Nag and Nagaina. The chapter ends with Rikki-tikki saving Teddy from Karait, a small but dangerous snake.

Lesson Goals

- Take a spelling pretest.
- Read "Rikki-Tikki-Tavi," Chapter 1.
- Make inferences about "Rikki-Tikki-Tavi," Chapter 1.
- Use a character's thoughts, words, and actions to describe a character.
- Use context clues to help figure out the meaning of unknown words.

GET READY

Introduction to "Rikki-Tikki-Tavi" (A)

Students will get a glimpse of what they will learn about in the lesson. They will also read the lesson goals and keywords. Have students select each keyword and preview its definition.

Spelling List 14 Pretest

Students will take a spelling pretest.

LEARNING COACH CHECK-IN Have students turn to Spelling List 14 Pretest in *Summit English Language Arts 4 Activity Book* and open the online Spelling Pretest activity. Online, students will listen to the spelling word, type the word in the space indicated, and then check their answer. In the activity book, students will write the correct spelling of the word in the tables provided and indicate with a ✓ or an ✘ if they spelled the word correctly or incorrectly online. Students will repeat this process with the remaining words.

As needed, help students with the interaction between the online activity and the activity book page until they become comfortable with what they need to do. As students practice their spelling words throughout the workshop, they should pay special attention to words they spelled incorrectly on the pretest.

This is the complete list of words students will be tested on.

/k/ spelled c, k, ck, or ch	Root *vis*	Heart Words
ache	invisible	Colorado
arctic	visible	Montana
campus	vision	
character	vista	
chorus		
mechanic		
speckled		
octopus		
package		
skeleton		
stomach		

NOTE   Have students keep their completed activity page in a safe place so they can refer to it later.

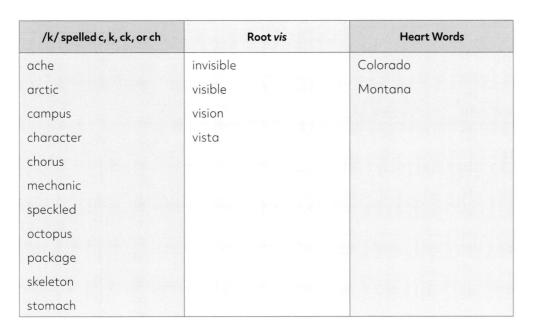

Before You Read "Rikki-Tikki-Tavi," Chapter 1

Students will be introduced to some key vocabulary words that they will encounter in the upcoming reading, learn some important historical background related to the reading, and answer questions to help them set a purpose for their reading.

READ

"Rikki-Tikki-Tavi," Chapter 1

Students will read Chapter 1 of "Rikki-Tikki-Tavi" by Rudyard Kipling in *Expeditions in Reading*.

Check-In: "Rikki-Tikki-Tavi," Chapter 1

Students will answer several questions to demonstrate their comprehension of Chapter 1 of "Rikki-Tikki-Tavi."

LEARN AND **TRY IT**

LEARN   Making Inferences

Students will learn about inferences and how to support inferences with details from the story.

TRY IT   Use Details to Support Inferences

Students will analyze passages and answer questions related to making inferences.

TRY IT   Apply: Making Inferences

Students will apply to a new work what they've learned about making inferences.

TRY IT   Write About a True Mongoose

Students will complete Write About a True Mongoose from *Summit English Language Arts 4 Activity Book*.

LEARNING COACH CHECK-IN   This activity page contains open-ended questions, so it's important that you review students' responses. Give students feedback, using the sample answers provided to guide you.

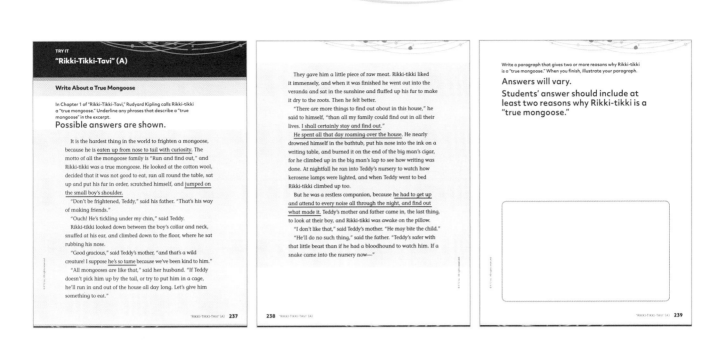

TRY IT   Practice Words from "Rikki-Tikki-Tavi," Chapter 1

Students will answer questions to demonstrate their understanding of the vocabulary words from the reading.

WRAP-UP

Questions About "Rikki-Tikki-Tavi," Chapter 1

Students will answer questions to show that they understand inferences.

"Rikki-Tikki-Tavi" (B)

Lesson Overview

ACTIVITY	ACTIVITY TITLE	TIME	ONLINE/OFFLINE
GET READY	Introduction to "Rikki-Tikki-Tavi" (B)	**1** minute	
	Spelling List 14 Activity Bank	**10** minutes	
	Recall "Rikki-Tikki-Tavi," Chapter 1	**5** minutes	
	Before You Read "Rikki-Tikki-Tavi," Chapter 2	**10** minutes	
READ	"Rikki-Tikki-Tavi," Chapter 2	**30** minutes	
	Check-In: "Rikki-Tikki-Tavi," Chapter 2	**5** minutes	
LEARN AND **TRY IT**	Author's Word Choice	**12** minutes	
	Analyze Author's Word Choice	**12** minutes	
	Apply: Word Choice	**15** minutes	
	Write About Author's Word Choice in "Rikki-Tikki-Tavi" **LEARNING COACH CHECK-IN**	**10** minutes	
	Practice Similes in "Rikki-Tikki-Tavi"	**8** minutes	
WRAP-UP	Questions About "Rikki-Tikki-Tavi," Chapter 2	**2** minutes	

Content Background

Students will read "Rikki-Tikki-Tavi," Chapter 2 by Rudyard Kipling. They will learn about author's word choice and how it affects our understanding of the story and its characters.

The words an author uses to describe a character help us picture in our minds what that character is like. For example, the author describes how Rikki-tikki moves with words like *bounding, jumped*, and *danced*. This descriptive language used by the author emphasizes that Rikki-tikki is constantly moving and ready to fight.

Advance Preparation

Gather students' completed Spelling List 14 Pretest activity page from "Rikki-Tikki-Tavi" (A). Students will refer to this page during Get Ready: Spelling List 14 Activity Bank.

"Rikki-Tikki-Tavi," Chapter 2 Synopsis

In Chapter 2, Rikki-tikki meets Chuchundra the muskrat and learns that the cobras Nag and Nagaina have found a way into the house. Rikki-tikki overhears the cobras' plan to kill the father. Rikki-tikki attacks Nag, and the fighting wakes up the father, who shoots and kills Nag. Rikki-tikki destroys Nagaina and her eggs. The chapter ends with Darzee the Tailorbird singing praises about Rikki-tikki.

KEYWORDS

simile – a comparison between two things using the words *like* or *as*; Example: I didn't hear him come in because he was as quiet as a mouse

Lesson Goals

- Practice spelling words.
- Finish reading "Rikki-Tikki-Tavi."
- Learn to analyze an author's word choice.
- Identify similes in context.

GET READY

Introduction to "Rikki-Tikki-Tavi" (B)

Students will get a glimpse of what they will learn about in the lesson. They will also read the lesson goals and keywords. Have students select each keyword and preview its definition.

Spelling List 14 Activity Bank

Students will practice all spelling words from the workshop by completing Spelling List 14 Activity Bank from *Summit English Language Arts 4 Activity Book*. Make sure students have their completed Spelling List 14 Pretest activity page from "Rikki-Tikki-Tavi" (A) to refer to during this activity.

Remind students to pay special attention to words they spelled incorrectly on the Spelling Pretest.

Worksheet pages shown:

GET READY
"Rikki-Tikki-Tavi" (B)

Spelling List 14 Activity Bank

Circle any words in the box that you did not spell correctly on the pretest. Using your circled words, complete one activity of your choice. Complete as much of the activity as you can in the time given.

If you spelled all words correctly on the pretest, complete your chosen activity with as many spelling words as you can.

ache	chorus	package	invisible	vista
arctic	mechanic	skeleton	visible	Colorado
campus	speckled	stomach	vision	Montana
character	octopus			

Spelling Activity Choices

Silly Sentences
1. Write a silly sentence using your words from the spelling word list.
2. Underline the spelling word in each sentence.
   Example: The dog was driving a car.
3. Correct any spelling errors.

Spelling Story
1. Write a very short story using your words from the spelling word list.
2. Underline the spelling words in the story.
3. Correct any spelling errors.

Riddle Me This
1. Write a riddle for your words from the spelling word list.
   Example: "I have a trunk, but it's not on my car."
2. Write the answer, which is your word, for each riddle.
   Example: Answer: elephant
3. Correct any spelling errors.

RunOnWord
1. Gather some crayons, colored pencils, or markers. Write each of your words, using a different color for each word, end to end as one long word.
   Example: dogcatbirdfishturtle
2. Rewrite the words correctly and with proper spacing.

Complete the activity that you chose.
My chosen activity:

Students should use this page to complete all steps in their chosen activity.

241 · 242 · 243

Recall "Rikki-Tikki-Tavi," Chapter 1

Students will answer some questions to review the reading that they have already completed.

Before You Read "Rikki-Tikki-Tavi," Chapter 2

Students will be introduced to some key similes that they will encounter in the upcoming reading and make a prediction about what will happen in Chapter 2 of "Rikki-Tikki-Tavi."

READ

"Rikki-Tikki-Tavi," Chapter 2

Students will read Chapter 2 of "Rikki-Tikki-Tavi" by Rudyard Kipling in *Expeditions in Reading.*

Check-In: "Rikki-Tikki-Tavi," Chapter 2

Students will answer several questions to demonstrate their comprehension of Chapter 2 of "Rikki-Tikki-Tavi."

LEARN AND TRY IT

LEARN   Author's Word Choice

Students will learn about author's word choice and how descriptive language helps us better understand and visualize the characters in a story.

TRY IT   Analyze Author's Word Choice

Students will analyze passages and answer questions related to author's word choice.

TRY IT   Apply: Word Choice

Students will apply to a new work what they've learned about identifying figurative language and author's word choice.

TRY IT   Write About Author's Word Choice in "Rikki-Tikki-Tavi"

Students will complete Write About Author's Word Choice in "Rikki-Tikki-Tavi" from *Summit English Language Arts 4 Activity Book*.

LEARNING COACH CHECK-IN   This activity page contains open-ended questions, so it's important that you review students' responses. Give students feedback, using the sample answers provided to guide you.

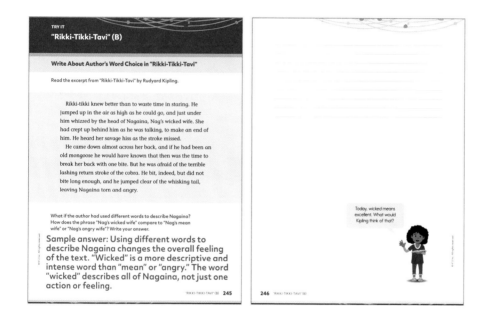

TRY IT   Practice Similes in "Rikki-Tikki-Tavi," Chapter 2

Students will practice identifying similes in the reading.

WRAP-UP

Question About "Rikki-Tikki-Tavi," Chapter 2

Students will answer a question to show that they understand author's word choice and similes.

"Rikki-Tikki-Tavi" (C)

Lesson Overview

ACTIVITY	ACTIVITY TITLE	TIME	ONLINE/OFFLINE
GET READY	Introduction to "Rikki-Tikki-Tavi" (C)	**1** minute	
	Spelling List 14 Review Game	**10** minutes	
	Recall "Rikki-Tikki-Tavi," Chapter 2	**5** minutes	
LEARN AND **TRY IT**	Comparing Text to Audio and Visual Representations	**30** minutes	
	Compare Text to Audio and Visual Representations	**20** minutes	
	Apply: Text and Illustrations	**15** minutes	
	Write About Comparing Versions of a Story **LEARNING COACH CHECK-IN**	**30** minutes	
	Practice Words from "Rikki-Tikki-Tavi"	**7** minutes	
WRAP-UP	Question About Comparing Text and Visuals	**2** minutes	

Content Background

Students will compare the text of "Rikki-Tikki-Tavi" to audio and visual representations. They will identify how the text helps direct the illustrations.

MATERIALS

Supplied
- *Summit English Language Arts 4 Activity Book*
  - Write About Comparing Versions of a Story

Lesson Goals

- Practice spelling words.
- Compare text to illustrations and audio recordings.
- Write a comparison.
- Practice vocabulary words.

GET READY

Introduction to "Rikki-Tikki-Tavi" (C)

Students will get a glimpse of what they will learn about in the lesson. They will also read the lesson goals.

Spelling List 14 Review Game

Students will practice all spelling words from the workshop.

Recall "Rikki-Tikki-Tavi," Chapter 2

Students will answer some questions to review the reading that they have already completed.

LEARN   Comparing Text to Audio and Visual Representations

Students will learn about comparing different representations of a story and identifying how audio and images reflect the descriptions in the text.

TRY IT   Compare Text to Audio and Visual Representations

Students will answer questions related to comparing the text of a story to an illustration.

TRY IT   Apply: Text and Illustrations

Students will apply to a new work what they've learned about comparing text of a story to illustrations.

TRY IT   Write About Comparing Versions of a Story

Students will complete Write About Comparing Versions of a Story from *Summit English Language Arts 4 Activity Book*.

LEARNING COACH CHECK-IN   This activity page contains open-ended questions, so it's important that you review students' responses. Give students feedback, using the sample answers provided to guide you.

TRY IT
"Rikki-Tikki-Tavi"(C)

Write About Comparing Versions of a Story

Think about a time you watched a movie based on a book. What was the title? Which version did you like better, the movie or the book? Write three reasons to explain your answer.

Answers will vary.

Students' answer should include three reasons why they preferred the book version or movie version.

"RIKKI-TIKKI-TAVI"(C) **247**

248 "RIKKI-TIKKI-TAVI"(C)

TRY IT Practice Words from "Rikki-Tikki-Tavi"

Students will answer questions to demonstrate their understanding of the vocabulary words from "Rikki-Tikki-Tavi."

Question About Comparing Text and Visuals

Students will answer a question to show that they understand how text and illustrations are related.

"Rikki-Tikki-Tavi" Wrap-Up

Lesson Overview

ACTIVITY	ACTIVITY TITLE	TIME	ONLINE/OFFLINE
GET READY	Introduction to "Rikki-Tikki-Tavi" Wrap-Up	**1** minute	
TRY IT	Write About Important Events in "Rikki-Tikki-Tavi" LEARNING COACH CHECK-IN	**30** minutes	
	Read and Record	**10** minutes	
	Review "Rikki-Tikki-Tavi"	**20** minutes	
QUIZ	"Rikki-Tikki-Tavi"	**30** minutes	
	Spelling List 14	**10** minutes	
WRAP-UP	More Language Arts Practice	**19** minutes	

Lesson Goals

- Write about important events in a text.
- Practice reading for fluency.
- Review concepts from the workshop.
- Take a quiz.
- Take a spelling quiz.

MATERIALS

Supplied
- *Summit English Language Arts 4 Activity Book*
  - Write About Important Events in "Rikki-Tikki-Tavi"

GET READY

Introduction to "Rikki-Tikki-Tavi" Wrap-Up

Students will read the lesson goals.

TRY IT

Write About Important Events in "Rikki-Tikki-Tavi"

Students will complete Write About Important Events in "Rikki-Tikki-Tavi" from *Summit English Language Arts 4 Activity Book*.

LEARNING COACH CHECK-IN This activity page contains open-ended questions, so it's important that you review students' responses. Give students feedback, using the sample answers provided to guide you.

TRY IT
"Rikki-Tikki-Tavi" Wrap-Up

Write About Important Events in "Rikki-Tikki-Tavi"

What do you think is the most important thing that happens in the story "Rikki-Tikki-Tavi"? How would the story change if this event did not occur? Write your answer.

Sample answer:

The most important event in "Rikki-Tikki-Tavi" is Rikki-tikki overhearing Nag and Nagaina's plan to kill Teddy's father. If Rikki-tikki didn't know the plan, then Nag may have been able to bite and kill Teddy's father. Without Rikki-tikki to stop them, Nag and Nagaina may have succeeded in their plan to take over the garden.

"RIKKI-TIKKI-TAVI" WRAP-UP **249**

250 "RIKKI-TIKKI-TAVI" WRAP-UP

Read and Record

Good readers read quickly, smoothly, and with expression. This is called *fluency*. Students will record themselves reading aloud. They will listen to their recording and think about how quick, smooth, and expressive they sound.

TIP Encourage students to rerecord as needed.

Review "Rikki-Tikki-Tavi"

Students will answer questions to review what they have learned about inferences, author's word choice, and comparing text to audio and illustrations.

QUIZ

"Rikki-Tikki-Tavi"

Students will complete the "Rikki-Tikki-Tavi" quiz.

Spelling List 14

Students will complete the Spelling List 14 quiz.

WRAP-UP

More Language Arts Practice

Students will practice skills according to their individual needs.

Big Ideas: Respond to a Prompt

Lesson Overview

Big Ideas lessons provide students the opportunity to further apply the knowledge acquired and skills learned throughout the unit workshops. Each Big Ideas lesson consists of these parts:

1. **Cumulative Review:** Students keep their skills fresh by reviewing prior content.

2. **Preview:** Students practice answering the types of questions they will commonly find on standardized tests.

3. **Synthesis:** Students complete an assignment that allows them to connect and apply what they have learned. Synthesis assignments vary throughout the course.

   In the Synthesis portion of this Big Ideas lesson, students will respond to an essay prompt based on reading selections. To respond meaningfully, students will need to use their own ideas as well as examples from the readings. Students' writing will be assessed in four categories: purpose and content; structure and organization; language and word choice; and grammar, usage, and mechanics.

   LEARNING COACH CHECK-IN   This is a graded assessment. Make sure students complete, review, and submit the assignment to their teacher.

All materials needed for this lesson are linked online and not provided in the Activity Book.

MATERIALS

Supplied
- Respond to a Prompt (printout)

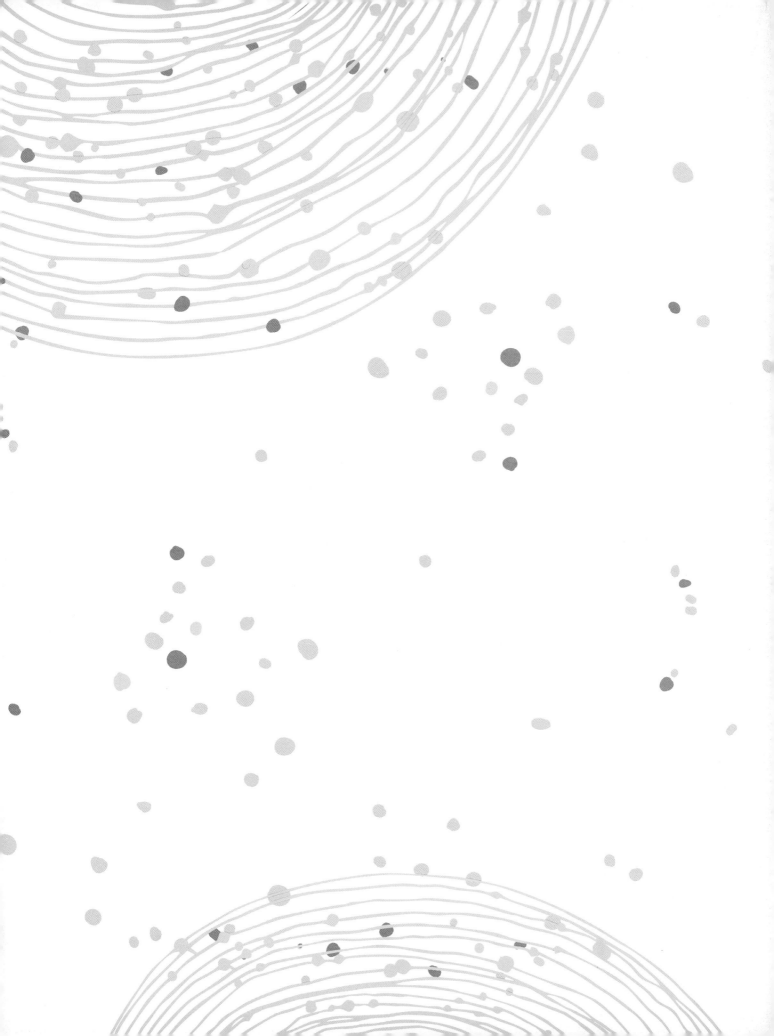

Quilting Bee

Latin Roots

Lesson Overview

ACTIVITY	ACTIVITY TITLE	TIME	ONLINE/OFFLINE
GET READY	Quilting Bee Unit Overview	**1** minute	🖥️
	Introduction to Latin Roots	**1** minute	🖥️
	Look Back at Latin Roots	**4** minutes	🖥️
LEARN AND **TRY IT**	Words That Come from Latin	**10** minutes	🖥️
	Practice Using Latin Roots	**10** minutes	🖥️
	Apply: Latin Roots **LEARNING COACH CHECK-IN**	**15** minutes	📄
	Go Write!	**15** minutes	📄
	Review Latin Roots	**15** minutes	🖥️
QUIZ	Latin Roots	**15** minutes	🖥️
WRAP-UP	More Language Arts Practice	**19** minutes	🖥️
	Go Read!	**15** minutes	🖥️ or 📄

Content Background

Students will learn about words that have the Latin roots *anima*, *hosp*, and *mar*. They will learn how knowing the meaning of a word's root can help them to determine the meaning of the word. They will also learn how context clues can help them determine the meaning of a word with a Latin root.

A root is a word part with a special meaning to which we can attach letters, prefixes, and suffixes to form a complete word. For example, *spec* is a root that means "to see." This is the root of the words *spectator* and *spectacles*. The meanings of these words are related to seeing because of the root *spec*.

It is important to know that a root cannot stand alone. It must have other letters or word parts attached to it to become a complete word. Thus, the root *hosp* is not a word on its own. But when other letters or word parts are attached, it is the foundation of words such as *hospitality* and *hospital*.

MATERIALS

Supplied
- *Summit English Language Arts 4 Activity Book*
- Apply: Latin Roots

Also Needed
- reading material for Go Read!

KEYWORDS

root – a word part with a special meaning to which prefixes and suffixes can be added; for example, *spec* is a root that means "see"

Advance Preparation

During the Go Read! activity, students will have the option of using the digital library. Allow extra time for students to make their reading selection, or have students make a selection before beginning the lesson.

Lesson Goals

- Use Latin roots to determine the meanings of words.
- Use context clues to determine the meanings of words.
- Read and write for pleasure.

GET READY

Quilting Bee Unit Overview

Students will read a summary of what they will learn in the Quilting Bee unit.

Introduction to Latin Roots

Students will get a glimpse of what they will learn about in the lesson. They will also read the lesson goals and keywords. Have students select each keyword and preview its definition.

Look Back at Latin Roots

Students will review the definition of a root. They will also review words they may have previously learned that are formed from common Latin roots.

LEARN AND TRY IT

LEARN   Words That Come from Latin

Students will learn the definitions of several words that have Latin roots. They will also learn how knowing the meaning of a root can help them define an unknown word and how context clues can help them define a word with a Latin root.

TRY IT   Practice Using Latin Roots

Students will analyze a passage and answer questions about words with Latin roots.

TRY IT   Apply: Latin Roots

Students will complete Apply: Latin Roots from *Summit English Language Arts 4 Activity Book*.

LEARNING COACH CHECK-IN   This activity page contains open-ended questions, so it's important that you review students' responses. Give students feedback, using the sample answers provided to guide you.

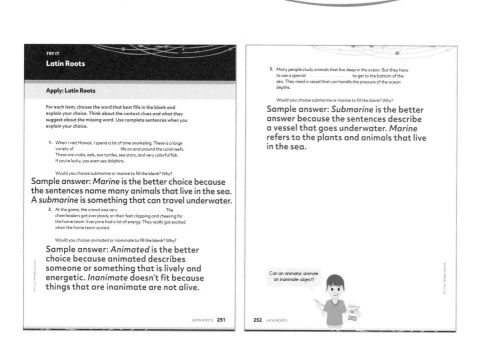

TRY IT   Go Write!

Students will write independently for pleasure. As they write, they should think about using words with Latin roots in their writing.

TRY IT   Review Latin Roots

Students will answer questions to review what they have learned about words with Latin roots.

QUIZ

Latin Roots

Students will complete the Latin Roots quiz.

WRAP-UP

More Language Arts Practice

Students will practice skills according to their individual needs.

Go Read!

Students will read for pleasure. They should choose a book or a magazine that interests them, or they may choose a selection from the digital library, linked in the online lesson.

Students should read for the entire time. Have students select something to read ahead of time to help them stay focused.

Quilting (A)

Lesson Overview

ACTIVITY	ACTIVITY TITLE	TIME	ONLINE/OFFLINE
GET READY	Introduction to Quilting (A)	**1** minute	🖥️
	Spelling List 15 Pretest **LEARNING COACH CHECK-IN**	**10** minutes	🖥️ and 📄
	Qulits in 60 seconds	**1** minute	🖥️
	Look Back at Fiction and Nonfiction	**4** minutes	🖥️
	Before You Read *The Quilting Bee*	**14** minutes	🖥️
READ	*The Quilting Bee*	**30** minutes	📄
	Check-In: *The Quilting Bee*	**5** minutes	🖥️
LEARN AND **TRY IT**	What Makes It Nonfiction?	**10** minutes	🖥️
	Features of Nonfiction	**10** minutes	🖥️
	Apply: Features of Nonfiction Text	**15** minutes	🖥️
	How Do You Do That? **LEARNING COACH CHECK-IN**	**10** minutes	📄
	Practice Words from *The Quilting Bee*	**8** minutes	🖥️
WRAP-UP	Question About *The Quilting Bee*	**2** minutes	🖥️

Content Background

Students will learn how to identify if a text is nonfiction. Nonfiction text is also called informational text because it provides information.

Nonfiction is about real things as opposed to fiction, which usually consists of made-up stories. Nonfiction text has many recognizable features. In *The Quilting Bee*, students will learn about captions, labels, and words printed in italics.

Informational text often has a specific text structure. The information in the text is organized or arranged in different ways. A common text structure, and one found in *The Quilting Bee*, is sequence. A text with a sequential structure tells the order in which things happen. This could include the steps for how to make something or for carrying out a procedure. For example, the beginning pages of *The Quilting Bee* explain the steps for making a quilt.

MATERIALS

Supplied
- *The Quilting Bee* by Gail Gibbons
- *Summit English Language Arts 4 Activity Book*
  - How Do You Do That?

The Quilting Bee Synopsis

The Quilting Bee by Gail Gibbons is a nonfiction picture book that introduces young readers to the world of quilting. It explains how to make a quilt and explores the history of quilting. The book describe the importance of quilting to pioneer families of the United States. The book also includes many traditional quilt patterns and describes what each pattern represents. The book connects the past to the present by describing quilting in modern times.

Lesson Goals

- Take a spelling pretest.
- Identify features of nonfiction text.
- Describe a sequence of steps.
- Identify sequential organization of a nonfiction text.
- Determine meanings of unfamiliar words in the reading.

KEYWORDS

informational text – text written to explain and give information on a topic

nonfiction – writing that presents facts and information in order to explain, describe, or persuade; for example, newspaper articles and biographies are nonfiction

sequence – the order in which things happen

structure – the way a piece of writing is organized

GET READY

Introduction to Quilting (A)

Students will get a glimpse of what they will learn about in the lesson. They will also read the lesson goals and keywords. Have students select each keyword and preview its definition.

Spelling List 15 Pretest

Students will take a spelling pretest.

LEARNING COACH CHECK-IN Have students turn to Spelling List 15 Pretest in *Summit English Language Arts 4 Activity Book* and open the online Spelling Pretest activity. Online, students will listen to the spelling word, type the word in the space indicated, and then check their answer. In the activity book, students will write the correct spelling of the word in the tables provided and indicate with a ✓ or an ✗ if they spelled the word correctly or incorrectly online. Students will repeat this process with the remaining words.

As needed, help students with the interaction between the online activity and the activity book page until they become comfortable with what they need to do. As students practice their spelling words throughout the workshop, they should pay special attention to words they spelled incorrectly on the pretest.

This is the complete list of words students will be tested on.

Words with /shul/ spelled *cial*	Words with /kw/ spelled *qu*	Root *cur*	Prefix *de–*	Heart Words
artificial	quarterly	concur	declaw	Arizona
official	quiet	current	deface	Mississippi
social	quotation	cursive	defrost	
commercial	squirrel	recur	dethrone	
facial	equal			
crucial	questions			
financial	squid			
	aqua			

NOTE   Have students keep their completed activity page in a safe place so they can refer to it later.

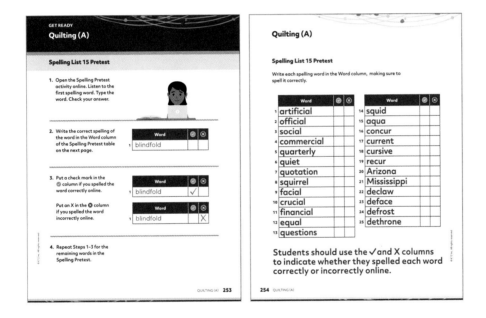

Before You Read *The Quilting Bee*

Students will be introduced to some key vocabulary words that they will encounter in the upcoming reading and answer questions to help them set a purpose for their reading.

READ

The Quilting Bee

Students will read *The Quilting Bee* by Gail Gibbons.

Check-In: *The Quilting Bee*

Students will answer questions to demonstrate their comprehension of *The Quilting Bee*.

LEARN AND TRY IT

LEARN   What Makes It Nonfiction?

Students will learn about features of nonfiction, or informational text, including how information in a nonfiction text can be organized.

TRY IT   Features of Nonfiction

Students will answer questions about nonfiction text features found in *The Quilting Bee*.

TRY IT   Apply: Features of Nonfiction Text

Students will apply to a new work what they have learned about nonfiction text features.

TRY IT   How Do You Do That?

Students will complete How Do You Do That? from *Summit English Language Arts 4 Activity Book*.

NOTE   Students will write the steps necessary to complete an action. They are offered a choice of two topics or they may choose their own. If students choose their own topic, they should check with you prior to writing to make sure their choice is a viable option for writing a sequence of steps.

LEARNING COACH CHECK-IN   This activity page contains open-ended questions, so it's important that you review students' responses. Give students feedback, using the sample answer provided to guide you.

TRY IT

Quilting (A)

How Do You Do That?

You have read the sequence of steps for making a quilt. Now, write the sequence of steps for making or doing something else. Use complete sentences in your response.

Choose between making toast or brushing your teeth. OR, choose your own action. Write the sequence of steps for completing one of these actions. You may write the steps in a paragraph, like in *The Quilting Bee*, or you may write numbered steps.

Sample answer: This is how you make toast. First, you have to take a slice of bread out of the bag. Then, put the slice of bread into a slot in the toaster. Push down on the lever so that the toaster will start cooking the bread. When the toast pops up, take it out of the toaster carefully so you don't burn yourself. Put the toast on a plate. Finally, spread some butter, jam, or whatever you like best on your toast. Then you get to eat it.

QUILTING (A) **255**

TRY IT Practice Words from *The Quilting Bee*

Students will answer questions to demonstrate their understanding of the vocabulary words from the reading.

Question About *The Quilting Bee*

Students will answer a question to show that they understand how text is organized in sequence.

Quilting (B)

Lesson Overview

ACTIVITY	ACTIVITY TITLE	TIME	ONLINE/OFFLINE
GET READY	Introduction to Quilting (B)	**1** minute	online
	Spelling List 15 Activity Bank	**9** minutes	offline
	Recall *The Quilting Bee*	**5** minutes	online
	Before You Read *Sweet Clara and the Freedom Quilt*	**10** minutes	online
READ	*Sweet Clara and the Freedom Quilt*	**30** minutes	offline
	Check-In: *Sweet Clara and the Freedom Quilt*	**5** minutes	online
LEARN AND **TRY IT**	Time Period Shapes the Story	**10** minutes	online
	Historical Era Influences the Story	**10** minutes	online
	Apply: Story Reflects Historical Time Period	**15** minutes	online
	Write a Summary of *Sweet Clara and the Freedom Quilt* **LEARNING COACH CHECK-IN**	**15** minutes	offline
	Practice Words from *Sweet Clara and the Freedom Quilt*	**8** minutes	online
WRAP-UP	Question About *Sweet Clara and the Freedom Quilt*	**2** minutes	online

Content Background

Students will read a work of historical fiction, *Sweet Clara and the Freedom Quilt* by Deborah Hopkinson. Works of historical fiction are made-up stories that include real events or people from history. Students will learn that *Sweet Clara and the Freedom Quilt* takes place during the historical time period of slavery. That is why the book is historical fiction.

This lesson will focus on how the institution of slavery influenced the author's choices of characters, setting, and events of the plot. For example, most of the characters in the book are enslaved people. The story takes place on a plantation and the events center on enslaved peoples' lives and actions. If this story had been set in another time or place in history, it would have been a very different story.

MATERIALS

Supplied
- *Sweet Clara and the Freedom Quilt* by Deborah Hopkinson
- *Summit English Language Arts 4 Activity Book*
  - Spelling List 15 Activity Bank
  - Write a Summary of *Sweet Clara and the Freedom Quilt*

Also Needed
- completed Spelling List 15 Pretest activity page from Quilting (A)

Advance Preparation

Gather students' completed Spelling List 15 Pretest activity page from Quilting (A). Students will refer to this page during Get Ready: Spelling List 15 Activity Bank.

KEYWORDS

dialect – a way of speaking that is particular to a certain group of people, place, or time

historical fiction – a story set in a historical time period that includes facts about real people, places, and events, but also contains fictional elements that add dramatic interest to the story

Sweet Clara and the Freedom Quilt Synopsis

Clara, a young enslaved girl, is separated from her mother and sent to a different plantation to be a field hand. At the new plantation Aunt Rachel, an enslaved woman, takes care of Clara. Working in the fields is back breaking, so Aunt Rachel teaches Clara to sew to get her out of the fields.

Clara becomes a seamstress in the Big House, where she learns that the Underground Railroad helps enslaved people reach freedom in the North. Clara collects scraps of cloth and snippets of information to create a quilt that will act as a map. Enslaved men and women can follow the map to the Ohio River, and then cross the river to connect with the Underground Railroad. When the quilt is complete, Clara escapes with another enslaved person, Young Jack. They leave the quilt behind so that other enslaved people can follow the map to freedom.

Lesson Goals

- Practice all spelling words.
- Explain how the historical context of a story influences the characters, setting, or plot.
- Identify traits of historical fiction, including words or phrases related to a historical time period.
- Determine meanings of unfamiliar words in the reading.

GET READY

Introduction to Quilting (B)

Students will get a glimpse of what they will learn about in the lesson. They will also read the lesson goals and keywords. Have students select each keyword and preview its definition.

Spelling List 15 Activity Bank

Students will practice all spelling words from the workshop by completing Spelling List 15 Activity Bank from *Summit English Language Arts 4 Activity Book*. Make sure students have their completed Spelling List 15 Pretest activity page from Quilting (A) to refer to during this activity.

Remind students to pay special attention to words they spelled incorrectly on the Spelling Pretest.

Recall *The Quilting Bee*

Students will answer questions to review the reading that they have already completed.

Before You Read *Sweet Clara and the Freedom Quilt*

Students will be introduced to some key vocabulary words that they will encounter in the upcoming reading and learn some important historical background related to the reading.

READ

Sweet Clara and the Freedom Quilt

Students will read *Sweet Clara and the Freedom Quilt* by Deborah Hopkinson.

Check-In: *Sweet Clara and the Freedom Quilt*

Students will answer several questions to demonstrate their comprehension of *Sweet Clara and the Freedom Quilt*.

LEARN   Time Period Shapes the Story

Students will learn how the time frame of a story can influence the characters, setting, and plot events.

TRY IT   Historical Era Influences the Story

Students will analyze passages and answer questions about how the historical era of slavery influences the story of *Sweet Clara and the Freedom Quilt*.

TRY IT   Apply: Story Reflects Historical Time Period

Students will apply to a new work what they've learned about how a story can reflect a historical time period.

TRY IT   Write a Summary of *Sweet Clara and the Freedom Quilt*

Students will complete Write a Summary of *Sweet Clara and the Freedom Quilt* from *Summit English Language Arts 4 Activity Book*.

LEARNING COACH CHECK-IN   This activity page contains an open-ended question, so it's important that you review students' responses. Give students feedback, using the sample summary provided to guide you.

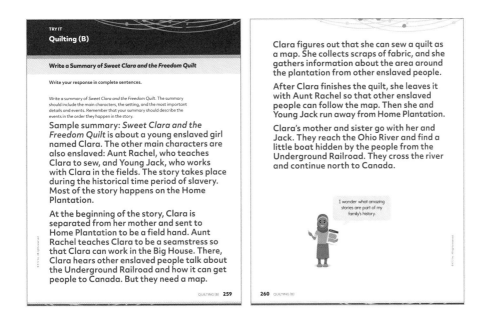

TRY IT   Practice Words from *Sweet Clara and the Freedom Quilt*

Students will answer questions to demonstrate their understanding of the vocabulary words from the reading.

Question About *Sweet Clara and the Freedom Quilt*

Students will answer a question to show that they understand how the historical time period of slavery influences the story.

Quilting (C)

Lesson Overview

ACTIVITY	ACTIVITY TITLE	TIME	ONLINE/OFFLINE
GET READY	Introduction to Quilting (C)	**1** minute	
	Spelling List 15 Practice	**9** minutes	
	Recall *Sweet Clara and the Freedom Quilt*	**5** minutes	
	Before You Read *The Keeping Quilt*	**10** minutes	
READ	*The Keeping Quilt*	**30** minutes	
	Check-In: *The Keeping Quilt*	**5** minutes	
LEARN AND **TRY IT**	Illustrations and Words Create Mood, Meaning	**10** minutes	
	Illustrations and Words Contribute to Story	**10** minutes	
	Apply: Author's Illustrations and Words	**15** minutes	
	Write About Illustrations **LEARNING COACH CHECK-IN**	**15** minutes	
	Practice Words from *The Keeping Quilt*	**8** minutes	
WRAP-UP	Question About *The Keeping Quilt*	**2** minutes	

Content Background

Students will read *The Keeping Quilt* by Patricia Polacco. They will learn how the illustrations in a story can create a certain mood or feeling. They will also learn how the illustrations and words of a story contribute to the story's meaning.

The illustrations in *The Keeping Quilt* are drawn in black and white. The only item in color is the quilt for which the story is named. The black-and-white illustrations often create a somber or serious mood. For example, an illustration early in the story shows a young Russian girl who has just immigrated to the United States. The expression on her face and the darkness of the black-and-white illustration convey a sad and serious mood.

The illustrations and words of the story contribute to the story's meaning. For example, the illustrations show the quilt being used for things such as a Sabbath tablecloth and a wedding canopy. This emphasizes the importance of traditions to the family in the story. Many words the author chose to use emphasize connections to her family's Russian and Jewish heritage.

MATERIALS

Supplied
- *The Keeping Quilt* by Patricia Polacco
- *Summit English Language Arts 4 Activity Book*
  - Write About Illustrations

KEYWORDS

mood – the emotions or feelings conveyed in a literary work

For example, the Russian word *babushka* is used to name a head scarf. Also, following Jewish tradition, each wedding ceremony in the story takes places under a *huppah*, a wedding canopy.

The Keeping Quilt Synopsis

When Anna and her family immigrate to the United States, they live in a crowded Jewish neighborhood in New York City. All Anna has from Russia is her dress and babushka, her head scarf. When Anna outgrows the dress, her mother uses it, the babushka, and old clothing from family members in Russia to make a quilt. The quilt acts as a connection to Anna's family members who remained in Russia. The quilt is passed down from generation to generation for almost a century. It is used for many things—a tablecloth, a wedding canopy, and a prop for imaginative play. It is also used to wrap each new child born into the family. At family gatherings, the story of the quilt is shared so all family members know their family's history and traditions.

Lesson Goals

- Practice all spelling words.
- Explain how words and illustrations create a mood and contribute to the meaning of a story.
- Determine meanings of unfamiliar words in the reading.

GET READY

Introduction to Quilting (C)
Students will get a glimpse of what they will learn about in the lesson. They will also read the lesson goals and keywords. Have students select each keyword and preview its definition.

Spelling List 15 Practice
Students will practice all spelling words from the workshop.

Recall *Sweet Clara and the Freedom Quilt*
Students will answer questions to review the reading that they have already completed.

Before You Read *The Keeping Quilt*

Students will be introduced to some key vocabulary words that they will encounter in the upcoming reading and learn some important cultural and historical background related to the reading.

READ

The Keeping Quilt

Students will read *The Keeping Quilt* by Patricia Polacco.

TIP   Remind students that the illustrations are very important to the story. Suggest that students spend time looking at the illustrations and thinking about how the illustrations make them feel.

Check-In: *The Keeping Quilt*

Students will answer questions to demonstrate their comprehension of *The Keeping Quilt*.

LEARN AND **TRY IT**

LEARN   Illustrations and Words Create Mood, Meaning

Students will learn how a story's illustrations can create a mood. They will also learn how the author's word choice and illustrations can contribute to the meaning of a story.

TRY IT   Illustrations and Words Contribute to Story

Students will analyze illustrations and answer questions about how the illustrations convey the mood of the story and contribute to the story's meaning. They will also analyze a passage and determine how the author's word choice conveys meaning.

TRY IT   Apply: Author's Illustrations and Words

Students will apply to a new work what they've learned about how the illustrations and words can convey a mood and contribute to the story's meaning.

TRY IT   Write About Illustrations

Students will complete Write About Illustrations from *Summit English Language Arts 4 Activity Book*.

LEARNING COACH CHECK-IN   This activity page contains open-ended questions, so it's important that you review students' responses. Give students feedback, using the sample answers provided to guide you.

TRY IT   Practice Words from *The Keeping Quilt*

Students will answer questions to demonstrate their understanding of the vocabulary words from the reading.

WRAP-UP

Question About *The Keeping Quilt*

Students will answer a question to show that they understand how the illustrations contribute to the meaning of the story.

Quilting (D)

Lesson Overview

ACTIVITY	ACTIVITY TITLE	TIME	ONLINE/OFFLINE
GET READY	Introduction to Quilting (D)	**1** minute	🖥️
	Spelling List 15 More Practice	**10** minutes	🖥️
	Recall *The Keeping Quilt*	**5** minutes	🖥️
LEARN AND **TRY IT**	Finding Specific Information	**13** minutes	🖥️
	Scan for Information	**10** minutes	🖥️
	Words and Illustrations Highlight Qualities	**13** minutes	🖥️
	Identify Qualities of Characters and Setting	**10** minutes	🖥️
	The Past Influences the Future	**13** minutes	🖥️
	Past Events Affect the Future	**10** minutes	🖥️
	Apply: Qualities of Characters and Setting	**15** minutes	🖥️
	Make a Family Tree **LEARNING COACH CHECK-IN**	**15** minutes	📄
WRAP-UP	Questions About *The Keeping Quilt*	**5** minutes	🖥️

Content Background

Students will complete activities for *The Keeping Quilt* by Patricia Polacco. They will learn about skimming and scanning to locate information in a text. They will use the skill of scanning to locate details that describe a character. They will learn how an author's choice of words and illustrations emphasize aspects of a character or a story's setting. They will also learn how events in a story influence events that occur later in the story.

Skimming and scanning are important skills for good readers. Skimming involves looking through a text quickly to get an overall idea of what it is about. For example, a reader may read just the first sentence of each paragraph in a text. This can give the reader an overview of the main idea of the text. Scanning a text involves looking through the text to find specific information. For example, a reader may need to answer the question about *The Keeping Quilt*, "How many months did it take for Anna to learn to speak

MATERIALS

Supplied
- *The Keeping Quilt* by Patricia Polacco
- *Summit English Language Arts 4 Activity Book*
  - Make a Family Tree

KEYWORDS

character – a person or animal in a story

setting – where and when a literary work takes place

English?" The student can scan for the target words *months*, *speak*, and *English*. This allows them to find the answer without having to spend time rereading the whole text.

The words an author uses emphasize aspects of a character or a setting. For example, in *The Keeping Quilt* the author uses the words *babushka* and *huppah*. These words emphasize Anna's Russian and Jewish heritage. Choices the author makes about illustrations do the same thing. For example, the illustration of all the people in Anna's New York City neighborhood emphasizes that the neighborhood is crowded. It also emphasizes that Anna's neighbors share her background.

In *The Keeping Quilt*, events that occur in earlier generations of the family affect later events. These later events would not have happened or would have happened differently had the earlier events not occurred. For example, when Great-Grandpa Sasha asks Anna to marry him, he gives her a handkerchief with a gold coin, a flower, and salt tied in it. These symbolize his hopes for his life with Anna. This becomes a family tradition that affects the weddings of future generations. These same items are placed in the bouquet of each bride.

Lesson Goals

- Practice all spelling words.
- Practice skimming and scanning to locate information.
- Explain how an author's word choice and illustrations emphasize aspects of a character and a story's setting.
- Explain how the past influences future events in a story.

.

GET READY

Introduction to Quilting (D)
Students will get a glimpse of what they will learn about in the lesson. They will also read the lesson goals and keywords. Have students select each keyword and preview its definition.

Spelling List 15 More Practice
Students will practice all spelling words from the workshop.

Recall *The Keeping Quilt*
Students will answer questions to review the reading that they have already completed.

LEARN   Finding Specific Information

Students will learn how the skills of skimming and scanning text can help them locate information.

TRY IT   Scan for Information

Students will scan passages to locate specific information.

TIP   Remind students that when they are scanning they do not have to read every single word. Instead, they need to focus on finding words in the text that match words in a question they must answer.

LEARN   Words and Illustrations Highlight Qualities

Students will learn how an author's choice of words and illustrations draw attention to qualities of characters and a story's setting.

TRY IT   Identify Qualities of Characters and Setting

Students will analyze passages and illustrations to determine how they emphasize qualities of a character or a story's setting.

LEARN   The Past Influences the Future

Students will learn how events in a story can influence events that happen later in the story.

TRY IT   Past Events Affect the Future

Students will analyze passages and answer questions about how past events are related to future events in a story.

TRY IT   Apply: Qualities of Characters and Setting

Students will apply to a new work what they've learned about how an author's choice of words and illustrations draw attention to qualities of characters and a story's setting.

TRY IT   Make a Family Tree

Students will complete Make a Family Tree from *Summit English Language Arts 4 Activity Book*. Students will first respond to a question about how the author of *The Keeping Quilt* is connected to past generations of her family. Then they will answer questions that will help them to fill in a family tree for the author's family.

LEARNING COACH CHECK-IN   This activity page contains open-ended questions, so it's important that you review students' responses. Give students feedback, using the sample answers provided to guide you.

Make a Family Tree

The Keeping Quilt is a story in which we can see how the past influences the future. The family's past generations are connected to future generations through the family's quilt and family traditions. Answer the questions, and then fill in a family tree that shows how the members of the author's family are related to each other.

1. How is the author of the story, Patricia Polacco, connected to past generations of her family and their traditions? Give at least two examples supported by details from the story.

Students' responses should include at least two of the following examples. One way Patricia is connected to her family is by using the quilt as a wedding huppah. Patricia's great grandmother, grandmother, and mother all used the quilt at their weddings. Then Patricia used it for her wedding. Another way Patricia is connected is with the things that she had in her wedding bouquet. When her great grandfather asked her great grandmother to marry him, he gave her a handkerchief containing a gold coin, a dried flower, and salt. After that, the women of each generation carried these same things in their bouquets. Patricia is also connected to her family by knowing

whose clothing was used for each part of the quilt. The story of the quilt and how it was made was passed down to family members over many, many years.

_____

_____

_____

_____

_____

2. Who does Anna marry?

Sasha

3. Who is Anna's daughter? Who does Anna's daughter marry?

Carle is Anna's daughter. She marries George.

4. Who is Carle's daughter?

Mary Ellen

5. Who is Mary Ellen's daughter?

Patricia

6. Who are Patricia's children?

Traci and Steven

7. Complete the family tree showing how each generation is connected to the other generations. Anna and Traci have been placed in the tree to help you get started.

```
Anna        Sasha
     Carle        George
           Mary Ellen
             Patricia
    Traci          Steven
```

WRAP-UP

Questions About *The Keeping Quilt*

Students will answer questions to show that they understand how to scan a text to locate specific information, how an illustration can emphasize aspects of a setting, and how past events influence later events in a story.

Quilting (E)

Lesson Overview

ACTIVITY	ACTIVITY TITLE	TIME	ONLINE/OFFLINE
GET READY	Introduction to Quilting (E)	**1** minute	🖥️
	Spelling List 15 Review Game	**10** minutes	📶
LEARN AND **TRY IT**	Compare and Contrast Works of Fiction	**17** minutes	🖥️
	Practice Comparing and Contrasting	**15** minutes	📶
	Compare and Contrast Fiction and Nonfiction	**17** minutes	🖥️
	Practice Comparing and Contrasting Fiction and Nonfiction	**15** minutes	📶
	Apply: Compare and Contrast Point of View	**23** minutes	🖥️
	What's the Same? What's Different? **LEARNING COACH CHECK-IN**	**20** minutes	📄
WRAP-UP	Question on Contrasting Text	**2** minutes	🖥️

Content Background

Students will compare and contrast works of fiction and nonfiction that share a similar topic. Students will first compare and contrast the two works of fiction, *Sweet Clara and the Freedom Quilt* and *The Keeping Quilt*. Then they will compare and contrast the works of fiction to the nonfiction book, *The Quilting Bee*.

Comparing texts means determining what is the same. Contrasting texts involves determining what is different. Comparing and contrasting texts is an important skill that builds a reader's critical thinking skills. It helps a reader remember important content. Focusing on important details when comparing and contrasting improves a reader's comprehension. Comparing and contrasting also provides a means for readers to organize their thinking when speaking or writing about text.

MATERIALS

Supplied
- *The Quilting Bee* by Gail Gibbons
- *Sweet Clara and the Freedom Quilt* by Deborah Hopkinson
- *The Keeping Quilt* by Patricia Polacco
- *Summit English Language Arts 4 Activity Book*
  - What's the Same? What's Different?

Lesson Goals

- Review all spelling words.

- Compare and contrast the point of view, illustrations, and language in two texts about similar topics.

- Compare and contrast ideas and information in fiction and nonfiction texts.

- Make connections between fiction and nonfiction texts with similar ideas.

- Determine the genre of a text.

GET READY

Introduction to Quilting (E)

Students will get a glimpse of what they will learn about in the lesson. They will also read the lesson goals and keywords. Have students select each keyword and preview its definition.

Spelling List 15 Review Game

Students will practice all spelling words from the workshop.

LEARN AND TRY IT

LEARN   Compare and Contrast Works of Fiction

Students will learn about the importance of comparing and contrasting. They will then learn what's the same and what's different in the point of view, illustrations, and author's word choice of two works of fiction that have a similar topic.

NOTE   While *The Keeping Quilt* is based on the experiences of the author's family, this book is classified as fiction.

TRY IT   Practice Comparing and Contrasting

Students will analyze passages and answer questions about comparing and contrasting two works of fiction.

LEARN   Compare and Contrast Fiction and Nonfiction

Students will learn about comparing and contrasting works of fiction and nonfiction that are similar in topic. They will learn how comparing and contrasting details can help readers determine if a text is fiction or nonfiction.

TRY IT Practice Comparing and Contrasting Fiction and Nonfiction

Students will analyze passages and answer questions that involve making connections, comparing and contrasting ideas, and determining the genre of a text.

TRY IT Apply: Compare and Contrast Point of View

Students will apply to new works what they've learned about comparing and contrasting the point of view from which texts are written.

TRY IT What's the Same? What's Different?

Students will complete What's the Same? What's Different? from *Summit English Language Arts 4 Activity Book*. Student will choose one of the fiction books, *Sweet Clara and the Freedom Quilt* or *The Keeping Quilt*, to compare with the nonfiction book *The Quilting Bee*.

LEARNING COACH CHECK-IN   This activity page contains open-ended questions, so it's important that you review students' responses. Give students feedback, using the sample answers provided to guide you.

TRY IT
Quilting (E)

What's the Same? What's Different?

Choose one of the fiction stories to compare with the nonfiction text *The Quilting Bee*. Then answer the questions to compare or contrast the fiction and nonfiction texts. Use complete sentences in your answers.

1. Circle the title of the book you will compare/contrast with *The Quilting Bee*.

    Sweet Clara and the Freedom Quilt   The Keeping Quilt

2. Is the point of view in the books the same or different? Explain.

Note: Sample answers include information from both fiction texts as a guide. Students' answers will need to include information from only one of the fiction stories.

The point of view is different. The narrator of *Sweet Clara* (or *The Keeping Quilt*) is a character in the story. The story is written in first-person point of view. The narrator of *The Quilting Bee* is outside of the story.

3. What is the same or different about the illustrations?

The illustrations in *The Quilting Bee* and *Sweet Clara* are the same because they are in color. The illustrations in *The Quilting Bee* and *The Keeping Quilt* are different. The illustrations in *The Quilting Bee* are completely in color. In *The Keeping Quilt*, they are mostly black and white with just a little bit of color.

QUILTING (E) **267**

---

4. What do the illustrations draw attention to in each story? Give an example from each book.

In *The Quilting Bee*, some of the drawings draw attention to how to make a quilt. For example, there's a drawing that shows the three layers of a quilt and what each layer is called. In *Sweet Clara*, the drawings show that the story is all about Clara making the quilt. In many of the drawings, she is either sewing or getting information to sew into the quilt. In *The Keeping Quilt*, the drawings focus on how the quilt is used for family traditions. For example, there are drawings that show family members getting married under the quilt.

5. Is the reason for making the quilt the same or different in each book? Explain the reason for making the quilt in each story.

The reason for making the quilt in each story is different. In *The Quilting Bee*, the quilt is made to be entered into a contest. In *Sweet Clara*, Clara makes the quilt into a map. Enslaved people can follow the map to escape from slavery. In *The Keeping Quilt*, the quilt is made to remember family that is far away.

268 QUILTING (E)

Question on Contrasting Text

Students will answer a question to show that they understand how to identify differences in texts.

Quilting Wrap-Up

Lesson Overview

ACTIVITY	ACTIVITY TITLE	TIME	ONLINE/OFFLINE
GET READY	Introduction to Quilting Wrap-Up	**1** minute	🖥️
TRY IT	Write About Quilts and History **LEARNING COACH CHECK-IN**	**25** minutes	📄
	Read and Record	**10** minutes	🖥️
	Review Quilting	**25** minutes	🖥️
QUIZ	Quilting	**30** minutes	🖥️
	Spelling List 15	**10** minutes	🖥️
WRAP-UP	More Language Arts Practice	**19** minutes	🖥️

Lesson Goals

- Write about connections to history in *The Quilting Bee*, *Sweet Clara and the Freedom Quilt*, and *The Keeping Quilt*.

- Review the stories *The Quilting Bee*, *Sweet Clara and the Freedom Quilt*, and *The Keeping Quilt*.

- Take a quiz on the reading skills and strategies learned in the Quilting workshop.

- Take a spelling quiz.

MATERIALS

Supplied
- *Summit English Language Arts 4 Activity Book*
  - Write About Quilts and History

GET READY

Introduction to Quilting Wrap-Up

Students will read the lesson goals.

TRY IT

Write About Quilts and History

Students will complete Write About Quilts and History from *Summit English Language Arts 4 Activity Book*.

This activity page contains open-ended questions, so it's important that you review students' responses. Give students feedback, using the sample answers provided to guide you.

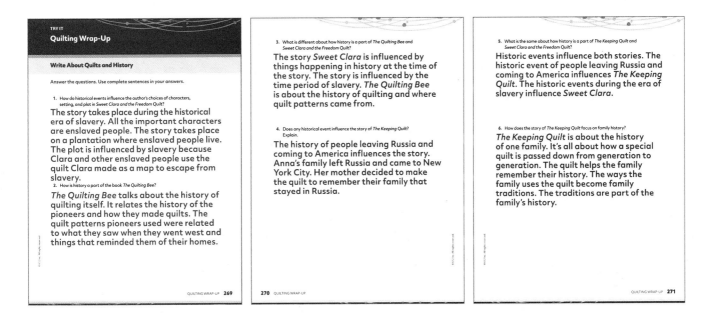

TRY IT
Quilting Wrap-Up

Write About Quilts and History

Answer the questions. Use complete sentences in your answers.

1. How do historical events influence the author's choices of characters, setting, and plot in *Sweet Clara and the Freedom Quilt*?

The story takes place during the historical era of slavery. All the important characters are enslaved people. The story takes place on a plantation where enslaved people live. The plot is influenced by slavery because Clara and other enslaved people use the quilt Clara made as a map to escape from slavery.

2. How is history a part of the book *The Quilting Bee*?

The Quilting Bee talks about the history of quilting itself. It relates the history of the pioneers and how they made quilts. The quilt patterns pioneers used were related to what they saw when they went west and things that reminded them of their homes.

QUILTING WRAP-UP **269**

3. What is different about how history is a part of *The Quilting Bee* and *Sweet Clara and the Freedom Quilt*?

The story *Sweet Clara* is influenced by things happening in history at the time of the story. The story is influenced by the time period of slavery. *The Quilting Bee* is about the history of quilting and where quilt patterns came from.

4. Does any historical event influence the story of *The Keeping Quilt*? Explain.

The history of people leaving Russia and coming to America influences the story. Anna's family left Russia and came to New York City. Her mother decided to make the quilt to remember their family that stayed in Russia.

270 QUILTING WRAP-UP

5. What is the same about how history is a part of *The Keeping Quilt* and *Sweet Clara and the Freedom Quilt*?

Historic events influence both stories. The historic event of people leaving Russia and coming to America influences *The Keeping Quilt*. The historic events during the era of slavery influence *Sweet Clara*.

6. How does the story of *The Keeping Quilt* focus on family history?

The Keeping Quilt is about the history of one family. It's all about how a special quilt is passed down from generation to generation. The quilt helps the family remember their history. The ways the family uses the quilt become family traditions. The traditions are part of the family's history.

QUILTING WRAP-UP **271**

Read and Record

Good readers read quickly, smoothly, and with expression. This is called *fluency*. Students will record themselves reading aloud. They will listen to their recording and think about how quick, smooth, and expressive they sound.

TIP Encourage students to rerecord as needed.

Review Quilting

Students will answer questions to review the reading skills and strategies learned in the Quilting workshop.

QUIZ

Quilting

Students will complete the Quilting quiz.

Spelling List 15

Students will complete the Spelling List 15 quiz.

WRAP-UP

More Language Arts Practice

Students will practice skills according to their individual needs.

Opinion Writing Skills (A)

Lesson Overview

ACTIVITY	ACTIVITY TITLE	TIME	ONLINE/OFFLINE
GET READY	Introduction to Opinion Writing Skills (A)	**2** minutes	🖥️
	Spelling List 16 Pretest **LEARNING COACH CHECK-IN**	**10** minutes	🖥️ and 📄
	Look Back at Prepositions	**5** minutes	🖥️
LEARN AND **TRY IT**	Use Prepositional Phrases	**15** minutes	🖥️
	Practice Using Prepositional Phrases	**10** minutes	🖥️
	Explore the Introduction and Organization of a Book Review	**15** minutes	🖥️
	Analyze the Introduction and Organization of a Book Review	**15** minutes	🖥️
	Begin Your Book Review **LEARNING COACH CHECK-IN**	**25** minutes	📄
WRAP-UP	Questions About Prepositional Phrases and Stating an Opinion	**3** minutes	🖥️
	Go Read!	**20** minutes	🖥️ or 📄

Content Background

Your opinion is what your think or feel about something. One way we can share our opinions with others is by writing about them. This type of writing is called *opinion writing*.

A *book review* is a form of opinion writing. Students will analyze how authors write book reviews and then apply those skills to their own opinion writing. In this lesson, students will focus on the introduction and organization of a book review.

Grammar, Usage, and Mechanics   Students will also begin learning about prepositional phrases. A prepositional phrase answers a question about something in a sentence such as "when?" or "where?" It begins with a preposition and ends with a noun or pronoun. The noun or pronoun is called the *object of the preposition*.

> **Example:** The scared dog ran **across the yard**.

MATERIALS

Supplied
- *Summit English Language Arts 4 Activity Book*
  - Spelling List 16 Pretest
  - Begin Your Book Review

Also Needed
- reading material for Go Read!

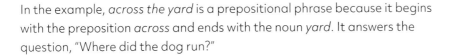

In the example, *across the yard* is a prepositional phrase because it begins with the preposition *across* and ends with the noun *yard*. It answers the question, "Where did the dog run?"

Advance Preparation

During the Go Read! activity, students will have the option of using the digital library. Allow extra time for students to make their reading selection, or have students make a selection before beginning the lesson.

Lesson Goals

- Take a spelling pretest.
- Form and use prepositional phrases.
- Explore how an author writes the introduction to and organizes a book review.
- Begin writing your own book review.
- Read for pleasure.

GET READY

Introduction to Opinion Writing Skills (A)

Students will get a glimpse of what they will learn about in the lesson. They will also read the lesson goals and keywords. Have students select each keyword and preview its definition.

Spelling List 16 Pretest

Students will take a spelling pretest.

LEARNING COACH CHECK-IN   Have students turn to Spelling List 16 Pretest in the activity book and open the online Spelling Pretest activity. Online, students will listen to the spelling word, type the word in the space indicated, and then check their answer. In the activity book, students will write the correct spelling of the word in the tables provided and indicate with a ✓ or an ✗ if they spelled the word correctly or incorrectly online. Students will repeat this process with the remaining words.

As needed, help students with the interaction between the online activity and the activity book page until they become comfortable with what they need to do. As students practice their spelling words throughout the workshop, they should pay special attention to the words they spelled incorrectly on the pretest.

This is the complete list of words students will be tested on.

Long e spelled *i*	Root *vent*	Heart Words
champion	avenue	Hawaii
curiosity	convention	Louisiana
librarian	vent	
machine	venture	
memorial		
trio		
piano		
patriot		
period		
radio		
trivia		

NOTE   Have students keep their completed activity page in a safe place so they can refer to it later.

GET READY
Opinion Writing Skills (A)

Spelling List 16 Pretest

1. Open the Spelling Pretest activity online. Listen to the first spelling word. Type the word. Check your answer.

2. Write the correct spelling of the word in the Word column of the Spelling Pretest table on the next page.

Word	✓	✗
1 blindfold		

3. Put a check mark in the ✓ column if you spelled the word correctly online.

Word	✓	✗
1 blindfold	✓	

Put an X in the ✗ column if you spelled the word incorrectly online.

Word	✓	✗
1 blindfold		X

4. Repeat Steps 1–3 for the remaining words in the Spelling Pretest.

OPINION WRITING SKILLS (A)   **273**

Opinion Writing Skills (A)

Spelling List 16 Pretest

Write each spelling word in the Word column, making sure to spell it correctly.

Word	✓	✗	Word	✓	✗
1 champion			10 radio		
2 curiosity			11 trivia		
3 librarian			12 avenue		
4 machine			13 convention		
5 memorial			14 vent		
6 trio			15 venture		
7 piano			16 Hawaii		
8 patriot			17 Louisiana		
9 period					

Students should use the ✓ and X columns to indicate whether they spelled each word correctly or incorrectly online.

274   OPINION WRITING SKILLS (A)

Look Back at Prepositions

Students will review the definition of a preposition and practice identifying prepositions.

LEARN   Use Prepositional Phrases

Students will learn how to form and use prepositional phrases.

TRY IT   Practice Using Prepositional Phrases

Students will answer questions about forming and using prepositional phrases. They will receive feedback on their answers.

LEARN   Explore the Introduction and Organization of a Book Review

Students will learn that a book review is a form of opinion writing and that a successful opinion piece always begins with a strong introduction. They will also briefly explore how this type of opinion writing is organized.

TRY IT   Analyze the Introduction and Organization of a Book Review

Students will answer questions about how a writer introduces and organizes a book review. They will receive feedback on their answers.

TRY IT   Begin Your Book Review

Students will complete Begin Your Book Review in *Summit English Language Arts 4 Activity Book*.

LEARNING COACH CHECK-IN   This activity page contains open-ended questions, so it's important that you review students' responses. Give students feedback, using the sample answers provided to guide you.

TRY IT
Opinion Writing Skills (A)

Begin Your Book Review

Use the prompt to answer the questions.
Sample answers are shown.
Prompt: Write a review of a book that you read recently.

1. Think about the piece you are reviewing.

 a. What is the title of the piece?
Samurai: A Feral Kitten's Journey to Find a Home
 b. Who is the author?
Rosemary Wood

 c. What is the piece about? Summarize the piece in 1 or 2 sentences.
This book is a true story about a wild kitten that was found and eventually adopted by Daniel and his wife Rosie.

2. Think about your opinion. Use complete sentences when answering the questions.

 a. What is your opinion of the piece you are reviewing?
This is an outstanding book!

OPINION WRITING SKILLS (A)   **275**

---

 b. How does the piece make you feel?
This book makes me feel happy.

 c. Why do you think and feel this way about the book?

See below.

3. Write an introduction to your book review. Use your answers to Questions 1 and 2 to help.

I think *Samurai: A Feral Kitten's Journey to Find a Home* by Rosemary Wood is an unusual and outstanding book. It tells the true story of a wild kitten that is found by a man while he's taking a walk in his neighborhood. The man and his wife know the kitten is hungry and needs a safe place to live. They lovingly and patiently do everything they can think of to get the kitten to come live with them. The realistic paintings that are on every page of the book really make the story come to life. I believe anyone who owns a cat or cares about animals would love this book.

276 OPINION WRITING SKILLS (A)

---

4. Think about how you would organize the remainder of your review. Then complete the outline. Write only one sentence in each box.

Reason 1:
This book tells a true story, which makes it hard to put down.

Reason 2:
The people who try to help the kitten are kind and dedicated to saving its life.

Reason 3:
The pictures that are on every page of the book really help the reader understand what the kitten experiences every day.

Conclusion:
I can't imagine anyone not enjoying this book.

OPINION WRITING SKILLS (A)   **277**

Additional answers

2c. The book is outstanding because it is about an unusual and interesting subject. It makes me feel happy because Daniel and Rosie are so kind to the poor kitten and never give up trying to take care of it.

NOTE Have students keep their completed activity page in a safe place so they can refer to it later.

WRAP-UP

Questions About Prepositional Phrases and Stating an Opinion

Students will answer questions to show that they understand how to use prepositional phrases and the elements of an introduction to a book review.

Go Read!

Students will read for pleasure. They should choose a book or a magazine that interests them, or they may choose a selection from the digital library, linked in the online lesson.

Students should read for the entire time. Have students select something to read ahead of time to help them stay focused.

Opinion Writing Skills (B)

Lesson Overview

ACTIVITY	ACTIVITY TITLE	TIME	ONLINE/OFFLINE
GET READY	Introduction to Opinion Writing Skills (B)	**2** minute	🖥️
	Spelling List 16 Activity Bank	**10** minutes	📄
LEARN AND **TRY IT**	Frequently Confused Words	**10** minutes	🖥️
	Use Frequently Confused Words	**10** minutes	🖥️
	Explore Facts and Details in a Book Review	**15** minutes	🖥️
	Analyze Facts and Details in a Book Review	**15** minutes	🖥️
	Support Reasons in Your Book Review **LEARNING COACH CHECK-IN**	**35** minutes	📄
WRAP-UP	Questions About Frequently Confused Words and Support	**3** minutes	🖥️
	Go Read!	**20** minutes	🖥️ or 📄

Content Background

Students will continue analyzing how authors write book reviews, which are a form of opinion writing, and then apply those skills to their own opinion writing. In this lesson, students will focus on supporting reasons for their opinions with facts.

Grammar, Usage, and Mechanics   Students will also explore frequently confused words, or *homophones*, which are words that sound alike but have different spellings and meanings.

Example: *there*, *their*, and *they're*

> **There** refers to a place: Park the car over **there**.

> **Their** is a possessive pronoun: I left my phone at **their** house.

> **They're** is a contraction of "they are": I think **they're** going to be late.

MATERIALS

Supplied
- *Summit English Language Arts 4 Activity Book*
  - Spelling List 16 Activity Bank
  - Support Reasons in Your Book Review

Also Needed
- completed Spelling List 16 Pretest activity page from Opinion Writing Skills (A)
- completed Begin Your Book Review activity page from Opinion Writing Skills (A)
- reading material for Go Read!

Advance Preparation

Gather students' completed Spelling List 16 Pretest activity page from Opinion Writing Skills (A). Students will refer to this page during Get Ready: Spelling List 16 Activity Bank.

Gather students' completed Begin Your Book Review activity page from Opinion Writing Skills (A). Students will refer to this page during Try It: Support Reasons in Your Book Review.

During the Go Read! activity, students will have the option of using the digital library. Allow extra time for students to make their reading selection, or have students make a selection before beginning the lesson.

Lesson Goals

- Practice all spelling words offline.
- Use frequently confused words correctly.
- Explore how an author supports reasons for opinions with facts and details in a book review.
- Support reasons with facts and details in your book review.
- Read for pleasure.

GET READY

Introduction to Opinion Writing Skills (B)

Students will get a glimpse of what they will learn about in the lesson. They will also read the lesson goals and keywords. Have students select each keyword and preview its definition.

Spelling List 16 Activity Bank

Students will practice all spelling words from the workshop by completing Spelling List 16 Activity Bank from *Summit English Language Arts 4 Activity Book*. Make sure students have their completed Spelling List 16 Pretest activity page from Opinion Writing Skills (A) to refer to during this activity.

Remind students to pay special attention to words they spelled incorrectly on the Spelling Pretest.

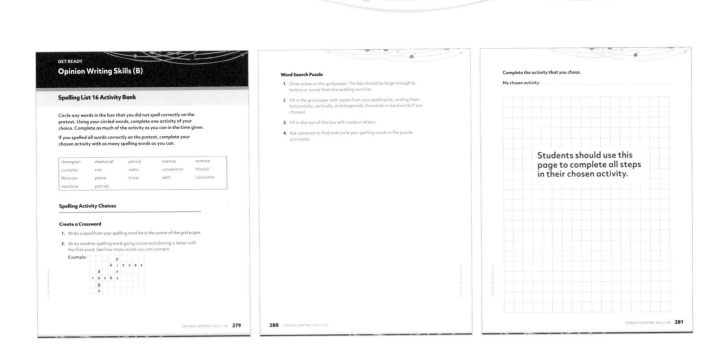

LEARN   Frequently Confused Words

Students will learn how to recognize and use frequently confused words.

TRY IT   Use Frequently Confused Words

Students will answer questions about frequently confused words. They will receive feedback on their answers.

LEARN   Explore Facts and Details in a Book Review

Students will learn how a writer supports opinions and reasons with facts and details in a book review.

TIP   A fact is a true statement that can be proven. A detail may or may not be a fact. It may be an example, definition, or other piece of information that provides clarity.

Fact: The main character in the book is nine years old, just like me.

Detail: I can relate to the way he spends hours riding his bike and climbing trees.

TRY IT   Analyze Facts and Details in a Book Review

Students will answer questions about how writers support reasons for their opinions with facts and details in a book review. They will receive feedback on their answers.

TRY IT   Support Reasons in Your Book Review

Students will complete Support Reasons in Your Book Review in *Summit English Language Arts 4 Activity Book*. Make sure students have their completed Begin Your Book Review activity page from Opinion Writing Skills (A) to refer to during this activity.

This activity page contains open-ended questions, so it's important that you review students' responses. Give students feedback, using the sample answers provided to guide you.

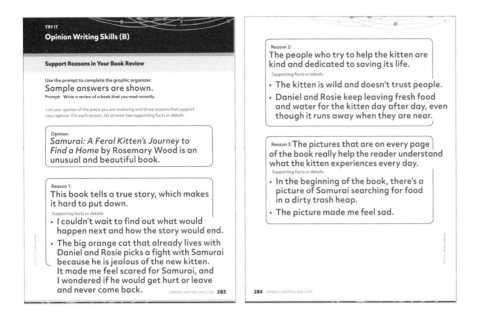

NOTE Have students keep their completed activity page in a safe place so they can refer to it later.

WRAP-UP

Questions About Frequently Confused Words and Support

Students will answer questions to show that they understand how to use frequently confused words correctly and how to support reasons in opinion writing.

Go Read!

Students will read for pleasure. They should choose a book or a magazine that interests them, or they may choose a selection from the digital library, linked in the online lesson.

Students should read for the entire time. Have students select something to read ahead of time to help them stay focused.

Opinion Writing Skills (C)

Lesson Overview

ACTIVITY	ACTIVITY TITLE	TIME	ONLINE/OFFLINE
GET READY	Introduction to Opinion Writing Skills (C)	**2** minute	
	Spelling List 16 Review Game	**10** minutes	
LEARN AND **TRY IT**	Use Helping Verbs	**10** minutes	
	Practice Using Helping Verbs	**10** minutes	
	Explore Linking and Conclusions in a Book Review	**15** minutes	
	Analyze Linking and Conclusions in a Book Review	**15** minutes	
	Conclude Your Book Review **LEARNING COACH CHECK-IN**	**35** minutes	
WRAP-UP	Questions About Helping Verbs and Linking Ideas	**3** minutes	
	Go Read!	**20** minutes	

Content Background

Students will continue analyzing how authors write book reviews, which are a form of opinion writing, and then apply those skills to their own opinion writing. In this lesson, students will focus on using transitions to connect ideas in their opinion piece and on writing a conclusion.

Grammar, Usage, and Mechanics Students will also explore helping verbs. A helping verb is a word that works with the main verb to show action or being. In the examples, *will*, *must*, and *can* are helping verbs. Notice how the helping verbs change the meaning of the main verb *dance*.

Examples: Benito **will** dance.

Benito **must** dance.

Benito **can** dance.

MATERIALS

Supplied
- *Summit English Language Arts 4 Activity Book*
  - Conclude Your Book Review

Also Needed
- completed Begin Your Book Review activity page from Opinion Writing Skills (A)
- completed Support Reasons in Your Book Review activity page from Opinion Writing Skills (B)
- reading material for Go Read!

Advance Preparation

Gather students' completed Begin Your Book Review activity page from Opinion Writing Skills (A) and Support Reasons in Your Book Review activity page from Opinion Writing Skills (B). Students will refer to these pages during Try It: Conclude Your Book Review.

During the Go Read! activity, students will have the option of using the digital library. Allow extra time for students to make their reading selection, or have students make a selection before beginning the lesson.

Lesson Goals

- Practice all spelling words online.
- Use helping verbs.
- Explore and analyze how an author uses transitions and writes a conclusion in a book review.
- Add transitions to your book review, and write a conclusion.
- Read for pleasure.

KEYWORDS

book review – a piece of writing that gives an opinion about a book and tells about it

conclusion – the final paragraph of a written work

helping verb – a word that works with the main verb to show action; for example, *has, have, will, do, did, can*

transition – a word, phrase, or clause that connects ideas

GET READY

Introduction to Opinion Writing Skills (C)

Students will get a glimpse of what they will learn about in the lesson. They will also read the lesson goals and keywords. Have students select each keyword and preview its definition.

Spelling List 16 Review Game

Students will practice all spelling words from the workshop.

LEARN AND TRY IT

Use Helping Verbs

Students will learn how to use helping verbs. They will learn that helping verbs change the meaning of main verbs to convey various conditions.

NOTE At this level, students are not expected to name all the various conditions that helping verbs create. For example, students do not need to know that the helping verb *could* is often used to express the conditional mood, but they should be able to describe generally that a helping verb changes the meaning of the main verb in a sentence.

TRY IT   Practice Using Helping Verbs

Students will answer questions about helping verbs. They will receive feedback on their answers.

LEARN   Explore Linking and Conclusions in a Book Review

Students will learn how a writer uses transitions to connect ideas and how to write a conclusion in a book review.

TIP   Transitions serve many purposes in opinion writing.

Purpose	Examples
Introduce opinion	*in my opinion*
Show order or importance of reasons	*first, finally*
Call out facts and details	*for example, in fact*
Conclude the piece	*in conclusion, to sum it up*

TRY IT   Analyze Linking and Conclusions in a Book Review

Students will answer questions about how writers use transitions to connect ideas and how to write a conclusion in a book review. They will receive feedback on their answers.

TRY IT   Conclude Your Book Review

Students will complete Conclude Your Book Review in *Summit English Language Arts 4 Activity Book*. Make sure students have their completed Begin Your Book Review activity page from Opinion Writing Skills (A) and Support Reasons in Your Book Review activity page from Opinion Writing Skills (B) to refer to during this activity.

LEARNING COACH CHECK-IN   This activity page contains open-ended questions, so it's important that you review students' responses. Give students feedback, using the sample answers provided to guide you.

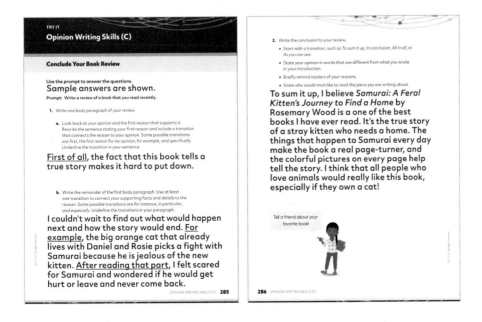

Questions About Helping Verbs and Linking Ideas

Students will answer questions to show that they understand how to use helping verbs and connect ideas with transitions in opinion writing.

Go Read!

Students will read for pleasure. They should choose a book or a magazine that interests them, or they may choose a selection from the digital library, linked in the online lesson.

Students should read for the entire time. Have students select something to read ahead of time to help them stay focused.

Opinion Writing Skills Wrap-Up

Lesson Overview

ACTIVITY	ACTIVITY TITLE	TIME	ONLINE/OFFLINE
GET READY	Introduction to Opinion Writing Skills Wrap-Up	**1** minute	🖥️
TRY IT	Use Opinion Writing Skills **LEARNING COACH CHECK-IN**	**35** minutes	📄
	Review Grammar Skills	**20** minutes	🖥️
QUIZ	Grammar and Opinion Writing Skills	**30** minutes	🖥️
	Spelling List 16	**10** minutes	🖥️
WRAP-UP	More Language Arts Practice	**9** minutes	🖥️
	Go Read!	**15** minutes	🖥️ or 📄

Lesson Goals

- Review prepositional phrases, frequently confused words, helping verbs, and opinion writing skills.

- Take a quiz on prepositional phrases, frequently confused words, helping verbs, and opinion writing skills.

- Take a spelling quiz.

MATERIALS

Supplied
- *Summit English Language Arts 4 Activity Book*
  - Use Opinion Writing Skills

GET READY

Introduction to Opinion Writing Skills Wrap-Up

Students will read the lesson goals.

TRY IT

Use Opinion Writing Skills

Students will complete Use Opinion Writing Skills in *Summit English Language Arts 4 Activity Book* to review the writing objectives that will be assessed on the quiz.

LEARNING COACH CHECK-IN This activity page contains open-ended questions, so it's important that you review students' responses. Give students feedback, using the sample answers provided to guide you.

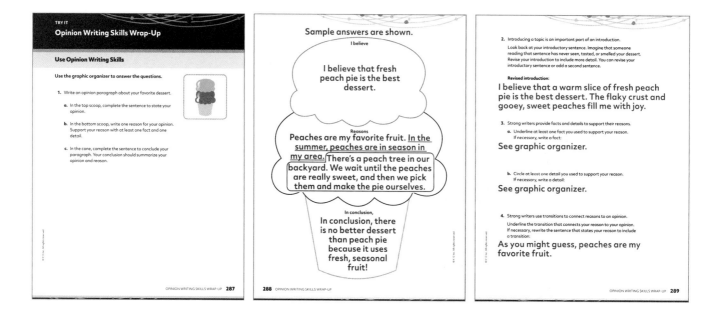

Review Grammar Skills

Students will answer questions to show that they understand how to use prepositional phrases, frequently confused words, and helping verbs.

QUIZ

Grammar and Opinion Writing Skills

Students will complete the Grammar and Opinion Writing Skills quiz.

Spelling List 16

Students will complete the Spelling List 16 quiz.

WRAP-UP

More Language Arts Practice

Students will practice skills according to their individual needs.

Go Read!

Students will read for pleasure. They should choose a book or a magazine that interests them, or they may choose a selection from the digital library, linked in the online lesson.

Students should read for the entire time. Have students select something to read ahead of time to help them stay focused.

Big Ideas: Mini-Project

Lesson Overview

Big Ideas lessons provide students the opportunity to further apply the knowledge and skills acquired throughout the unit workshops. Each Big Ideas lesson consists of three parts:

1. **Cumulative Review:** Students keep their skills fresh by reviewing prior content.

2. **Preview:** Students practice answering the types of questions they will commonly find on standardized tests.

3. **Synthesis:** Students complete an assignment that allows them to interweave and apply what they've learned. These synthesis assignments will vary throughout the course.

In the Synthesis portion of this Big Ideas lesson, students will complete a small, creative project designed to tie together concepts and skills that students have encountered across workshops. These small projects are designed to deepen students' understanding of those concepts and skills.

LEARNING COACH CHECK-IN Make sure students complete, review, and submit the assignment to their teacher.

All materials needed for this lesson are linked online and not provided in the Activity Book.

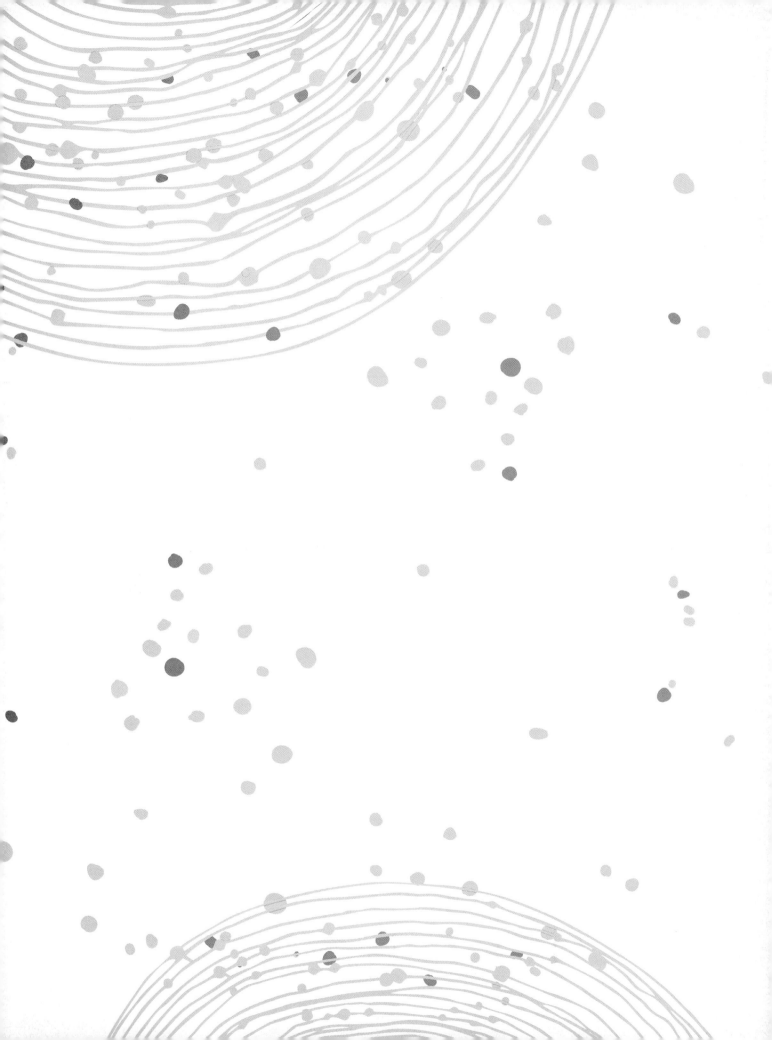

Choice Reading Project

Choice Reading Project

Workshop Overview

This unique reading workshop is designed to build students' comprehension and critical-thinking skills as they read a work or works of their choice and complete a related project. Research indicates that opportunities for choice enhance student performance and motivate readers.

Students will select a project and corresponding book or books from a bank of options. All but one of the projects will require you to acquire a book on your own. The remaining project option will use a book or books available in the digital library linked in the online lesson. Discuss the choices with students to help ensure that they select an option that interests them. To help students make a choice, the online lessons include synopses of the books and descriptions of the related projects.

Other than the standard Spelling activities embedded throughout the workshop (and described on the following pages), students will encounter different lesson content depending on which project they choose. Therefore, this Lesson Guide does not contain detailed activity descriptions for each lesson of this workshop. Regardless of which project students choose, they will complete project work that includes reading, research, writing, and creation of a final product, which they will submit to their teacher.

All materials needed for the choice reading project are linked online and not provided in the Activity Book.

Advance Preparation

If students select a project that requires acquiring a book on your own, you will need to acquire the book before students begin the workshop.

MATERIALS

Supplied
- project packet (printout)

Also Needed
- students' chosen book or books

Choice Reading Project: Spelling

ACTIVITY	LESSON	ACTIVITY TITLE	TIME	ONLINE/OFFLINE
GET READY	1	Spelling List 17 Pretest **LEARNING COACH CHECK-IN**	**10** minutes	and
	2	Spelling List 17 Activity Bank	**10** minutes	
	3	Spelling List 17 Practice	**10** minutes	
	4	Spelling List 17 Review Game	**10** minutes	
QUIZ	5	Spelling List 17	**10** minutes	
GET READY	6	Spelling List 18 Pretest **LEARNING COACH CHECK-IN**	**10** minutes	and
	7	Spelling List 18 Activity Bank	**10** minutes	
	8	Spelling List 18 Practice	**10** minutes	
	9	Spelling List 18 Review Game	**10** minutes	
QUIZ	10	Spelling List 18	**10** minutes	

GET READY

Lesson 1   Spelling List 17 Pretest

Students will take a spelling pretest.

LEARNING COACH CHECK-IN   Have students turn to Spelling List 17 Pretest in *Summit English Language Arts 4 Activity Book* and open the online Spelling Pretest activity. Online, students will listen to the spelling word, type the word in the space indicated, and then check their answer. In the activity book, students will write the correct spelling of the word in the tables provided and indicate with a ✓ or an ✗ if they spelled the word correctly or incorrectly online. Students will repeat this process with the remaining words.

As needed, help students with the interaction between the online activity and the activity book page until they become comfortable with what they need to do. As students practice their spelling words throughout Lessons 2–4 of the workshop, they should pay special attention to words they spelled incorrectly on the pretest.

MATERIALS

Supplied
- *Summit English Language Arts 4 Activity Book*
  - Spelling List 17 Pretest
  - Spelling List 17 Activity Bank
  - Spelling List 18 Pretest
  - Spelling List 18 Activity Bank

This is the complete list of words students will be tested on in the Lesson 5 quiz.

Soft c	Root *script*	Suffix *–able*	Heart Words
absence	description	acceptable	Indiana
ancestor	manuscript	honorable	Missouri
citizen	prescription	predictable	
conceited	script	respectable	
fragrance	transcript		
recent			
rejoice			
scene			
science			
twice			

NOTE Have students keep their completed activity page in a safe place so they can refer to it later.

Choice Reading Project (A)

GET READY

Spelling List 17 Pretest

1. Open the Spelling Pretest activity online. Listen to the first spelling word. Type the word. Check your answer.

2. Write the correct spelling of the word in the Word column of the Spelling Pretest table on the next page.

Word	✓	✗
1 blindfold		

3. Put a check mark in the ✓ column if you spelled the word correctly online.

Word	✓	✗
1 blindfold	✓	

Put an X in the ✗ column if you spelled the word incorrectly online.

Word	✓	✗
1 blindfold		X

4. Repeat Steps 1–3 for the remaining words in the Spelling Pretest.

CHOICE READING PROJECT (A) **291**

Choice Reading Project (A)

Spelling List 17 Pretest

Write each spelling word in the Word column, making sure to spell it correctly.

Word	✓	✗	Word	✓	✗
1 absence			12 manuscript		
2 ancestor			13 prescription		
3 citizen			14 script		
4 conceited			15 transcript		
5 fragrance			16 Indiana		
6 recent			17 Missouri		
7 rejoice			18 acceptable		
8 scene			19 honorable		
9 science			20 predictable		
10 twice			21 respectable		
11 description					

Students should use the ✓ and X columns to indicate whether they spelled each word correctly or incorrectly online.

292 CHOICE READING PROJECT (A)

Lesson 2   Spelling List 17 Activity Bank

Students will practice all spelling words from Spelling List 17 by completing Spelling List 17 Activity Bank from *Summit English Language Arts 4 Activity Book*. Make sure students have their completed Spelling List 17 Pretest activity page to refer to during this activity.

Remind students to pay special attention to words they spelled incorrectly on the Spelling Pretest.

GET READY

Choice Reading Project (B)

Spelling List 17 Activity Bank

Circle any words in the box that you did not spell correctly on the pretest. Using your circled words, complete one activity of your choice. Complete as much of the activity as you can in the time given.

If you spelled all words correctly on the pretest, complete your chosen activity with as many spelling words as you can.

absence	recent	twice	script	acceptable
ancestor	rejoice	description	transcript	honorable
citizen	scene	manuscript	Indiana	predictable
conceited	science	prescription	Missouri	respectable
fragrance				

Spelling Activity Choices

Vowel-Free Words

1. In the left column, write only the consonants in each word and put a dot where each vowel should be.
2. Spell each word out loud, stating which vowels should be in the places you wrote dots.
3. In the right column, rewrite the entire spelling word.
4. Correct any spelling errors.

CHOICE READING PROJECT (B) 293

Alphabetizing

1. In the left column, write your words from the spelling word list in alphabetical order.
2. Correct any spelling errors.

Parts of Speech

1. In the left column, write the words from your spelling list that are nouns.
2. In the right column, write all the other words from your spelling list and label each word's part of speech.
3. Correct any spelling errors.

Uppercase and Lowercase

1. In the left column, write each of your words in all capital (uppercase) letters.
2. In the right column, write each of your words in all lowercase letters.
3. Correct any spelling errors.

294 CHOICE READING PROJECT (B)

Complete the activity that you chose.

My chosen activity:

1.
2.
3.
4.
5.
6.
7.
8.
9.
10.
11.
12.
13.
14.
15.
16.
17.
18.
19.
20.
21.
22.
23.
24.
25.

Students should use this page to complete all steps in their chosen activity.

CHOICE READING PROJECT (B) 295

Lesson 3   Spelling List 17 Practice

Students will practice all spelling words from Spelling List 17.

Lesson 4   Spelling List 17 Review Game

Students will practice all spelling words from Spelling List 17.

QUIZ

Lesson 5   Spelling List 17

Students will complete the Spelling List 17 quiz.

GET READY

Lesson 6   Spelling List 18 Pretest

Students will take a spelling pretest.

LEARNING COACH CHECK-IN   Have students turn to Spelling List 18 Pretest in *Summit English Language Arts 4 Activity Book* and open the online Spelling Pretest activity. Online, students will listen to the spelling word, type the word in the space indicated, and then check their answer. In the activity book, students will write the correct spelling of the word in the tables provided and indicate with a ✓ or an ✗ if they spelled the word correctly or incorrectly online. Students will repeat this process with the remaining words.

As needed, help students with the interaction between the online activity and the activity book page until they become comfortable with what they need to do. As students practice their spelling words throughout Lessons 7–9 of the workshop, they should pay special attention to words they spelled incorrectly on the pretest.

This is the complete list of words students will be tested on in the Lesson 10 quiz.

Adding Suffixes to Silent e	Root *cap*	Suffix *–tion*	Heart Words
announcement	capsule	humiliation	North Carolina
balanced	captivate	location	West Virginia
immediately	captive	occupation	
likely	capture	starvation	
motivated	capacity		
probing			
relieved			
sharing			
sincerely			
tasteful			

NOTE   Have students keep their completed activity page in a safe place so they can refer to it later.

GET READY
Choice Reading Project (F)

Spelling List 18 Pretest

1. Open the Spelling Pretest activity online. Listen to the first spelling word. Type the word. Check your answer.

2. Write the correct spelling of the word in the Word column of the Spelling Pretest table on the next page.

Word	✓	✗
1 blindfold		

3. Put a check mark in the ✓ column if you spelled the word correctly online.

Word	✓	✗
1 blindfold	✓	

Put an X in the ✗ column if you spelled the word incorrectly online.

Word	✓	✗
1 blindfold		✗

4. Repeat Steps 1–3 for the remaining words in the Spelling Pretest.

CHOICE READING PROJECT (F)   **297**

Choice Reading Project (F)

Spelling List 18 Pretest

Write each spelling word in the Word column, making sure to spell it correctly.

Word	✓	✗	Word	✓	✗
1 announcement			12 captivate		
2 balanced			13 captive		
3 immediately			14 capture		
4 likely			15 capacity		
5 motivated			16 North Carolina		
6 probing			17 West Virginia		
7 relieved			18 humiliation		
8 sharing			19 location		
9 sincerely			20 occupation		
10 tasteful			21 starvation		
11 capsule					

Students should use the ✓ and X columns to indicate whether they spelled each word correctly or incorrectly online.

298   CHOICE READING PROJECT (F)

Lesson 7   Spelling List 18 Activity Bank

Students will practice all spelling words from Spelling List 18 by completing Spelling List 18 Activity Bank from *Summit English Language Arts 4 Activity Book*. Make sure students have their completed Spelling List 18 Pretest activity page to refer to during this activity.

Remind students to pay special attention to words they spelled incorrectly on the Spelling Pretest.

GET READY
Choice Reading Project (G)

Spelling List 18 Activity Bank

Circle any words in the box that you did not spell correctly on the pretest. Using your circled words, complete one activity of your choice. Complete as much of the activity as you can in the time given.

If you spelled all words correctly on the pretest, complete your chosen activity with as many spelling words as you can.

announcement	probing	tasteful	capture	humiliation
balanced	relieved	capsule	capacity	location
immediately	sharing	captivate	North Carolina	occupation
likely	sincerely	captive	West Virginia	starvation
motivated				

Spelling Activity Choices

Hidden Words

1. Draw a picture and "hide" as many words from the Spelling Word List as they can inside the picture.
2. See if others can find the words within the picture.

Triangle Spelling
Write each word in a triangle.

Ghost Words

1. Use a white crayon to write each spelling word.
2. Go over the white crayon writing with a colored marker.

CHOICE READING PROJECT (G)   **299**

300   CHOICE READING PROJECT (G)

Complete the activity that you chose.

My chosen activity:

Students should use this page to complete all steps in their chosen activity.

Lesson 8   Spelling List 18 Practice

Students will practice all spelling words from Spelling List 18.

Lesson 9   Spelling List 18 Review Game

Students will practice all spelling words from Spelling List 18.

QUIZ

Lesson 10   Spelling List 18

Students will complete the Spelling List 18 quiz.

Latin Affixes

Lesson Overview

ACTIVITY	ACTIVITY TITLE	TIME	ONLINE/OFFLINE
GET READY	Introduction to Latin Affixes	**1** minute	
	Look Back at Affixes	**4** minutes	
LEARN AND **TRY IT**	Words with Latin Affixes	**10** minutes	
	Define Words with Latin Affixes	**10** minutes	
	Apply: Latin Affixes **LEARNING COACH CHECK·IN**	**15** minutes	
	Go Write!	**15** minutes	
	Review Latin Affixes	**15** minutes	
QUIZ	Latin Affixes	**15** minutes	
WRAP-UP	More Language Arts Practice	**20** minutes	
	Go Read!	**15** minutes	

Content Background

Students will learn about words that have the Latin affixes *non*, *ance*, and *ous*. They will learn how knowing the meaning of a word's affix can help them determine the meaning of the word. They will also learn how context clues can help them determine the meaning of a word with a Latin affix.

An affix is a word part that has a special meaning. It can be found at the beginning or ending of a word. An affix is not a word on its own. It must be attached to a base word or root to make a word. Many affixes commonly used in English have come from Latin.

Prefixes and suffixes fall under the category of affixes. A prefix is an affix that comes at the beginning of a word. For example, the prefix *non* comes at the beginning of the word *nonfiction*. Since the prefix *non* means "not," the word *nonfiction* means "not fiction."

A suffix is an affix that comes at the end of a word. For example, the suffix *ous* comes at the end of the word *famous*. Since the suffix *ous* means "having the quality of; characterized by," the word *famous* means "having the quality of fame or characterized by fame."

MATERIALS

Supplied
- *Summit English Language Arts 4 Activity Book*
  - Apply: Latin Affixes

Also Needed
- reading material for Go Read!

Advance Preparation

During the Go Read! activity, students will have the option of using the digital library. Allow extra time for students to make their reading selection, or have students make a selection before beginning the lesson.

Lesson Goals

- Use Latin affixes to determine the meanings of words.
- Use context clues to determine the meanings of words.
- Read and write for pleasure.

KEYWORDS

affix – a word part attached to a root or base word to create a new word

prefix – a word part with its own meaning that can be added to the beginning of a base word or root to make a new word with a different meaning

suffix – a word part added to the end of a base word or root that changes the meaning or part of speech of a word

GET READY

Introduction to Latin Affixes

Students will get a glimpse of what they will learn about in the lesson. They will also read the lesson goals and keywords. Have students select each keyword and preview its definition.

Look Back at Affixes

Students will review the definition of an affix. They will also practice the prerequisite skill of identifying words with an affix and identifying definitions of words with common affixes.

LEARN AND TRY IT

LEARN   Words with Latin Affixes

Students will learn the definition of several words that have Latin affixes. They will also learn that knowing the meaning of an affix can help them define an unknown word and how context clues can help them define a word with a Latin affix.

SUPPORT   For students having difficulty recognizing that prefixes and suffixes are types of affixes, use a simple model to demonstrate that items can belong to a category. For example, write the category "clothing" on the board. Under the heading "clothing," write the items "shirts" and "pants." Then write the category "affixes." Under the heading "affixes," write "prefixes" and "suffixes."

TRY IT   Define Words with Latin Affixes

Students will use context clues and the meanings of Latin affixes to determine the meanings of words in a passage.

TRY IT   Apply: Latin Affixes

Students will complete Apply: Latin Affixes from *Summit English Language Arts 4 Activity Book*.

This activity page contains open-ended questions, so it's important that you review students' responses. Give students feedback, using the sample answers provided to guide you.

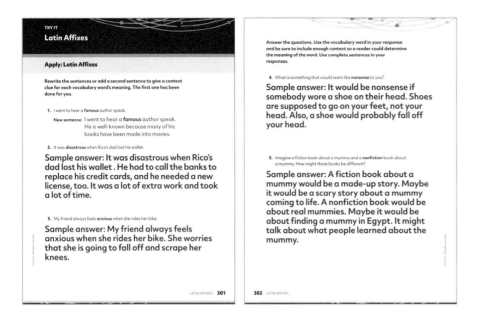

TRY IT   Go Write!

Students will write independently for pleasure. As they write, they should think about using words with Latin affixes in their writing.

TRY IT   Review Latin Affixes

Students will answer questions to review what they have learned about words with Latin affixes.

QUIZ

Latin Affixes

Students will complete the Latin Affixes quiz.

WRAP-UP

More Language Arts Practice

Students will practice skills according to their individual needs.

Go Read!

Students will read for pleasure. They should choose a book or a magazine that interests them, or they may choose a selection from the digital library, linked in the online lesson.

Students should read for the entire time. Have students select something to read ahead of time to help them stay focused.

Opinion Writing: Prewriting (A)

Lesson Overview

ACTIVITY	ACTIVITY TITLE	TIME	ONLINE/OFFLINE
GET READY	Introduction to Opinion Writing: Prewriting (A)	**2** minutes	📶
	Spelling List 19 Pretest **LEARNING COACH CHECK-IN**	**10** minutes	📶 and 📄
	Look Back at Pronouns	**10** minutes	📶
LEARN AND **TRY IT**	Relative Pronouns	**15** minutes	📶
	Use Relative Pronouns	**15** minutes	📶
	Explore a Student's Opinion Essay	**20** minutes	📶
	Brainstorming for an Opinion Essay	**15** minutes	📶
	Brainstorm for Your Opinion Essay **LEARNING COACH CHECK-IN**	**30** minutes	📄
WRAP-UP	Questions About Relative Pronouns and Brainstorming	**3** minutes	📶

Content Background

Students will begin working on an **opinion essay** about a topic of their choice. They will complete this assignment over the course of several lessons by following the writing process. Students will begin by prewriting.

Writing Process

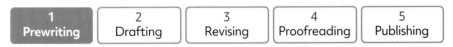

| 1 Prewriting | 2 Drafting | 3 Revising | 4 Proofreading | 5 Publishing |

During **prewriting**, writers choose a topic, conduct research, and create a plan for their writing assignment. In this lesson, students will complete the first part of prewriting, choosing a topic. To do that, they'll **brainstorm** by listing several opinions and answering questions to evaluate them.

Grammar, Usage, and Mechanics Students will learn how to recognize and use relative pronouns. A relative pronoun is a pronoun such as *who* or *which* that introduces a dependent clause.

The relative pronouns *who* and *whom* refer to a person or people. The relative pronouns *that* and *which* usually refer to animals or things.

> **Example:** She's the lady **who** sold me the flowers.

> **Example:** What did you do with the book **that** I gave you?

Advance Preparation

Gather a folder that students can use to keep all notes and activity pages related to their opinion essay.

Lesson Goals

- Take a spelling pretest.
- Learn to use relative pronouns.
- Explore a model opinion essay.
- Analyze how an author brainstorms.
- Brainstorm topics for your opinion essay.

GET READY

Introduction to Opinion Writing: Prewriting (A)

Students will get a glimpse of what they will learn about in the lesson. They will also read the lesson goals and keywords. Have students select each keyword and preview its definition.

Spelling List 19 Pretest

Students will take a spelling pretest.

LEARNING COACH CHECK-IN   Have students turn to Spelling List 19 Pretest in *Summit English Language Arts 4 Activity Book* and open the online Spelling Pretest activity. Online, students will listen to the spelling word, type the word in the space indicated, and then check their answer. In the activity book, students will write the correct spelling of the word in the tables provided and indicate with a ✓ or an ✗ if they spelled the word correctly or incorrectly online. Students will repeat this process with the remaining words.

As needed, help students with the interaction between the online activity and the activity book page until they become comfortable with what they need to do. As students practice their spelling words throughout the workshop, they should pay special attention to words they spelled incorrectly on the pretest.

This is the complete list of words students will be tested on.

y + Vowel Suffixes	Root *cred*	Suffix *–ist*	Heart Words
betrayed	credible	dentist	California
cozier	credit	journalist	Minnesota
displaying	discredit	scientist	
heaviest	incredible	violinist	
laziest		nutritionist	
relaying			
supplying			
surveyed			
angrier			
worrying			

NOTE   Have students keep their completed activity page in a safe place so they can refer to it later.

GET READY
Opinion Writing: Prewriting (A)

Spelling List 19 Pretest

1. Open the Spelling Pretest activity online. Listen to the first spelling word. Type the word. Check your answer.

2. Write the correct spelling of the word in the Word column of the Spelling Pretest table on the next page.

Word		
1 blindfold		

3. Put a check mark in the ☺ column if you spelled the word correctly online.

Word		
1 blindfold	✓	

Put an X in the ☒ column if you spelled the word incorrectly online.

Word		
1 blindfold		X

4. Repeat Steps 1–3 for the remaining words in the Spelling Pretest.

OPINION WRITING: PREWRITING (A)   **303**

Opinion Writing: Prewriting (A)

Spelling List 19 Pretest

Write each spelling word in the Word column, making sure to spell it correctly.

Word				Word		
1 betrayed				12 credit		
2 cozier				13 discredit		
3 displaying				14 incredible		
4 heaviest				15 California		
5 laziest				16 Minnesota		
6 relaying				17 dentist		
7 supplying				18 journalist		
8 surveyed				19 scientist		
9 angrier				20 violinist		
10 worrying				21 nutritionist		
11 credible						

Students should use the ✓ and X columns to indicate whether they spelled each word correctly or incorrectly online.

304   OPINION WRITING: PREWRITING (A)

Look Back at Pronouns

Students will practice the prerequisite skill of recognizing and correctly using pronouns.

LEARN AND TRY IT

LEARN   Relative Pronouns

Students will learn how to recognize and use relative pronouns.

TRY IT   Use Relative Pronouns

Students will answer questions about recognizing and using relative pronouns. They will receive feedback on their answers.

LEARN   Explore a Student's Opinion Essay

To help them better understand their writing assignment, students will read a model opinion essay and explore the elements that make it successful.

> **TIP**   The genre of the writing assignment for this workshop is the opinion essay. It is not, however, a *persuasive* essay. In opinion writing, writers use facts and details to support their opinion. In persuasive writing, writers choose the most favorable pieces of evidence to convince others of their opinion.

LEARN   Brainstorming for an Opinion Essay

Students will closely investigate brainstorming, which is the first part of the prewriting step of the writing process.

TRY IT   Brainstorm for Your Opinion Essay

Students will complete Brainstorm for Your Opinion Essay from *Summit English Language Arts 4 Activity Book*.

> **LEARNING COACH CHECK-IN**   Review students' responses. Ensure that students have selected a topic for their opinion essay that meets the criteria listed in Question 4 on the activity page. When students have completed the page, they should store it in a folder so that they can refer to it throughout the writing process.

> **NOTE**   In addition to the brainstorming activity, this activity page contains the instructions for the opinion essay. Students should read the instructions carefully, but in this lesson, they should complete the brainstorming activity only (not the entire assignment). If you or students wish, you can download and print another copy of the Opinion Essay Instructions online.

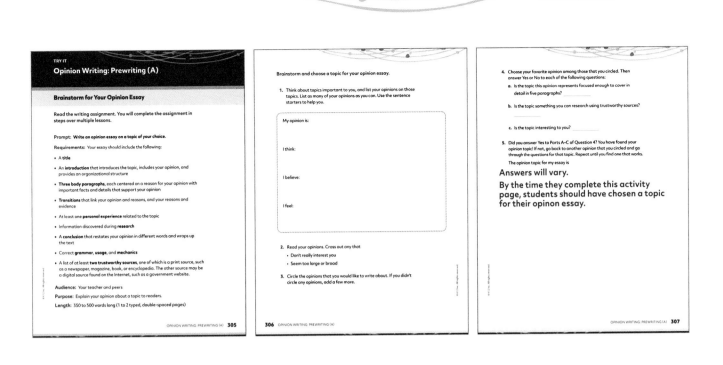

WRAP-UP

Questions About Relative Pronouns and Brainstorming

Students will answer questions to show that they understand how to recognize and use relative pronouns and how to brainstorm a topic for an opinion essay.

Opinion Writing: Prewriting (B)

Lesson Overview

ACTIVITY	ACTIVITY TITLE	TIME	ONLINE/OFFLINE
GET READY	Introduction to Opinion Writing: Prewriting (B)	**2** minutes	🖥️
	Spelling List 19 Activity Bank	**10** minutes	📄
LEARN AND **TRY IT**	Relative Adverbs	**10** minutes	🖥️
	Use Relative Adverbs	**10** minutes	🖥️
	Researching an Opinion Essay	**15** minutes	🖥️
	Conduct Research for Your Opinion Essay **LEARNING COACH CHECK-IN**	**50** minutes	🖥️ and 📄
WRAP-UP	Questions About Relative Adverbs and Research	**3** minutes	🖥️
	Go Read!	**20** minutes	🖥️ or 📄

Content Background

Students continue to work on an **opinion essay**, an assignment they will complete over the course of several lessons by following the writing process.

Writing Process

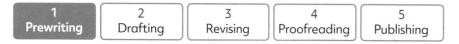

| 1 Prewriting | 2 Drafting | 3 Revising | 4 Proofreading | 5 Publishing |

In this lesson, students will continue prewriting by conducting research. Students will create a **research question** that will guide and focus their research and that their essay will answer. To generate their research question, they will ask themselves, "What question do I need to answer to support my opinion?" Next, they will find trustworthy print and digital sources with information about their topic. They will take notes on their topic, using at least two sources.

Grammar, Usage, and Mechanics Students will explore the relative adverbs *where*, *when*, and *why*. These relative adverbs introduce dependent clauses that relate to the place, the time, or the reason an action took place.

> **Example:** This is the park **where** we play soccer.

> **Example:** I remember the time **when** I broke my arm

MATERIALS

Supplied
- *Summit English Language Arts 4 Activity Book*
  - Spelling List 19 Activity Bank
  - Conduct Research for Your Opinion Essay
- Opinion Essay Instructions (printout)

Also Needed
- completed Spelling List 19 Pretest activity page from Opinion Writing: Prewriting (A)
- folder for organizing opinion writing assignment pages
- reading material for Go Read!

Advance Preparation

Gather students' completed Spelling List 19 Pretest activity page from Opinion Writing: Prewriting (A). Students will refer to this page during Get Ready: Spelling List 19 Activity Bank.

Gather the folder that students are using to store the activity pages related to their opinion essay. The folder should contain the following:

- Students' completed Brainstorm for Your Opinion Essay activity page from Opinion Writing: Prewriting (A)

Students will need to complete their own research during Try It: Research Your Opinion Essay. Make sure students have access to trustworthy research sources. You may choose to complete the activity at a library.

During the Go Read! activity, students will have the option of using the digital library. Allow extra time for students to make their reading selection, or have students make a selection before beginning the lesson.

Lesson Goals

- Practice all spelling words offline.
- Explore and use relative adverbs.
- Learn how to conduct research.
- Research the topic of your opinion essay.
- Read for pleasure.

GET READY

Introduction to Opinion Writing: Prewriting (B)

Students will get a glimpse of what they will learn about in the lesson. They will also read the lesson goals and keywords. Have students select each keyword and preview its definition.

Spelling List 19 Activity Bank

Students will practice all spelling words from the workshop by completing Spelling List 19 Activity Bank from *Summit English Language Arts 4 Activity Book*. Make sure students have their completed Spelling List 19 Pretest activity page from Opinion Writing: Prewriting (A) to refer to during this activity.

Remind students to pay special attention to words they spelled incorrectly on the Spelling Pretest.

Spelling List 19 Activity Bank

Circle any words in the box that you did not spell correctly on the pretest. Using your circled words, complete one activity of your choice. Complete as much of the activity as you can in the time given.

If you spelled all words correctly on the pretest, complete your chosen activity with as many spelling words as you can.

betrayed	relaying	worrying	incredible	journalist
cozier	supplying	credible	California	scientist
displaying	surveyed	credit	Minnesota	violinist
heaviest	angrier	discredit	dentist	nutritionist
laziest				

Spelling Activity Choices

Create a Crossword

1. Write a word from your spelling word list in the center of the grid paper.
2. Write another spelling word going across and sharing a letter with the first word. See how many words you can connect.

Example:

OPINION WRITING: PREWRITING (B) **309**

Word Search Puzzle

1. Draw a box on the grid paper. The box should be large enough to hold your words from the spelling word list.
2. Fill in the grid paper with words from your spelling list, writing them horizontally, vertically, and diagonally (forward and backward if you choose).
3. Fill in the rest of the box with random letters.
4. Ask someone to find and circle your spelling words in the puzzle you made.

310 OPINION WRITING: PREWRITING (B)

Complete the activity that you chose.

My chosen activity:

Students should use this page to complete all steps in their chosen activity.

OPINION WRITING: PREWRITING (B) **311**

LEARN AND TRY IT

LEARN   Relative Adverbs

Students will explore and use relative adverbs.

TRY IT   Use Relative Adverbs

Students will answer questions about relative adverbs. They will receive feedback on their answers.

LEARN   Researching an Opinion Essay

Students will learn how to come up with an effective research question and conduct research. They will focus on how to choose trustworthy sources and take notes. They will also learn how personal experience can be incorporated into a researched piece of writing.

TIP   Tell students that major newspapers, such as the *New York Times*, the *Washington Post*, and the *Chicago Tribune* are all trustworthy sources. Likewise, government websites, such as those run by the Library of Congress and other agencies, contain reliable and useful information. Print reference books, such as *Encyclopedia Britannica* and the *World Book Encyclopedia*, are also credible sources of information.

TRY IT   Conduct Research for Your Opinion Essay

Students will complete Conduct Research for Your Opinion Essay in *Summit English Language Arts 4 Activity Book*. Make sure students have their completed Brainstorm for Your Opinion Essay activity page from Opinion Writing: Prewriting (A) to refer to during this activity.

LEARNING COACH CHECK-IN Review students' responses. Ensure that students have created an effective research question that meets the criteria on the activity page. Then ensure that students have found and taken notes from two appropriate and trustworthy sources, one of which should be a print source. When students have completed the pages with their notes, they should store them in a folder so that they can refer to them throughout the writing process.

NOTE If you or students wish, you can download and print another copy of the Opinion Essay Instructions online. Additional sheets for Research Notes are also available online.

TRY IT

Opinion Writing: Prewriting (B)

Conduct Research for Your Opinion Essay

Follow these steps to write a research question.

1. Write the opinion that you are supporting in your opinion essay.

   Sample opinion:
   I think that cats make an ideal pet.

   Opinion:
   _____
   _____

2. Write a question that you can research to support your opinion.

   Sample research question:
   What traits do cats possess that make them good pets?

   Research question:
   _____
   _____

Follow these steps to conduct research. Record information on the Research Notes pages that follow. Use one page per source.

3. Identify at least two sources. Record the title, author, publisher, and URL of each source.
   - One source must be a print source, such as a book, an article originally published in a newspaper or magazine, a pamphlet, or an encyclopedia article.
   - One source must be a digital source found on the Internet.

4. As you read each source, take notes about information related to your research question.
   - Write your notes in your own words.
   - If you find a direct quotation that you think you might use in your essay, record the quotation, word for word, in quotation marks. Also record the name of the person you are quoting.

   I'm searching for facts about how much cats love laundry baskets.

Research Notes

Source

Title: _____

Author: _____

Published by: _____

URL (if necessary): _____

Notes

Key Information Written in Your Own Words:
_____
_____
_____
_____

Direct Quotation:
_____
_____

Person Quoted: _____

Research Notes

Source

Title: _____

Author: _____

Published by: _____

URL (if necessary): _____

Notes

Key Information Written in Your Own Words:
_____
_____
_____
_____

Direct Quotation:
_____
_____

Person Quoted: _____

Questions About Relative Adverbs and Research

Students will answer questions to show that they understand how to use relative adverbs correctly and how to conduct research for an opinion essay.

Go Read!

Students will read for pleasure. They should choose a book or a magazine that interests them, or they may choose a selection from the digital library, linked in the online lesson.

Students should read for the entire time. Have students select something to read ahead of time to help them stay focused.

Opinion Writing: Prewriting (C)

Lesson Overview

ACTIVITY	ACTIVITY TITLE	TIME	ONLINE/OFFLINE
GET READY	Introduction to Opinion Writing: Prewriting (C)	**2** minutes	
	Spelling List 19 Practice	**10** minutes	
	Dogs Make the Best Pets	**10** minutes	
LEARN AND **TRY IT**	Prewriting an Opinion Essay	**15** minutes	
	Prewrite Your Opinion Essay **LEARNING COACH CHECK-IN**	**60** minutes	
WRAP-UP	Question About Prewriting an Opinion Essay	**3** minutes	
	Go Read!	**20** minutes	

Content Background

Students will continue to work on their **opinion essay**, an assignment that they will complete over the course of several lessons by following the writing process.

Writing Process

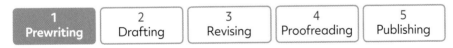

During **prewriting**, writers choose an opinion, create a research question, conduct research, and create a plan for their writing assignment. In this lesson, students will organize their research and ideas using a graphic organizer.

First, students will gather the notes they took during research. They will use these notes to help them create a plan for their opinion essay by completing a graphic organizer provided to them in their activity book. The graphic organizer will allow them to organize information in the same order in which they will present it in their essay. The graphic organizer will also help students group together related information, including information gathered during research and relevant personal experience.

Remind students that it is not necessary to write in complete sentences when completing a graphic organizer.

MATERIALS

Supplied
- *Summit English Language Arts 4 Activity Book*
  - Prewrite Your Opinion Essay
- Opinion Essay Instructions (printout)

Also Needed
- folder for organizing opinion writing assignment pages
- reading material for Go Read!

Advance Preparation

Gather the folder that students are using to keep all notes and activity pages related to their opinion essay. The folder should contain the following:

- Students' completed Brainstorm for Your Opinion Essay activity page from Opinion Writing: Prewriting (A)

- Students' completed research notes from Opinion Writing: Prewriting (B)

During the Go Read! activity, students will have the option of using the digital library. Allow extra time for students to make their reading selection, or have students make a selection before beginning the lesson.

Lesson Goals

- Practice spelling words online.

- Practice grammar skills by editing a passage.

- Learn how to organize an opinion essay.

- Complete a graphic organizer for your opinion essay.

- Read for pleasure.

GET READY

Introduction to Opinion Writing: Prewriting (C)

Students will get a glimpse of what they will learn about in the lesson. They will also read the lesson goals and keywords. Have students select each keyword and preview its definition.

Spelling List 19 Practice

Students will practice all spelling words from the workshop.

Dogs Make the Best Pets

Students will edit a short passage to practice applying grammar skills. This passage contains errors and opportunities to improve the writing related to relative pronouns, relative adverbs, frequently confused words, and subject-verb agreement.

LEARN   Prewriting an Opinion Essay

Students will learn about completing a graphic organizer, which is part of the prewriting step in the writing process. They will focus on how to use their notes to complete the graphic organizer and how to group related information together.

TRY IT   Prewrite Your Opinion Essay

Students will complete Prewrite Your Opinion Essay from *Summit English Language Arts 4 Activity Book*. Make sure students have their completed Brainstorm for Your Opinion Essay activity page from Opinion Writing: Prewriting (A) and their research notes from Opinion Writing: Prewriting (B) to refer to during this activity.

LEARNING COACH CHECK-IN   Review students' responses. Ensure that students have completed the graphic organizer in a way that meets the criteria on the activity page. That means making certain that (1) they have used notes taken during research and relevant personal experience; (2) they have put their ideas in the appropriate order for a five-paragraph essay; and (3) they have grouped together related information. When students have completed their graphic organizer, they should store it in the folder they are using to organize their writing assignment pages.

NOTE   If you or students wish, you can download and print another copy of the Opinion Essay Instructions online.

Question About Prewriting an Opinion Essay

Students will answer a question to show that they understand how to complete a graphic organizer.

Go Read!

Students will read for pleasure. They should choose a book or a magazine that interests them, or they may choose a selection from the digital library, linked in the online lesson.

Students should read for the entire time. Have students select something to read ahead of time to help them stay focused.

Opinion Writing: Drafting (A)

Lesson Overview

ACTIVITY	ACTIVITY TITLE	TIME	ONLINE/OFFLINE
GET READY	Introduction to Opinion Writing: Drafting (A)	**2** minutes	
	Spelling List 19 Review Game	**10** minutes	
	Sleepaway Camp	**10** minutes	
LEARN AND **TRY IT**	Drafting an Opinion Essay	**15** minutes	
	Draft Your Opinion Essay **LEARNING COACH CHECK-IN**	**60** minutes	
WRAP-UP	Question About Drafting an Opinion Essay	**3** minutes	
	Go Read!	**20** minutes	

Content Background

Students will continue working on their **opinion essay**. They will complete this assignment over the course of several lessons by following the writing process. In this lesson, students will begin drafting their essay.

Writing Process

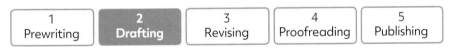

| 1 Prewriting | 2 **Drafting** | 3 Revising | 4 Proofreading | 5 Publishing |

During **drafting**, students will use their notes and their completed graphic organizer as guides as they write a rough draft of their opinion essay. Students are expected to write about half of their rough draft in this lesson (although they may write more, if they wish). They will have time to finish and submit their draft in Opinion Writing: Drafting (B).

Advance Preparation

Gather the folder that students are using to store the activity pages related to their opinion essay. The folder should contain the following:

• Students' completed Brainstorm for Your Opinion Essay activity page from Opinion Writing: Prewriting (A)

• Students' completed research notes from Opinion Writing: Prewriting (B)

- Students' completed Prewrite Your Opinion Essay activity page from Opinion Writing: Prewriting (C)

During the Go Read! activity, students will have the option of using the digital library. Allow extra time for students to make their reading selection, or have students make a selection before beginning the lesson.

Lesson Goals

- Practice all spelling words online.

- Practice grammar skills by editing a passage.

- Explore how to draft an opinion essay.

- Begin to draft your opinion essay.

- Read for pleasure.

GET READY

Introduction to Opinion Writing: Drafting (A)
Students will get a glimpse of what they will learn about in the lesson. They will also read the lesson goals and keywords. Have students select each keyword and preview its definition.

Spelling List 19 Review Game
Students will practice all spelling words from the workshop.

Sleepaway Camp
Students will edit a short passage to practice applying grammar skills. This passage contains errors and opportunities to improve the writing related to relative pronouns, relative adverbs, frequently confused words, and subject-verb agreement.

LEARN AND TRY IT

LEARN Drafting an Opinion Essay
Students will explore how a student drafts an opinion essay, using her graphic organizer and her notes to guide her.

TRY IT Draft Your Opinion Essay
Students will complete half of their first draft using Draft Your Opinion Essay in *Summit English Language Arts 4 Activity Book*. If students wish, they may complete more than half of their draft.

Make sure students have their completed Brainstorm for Your Opinion Essay activity page from Opinion Writing: Prewriting (A), their research notes from Opinion Writing: Prewriting (B), and their Prewrite Your Opinion Essay activity page from Opinion Writing: Prewriting (C) to refer to during this activity.

LEARNING COACH CHECK-IN   Review students' responses. Ensure that students' draft is in line with the assignment criteria outlined on the Brainstorm for Your Opinion Essay activity page. If necessary, remind students not to focus on perfection at this stage of the writing process. Students should store their draft in the folder they are using to organize their writing assignment pages.

NOTE   If you or students wish, you can download and print another copy of the Opinion Essay Instructions online. Additional sheets of Drafting Paper are also available online.

TRY IT
Opinion Writing: Drafting (A)

Draft Your Opinion Essay

Using your notes and your graphic organizer to guide you, write the first draft of your opinion essay. Write only on the white rows. You will use the purple rows for revisions later.

Title

start here ►

Students should write their draft in the white rows only.

keep writing ►

Draft Page 1

OPINION WRITING: DRAFTING (A)   **319**

320   OPINION WRITING: DRAFTING (A)

keep writing ►

Draft Page 2

keep writing ►

Draft Page 3

OPINION WRITING: DRAFTING (A)   **321**

322   OPINION WRITING: DRAFTING (A)

Draft Page 4

Question About Drafting an Opinion Essay

Students will answer a question to show that they understand how to draft an opinion essay.

Go Read!

Students will read for pleasure. They should choose a book or a magazine that interests them, or they may choose a selection from the digital library, linked in the online lesson.

Students should read for the entire time. Have students select something to read ahead of time to help them stay focused.

Opinion Writing: Drafting (B)

Lesson Overview

ACTIVITY	ACTIVITY TITLE	TIME	ONLINE/OFFLINE
GET READY	Introduction to Opinion Writing: Drafting (B)	**1** minute	
TRY IT	Review Relative Pronouns and Relative Adverbs	**10** minutes	
QUIZ	Relative Pronouns and Relative Adverbs	**20** minutes	
	Spelling List 19	**10** minutes	
TRY IT	Finish Drafting Your Opinion Essay **LEARNING COACH CHECK-IN**	**60** minutes	
WRAP-UP	Turn In Your Opinion Essay Draft	**1** minute	
	More Language Arts Practice	**8** minutes	
	Go Read!	**10** minutes	

Content Background

Students will continue working on their **opinion essay** about a topic of their choice. In this lesson, students will finish and submit their rough draft. They will revise, proofread, and publish their essay in a future workshop.

Writing Process

| 1 Prewriting | 2 **Drafting** | 3 Revising | 4 Proofreading | 5 Publishing |

Advance Preparation

Gather the folder that students are using to store the activity pages related to their opinion essay. The folder should contain the following:

- Students' completed Brainstorm for Your Opinion Essay activity page from Opinion Writing: Prewriting (A)

- Students' completed research notes from Opinion Writing: Prewriting (B)

- Students' completed Prewrite Your Opinion Essay activity page from Opinion Writing: Prewriting (C)

- Students' in-progress Draft Your Opinion Essay activity page from Opinion Writing: Drafting (A)

Lesson Goals

- Review relative pronouns and relative adverbs.

- Take a quiz on relative pronouns and relative adverbs.

- Take a spelling quiz.

- Finish and submit the rough draft of your opinion essay.

GET READY

Introduction to Opinion Writing: Drafting (B)

Students will read the lesson goals.

TRY IT

Review Relative Pronouns and Relative Adverbs

Students will answer questions to review what they have learned about the use of relative pronouns and relative adverbs.

QUIZ

Relative Pronouns and Relative Adverbs

Students will complete the Relative Pronouns and Relative Adverbs quiz.

Spelling List 19

Students will complete the Spelling List 19 quiz.

TRY IT

Finish Drafting Your Opinion Essay

Students will complete the rough draft of their opinion essay. Students should gather the Draft Your Opinion Essay activity page that they started in Opinion Writing: Drafting (A) and complete it.

Make sure students also have their completed Brainstorm for Your Opinion Essay activity page from Opinion Writing: Prewriting (A), their research notes from Opinion Writing: Prewriting (B), and their Prewrite Your Opinion Essay activity page from Opinion Writing: Prewriting (C) to refer to during this activity.

LEARNING COACH CHECK-IN   Review students' draft. Ensure that students' draft is in line with the assignment criteria outlined on the Brainstorm for Your Opinion Essay activity page. If necessary, remind students not to focus on perfection at this stage of the writing process. Students should store a copy of their draft in the folder they are using to organize their writing assignment pages.

NOTE   If you or students wish, you can download and print another copy of the Opinion Essay Instructions online. Additional sheets of Drafting Paper are also available online.

TRY IT
Opinion Writing: Drafting (A)

Draft Your Opinion Essay

Using your notes and your graphic organizer to guide you, write the first draft of your opinion essay. Write only on the white rows. You will use the purple rows for revisions later.

Title

start here ▶

Students should write their draft in the white rows only.

keep writing ▶

Draft Page 1

OPINION WRITING: DRAFTING (A) **319**

---

keep writing ▶

Draft Page 2

320 OPINION WRITING: DRAFTING (A)

---

keep writing ▶

Draft Page 3

OPINION WRITING: DRAFTING (A) **321**

Draft Page 4

322 OPINION WRITING: DRAFTING (A)

Turn In Your Opinion Essay Draft

Students will submit their writing assignment to their teacher.

More Language Arts Practice

Students will practice skills according to their individual needs.

Go Read!

Students will read for pleasure. They should choose a book or a magazine that interests them, or they may choose a selection from the digital library, linked in the online lesson.

Students should read for the entire time. Have students select something to read ahead of time to help them stay focused.

Big Ideas: Critical Skills Assignment

Lesson Overview

Big Ideas lessons provide students the opportunity to further apply the knowledge acquired and skills learned throughout the unit workshops. Each Big Ideas lesson consists of these parts:

1. **Cumulative Review:** Students keep their skills fresh by reviewing prior content.

2. **Preview:** Students practice answering the types of questions they will commonly find on standardized tests.

3. **Synthesis:** Students complete an assignment that allows them to connect and apply what they have learned. Synthesis assignments vary throughout the course.

   In the Synthesis portion of this Big Ideas lesson, students will read new selections. They will answer literal and inferential comprehension questions and complete writing questions that ask for short responses about the reading selections. Students should refer to the selections while answering the questions, because the questions emphasize using textual evidence. The questions call for students to demonstrate critical thinking, reading, and writing skills.

   LEARNING COACH CHECK-IN   This is a graded assessment. Make sure students complete, review, and submit the assignment to their teacher.

All materials needed for this lesson are linked online and not provided in the Activity Book.

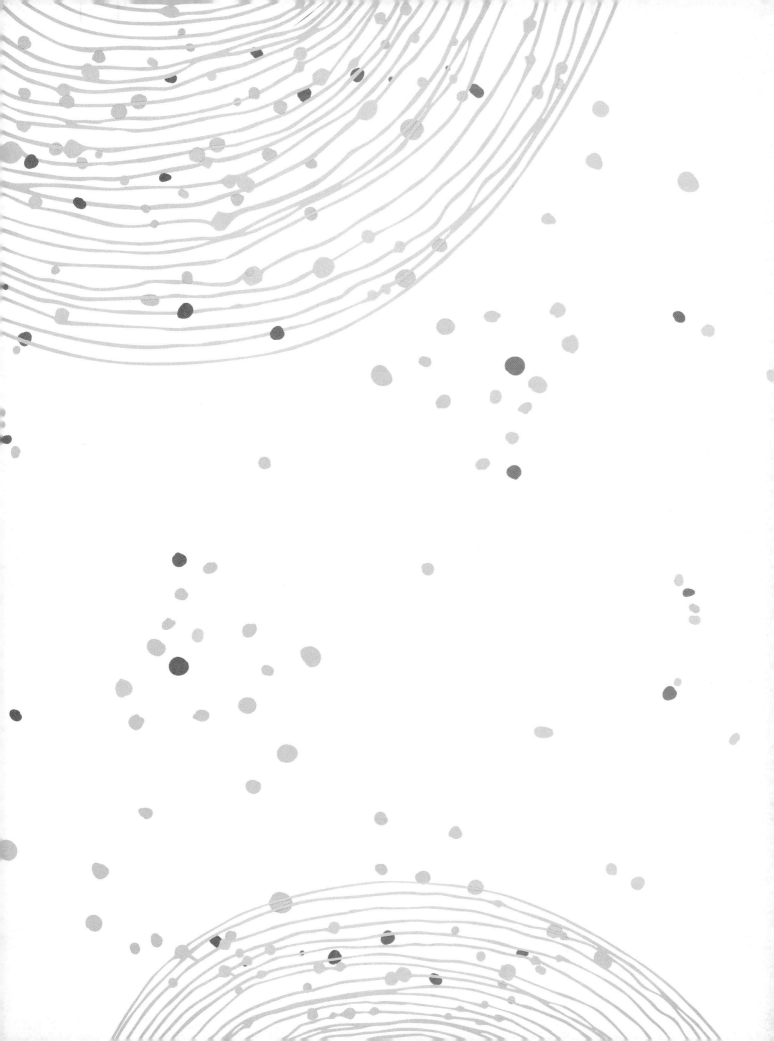

Men and Women
of Character

Pink and Say

Lesson Overview

ACTIVITY	ACTIVITY TITLE	TIME	ONLINE/OFFLINE
GET READY	Men and Woman of Character Unit Overview	**1** minute	🖥️
	Introduction to *Pink and Say*	**1** minute	🖥️
	Spelling List 20 Pretest **LEARNING COACH CHECK-IN**	**10** minutes	🖥️ and 📄
	Brave in 60 Seconds	**1** minute	🖥️
	Before You Read *Pink and Say*	**14** minutes	🖥️
READ	*Pink and Say*	**30** minutes	📄
	Check-In: *Pink and Say*	**8** minutes	🖥️
LEARN AND **TRY IT**	Pink and Say Perspectives	**10** minutes	🖥️
	Identifying Perspectives in *Pink and Say*	**10** minutes	🖥️
	Apply: Identify Perspectives	**15** minutes	🖥️
	Write from Another Character's Perspective **LEARNING COACH CHECK-IN**	**10** minutes	📄
	Practice Words from *Pink and Say*	**8** minutes	🖥️
WRAP-UP	Question About *Pink and Say*	**2** minutes	🖥️

Content Background

Students will read a work of historical fiction, *Pink and Say*. This lesson will focus on students identifying the author's perspective, or viewpoint, as well as the perspectives of characters in a story. They will also focus on making and modifying predictions before and after they read.

Students will learn about the differences between an author's and character's perspective and how they affect readers' understanding of the story. An author's perspective involves the different beliefs, opinions, attitudes, or biases that he or she may bring to a text. For instance, in the story, the author learns of the tale from her family members. But the reader needs to keep in mind that the author heard the story after a lot of time had passed, and this may affect how the story is told.

MATERIALS

Supplied
- *Pink and Say* by Patricia Polacco
- *Summit English Language Arts 4 Activity Book*
- Spelling List 20 Pretest
- Write from Another Character's Perspective

On the other hand, a character's perspective is his or her feelings, beliefs, attitudes, or opinions on a topic, issue, or experience in a story. For example, in the story, Pinkus (Pink) and Sheldon (Say) have different perspectives on the Civil War. These different perspectives influence the events of the story and each character's actions.

Finally, before reading, students will establish a focus for their reading by making a prediction about what they think will happen in the story. After reading, students will reflect on their prediction and either confirm it was correct or modify it to reflect the details they learned while they read.

Pink and Say Synopsis

Pink and Say is about two teenagers who become soldiers in the Civil War. Each enters the war for different reasons. Pinkus is an enslaved person who wants to fight to help get rid of slavery. Sheldon offers to hold the staff (or flag) in his outfit and ends up having to fight because too many deaths dwindle troop numbers. Afraid, Sheldon attempts to run away, gets shot in the leg, and is left to die in a field. Pinkus, having lost his own troop, stumbles upon Sheldon. He carries Sheldon to his mother's house to help nurse him back to health. From then on, they become Pink and Say and develop a friendship. Despite this friendship and eventual decision to rejoin the fighting, Pink and Say are discovered by marauders of the Confederate army. Pink's mother is murdered, Say is imprisoned in the Confederate camp, and Pink is executed. After Say is released, he lives a long life and the story of Pink and Say is passed down through the generations in his family.

Lesson Goals

- Take a spelling pretest.
- Identify author and character perspectives in a story.
- Make and modify predictions before and after reading.
- Determine the meaning of words using context.

GET READY

Men and Women of Character Unit Overview
Students will read a summary of what they will learn in the Men and Women of Character unit.

Introduction to *Pink and Say*

Students will get a glimpse of what they will learn about in the lesson. They will also read the lesson goals and keywords. Have students select each keyword and preview its definition.

Spelling List 20 Pretest

Students will take a spelling pretest.

LEARNING COACH CHECK-IN   Have students turn to Spelling List 20 Pretest in *Summit English Language Arts 4 Activity Book* and open the online Spelling Pretest activity. Online, students will listen to the spelling word, type the word in the space indicated, and then check their answer. In the activity book, students will write the correct spelling of the word in the tables provided andindicate with a ✓ or an ✗ if they spelled the word correctly or incorrectly online. Students will repeat this process with the remaining words.

As needed, help students with the interaction between the online activity and the activity book page until they become comfortable with what they need to do. As students practice their spelling words throughout the workshop, they should pay special attention to words they spelled incorrectly on the pretest.

This is the complete list of words students will be tested on.

y-Ending Plural Nouns	Root *sens*	Suffix *–or*	Heart Words
counties	nonsense	collector	Massachusetts
diaries	sensational	counselor	Washington
highways	sensible	director	
hobbies	sensitive	governor	
holidays		senator	
journeys			
kidneys			
libraries			
territories			
valleys			
activities			
daisies			
birthdays			
supplies			

NOTE Have students keep their completed activity page in a safe place so they can refer to it later.

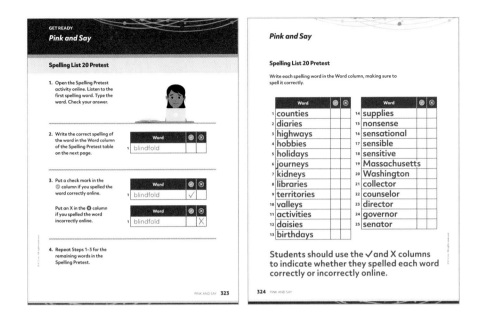

Brave in 60 Seconds

Students will watch a short video designed to spark their interest in upcoming topics.

Before You Read *Pink and Say*

Students will be introduced to some key vocabulary words that they will encounter in the upcoming reading, learn some important historical background related to the reading, and make predictions to help them set a purpose for their reading.

READ

Pink and Say

Students will read *Pink and Say* by Patricia Polacco.

NOTE This story takes place during the Civil War and touches on many sensitive subjects. There are explicit mentions of slavery, racism, violence, and death.

Check-In: *Pink and Say*

Students will answer several questions to demonstrate their comprehension of *Pink and Say*.

LEARN *Pink and Say* Perspectives

Students will learn how to identify the author's and characters' perspectives by using details from the story.

TRY IT Identifying Perspectives in *Pink and Say*

Students will analyze passages and answer questions that involve identifying the author's and characters' perspectives in the story.

TRY IT Apply: Identify Perspectives

Students will apply to a new work what they've learned about how to identify an author's and characters' perspectives.

TRY IT Write from Another Character's Perspective

Students will complete Write from Another Character's Perspective from *Summit English Language Arts 4 Activity Book*.

LEARNING COACH CHECK-IN   This activity page contains an open-ended prompt, so it's important that you review students' responses. Give students feedback, using the sample answers provided to guide you.

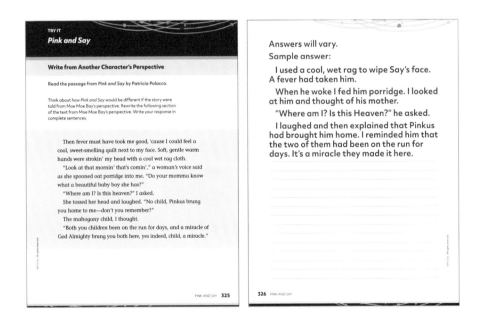

TRY IT Practice Words from *Pink and Say*

Students will answer questions to demonstrate their understanding of the vocabulary words from *Pink and Say*.

Question About *Pink and Say*

Students will answer a question to show that they understand how to identify characters' perspectives in *Pink and Say*.

Pink and Say Wrap-Up

Lesson Overview

ACTIVITY	ACTIVITY TITLE	TIME	ONLINE/OFFLINE
GET READY	Introduction to *Pink and Say* Wrap-Up	**1** minute	
	Spelling List 20 Activity Bank	**10** minute	
TRY IT	Write About the Author's Perspective in *Pink and Say* **LEARNING COACH CHECK-IN**	**29** minutes	
	Read and Record	**15** minutes	
	Review *Pink and Say*	**15** minutes	
QUIZ	*Pink and Say*	**30** minutes	
WRAP-UP	More Language Arts Practice	**20** minutes	

Advance Preparation

Gather students completed Spelling List 20 Pretest activity page from *Pink and Say*. Students will refer to this page during the Spelling List 20 Activity Bank.

Lesson Goals

- Answer questions about the author's perspective in *Pink and Say*.

- Practice reading aloud to develop fluency.

- Practice all spelling words offline.

- Take a quiz on characters, setting, events, and theme in *Pink and Say*.

MATERIALS

Supplied
- *Pink and Say* by Patricia Polacco
- *Summit English Language Arts 4 Activity Book*
  - Spelling List 20 Activity Bank
  - Write About the Author's Perspective in *Pink and Say*

Also Needed
- completed Spelling List 20 Pretest activity page from *Pink and Say*

GET READY

Introduction to *Pink and Say* Wrap-Up

Students will read the lesson goals.

Spelling List 20 Activity Bank

Students will practice all spelling words from the workshop by completing Spelling List 20 Activity Bank from *Summit English Language Arts 4 Activity Book*. Make sure students have their completed Spelling List 20 Pretest activity page from the *Pink and Say* lesson to refer to during this activity.

Remind students to pay special attention to words they spelled incorrectly on the Spelling Pretest.

TRY IT

Write About the Author's Perspective in *Pink and Say*

Students will complete Write About Author's Perspective in *Pink and Say* from *Summit English Language Arts 4 Activity Book*.

LEARNING COACH CHECK-IN This activity page contains open-ended questions, so it's important that you review students' responses. Give students feedback, using the sample answers provided to guide you.

Additional answers

5. Answers will vary.

   Example answer: The words that the author chose to reveal what happened to Pinkus shows that she feels sad. She states, "for him there was to be no wife, no children nor grandchildren to remember him." By saying what Pinkus could never have, compared to what Sheldon did have, she reveals how tragic Pinkus's end was. Also, by showing that there were no relatives to remember him, she makes it clear how important it was that the she write his story.

Read and Record

Good readers read quickly, smoothly, and with expression. This is called *fluency*. Students will record themselves reading aloud. They will listen to their recording and think about how quick, smooth, and expressive they sound.

TIP   Encourage students to rerecord as needed.

Review *Pink and Say*

Students will answer questions to review what they have learned about *Pink and Say*.

QUIZ

Pink and Say

Students will complete the *Pink and Say* quiz.

WRAP-UP

More Language Arts Practice

Students will practice skills according to their individual needs.

"Ibrahim"

Lesson Overview

ACTIVITY	ACTIVITY TITLE	TIME	ONLINE/OFFLINE
GET READY	Introduction to "Ibrahim"	**1** minute	online
	Spelling List 20 Practice	**10** minutes	online
	Before You Read "Ibrahim"	**14** minutes	online
READ	"Ibrahim"	**30** minutes	offline
	Check-In: "Ibrahim"	**5** minutes	online
LEARN AND TRY IT	Inferences and Conclusions	**15** minutes	online
	Making Inferences and Drawing Conclusions	**10** minutes	online
	Apply: Make Inferences and Draw Conclusions	**15** minutes	online
	Write About Inferences and Conclusions LEARNING COACH CHECK-IN	**10** minutes	offline
	Practice Words from "Ibrahim"	**8** minutes	online
WRAP-UP	Question About "Ibrahim"	**2** minutes	online

Content Background

Students will read a work of realistic fiction, "Ibrahim." The lesson will focus on making inferences, and then modifying those inferences based on new information. Students will then learn how inferences can lead to drawing conclusions.

An inference is an assumption, or a logical guess, based on text information and our own experiences. For example, in the story "Ibrahim," Mary finds a five-year-old boy all by himself in the middle of nowhere. Based on the details, we can infer that the boy is lost. As we read further, we learn that Ibrahim eats three granola bars and drinks a canteen full of water. With this information we can modify our inference to include that he has not had any food or water since he got lost. Based on Mary's actions, we can make inferences about her character—she is kind and generous, and she is very concerned about Ibrahim.

Making inferences helps us draw conclusions. A conclusion is a decision reached that is based on inferences. It's the next logical step about what could happen as a result of what we have inferred. For example, we have

inferred that Ibrahim is lost, that Mary is a kind and generous person, and that Mary is concerned about Ibrahim. We can draw the conclusion that Mary will help Ibrahim and try to find his home.

"Ibrahim" Synopsis

While stationed in Iraq in 2003, Mary Bolger and her patrol find five-year-old Ibrahim alone by the roadside. He is lost and in the middle of nowhere. With the help of a translator, Ibrahim explains that he fell asleep in the back of a truck two days earlier and woke up in the city. He doesn't know where he lives. The adults are stumped. But on a phone call home to the United States, Mary's seven-year-old daughter suggests that Ibrahim draw a picture of his home. With information from Ibrahim's picture, the support of her superior officer, and some luck, Mary succeeds in reuniting Ibrahim with his mother.

Lesson Goals

- Practice all spelling words.
- Make and modify inferences about a story.
- Draw conclusions based on inferences about a story.
- Determine meanings of unfamiliar words in the reading.

GET READY

Introduction to "Ibrahim"
Students will get a glimpse of what they will learn about in the lesson. They will also read the lesson goals and keywords. Have students select each keyword and preview its definition.

NOTE   The story takes place in 2003 at the beginning of the war in Iraq. It does not include any violence or judgments about the war or the political situation during that time period.

Spelling List 20 Practice
Students will practice all spelling words from the workshop.

Before You Read "Ibrahim"

Students will be introduced to key vocabulary words that they will encounter in the upcoming reading and learn some important background related to the reading.

"Ibrahim"

Students will read "Ibrahim" in *Expeditions in Reading*.

Check-In: "Ibrahim"

Students will answer questions to demonstrate their comprehension of "Ibrahim."

LEARN AND TRY IT

LEARN   Inferences and Conclusions

Students will learn how to use text information combined with personal experiences to make and modify inferences. They will then learn how to draw conclusions based on inferences.

TRY IT   Making Inferences and Drawing Conclusions

Students will analyze passages and answer questions that involve making and modifying inferences and drawing conclusions.

TRY IT   Apply: Make Inferences and Draw Conclusions

Students will apply to a new work what they've learned about making inferences and drawing conclusions.

TRY IT   Write About Inferences and Conclusions

Students will complete Write About Inferences and Conclusions from *Summit English Language Arts 4 Activity Book*.

LEARNING COACH CHECK-IN   This activity page contains open-ended questions, so it's important that you review students' responses. Give students feedback, using the sample answers provided to guide you.

TRY IT   Practice Words from "Ibrahim"

Students will answer questions to demonstrate their understanding of the vocabulary words from the reading.

WRAP-UP

Question About "Ibrahim"

Students will answer a question to show that they understand how to make an inference.

"Ibrahim" Wrap-Up

Lesson Overview

ACTIVITY	ACTIVITY TITLE	TIME	ONLINE/OFFLINE
GET READY	Introduction to "Ibrahim" Wrap-Up	**1** minute	🖥️
TRY IT	Spelling List 20 More Practice	**10** minutes	🖥️
	Write About Theme in "Ibrahim" **LEARNING COACH CHECK-IN**	**29** minutes	📄
	Read and Record	**15** minutes	🖥️
	Review "Ibrahim"	**15** minutes	🖥️
QUIZ	"Ibrahim"	**30** minutes	🖥️
WRAP-UP	More Language Arts Practice	**20** minutes	🖥️

Lesson Goals

- Practice all spelling words.
- Write about a theme in "Ibrahim."
- Practice reading aloud to develop fluency.
- Review the story "Ibrahim."
- Take a quiz on inferences, conclusions, and content from the story "Ibrahim."

MATERIALS

Supplied
- *Summit English Language Arts 4 Expeditions in Reading*
- *Summit English Language Arts 4 Activity Book*
  - Write About Theme in "Ibrahim"

GET READY

Introduction to "Ibrahim" Wrap-Up

Students will read the lesson goals.

Spelling List 20 More Practice

Students will practice all spelling words from the workshop.

Write About Theme in "Ibrahim"

Students will complete Write About Theme in "Ibrahim" from *Summit English Language Arts 4 Activity Book*.

LEARNING COACH CHECK-IN   This activity page contains open-ended questions, so it's important that you review students' responses. Give students feedback, using the sample answers provided to guide you.

TRY IT
"Ibrahim" Wrap-Up

Write About Theme in "Ibrahim"

Write your responses in complete sentences.

1. What is Ibrahim's problem in the story?
Ibrahim is lost and he doesn't know where he lives.

2. What are some of the ways that Mary helps Ibrahim?
Mary helps Ibrahim in lots of ways. She gives him food and water. She brings him back to the base and takes care of him there for two days. She helps figure out where Ibrahim lives. Then she takes him back to his home and helps him find his mother.

3. Who are some of the other people that help Ibrahim, and how do they help him?
Lieutenant Ramirez helps Ibrahim by giving Mary permission to bring him to their base. He also helps by arranging for Mary to be in a convoy so she can take Ibrahim home. Mary's daughter Alice helps. It was her idea to have Ibrahim draw a picture of where

"IBRAHIM" WRAP-UP **337**

he lives. The translator, Malik, helps by talking to Ibrahim. Malik asks a lot of questions about Ibrahim's home while Ibrahim draws his picture. Malik and Mary then figure out where Ibrahim might live.

4. Based on your answers to Questions 1–3, what is one of the themes of "Ibrahim"? Circle your choice.

Most people are able to solve problems on their own.

When people work together they can solve problems.

When people work together they can solve problems.

338   "IBRAHIM" WRAP-UP

Read and Record

Good readers read quickly, smoothly, and with expression. This is called *fluency*. Students will record themselves reading aloud. They will listen to their recording and think about how quick, smooth, and expressive they sound.

TIP   Encourage students to rerecord as needed.

Review "Ibrahim"

Students will answer questions to review what they have learned about making inferences and drawing conclusions. They will also review content from the story.

"Ibrahim"

Students will complete the "Ibrahim" quiz.

More Language Arts Practice

Students will practice skills according to their individual needs.

Baseball Saved Us

Lesson Overview

ACTIVITY	ACTIVITY TITLE	TIME	ONLINE/OFFLINE
GET READY	Introduction to *Baseball Saved Us*	**1** minute	🖥
	Spelling List 20 Review Game	**10** minutes	🖥
	Before You Read *Baseball Saved Us*	**14** minutes	🖥
READ	*Baseball Saved Us*	**30** minutes	📄
	Check-In: *Baseball Saved Us*	**5** minutes	🖥
LEARN AND **TRY IT**	Cause-and-Effect Relationships	**10** minutes	🖥
	Cause and Effect in *Baseball Saved Us*	**10** minutes	🖥
	Apply: Identifying Cause-and-Effect Relationships	**15** minutes	🖥
	How Do Cause and Effect Affect Character? **LEARNING COACH CHECK-IN**	**15** minutes	📄
	Practice Words from *Baseball Saved Us*	**8** minutes	🖥
WRAP-UP	Question About *Baseball Saved Us*	**2** minutes	🖥

Content Background

Students will read a work of historical fiction, *Baseball Saved Us* by Ken Mochizuki. This lesson will focus on identifying the different cause-and-effect relationships within this story. Students will learn two ways that readers determine cause-and-effect relationships.

For one, the author will directly state cause and effect within the details of the story. For example, in the story *Baseball Saved Us*, the main character (later known as "Shorty") asks his father why they were sent away to the camp. The reason that the father gives (the government does not trust Japanese Americans) is the cause of this event, which is directly stated in the text.

Other times, readers will have to make and modify inferences based on the information the author gives to determine the cause and effect of an event. An inference is an assumption, or logical guess, based on the text information and our own experiences or prior knowledge. For example, while the main character was in school, kids started calling him names and ignoring him, even though he didn't do anything wrong. The detail, "At the same time the

MATERIALS

Supplied
- *Baseball Saved Us* by Ken Mochizuki
- *Summit English Language Arts 4 Activity Book*
  - How Do Cause and Effect Affect Character?

radio kept talking about some place far away called Pearl Harbor," helps us modify inferences about why the kids call him names. These two pieces of information helps us make an inference as to why the main character was being treated differently.

Baseball Saved Us Synopsis

After the attack on Pearl Harbor during World War II, Japanese Americans were sent to internment camps because the U.S. government did not trust that they were loyal citizens. The main character and his family are forced to relocate from their homes to the middle of nowhere with less-than-ideal living conditions. To help with the boredom, the main character's father comes up with the idea to build a baseball field in the camp. Not only does the main character work at becoming a better ball player, but through baseball he can handle any challenge that life throws at him.

Lesson Goals

- Practice all spelling words online.
- Determine the meaning of multiple-meaning words.
- Make and modify inferences based on details in a text.
- Identify cause-and-effect relationships in a story.

GET READY

Introduction to *Baseball Saved Us*
Students will get a glimpse of what they will learn about in the lesson. They will also read the lesson goals and keywords. Have students select each keyword and preview its definition.

Spelling List 20 Review Game
Students will practice all spelling words from the workshop.

Before You Read *Baseball Saved Us*
Students will be introduced to some key vocabulary words that they will encounter in the upcoming reading, learn some important historical background related to the reading, and make an inference to help them set a focus for their reading.

Baseball Saved Us

Students will read *Baseball Saved Us* by Ken Mochizuki.

NOTE This story takes place during World War II, after the attack on Pearl Harbor by Japan. The story outlines the experiences a Japanese American person could have gone through in an internment camp and living in the United States. While there is no violence depicted, there are moments of discrimination and bullying, which may be a sensitive topic for students.

Check-In: *Baseball Saved Us*

Students will answer several questions to demonstrate their comprehension of *Baseball Saved Us*.

LEARN AND TRY IT

LEARN Cause-and-Effect Relationships

Students will learn how to use details from the text to identify cause-and-effect relationships from the story. They will also learn how to make inferences to help identify cause-and-effect relationships that are not directly stated by the author.

TRY IT Cause and Effect in *Baseball Saved Us*

Students will analyze passages and answer questions that involve identifying causes and their effects, using either explicit details from the text or making inferences.

TRY IT Apply: Identify Cause-and-Effect Relationships

Students will apply to a new work what they've learned about identifying cause and effect.

TRY IT How Do Cause and Effect Affect Character?

Students will complete How Do Cause and Effect Affect Character? from *Summit English Language Arts 4 Activity Book*.

LEARNING COACH CHECK-IN This activity page contains open-ended questions, so it's important that you review students' responses. Give students feedback, using the sample answers provided to guide you.

TRY IT   Practice Words from *Baseball Saved Us*

Students will answer questions to demonstrate their understanding of the vocabulary words from *Baseball Saved Us*.

WRAP-UP

Question About *Baseball Saved Us*

Students will answer a question to show that they understand cause-and-effect relationships in *Baseball Saved Us*.

Baseball Saved Us Wrap-Up

Lesson Overview

ACTIVITY	ACTIVITY TITLE	TIME	ONLINE/OFFLINE
GET READY	Introduction to *Baseball Saved Us* Wrap-Up	**1** minute	
TRY IT	Write About Theme in *Baseball Saved Us* **LEARNING COACH CHECK-IN**	**29** minutes	
	Read and Record	**15** minutes	
	Review *Baseball Saved Us*	**15** minutes	
QUIZ	*Baseball Saved Us*	**30** minutes	
	Spelling List 20	**10** minutes	
WRAP-UP	More Language Arts Practice	**20** minutes	

Lesson Goals

- Write about theme in *Baseball Saved Us* using details from the text.

- Practice reading aloud to develop fluency.

- Review the story *Baseball Saved Us*.

- Take a quiz on the characters, setting, plot, cause and effect, and theme in the story.

- Take a spelling quiz.

MATERIALS

Supplied
- *Baseball Saved Us* by Ken Mochizuki
- *Summit English Language Arts 4 Activity Book*
  - Write About Theme in *Baseball Saved Us*

GET READY

Introduction to *Baseball Saved Us* Wrap-Up

Students will read the lesson goals.

TRY IT

Write About Theme in *Baseball Saved Us*

Students will complete Write About Theme in *Baseball Saved Us* from *Summit English Language Arts 4 Activity Book*.

LEARNING COACH CHECK-IN This activity page contains open-ended questions, so it's important that you review students' responses. Give students feedback, using the sample answers provided to guide you.

TRY IT
Baseball Saved Us Wrap-Up

Write About Theme in *Baseball Saved Us*

Write your responses in complete sentences.

1. What is one of the themes in the book *Baseball Saved Us*? Write a paragraph explaining the theme.

Possible themes of *Baseball Saved Us* include that it takes determination to overcome obstacles and challenges and that determination and team support help when facing bullies.

2. What details from the story support the theme you identified in Question 1?

Example answer:

One theme of *Baseball Saved Us* is determination helps us overcome obstacles and challenges. Many characters deal with challenges that affect their character and actions.

In the camp, the conditions were bad for Shorty and his family. Everyone had to stand in line for food and to use the bathroom. They lived in barracks, which were small and had no walls. To help deal with this, Shorty's father came up with the idea to build a baseball field for the camp.

Another theme in the story is that determination and team support help when facing bullies. When Shorty was in school before coming to the camp, he was picked on for his height and always picked last to be on teams.

Also, during a game with his new team after returning from camp, the crowd calls him names and doesn't believe that he can do well. Shorty practices hard, believes in himself, and listens to his teammates' support to overcome the words of the crowd.

BASEBALL SAVED US WRAP-UP **343** | **344** BASEBALL SAVED US WRAP-UP | BASEBALL SAVED US WRAP-UP **345**

Read and Record

Good readers read quickly, smoothly, and with expression. This is called *fluency*. Students will record themselves reading aloud. They will listen to their recording and think about how quick, smooth, and expressive they sound.

TIP Encourage students to rerecord as needed.

Review *Baseball Saved Us*

Students will answer questions to review what they have learned about the characters, setting, plot, causes of and effects on events in, and theme of *Baseball Saved Us*.

QUIZ

Baseball Saved Us

Students will complete the *Baseball Saved Us* quiz.

Spelling List 20

Students will complete the Spelling List 20 quiz.

More Language Arts Practice

Students will practice skills according to their individual needs.

Opinion Writing: Revising

Lesson Overview

ACTIVITY	ACTIVITY TITLE	TIME	ONLINE/OFFLINE
GET READY	Introduction to Opinion Writing: Revising	**2** minutes	📶
	Explore a Student's Opinion Essay	**15** minutes	📶
LEARN AND **TRY IT**	Revising an Opinion Essay	**20** minutes	🖥️
	Revise Your Opinion Essay LEARNING COACH CHECK-IN	**60** minutes	📄
WRAP-UP	Question About Revising an Opinion Essay	**3** minutes	📶
	Go Read!	**20** minutes	📶 or 📄

Content Background

Students will continue working on their **opinion essay** about a topic of their choice. In this lesson, students will **revise** their rough draft.

Writing Process

| 1 Prewriting | 2 Drafting | **3 Revising** | 4 Proofreading | 5 Publishing |

To revise their essays, students will use a checklist. The checklist focuses on organization (*Are supporting facts and details grouped in the correct body paragraphs?*) and content (*Do I use enough facts and details, including at least one personal experience, to support each reason?*). At the end of this lesson, students will be ready to proofread their essays for grammar, usage, and mechanics.

Students may not understand the difference between revising and proofreading. When revising, writers focus on large issues, such as the order of ideas or the choice of transitions. When proofreading, writers fix errors in grammar, usage, and mechanics, such as spelling or punctuation mistakes. Encourage students to focus on revision during this lesson. In the next lesson, students will proofread their essays.

MATERIALS

Supplied
- *Summit English Language Arts 4 Activity Book*
  - Revise Your Opinion Essay
- Opinion Essay: Revision Feedback Sheet (printout)
- Opinion Essay Instructions (printout)

Also Needed
- folder in which students are storing opinion essay writing assignment pages
- reading material for Go Read!

Advance Preparation

Gather the folder that students are using to store the activity pages related to their opinion essay. The folder should contain the following:

- Students' completed Brainstorm for Your Opinion Essay activity page from Opinion Writing: Prewriting (A)

- Students' completed research notes from Opinion Writing: Prewriting (B)

- Students' completed Prewrite Your Opinion Essay activity page from Opinion Writing: Prewriting (C)

- Students' completed rough draft from Opinion Writing: Drafting (B)

Prior to the Revise Your Opinion Essay activity in this lesson, read students' rough draft and complete Opinion Essay: Revision Feedback Sheet.

During the Go Read! activity, students will have the option of using the digital library. Allow extra time for students to make their reading selection, or have students make a selection before beginning the lesson.

Lesson Goals

- Use a checklist to revise your essay.

- Read for pleasure.

GET READY

Introduction to Opinion Writing: Revising

Students will get a glimpse of what they will learn about in the lesson. They will also read the lesson goals and keywords. Have students select each keyword and preview its definition.

Explore a Student's Opinion Essay

Students will review the prerequisite skill of how to organize an opinion essay.

LEARN AND TRY IT

LEARN Revising an Opinion Essay

Students will learn about revising, including how to use a revision checklist. Through a guided activity, they will revise a sample student opinion essay.

TRY IT   Revise Your Opinion Essay

Students will complete Revise Your Opinion Essay from *Summit English Language Arts 4 Activity Book*. They will need their completed rough draft from Opinion Writing: Drafting (B).

LEARNING COACH CHECK-IN   Guide students through the revision process.

1. Gather and use the Opinion Essay: Revision Feedback Sheet that you filled out to guide a discussion with students.

   - Tell students the strengths of their essay. Provide positive comments about the ideas, language, detail, or other elements of the essay that you enjoyed.

   - Walk through your feedback with students.

   - As you discuss your feedback, encourage students to actively revise their draft in response. Reassure students that it's okay to remove or move around ideas and sentences. Students should revise their draft directly on the page, using the lines they left blank.

2. Have students review their draft once more, using the Revise Your Opinion Essay activity page.

   - For students having difficulty recognizing areas they should revise, suggest a revision, and think aloud to model your revising. For example: *This fact doesn't sound right here. It really goes with the ideas in the second paragraph. Let's move it there, or else the reader might get confused. Can you find any other facts or details that are out of place?*

3. Make sure students store their revised draft in the folder they are using to organize their writing assignment pages.

TIP   Remind students to focus on the checklist questions. Emphasize that they should not worry about spelling, punctuation, grammar, and so on.

NOTE   If you or students wish, you can download and print another copy of the Opinion Essay Instructions online.

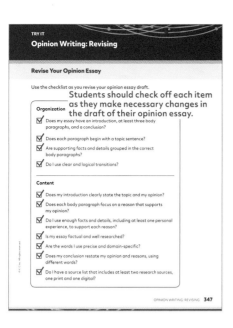

WRAP-UP

Question About Revising

Students will answer a question to show that they understand a key revision skill.

Go Read!

Students will read for pleasure. They should choose a book or a magazine that interests them, or they may choose a selection from the digital library, linked in the online lesson.

Students should read for the entire time. Have students select something to read ahead of time to help them stay focused.

Opinion Writing: Proofreading

Lesson Overview

ACTIVITY	ACTIVITY TITLE	TIME	ONLINE/OFFLINE
GET READY	Introduction to Opinion Writing: Proofreading	**2** minutes	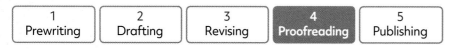
	Review Grammar Skills	**20** minutes	
LEARN AND **TRY IT**	Proofreading an Opinion Essay	**15** minutes	
	Proofread Your Opinion Essay LEARNING COACH CHECK-IN	**60** minutes	
WRAP-UP	Question About Proofreading an Opinion Essay	**3** minutes	
	Go Read!	**20** minutes	or

Content Background

Students will continue working on their **opinion essay** about a topic of their choice. In this lesson, students will **proofread** their revised rough draft.

Writing Process

1 Prewriting	2 Drafting	3 Revising	**4 Proofreading**	5 Publishing

To proofread their essays, students will use a checklist. The checklist focuses on grammar (*Are all sentences complete and correct?*), usage (*Are helping verbs used correctly, such as using* can *vs.* could *to express a particular meaning?*), and mechanics (*Is every word spelled correctly, including frequently confused words?*). After completing this lesson, students will be ready to prepare a clean copy of their essay.

Proofreading is sometimes called *editing*.

Advance Preparation

Gather the folder that students are using to store the activity pages related to their opinion essay. The folder should contain the following:

- Students' completed Brainstorm for Your Opinion Essay activity page from Opinion Writing: Prewriting (A)

- Students' completed research notes from Opinion Writing: Prewriting (B)

MATERIALS

Supplied

- *Summit English Language Arts 4 Activity Book*
  - Proofread Your Opinion Essay
- Opinion Essay: Proofreading Feedback Sheet (printout)
- Opinion Essay Instructions (printout)

Also Needed

- folder in which students are storing opinion essay writing assignment pages
- reading material for Go Read!

- Students' completed Prewrite Your Opinion Essay activity page from Opinion Writing: Prewriting (C)

- Students' revised draft from Opinion Writing: Revising

Prior to the Proofread Your Opinion Essay activity in this lesson, read students' revised draft. As you read, complete the Opinion Essay: Proofreading Feedback Sheet.

During the Go Read! activity, students will have the option of using the digital library. Allow extra time for students to make their reading selection, or have students make a selection before beginning the lesson.

KEYWORDS

opinion – something that a person thinks or believes but that cannot be proven to be true

proofreading – the stage or step of the writing process in which the writer checks for errors in grammar, punctuation, capitalization, and spelling

Lesson Goals

- Use a checklist to proofread your essay.

- Read for pleasure.

GET READY

Introduction to Opinion Writing: Proofreading
Students will get a glimpse of what they will learn about in the lesson. They will also read the lesson goals and keywords. Have students select each keyword and preview its definition.

Review Grammar Skills
Students will review prerequisite grammar skills.

LEARN AND TRY IT

LEARN Proofreading an Opinion Essay
Students will learn about proofreading, including how to use a proofreading checklist. Through a guided activity, they will proofread a sample student opinion essay.

TRY IT Proofread Your Opinion Essay
Students will complete Proofread Your Opinion Essay in *Summit English Language Arts 4 Activity Book*. They will need their revised rough draft from Opinion Writing: Revising.

LEARNING COACH CHECK-IN   Guide students through the proofreading process.

1. Have students read their draft aloud, listening for errors such as missing words, incomplete sentences, and agreement errors. As students catch errors, have them fix the errors.

   - For students having difficultly noticing errors as they read aloud, model the process. Slowly read a sentence aloud. Pause and model your thinking when you encounter an error. For example, *"Needs to change." This sentence sounds wrong. What needs to change? The subject is missing. Since the topic is throwing away paper instead of recycling it, I'll write "This practice" at the beginning of the sentence and lowercase the word "needs."*

2. Have students review their revised draft once more, using the Proofread Your Opinion Essay activity page.

3. Review with students your comments on the Opinion Essay: Proofreading Feedback Sheet. Praise students for the errors that they caught, and guide students to recognize any errors that they have not yet fixed.

4. Have students store their edited draft in the folder they are using to organize their writing assignment pages.

OPTIONAL   Have students exchange revised essays with a peer and use the Proofread Your Opinion Essay activity page to proofread each other's essays.

NOTE   If you or students wish, you can download and print another copy of the Opinion Essay Instructions online.

TRY IT

Opinion Writing: Proofreading

Proofread Your Opinion Essay

Use the checklist as you proofread your revised opinion essay draft.

Students should check off each item as they make necessary changes in their revised draft.

Grammar and Usage

- ☑ Are all sentences complete and correct?
- ☑ Are there any missing or extra words?
- ☑ Are helping verbs used correctly, such as using can vs. could to express a particular meaning?
- ☑ Are prepositional phrases used to add information to sentences?
- ☑ Are relative pronouns and relative adverbs used correctly?
- ☑ Are there other grammatical or usage errors?

Mechanics

- ☑ Is every word spelled correctly, including frequently confused words?
- ☑ Does every sentence begin with a capital letter and end with the appropriate punctuation?
- ☑ Is punctuation used thoughtfully and effectively?
- ☑ Are the titles of works in the source list capitalized correctly?
- ☑ Are there other punctuation or capitalization errors?

OPINION WRITING: PROOFREADING **349**

Question About Proofreading

Students will answer a question to show that they understand a key proofreading skill.

Go Read!

Students will read for pleasure. They should choose a book or a magazine that interests them, or they may choose a selection from the digital library, linked in the online lesson.

Students should read for the entire time. Have students select something to read ahead of time to help them stay focused.

Opinion Writing: Publishing

Lesson Overview

ACTIVITY	ACTIVITY TITLE	TIME	ONLINE/OFFLINE
GET READY	Introduction to Opinion Writing: Publishing	**1** minute	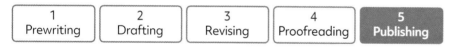
LEARN AND **TRY IT**	Publishing an Opinion Essay	**20** minutes	
	Publish Your Opinion Essay	**60** minutes	
WRAP-UP	Turn In Your Opinion Essay	**1** minute	
	More Language Arts Practice	**18** minutes	
	Go Read!	**20** minutes	

Content Background

Students will continue working on their **opinion essay** about a topic of their choice. In this lesson, students will **publish** their essay. Then they will submit their completed essay to their teacher.

Writing Process

1 Prewriting	2 Drafting	3 Revising	4 Proofreading	5 Publishing

Students will need to type their opinion essays using a word-processing program. They will complete an activity to review basic word-processing skills, such as using a keyboard and saving a document.

Advance Preparation

Gather the folder that students are using to store the activity pages related to their opinion essay. The folder should contain the following:

- Students' completed Brainstorm for Your Opinion Essay activity page from Opinion Writing: Prewriting (A)

- Students' completed research notes from Opinion Writing: Prewriting (B)

- Students' completed Prewrite Your Opinion Essay activity page from Opinion Writing: Prewriting (C)

- Students' revised and edited draft from Opinion Writing: Proofreading

MATERIALS

Supplied
- Opinion Essay Instructions (printout)

Also Needed
- folder in which students are storing opinion essay writing assignment pages
- reading material for Go Read!

KEYWORDS

opinion – something that a person thinks or believes but that cannot be proven to be true

publishing – the stage or step of the writing process in which the writer makes a clean copy of the piece and shares it

During the Go Read! activity, students will have the option of using the digital library. Allow extra time for students to make their reading selection, or have students make a selection before beginning the lesson.

Lesson Goals

- Type your opinion essay.
- Submit your opinion essay to your teacher.
- Read for pleasure.

GET READY

Introduction to Opinion Writing: Publishing

Students will read the lesson goals and keywords.

LEARN AND TRY IT

LEARN   Publishing an Opinion Essay

Students will learn about word-processing skills in preparation for typing their opinion essay.

TRY IT   Publish Your Opinion Essay

Students will type a final copy of their opinion essay. Students should gather their revised and proofread draft, and they should type it using a word-processing program.

NOTE   If you or students wish, you can download and print another copy of the Opinion Essay Instructions online.

WRAP-UP

Turn In Your Opinion Essay

Students will submit their writing assignment to their teacher.

More Language Arts Practice

Students will practice skills according to their individual needs.

Go Read!

Students will read for pleasure. They should choose a book or magazine that interests them, or they may choose a selection from the digital library, linked in the online lesson.

Students should read for the entire time. Have students select something to read ahead of time to help them stay focused.

Greek Roots

Lesson Overview

ACTIVITY	ACTIVITY TITLE	TIME	ONLINE/OFFLINE
GET READY	Introduction to Greek Roots	**1** minute	🖥️
	Look Back at Roots	**4** minutes	🖥️
LEARN AND **TRY IT**	Words That Come from Greek	**10** minutes	🖥️
	Practice Using Greek Roots	**10** minutes	🖥️
	Apply: Greek Roots LEARNING COACH CHECK-IN	**15** minutes	📄
	Go Write!	**15** minutes	📄
	Review Greek Roots	**15** minutes	🖥️
QUIZ	Greek Roots	**15** minutes	🖥️
WRAP-UP	More Language Arts Practice	**19** minutes	🖥️
	Go Read!	**15** minutes	🖥️ or 📄

Content Background

Students will learn about words that have the Greek roots *phon*, *derm*, and *hydro*. They will learn how knowing the meaning of a word's root can help them determine the meaning of the word. They will also learn how context clues can help them determine the meaning of a word with a Greek root.

A root is a word part with a special meaning, to which we can attach letters, prefixes, and suffixes to form a complete word. For example, *bio* is a root that means "life." This is the root of the word *biography*, which is the written story of somebody's life.

It is important to know that a root cannot stand alone. It must have other letters or word parts attached to it to become a complete word. Thus, the root *derm* is not a word on its own. But when other letters or word parts are attached, it is the foundation of words such as *epidermis* and *dermatology*.

Advance Preparation

During the Go Read! activity, students will have the option of using the digital library. Allow extra time for students to make their reading selection, or have students make a selection before beginning the lesson.

Lesson Goals

- Use Greek roots to determine the meanings of words.
- Use context clues to determine the meanings of words.
- Read and write for pleasure.

GET READY

Introduction to Greek Roots

Students will get a glimpse of what they will learn about in the lesson. They will also read the lesson and keywords. Have students select each keyword and preview its definition.

Look Back at Roots

Students will review the definition of a root. They will also review words they may have previously learned that are formed with common roots.

LEARN AND TRY IT

LEARN   Words That Come from Greek

Students will learn the definition of several words that have Greek roots. They will also learn how the meaning of a root can help them to define an unknown word and how context clues can help them to define a word with a Greek root.

TIP   Point out to students that a root such as *hydro* may drop the letter *o* when suffixes are added. For example, the word *hydrant* drops the letter *o* from the root *hydro*, and then adds the suffix *–ant*.

TRY IT   Practice Using Greek Roots

Students will practice breaking down words formed with Greek roots and affixes to determine the meanings of words. They will also use context clues combined with knowledge of Greek roots to define words.

TRY IT   Apply: Greek Roots

Students will complete Apply: Greek Roots from *Summit English Language Arts 4 Activity Book*.

LEARNING COACH CHECK-IN   This activity page contains open-ended questions, so it's important that you review students' responses. Give students feedback, using the example answers provided to guide you.

Apply: Greek Roots

Answer the questions. Use complete sentences in your responses to questions that ask for an explanation.

1. The word *hydrate* means "to give water to or to drink water." Which word means the opposite of *hydrate*—*hydrant* or *dehydrate*? Explain why that word is the opposite of *hydrate*.

Example answer:

The word dehydrate is the opposite of hydrate. Hydrate means to give water to, but dehydrate means to remove water from.

2. The prefix *re-* means "again." What word could you form that means "to give water to again"?

rehydrate

3. Why might you need to rehydrate a plant? Explain how you would do it. Be sure to use the word *rehydrate* in your answer.

Example answer:

You might need to rehydrate a plant if it hasn't been watered in a while. Maybe the plant has dried out. You would rehydrate a plant by giving it water.

4. Who is more likely to use a *hydrant*—a police officer or a firefighter? Why? In your answer, be sure to explain how a hydrant is used.

Example answer:

A firefighter is more likely to use a hydrant than a police officer because water comes out of a hydrant. A firefighter needs water to put out fires. A hydrant gets water from the main water pipes. A firefighter has to hook up a hose to the hydrant. Then he can get water from the hydrant to put out a fire.

5. The definition of *dermatology* is "the science of or the study of the skin." The definition of *biology* is "the science of or the study of life." What word means the "the science or study of water"?

hydrology

6. List two additional words that contain the Greek root *hydro*. You may want to refer to a dictionary.

Accept any reasonable answer. Possible answers include: hydropower, hydroelectric, hydrotherapy, hydrogen, hydroplane

TRY IT   Go Write!

Students will write independently for pleasure. As they write, they should think about using words with Greek roots in their writing.

TRY IT   Review Greek Roots

Students will answer questions to review what they have learned about words with Greek roots.

QUIZ

Greek Roots

Students will complete the Greek Roots quiz.

WRAP-UP

More Language Arts Practice

Students will practice skills according to their individual needs.

Go Read!

Students will read for pleasure. They should choose a book or a magazine that interests them, or they may choose a selection from the digital library, linked in the online lesson.

Students should read for the entire time. Have students select something to read ahead of time to help them stay focused.

"Maria Gonzalez, Modern Hero"

Lesson Overview

ACTIVITY	ACTIVITY TITLE	TIME	ONLINE/OFFLINE
GET READY	Introduction to "Maria Gonzalez, Modern Hero"	**1** minute	🖥️
	Spelling List 21 Pretest **LEARNING COACH CHECK-IN**	**10** minutes	🖥️ and 📄
	Before You Read "Maria Gonzalez, Modern Hero"	**14** minute	🖥️
READ	"Maria Gonzalez, Modern Hero"	**30** minutes	📄
	Check-In: "Maria Gonzalez, Modern Hero"	**5** minutes	🖥️
LEARN AND **TRY IT**	Allusions in "Maria Gonzalez, Modern Hero"	**15** minutes	🖥️
	Identify and Describe Allusions	**10** minutes	🖥️
	Apply: Allusions	**15** minutes	🖥️
	A Herculean Task **LEARNING COACH CHECK-IN**	**10** minutes	📄
	Practice Words from "Maria Gonzalez, Modern Hero"	**8** minutes	🖥️
WRAP-UP	Question About "Maria Gonzalez, Modern Hero"	**2** minutes	🖥️

Content Background

Students will learn about allusions in text. An allusion is a reference to a significant literary or historical figure. It can also be a reference to a well-known place, event, or statement. Allusions are references that make ideas easier to understand. One example of an allusion is the statement, "I don't think we're in Kansas anymore." It's an allusion to *The Wizard of Oz*, and it means that everything is unfamiliar and different.

Students will learn about allusions to characters in mythology. Often, allusions to mythological characters are related to those characters' qualities or actions. For example, the allusions "a Herculean task" and "a Herculean effort" refer to the Greek hero Hercules. Hercules was very strong, and he was required to perform twelve labors that were extremely difficult. These labors included defeating the Hydra, a nine-headed snake, and capturing Cerberus, the three-headed dog that guards the underworld. So a Herculean task is a task that is extremely difficult and almost impossible to complete. A Herculean effort refers to the great effort and strength required to complete a difficult task.

"Maria Gonzalez, Modern Hero" Synopsis

In most ways, Maria Gonzalez is a typical nine-year-old. She's bright, has many friends, sings in the choir, and plays basketball. But she does all of this in a wheelchair. When she feels down, she cheers herself up by reading the myths of ancient Greece and Rome. Maria feels a special connection to Athena, the Greek goddess of wisdom and heroism. She imagines herself to be like Athena, using daring and intelligence to save the day. Then one day, Maria has the chance to do just that as she stops a criminal in his tracks.

Lesson Goals

- Take a spelling pretest.
- Identify words and phrases that allude to characters in mythology.
- Describe how allusions to mythological characters affect the meaning of text.
- Determine meanings of unfamiliar words in the reading.

GET READY

Introduction to "Maria Gonzalez, Modern Hero"

Students will get a glimpse of what they will learn about in the lesson. They will also read the lesson goals and keywords. Have students select each keyword and preview its definition.

Spelling List 21 Pretest

Students will take a spelling pretest.

LEARNING COACH CHECK-IN   Have students turn to Spelling List 21 Pretest in *Summit English Language Arts 4 Activity Book* and open the online Spelling Pretest activity. Online, students will listen to the spelling word, type the word in the space indicated, and then check their answer. In the activity book, students will write the correct spelling of the word in the tables provided and indicate with a ✓ or an ✗ if they spelled the word correctly or incorrectly online. Students will repeat this process with the remaining words.

As needed, help students with the interaction between the online activity and the activity book page until they become comfortable with what they need to do. As students practice their spelling words throughout the workshop, they should pay special attention to words they spelled incorrectly on the pretest.

This is the complete list of words students will be tested on.

/f/ Spelled *ph*	/g/ Spelled *gu*	Root *aud*	Heart Words
dolphin	guard	audible	Idaho
hyphen	guess	audience	South Dakota
philosophy	guest	audio	
photograph	guide	audition	
trophy	guilty		
	guitar		

NOTE Have students keep their completed activity page in a safe place so they can refer to it later.

Before You Read "Maria Gonzalez, Modern Hero"

Students will be introduced to some key vocabulary words that they will encounter in the upcoming reading and learn some important background related to the reading.

READ

"Maria Gonzalez, Modern Hero"

Students will read "Maria Gonzalez, Modern Hero" in *Expeditions in Reading*.

Check-In: "Maria Gonzalez, Modern Hero"

Students will answer questions to demonstrate their comprehension of "Maria Gonzalez, Modern Hero."

LEARN AND TRY IT

LEARN   Allusions in "Maria Gonzalez, Modern Hero"

Students will learn about allusions to characters from mythology. They will learn how allusions can give a reader a better understanding of a story and a story's characters.

TRY IT   Identify and Describe Allusions

Students will identify allusions in text and determine how the allusions contribute to a story's meaning.

TRY IT   Apply: Allusions

Students will apply to a new work what they've learned about allusions to characters in mythology.

TRY IT   A Herculean Task

Students will complete A Herculean Task from *Summit English Language Arts 4 Activity Book*.

SUPPORT   For students having difficulty thinking of a Herculean task to write about, suggest that they think about something that is difficult for them to do. Help them understand that any task that is difficult and takes a great deal of effort to complete could be considered a Herculean task for them. It does not have to be a task that takes superhuman effort to complete.

LEARNING COACH CHECK-IN   This activity page contains an open-ended question, so it's important that you review students' responses. Give students feedback, using the sample answers provided to guide you.

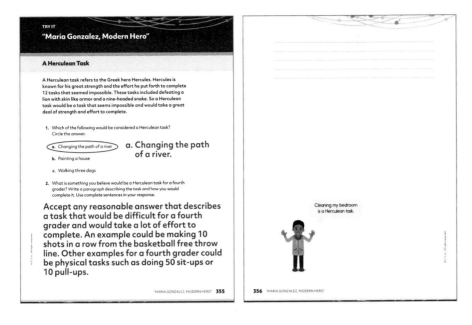

TRY IT   Practice Words from "Maria Gonzalez, Modern Hero"

Students will answer questions to demonstrate their understanding of the vocabulary words from the reading.

WRAP-UP

Question About "Maria Gonzalez, Modern Hero"

Students will answer a question to show that they are able to identify an allusion to a character from mythology.

"Maria Gonzalez, Modern Hero" Wrap-Up

Lesson Overview

ACTIVITY	ACTIVITY TITLE	TIME	ONLINE/OFFLINE
GET READY	Introduction to "Maria Gonzalez, Modern Hero" Wrap-Up	**1** minute	
TRY IT	Spelling List 21 Activity Bank	**10** minutes	
	Match Them Up **LEARNING COACH CHECK-IN**	**29** minutes	
	Read and Record	**15** minutes	
	Review "Maria Gonzalez, Modern Hero"	**15** minutes	
QUIZ	"Maria Gonzalez, Modern Hero"	**30** minutes	
WRAP-UP	More Language Arts Practice	**20** minutes	

Advance Preparation

Gather students' completed Spelling List 21 Pretest activity page from "Maria Gonzalez, Modern Hero." Students will refer to this page during Get Ready: Spelling List 21 Activity Bank.

Lesson Goals

- Practice all spelling words.
- Match characters from mythology to descriptions of people, and explain why they match.
- Practice reading aloud to develop fluency.
- Review the story "Maria Gonzalez, Modern Hero."
- Take a quiz on allusions and content from the story "Maria Gonzalez, Modern Hero."

GET READY

Introduction to "Maria Gonzalez, Modern Hero" Wrap-Up

Students will read the lesson goals.

Spelling List 21 Activity Bank

Students will practice all spelling words from the workshop by completing Spelling List 21 Activity Bank from *Summit English Language Arts 4 Activity Book*. Make sure students have their completed Spelling List 21 Pretest activity page from "Maria Gonzalez, Modern Hero" to refer to during this activity.

Remind students to pay special attention to words they spelled incorrectly on the Spelling Pretest.

GET READY
"Maria Gonzalez, Modern Hero" Wrap-Up

Spelling List 21 Activity Bank

Circle any words in the box that you did not spell correctly on the pretest. Using your circled words, complete one activity of your choice. Complete as much of the activity as you can in the time given.

If you spelled all words correctly on the pretest, complete your chosen activity with as many spelling words as you can.

dolphin	trophy	guide	audible	audition
hyphen	guard	guilty	audience	Idaho
philosophy	guess	guitar	audio	South Dakota
photograph	guest			

Spelling Activity Choices

Silly Sentences

1. Write a silly sentence using your words from the spelling word list.

2. Underline the spelling word in each sentence.
   Example: The dog was <u>driving</u> a car.

3. Correct any spelling errors.

"MARIA GONZALEZ, MODERN HERO" WRAP-UP **357**

Spelling Story

1. Write a very short story using your words from the spelling word list.

2. Underline the spelling words in the story.

3. Correct any spelling errors.

Riddle Me This

1. Write a riddle for your words from the spelling word list.
   Example: "I have a trunk, but it's not on my car."

2. Write the answer, which is your word, for each riddle.
   Example: Answer: elephant

3. Correct any spelling errors.

RunOnWord

1. Gather some crayons, colored pencils, or markers. Write each of your words, using a different color for each word, end to end as one long word.
   Example: dogcatbirdfishturtle

2. Rewrite the words correctly and with proper spacing.

358 "MARIA GONZALEZ, MODERN HERO" WRAP-UP

Complete the activity that you chose.

My chosen activity:

Students should use this page to complete all steps in their chosen activity.

"MARIA GONZALEZ, MODERN HERO" WRAP-UP **359**

TRY IT

Match Them Up

Students will complete Match Them Up from *Summit English Language Arts 4 Activity Book*.

LEARNING COACH CHECK-IN   This activity page contains open-ended questions, so it's important that you review students' responses. Give students feedback, using the sample answers provided to guide you.

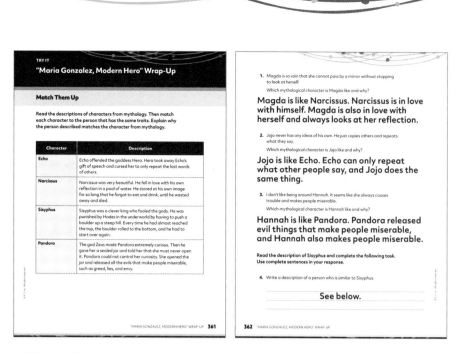

Additional answers

4. Students' responses should describe a person who has trouble completing tasks and often must start over. Example answer: Will never finishes anything. Whenever he gets close to completing a job, something goes wrong, and he has to start over again.

Read and Record

Good readers read quickly, smoothly, and with expression. This is called *fluency*. Students will record themselves reading aloud. They will listen to their recording and think about how quick, smooth, and expressive they sound.

TIP Encourage students to rerecord as needed.

Review "Maria Gonzalez, Modern Hero"

Students will review what they have learned about allusions to characters from mythology. They will also review content from the story.

QUIZ

"Maria Gonzalez, Modern Hero"

Students will complete the "Maria Gonzalez, Modern Hero" quiz.

WRAP-UP

More Language Arts Practice

Students will practice skills according to their individual needs.

"Grace"

Lesson Overview

ACTIVITY	ACTIVITY TITLE	TIME	ONLINE/OFFLINE
GET READY	Introduction to "Grace"	**1** minute	
	Spelling List 21 Review Game	**10** minutes	
	Before You Read "Grace"	**14** minutes	
READ	"Grace"	**30** minutes	
	Check-In: "Grace"	**5** minutes	
LEARN AND **TRY IT**	Words Matter: Author's Word Choice	**15** minutes	
	Word Choice	**10** minutes	
	Apply: Author's Word Choice	**15** minutes	
	Write a Summary of "Grace" **LEARNING COACH CHECK-IN**	**10** minutes	
	Practice Words from "Grace"	**8** minutes	
WRAP-UP	Question About "Grace"	**2** minutes	

Content Background

Students will learn how an author's choice of words influences a story and a reader's experience reading it. An author's choice of words is very deliberate. Some words are used to set a mood. For example, when the author describes a room as having a gloomy orange tint, it creates a gloomy mood in the story.

Other words and phrases, such as figurative language, create vivid images and help a reader better understand a story and its characters. For example, the character Grace dreads hearing her mother use her full name because the words "pierce her like an arrow to the heart." This simile provides insight into how painful it is for Grace to disappoint her mother.

An author's specific choice of words assists a reader to make inferences. For example, Grace's dad says he doesn't want to face her mom's wrath, but he says it with a wink. We might infer that Grace's mom is going to get angry, but the addition of the word "wink" leads to the inference that Grace's dad is joking and her mother won't get too angry.

MATERIALS

Supplied
- *Summit English Language Arts 4 Expeditions in Reading*
- *Summit English Language Arts 4 Activity Book*
  - Write a Summary of "Grace"

Finally, students will learn how a past event can influence future events in a story. For example, at the beginning of the story, Grace is sitting in her room crying. As we read further, we learn that the past event of Grace lying about her sister getting hurt has resulted in her being sent to her room.

KEYWORDS

figurative language – words that describe something by comparing it to something completely different; for example: "Rain fell in buckets, and the streets looked like rivers."

infer – to use clues and what you already know to make a guess

inference – a guess that readers make using the clues that an author gives them in a piece of writing

"Grace" Synopsis

As Grace sits in her room waiting for her mother to arrive home, she is crying. She is very worried about her mother being disappointed in her. As the story goes back in time, we learn that earlier in the day, Grace and her sister Karen built a catapult out of toys scattered in the family basement. Grace then made a poor decision, which led to her sister getting hurt. When Grace lied to her father about what happened, he sent her to her room to wait for her mother. When her mother arrives, she tells Grace a story about building a crane when she was Grace's age. She ended up breaking the taillight on her father's car and getting in trouble. But she got in trouble for lying to her father, not for breaking the light. Grace's mother explains that it's important to be safe when building things and to always tell the truth.

Lesson Goals

- Practice all spelling words.
- Explain how the author's word choice sets the mood in a story.
- Make inferences about characters and events in a story.
- Use context clues to determine the meaning of figurative language.
- Determine how past events influence future events in a story.
- Write a summary of "Grace."
- Determine meanings of unfamiliar words in the reading.

Introduction to "Grace"
Students will get a glimpse of what they will learn about in the lesson. They will also read the lesson goals and keywords. Have students select each keyword and preview its definition.

Spelling List 21 Review Game

Students will practice all spelling words from the workshop.

Before You Read "Grace"

Students will be introduced to some key vocabulary words that they will encounter in the upcoming reading.

READ

"Grace"

Students will read "Grace" in *Expeditions in Reading*.

Check-In: "Grace"

Students will answer questions to demonstrate their comprehension of "Grace."

LEARN AND TRY IT

LEARN   Words Matter

Students will learn about an author's word choice. They will learn how the words an author uses can create a mood, how figurative language can help a reader understand characters and events, and how specific language can help a reader make inferences. Students will also learn how a past event can influence a future event in a story.

> **SUPPORT**   For students having difficulty recognizing that an event described in the middle of the story actually happened before the events in the beginning, help them to create a time line of the story's events. Seeing a graphic representation of the order of events will help them understand that the author uses a flashback to describe past events.

TRY IT   Word Choice

Students will analyze passages to determine the meaning of figurative language, how word choice creates a mood, and how to use the author's words to make inferences. They will also determine how a past event influences a future event.

TRY IT   Apply: Author's Word Choice

Students will apply to a new work what they've learned about an author's word choice.

TRY IT   Write a Summary of "Grace"

Students will complete Write a Summary of "Grace" in *Summit English Language Arts 4 Activity Book*.

> **LEARNING COACH CHECK-IN**   This activity page contains an open-ended question, so it's important that you review students' responses. Give students feedback, using the sample answers provided to guide you.

TRY IT   Practice Words from "Grace"

Students will answer questions to demonstrate their understanding of the vocabulary
words from the reading.

WRAP-UP

Question About "Grace"

Students will answer a question to show that they know how to make an inference.

"Grace" Wrap-Up

Lesson Overview

ACTIVITY	ACTIVITY TITLE	TIME	ONLINE/OFFLINE
GET READY	Introduction to "Grace" Wrap-Up	**1** minute	
TRY IT	Write About Theme in "Grace" LEARNING COACH CHECK-IN	**29** minutes	
	Read and Record	**15** minutes	
	Review "Grace"	**15** minutes	
QUIZ	"Grace"	**30** minutes	
	Spelling List 21	**10** minutes	
WRAP-UP	More Language Arts Practice	**20** minutes	

Lesson Goals

- Write about a theme in "Grace."
- Practice reading aloud to develop fluency.
- Review the story "Grace."
- Take a quiz on author's word choice, figurative language, making inferences, and content from the story "Grace."
- Take a spelling quiz.

MATERIALS

Supplied
- *Summit English Language Arts 4 Expeditions in Reading*
- *Summit English Language Arts 4 Activity Book*
  - Write About Theme in "Grace"

GET READY

Introduction to "Grace" Wrap-Up

Students will read the lesson goals.

TRY IT

Write About Theme in "Grace"

Students will complete Write About Theme in "Grace" from *Summit English Language Arts 4 Activity Book*.

SUPPORT   For students having difficulty determine the story's theme, ask them to think about the main reason Grace got in trouble (for lying) and what lesson Grace learned from her experience.

LEARNING COACH CHECK-IN   This activity page contains an open-ended question, so it's important that you review students' responses. Give students feedback, using the sample answer provided to guide you.

TRY IT

"Grace" Wrap-Up

Write About Theme in "Grace"

Write your responses in complete sentences.

What is a theme the author conveys in "Grace"? Write a paragraph explaining the theme. Be sure to include examples of how the actions of the story's characters support the theme.

Example answer:

A theme in the story "Grace" is that it's always best to tell the truth and not lie. Grace's actions show that it is not good to lie. First, she lied to her dad about not throwing things when she and Karen were playing. Right after that, Karen got hurt. Then Grace lied to her dad and said she didn't know how Karen got hurt. That's why her dad sent her to her room. When Grace's mom was her age, she also got in trouble for lying. She broke the taillight on her father's car. She didn't get in trouble for breaking the light. She got in trouble for lying about it. The actions of Grace and her mother show that you should not lie and that it's best to always tell the truth.

'GRACE' WRAP-UP **365**

366 'GRACE' WRAP-UP

Read and Record

Good readers read quickly, smoothly, and with expression. This is called *fluency*. Students will record themselves reading aloud. They will listen to their recording and think about how quick, smooth, and expressive they sound.

TIP   Encourage students to rerecord as needed.

Review "Grace"

Students will answer questions to review what they have learned about an author's word choice, figurative language, and making inferences. They will also review content from the story.

QUIZ

"Grace"

Students will complete the "Grace" quiz.

Spelling List 21

Students will complete the Spelling List 21 quiz.

WRAP-UP

More Language Arts Practice

Students will practice skills according to their individual needs.

Big Ideas: Respond to a Prompt

Lesson Overview

Big Ideas lessons provide students the opportunity to further apply the knowledge acquired and skills learned throughout the unit workshops. Each Big Ideas lesson consists of these parts:

1. **Cumulative Review:** Students keep their skills fresh by reviewing prior content.

2. **Preview:** Students practice answering the types of questions they will commonly find on standardized tests.

3. **Synthesis:** Students complete an assignment that allows them to connect and apply what they have learned. Synthesis assignments vary throughout the course.

   In the Synthesis portion of this Big Ideas lesson, students will respond to an essay prompt based on reading selections. To respond meaningfully, students will need to use their own ideas as well as examples from the readings. Students' writing will be assessed in four categories: purpose and content; structure and organization; language and word choice; and grammar, usage, and mechanics.

   LEARNING COACH CHECK-IN   This is a graded assessment. Make sure students complete, review, and submit the assignment to their teacher.

All materials needed for this lesson are linked online and not provided in the Activity Book.

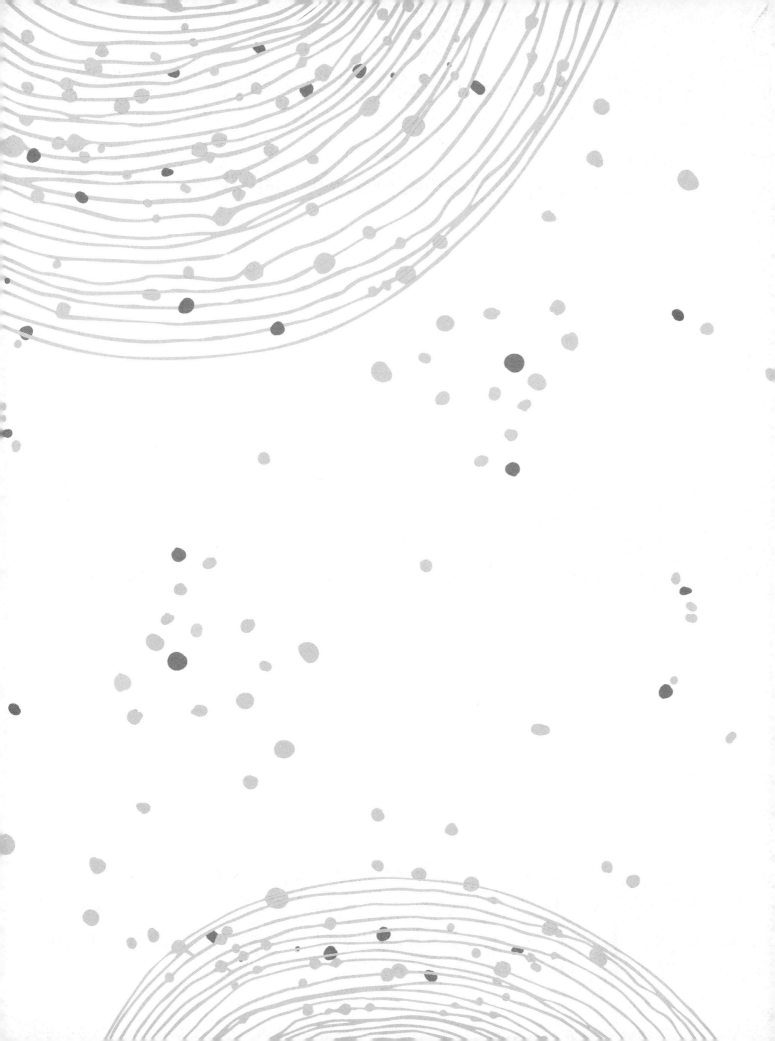

Healthy and Safe

Presentation Skills (A)

Lesson Overview

ACTIVITY	ACTIVITY TITLE	TIME	ONLINE/OFFLINE
GET READY	Healthy and Safe Unit Overview	**1** minute	
	Introduction to Presentation Skills (A)	**1** minute	
	Look Back at Formal and Informal English	**4** minutes	
LEARN AND **TRY IT**	Different Types of Language	**10** minutes	
	Identify Different Types of Language	**10** minutes	
	Retelling an Experience	**15** minutes	
	Analyze How an Experience Is Retold	**15** minutes	
	Tell About an Experience **LEARNING COACH CHECK-IN**	**35** minutes	
WRAP-UP	Questions About Language and Storytelling	**4** minutes	
	Go Read!	**25** minutes	or

Content Background

Students will explore presentation, or speaking, skills. Presentation skills are the skills one needs to deliver an effective and engaging speech to a particular audience.

Students will learn skills related to the organization and content of a speech. They will learn how to effectively tell about an experience by organizing their information so that it has a clear beginning, middle, and end. They will learn that descriptions, or details that evoke the five senses, are especially effective in speech. They will also learn that any details they include in a speech should be relevant to the speech's theme or main idea.

Students will use the skills they learn to tell about an experience that they had. In fact, they will tell about the experience twice, once using informal language, and once using formal language.

Grammar, Usage, and Mechanics Students will learn about the difference between formal and informal language, including when it is appropriate to use each type of language. Formal language is precise and academic,

MATERIALS

Supplied
- *Summit English Language Arts 4 Activity Book*
  - Tell About an Experience

Also Needed
- reading material for Go Read!

and it does not include slang or contractions. Informal language is more conversational and may include slang or contractions.

Formal: Would you care to join me for lunch?

Informal: Want to grab some lunch?

Advance Preparation

Try It: Tell About an Experience specifies that students deliver a speech to their Learning Coach.

During the Go Read! activity, students will have the option of using the digital library. Allow extra time for students to make their reading selection, or have students make a selection before beginning the lesson.

Lesson Goals

- Explore formal and informal language.
- Analyze the ideas and organization of a speech.
- Give your own formal and informal speeches on the same topic.
- Read for pleasure.

description – writing that uses words that show how something looks, sounds, feels, tastes, or smells

formal language – the choice of words, phrases, and sentences that adhere to the conventional standards of grammar, usage, and mechanics

informal language – language that may include, for example, personal feeling, slang, contractions, humor, and fragments

GET READY

Healthy and Safe Unit Overview
Students will read a summary of what they will learn in the Healthy and Safe unit.

Introduction to Presentation Skills (A)
Students will get a glimpse of what they will learn about in the lesson. They will also read the lesson goals and keywords. Have students select each keyword and preview its definition.

Look Back at Formal and Informal English
Students will practice the prerequisite skill of recognizing the difference between formal and informal language.

LEARN Different Types of Language

Students will explore elements of formal and informal language, including when it is appropriate to use one or the other, in both speech and writing.

TRY IT Identify Different Types of Language

Students will practice determining which type of language would be best to use in a given situation. They will receive feedback on their answers.

LEARN Retelling an Experience

Students will listen to a speech about an experience that is described formally. Then they will listen to the same experience described informally. They will explore the elements that make the speeches formal or informal.

Then students will explore the content and organization of the speeches. They will learn that speeches have a clear beginning, middle, and end. They will focus on using relevant, descriptive details that support the speech's main idea or theme and influence listeners.

TRY IT Analyze How an Experience Is Retold

Students will listen to a short speech about an experience and answer questions about its content and organization. They will receive feedback on their answers.

TRY IT Tell About an Experience

Students will complete Tell About an Experience from *Summit English Language Arts 4 Activity Book*. They will plan a short speech and then deliver the speech twice—first using informal language and then using formal language.

LEARNING COACH CHECK-IN As part of this activity, students will deliver speeches to you. Encourage students by pointing out things that they did well during their speeches. Offer words of encouragement if students appear nervous or shy about speaking aloud.

TIP Students can speak to an audience—even a virtual one! If possible, encourage students to present their speeches to a friend or a relative near or far.

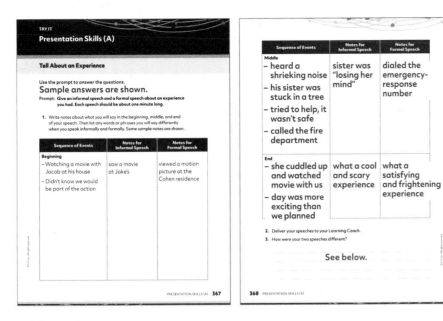

Additional answers

3. Possible answer: In my formal speech, I used precise words instead of slang, such as "residence," and I used whole words like "I have" instead of contractions. In my informal speech, I used slang words such as "a blast" and contractions like "didn't."

WRAP-UP

Questions About Language and Storytelling

Students will answer questions to show that they understand formal and informal language and elements of storytelling.

Go Read!

Students will read for pleasure. They should choose a book or a magazine that interests them, or they may choose a selection from the digital library, linked in the online lesson.

Students should read for the entire time. Have students select something to read ahead of time to help them stay focused.

Presentation Skills (B)

Lesson Overview

ACTIVITY	ACTIVITY TITLE	TIME	ONLINE/OFFLINE
GET READY	Introduction to Presentation Skills (B)	**1** minute	🖥
LEARN AND **TRY IT**	Choose the Type of Language	**10** minutes	🖥
	Practice Choosing the Type of Language	**10** minutes	🖥
	Clarity and Pace	**15** minutes	🖥
	Analyze Clarity and Pace	**15** minutes	🖥
	Read Aloud Like a Pro **LEARNING COACH CHECK-IN**	**35** minutes	🖥 and 📄
WRAP-UP	Questions About Language and Pace	**4** minutes	🖥
	Go Read!	**30** minutes	🖥 and 📄

Content Background

Students will continue to learn about presentation skills. In this lesson, they will focus on skills related to the mechanics of speaking: speaking at an understandable pace and speaking clearly. Pace refers to how quickly or slowly someone speaks. Clarity refers to the correct pronunciation of words, as well as speaking at an appropriate volume.

To practice the presentation skills they learn in this lesson, students will record themselves reading aloud an excerpt from the story "Cinderella." They will listen to their recording and critique their pace and clarity.

Advance Preparation

During the Go Read! activity, students will have the option of using the digital library. Allow extra time for students to make their reading selection, or have students make a selection before beginning the lesson.

> ### MATERIALS
>
> **Supplied**
> - *Summit English Language Arts 4 Activity Book*
>   - Read Aloud Like a Pro
>
> **Also Needed**
> - reading material for Go Read!

Lesson Goals

- Decide whether formal or informal language is appropriate for a given situation.

- Analyze a speaker's pace and clarity.

- Read aloud a passage with appropriate pace and clarity.

- Read for pleasure.

GET READY

Introduction to Presentation Skills (B)

Students will get a glimpse of what they will learn about in the lesson. They will also read the lesson goals and keywords. Have students select each keyword and preview its definition.

LEARN AND TRY IT

LEARN   Choose the Type of Language

Students will learn how to evaluate whether language is appropriate for formal or informal situations.

TRY IT   Practice Choosing the Type of Language

Students will evaluate whether language is appropriate for formal or informal situations. They will receive feedback on their answers.

LEARN   Clarity and Pace

Students will learn what it means to speak clearly and at an understandable pace. They will explore how audience and purpose affect a speaker's clarity and pace.

TIP   Speaking too quickly is a common problem for many speakers.

TRY IT   Analyze Clarity and Pace

Students will answer questions about speaking clearly and at an understandable pace. They will receive feedback on their answers.

TRY IT   Read Aloud Like a Pro

Students will complete Read Aloud Like a Pro from *Summit English Language Arts 4 Activity Book*.

NOTE   Students will record themselves reading aloud a passage using an online recording tool. Then they will listen to their recording, think about

improvements they can make, and read and record the passage again. Ensure that students have access to a computer while completing the activity.

LEARNING COACH CHECK-IN　Encourage students to read aloud the passage to you, or listen to their recorded passage. Give students feedback, using Question 2 on the activity page as a guide.

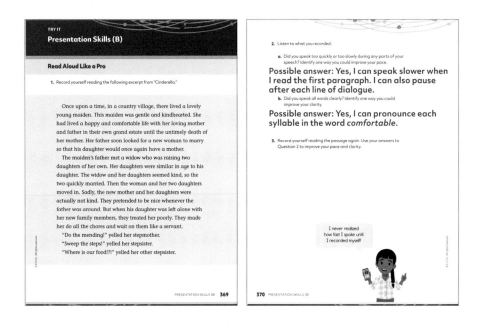

TRY IT
Presentation Skills (B)

Read Aloud Like a Pro

1. Record yourself reading the following excerpt from "Cinderella."

Once upon a time, in a country village, there lived a lovely young maiden. This maiden was gentle and kindhearted. She had lived a happy and comfortable life with her loving mother and father in their own grand estate until the untimely death of her mother. Her father soon looked for a new woman to marry so that his daughter would once again have a mother.

The maiden's father met a widow who was raising two daughters of her own. Her daughters were similar in age to his daughter. The widow and her daughters seemed kind, so the two quickly married. Then the woman and her two daughters moved in. Sadly, the new mother and her daughters were actually not kind. They pretended to be nice whenever the father was around. But when his daughter was left alone with her new family members, they treated her poorly. They made her do all the chores and wait on them like a servant.

"Do the mending!" yelled her stepmother.

"Sweep the steps!" yelled her stepsister.

"Where is our food!?!" yelled her other stepsister.

PRESENTATION SKILLS (B)　**369**

370　PRESENTATION SKILLS (B)

2. Listen to what you recorded.

   a. Did you speak too quickly or too slowly during any parts of your speech? Identify one way you could improve your pace.

   Possible answer: Yes, I can speak slower when I read the first paragraph. I can also pause after each line of dialogue.

   b. Did you speak all words clearly? Identify one way you could improve your clarity.

   Possible answer: Yes, I can pronounce each syllable in the word *comfortable*.

3. Record yourself reading the passage again. Use your answers to Question 2 to improve your pace and clarity.

I never realized how fast I spoke until I recorded myself!

WRAP-UP

Questions About Language and Pace

Students will answer questions to show that they understand how to choose language appropriate for a given situation and how to speak at an appropriate pace.

Go Read!

Students will read for pleasure. They should choose a book or a magazine that interests them, or they may choose a selection from the digital library, linked in the online lesson.

Students should read for the entire time. Have students select something to read ahead of time to help them stay focused.

Presentation Skills Wrap-Up

Lesson Overview

ACTIVITY	ACTIVITY TITLE	TIME	ONLINE/OFFLINE
GET READY	Introduction to Presentation Skills Wrap-Up	**1** minute	🖥️
TRY IT	Use Presentation Skills **LEARNING COACH CHECK-IN**	**40** minutes	🖥️ and 📄
	Review Formal and Informal Language	**20** minutes	🖥️
QUIZ	Formal and Informal Language and Presentation Skills	**30** minutes	🖥️
WRAP-UP	More Language Arts Practice	**9** minutes	🖥️
	Go Read!	**15** minutes	🖥️ or 📄

Lesson Goals

- Review presentation skills by responding to a speaking prompt.

- Review how to use formal and informal language appropriately.

- Take a quiz on using formal and informal language and presentation skills.

MATERIALS

Supplied
- *Summit English Language Arts 4 Activity Book*
  - Use Presentation Skills

GET READY

Introduction to Presentation Skills Wrap-Up
Students will read the lesson goals.

TRY IT

Use Presentation Skills
Students will complete Use Presentation Skills from *Summit English Language Arts 4 Activity Book*.

NOTE This activity involves planning a short speech, recording that speech using the online recording tool, and then listening to the speech and answering reflection questions. Ensure that students have access to a computer while completing the activity.

LEARNING COACH CHECK-IN Encourage students to present their speech to you, or listen to their recorded speech. Give them specific feedback about their speaking pace and clarity. Additionally, give them feedback about the content of their speech, including how well they organized their ideas, used descriptive details, and used appropriate language (formal or informal) for their chosen audience and purpose.

TRY IT
Presentation Skills Wrap-Up

Use Presentation Skills

Use the picture prompt to answer the questions.
Possible answers are shown.

1. You will tell a story about something that is happening in the picture.

a. Identify the audience for your story. (Be imaginative! Feel free to pretend you're speaking to the Queen of England or to a room of preschoolers.)

My audience is my little brother and sister.

b. Identify the purpose of your story. Is it to entertain? To inform?

My purpose is to entertain.

PRESENTATION SKILLS WRAP-UP **371**

---

c. Given your audience and purpose, will you use formal or informal language? Explain.

I will use informal language because that will be easier for my young audience to understand. Also, I am trying to entertain, so I want to sound conversational. It is okay if I use slang—I am not trying to be informative.

2. Write notes that you can use as you tell the story. You may include details that are not shown in the picture. Have fun with it!

Beginning

Answers will vary.

Middle

End

372 PRESENTATION SKILLS WRAP-UP

---

3. Record your speech.
- Use formal or informal language depending on your audience and purpose.
- Refer to your graphic organizer from Question 2 as you speak.
- Speak clearly and at an understandable pace.

4. Listen to your speech.

a. Describe two strengths of your speech.

I spoke at an understandable pace for my audience. My story was well organized with a clear beginning, middle, and end.

b. Describe two ways you could improve your speech.

I could have used more descriptive details to bring my story to life. There were also a couple of words that I could have spoken more clearly.

PRESENTATION SKILLS WRAP-UP **373**

Review Formal and Informal Language

Students will answer questions to review what they have learned about formal and informal language.

QUIZ

Formal and Informal Language and Presentation Skills

Students will complete the Formal and Informal Language and Presentation Skills quiz.

WRAP-UP

More Language Arts Practice

Students will practice skills according to their individual needs.

Go Read!

Students will read for pleasure. They should choose a book or a magazine that interests them, or they may choose a selection from the digital library, linked in the online lesson.

Students should read for the entire time. Have students select something to read ahead of time to help them stay focused.

"Why Kids Should Eat Healthy and Exercise"

Lesson Overview

ACTIVITY	ACTIVITY TITLE	TIME	ONLINE/OFFLINE
GET READY	Introduction to "Why Kids Should Eat Healthy and Exercise"	**1** minute	📶
	Spelling List 22 Pretest **LEARNING COACH CHECK-IN**	**10** minutes	📶 and 📄
	Trustworthy Internet Sites in 60 Seconds	**1** minute	📶
	Before You View "Why Kids Should Eat Healthy and Exercise"	**14** minutes	📶
LEARN AND **TRY IT**	"Why Kids Should Eat Healthy and Exercise"	**5** minutes	📶
	Check-In: "Why Kids Should Eat Healthy and Exercise"	**5** minutes	📶
	Apply Reading Strategies to Video	**10** minutes	📶
	Videos Have Main Ideas, Too	**10** minutes	📶
	Apply: Main Idea of a Video	**15** minutes	📶
	Plan a Media Message **LEARNING COACH CHECK-IN**	**47** minutes	📄
WRAP-UP	Question About "Why Kids Should Eat Healthy and Exercise"	**2** minutes	📶

Content Background

Students will watch a short video called "Why Kids Should Eat Healthy and Exercise." Students will learn that they can apply reading strategies to analyzing a video. Prior to viewing, they will make an inference about the content of the video based on the title. An *inference* is a logical guess based on clues from, in this case, a video and what students already know. For example, they can make an inference that a video titled "Why Kids Should Eat Healthy and Exercise" will be about the benefits of eating right and exercising.

Students will also analyze the video to determine main ideas and supporting details. The main idea is the most important point the video makes. In this video, each section has a main idea. For example, the main idea of the section of the video titled "What are the five food groups?" is that eating foods from all five food groups is important for your body.

Supporting details are the key details that give important information about the main idea. For example, one supporting detail for the main idea that eating foods from all five food groups is important for your body is that foods from all five food groups give your body vitamins.

KEYWORDS

infer – to use clues and what you already know to make a guess

inference – a guess that readers make using the clues that an author gives them in a piece of writing

main idea – the most important point the author makes; it may be stated or unstated

media – all the ways by which something can be shown, shared, or expressed

supporting detail – a detail that gives more information about a main idea

"Why Kids Should Eat Healthy and Exercise" Synopsis

This short public service announcement video provides information on why it's important for kids to eat healthy foods and exercise. The video begins by introducing the idea that healthy eating helps kids' school performance and helps their bodies to grow and be strong. The video names the five food groups: vegetables, fruits, grains, protein foods, and dairy. It explains that there are foods kids should eat only sometimes and healthy foods that they can eat any time. Finally, it describes ways that kids can get 60 minutes of exercise a day.

Lesson Goals

- Take a spelling pretest.

- Make, modify, or confirm inferences about a media message.

- Determine main idea and supporting details of a media message.

- Choose a topic of interest and plan a media message that includes a main idea and supporting details.

Introduction to "Why Kids Should Eat Healthy and Exercise"
Students will get a glimpse of what they will learn about in the lesson. They will also read the lesson goals and keywords. Have students select each keyword and preview its definition.

Spelling List 22 Pretest
Students will take a spelling pretest.

LEARNING COACH CHECK-IN   Have students turn to Spelling List 22 Pretest in *Summit English Language Arts 4 Activity Book* and open the online Spelling Pretest activity. Online, students will listen to the spelling word, type the word in the space indicated, and then check their answer. In the activity book, students will write the correct spelling of the word in the tables provided and indicate with a ✓ or an ✗ if they spelled the word correctly or incorrectly online. Students will repeat this process with the remaining words.

As needed, help students with the interaction between the online activity and the activity book page until they become comfortable with what they need to do. As students practice their spelling words throughout the workshop, they should pay special attention to words they spelled incorrectly on the pretest.

This is the complete list of words students will be tested on.

/oi/ Spelled *oi* or *oy*	Base Word *form*	Heart Words
annoy	conform	Maryland
coil	form	Oregon
coinage	formal	
disappoint	deform	
employ	formula	
exploit		
ointment		
poison		
royal		
voyage		

NOTE   Have students keep their completed activity page in a safe place so they can refer to it later.

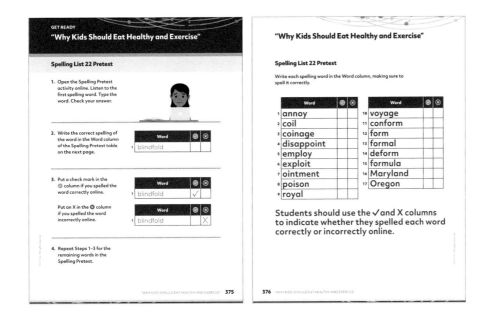

Trustworthy Internet Sites in 60 Seconds

Students will watch a short video designed to educate them on how to tell if information on a website can be trusted.

Before You View "Why Kids Should Eat Healthy and Exercise"

Students will answer questions in which they will make an inference about the content of a video and set a purpose for watching it.

LEARN AND TRY IT

LEARN   "Why Kids Should Eat Healthy and Exercise"

Students will view the public service announcement video "Why Kids Should Eat Healthy and Exercise."

LEARN   Check-In: "Why Kids Should Eat Healthy and Exercise"

Students will answer questions to demonstrate their comprehension of the video "Why Kids Should Eat Healthy and Exercise."

LEARN   Apply Reading Strategies to Video

Students will learn that reading strategies can be applied to help them analyze a video. They will learn that they can make and then either confirm or modify inferences about video content. They will also learn how to determine the main idea and supporting details of a media message.

TRY IT   Videos Have Main Ideas, Too

Students will analyze a section of the video "Why Kids Should Eat Healthy and Exercise." They will determine the main idea and supporting details of the video clip.

TIP   Remind students that the main idea is what the video clip is mostly about. To check if they have found the main idea, they can test their idea in the following way. Have them state what they believe is the main idea. Then ask them to review each statement in that section of the video (it may be easier to refer to the video transcript for this step). Ask, "Is that statement related to the main idea you said?" If students can answer "yes" for most of the details in that section, then they have correctly determined the main idea.

TRY IT   Apply: Main Idea of a Video

Students will view another video and apply what they've learned about determining the main idea and supporting details of a media message.

TRY IT   Plan a Media Message

Students will complete Plan a Media Message from *Summit English Language Arts 4 Activity Book*. Students will plan out a media message that includes a main idea and supporting details. Students may choose among the three topics provided or come up with their own topic. They will determine the main point, or main idea, that they want

to convey in their media message. They will then decide on three details that support their main idea and images they would shoot for each supporting detail if they were to produce a real video.

LEARNING COACH CHECK-IN This activity page contains tasks that will be a reference for writing a script later, so it's important that you review students' responses. Give students feedback, using the sample answers provided to guide you.

NOTE Have students keep their completed activity page in a safe place so they can refer to it later.

TRY IT
"Why Kids Should Eat Healthy and Exercise"

Plan a Media Message

Use the prompt to answer the questions.

Prompt: Create a media message on a topic of your choice.
This video should share an important message for kids.
Note: You will not actually create this video.

1. Choose a topic for your media message. Choose from the following topics or come up with a topic of your own.
   - The best sport to play is [name of sport].
   - Why [name of food] is healthy food choice
   - Why a [name of animal] is a good pet

The topic of my media message will be

Answers will vary.

2. What is the main point, or the main idea, that you want to convey in your media message?

Answers will vary. Sample answer: The main idea of my video is why a dog is a good pet.

"WHY KIDS SHOULD EAT HEALTHY AND EXERCISE" **377**

Answers will vary.
Sample answers are given in the chart.

3. Complete the chart. List three details that support your media message. Describe video images that support each detail.

Supporting Details	Video Images for Supporting Detail
Supporting Detail 1 A dog gives you love and makes you feel good.	A family is around a dog, petting the dog. The dog is wagging its tail and licking family members.
Supporting Detail 2 You get exercise when you have a dog.	A boy and girl are playing with a dog. They are running and throwing a ball. Then, the whole family is on a walk with the dog.
Supporting Detail 3 A dog can protect your home and family.	A burglar is about to break into the window of a house. Then, the dog starts barking, and the burglar runs away.

378 "WHY KIDS SHOULD EAT HEALTHY AND EXERCISE"

WRAP-UP

Question About "Why Kids Should Eat Healthy and Exercise"

Students will answer a question to show that they understand how to determine the main idea of a media message.

"Why Kids Should Eat Healthy and Exercise" Wrap-Up

Lesson Overview

ACTIVITY	ACTIVITY TITLE	TIME	ONLINE/OFFLINE
GET READY	Introduction to "Why Kids Should Eat Healthy..." Wrap-Up	**1** minute	
	Spelling List 22 Activity Bank	**10** minutes	
TRY IT	Write a Script for a Media Message **LEARNING COACH CHECK-IN**	**30** minutes	
	Read and Record	**10** minutes	
	Review "Why Kids Should Eat Healthy and Exercise"	**20** minutes	
QUIZ	"Why Kids Should Eat Healthy and Exercise"	**30** minutes	
WRAP-UP	More Language Arts Practice	**19** minutes	

Advance Preparation

Gather students' completed Spelling List 22 Pretest activity page from "Why Kids Should Eat Healthy and Exercise." Students will refer to this page during Get Ready: Spelling List 22 Activity Bank.

Gather students' completed Plan a Media Message activity page from "Why Kids Should Eat Healthy and Exercise." Students will refer to this page during Try It: Write a Script for a Media Message.

Lesson Goals

- Practice all spelling words.
- Write a script for a media message.
- Practice reading aloud to develop fluency.
- Review the video "Why Kids Should Eat Healthy and Exercise."
- Take a quiz on making, modifying, and confirming inferences, and on main idea and supporting details.

Introduction to "Why Kids Should Eat Healthy and Exercise" Wrap-Up

Students will read the lesson goals.

Spelling List 22 Activity Bank

Students will practice all spelling words from the workshop by completing Spelling List 22 Activity Bank from *Summit English Language Arts 4 Activity Book*. Make sure students have their completed Spelling List 22 Pretest activity page from "Why Kids Should Eat Healthy and Exercise" to refer to during this activity.

Remind students to pay special attention to words they spelled incorrectly on the Spelling Pretest.

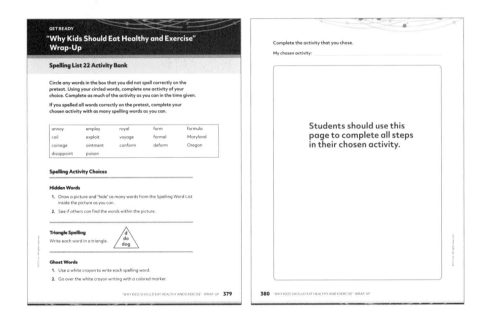

TRY IT

Write a Script for a Media Message

Students will complete Write a Script for a Media Message from *Summit English Language Arts 4 Activity Book*. Make sure students have their completed Plan a Media Message activity page from "Why Kids Should Eat Healthy and Exercise" to refer to during this activity.

TIP   Encourage students to keep their narration simple. The introduction could be as simple as one sentence such as, "Hi, I'm [student name] and I'm here to tell you why …."

LEARNING COACH CHECK-IN   Each student will have a different response to this activity page, so it's important that you review students' responses. Give students feedback, using the sample answers provided to guide you.

Worksheet Pages

Additional answers

What will the title card for Detail 1 say?

What will narrator say? Dogs are very loveable animals. It's easy to love them. You can tell they love you when they wag their tails, and they get excited when you come home. Petting and snuggling with a dog makes you feel good. It makes you feel happy and relaxed.

What images will appear? A dog is wagging its tail and acting excited as a boy walks in the front door of a house. Then the boy is shown snuggling with the dog. Both the boy and dog look happy and relaxed.

What will the title card for Detail 2 say?

What will narrator say? You know how your parents are always telling you to go outside and get some exercise? It's easy when you have a dog. You can spend hours throwing balls and running around with a dog. Also, everybody can take the dog for a walk. That way, the whole family gets exercise and spends time together.

What images will appear? A boy and girl playing with a dog—they run with the dog and throw balls for the dog to chase. Then, a whole family is shown walking a dog on a path through a park.

Read and Record

Good readers read quickly, smoothly, and with expression. This is called *fluency*. Students will record themselves reading aloud. They will listen to their recording and think about how quick, smooth, and expressive they sound.

TIP Encourage students to rerecord as needed.

Review "Why Kids Should Eat Healthy and Exercise"

Students will answer questions to review what they have learned about making, confirming, or modifying inferences. They will also answer questions to review determining the main idea and supporting details of a media message.

QUIZ

"Why Kids Should Eat Healthy and Exercise"

Students will complete the "Why Kids Should Eat Healthy and Exercise" quiz.

WRAP-UP

More Language Arts Practice

Students will practice skills according to their individual needs.

Staying Safe While Being Active

Lesson Overview

ACTIVITY	ACTIVITY TITLE	TIME	ONLINE/OFFLINE
GET READY	Introduction to Staying Safe While Being Active	**1** minute	🖥️
	Spelling List 22 Review Game	**10** minutes	🖥️
	Before You Read Safety Equipment	**14** minutes	🖥️
READ	Safety Equipment	**20** minutes	🖥️
	Check-In: Safety Equipment	**5** minutes	🖥️
LEARN AND **TRY IT**	Interactive Web Pages	**15** minutes	🖥️
	Web Page Elements	**10** minutes	🖥️
	Apply: Interact with a Web Page LEARNING COACH CHECK-IN	**15** minutes	🖥️
	Write About Safety Equipment LEARNING COACH CHECK-IN	**20** minutes	🖥️ and 📄
	Practice Words Related to the Internet	**8** minutes	🖥️
WRAP-UP	Question About Safety Equipment	**2** minutes	🖥️

Content Background

Students will explore the Safety Equipment web page, which is part of the girlshealth.gov website.

Students will learn terminology related to the Internet and web pages. They will learn to identify elements of a web page, including the page's address and navigation bar. They will learn that a web page is interactive because hyperlinks, or links, respond to the action of being selected. For example, selecting a link on a web page may take the user to a different web page within the same website or to a different location on the same web page.

Students will also learn how information presented on a web page contributes to their understanding. For example, the diagram of safety equipment on the Safety Equipment web page improves students' understanding of safety equipment by showing what each piece of gear looks like and where it is worn.

MATERIALS

Supplied
- *Summit English Language Arts 4 Activity Book*
  - Write About Safety Equipment

Advance Preparation

Students will need to visit a website of their choice during Apply: Interact with a Web Page. Help students find a trustworthy website to use to complete this activity.

Safety Equipment Synopsis

The interactive web page Safety Equipment is part of the girlshealth.gov website. The web page includes a large diagram of a girl wearing several items of safety gear. The diagram includes hyperlinks for each type of equipment shown. When selected, each link takes the reader to text that explains the purpose for each piece of safety gear and the different sports or activities for which the gear should be worn.

Lesson Goals

- Practice all spelling words.
- Define *interactive web pages* and determine meanings of related words.
- Use symbols or graphics to interpret information on a web page.
- Understand and make inferences made about information presented on a web page.

GET READY

Introduction to Staying Safe While Being Active
Students will get a glimpse of what they will learn about in the lesson. They will also read the lesson goals and keywords. Have students select each keyword and preview its definition.

Spelling List 22 Review Game
Students will practice all spelling words from the workshop.

Before You Read Safety Equipment
Students will be introduced to some key vocabulary words related to using the Internet and interacting with web pages. Students will learn some background information about elements of web pages and how to navigate a web page. They will also answer questions that ask them to make inferences about the content of a website and web page.

READ

Safety Equipment

Students will read the text of the Safety Equipment web page.

Check-In: Safety Equipment

Students will answer questions to demonstrate their comprehension of the content of the Safety Equipment web page.

LEARN AND TRY IT

LEARN   Interactive Web Pages

Students will learn about the elements of a web page and what makes a web page interactive. They will learn how interactive elements allow them to navigate a website or web page. They will also learn how elements of a web page can support their understanding and the differences between searching for information on a website and in a book.

NOTE   The only active links on the Safety Equipment web page are those around the diagram of the girl wearing safety gear. These links take the reader to text on the same web page that gives information on each piece of safety gear. If students seem to struggle with understanding how elements such as the website title or the navigation bar function, model using these elements with a website that you deem to be appropriate for students.

TRY IT   Web Page Elements

Students will answer questions to demonstrate their knowledge of interactive web page elements and how those elements support their understanding of content.

TRY IT   Apply: Interact with a Web Page

Students will visit another website to practice what they've learned about interacting with web pages and interactive components.

LEARNING COACH CHECK-IN   Students will need to visit a website of their choice to complete this activity. Help students find a trustworthy website. Examples of trustworthy websites include government websites, such as those run by the Library of Congress or the National Institutes of Health.

TRY IT   Write About Safety Equipment

Students will complete Write About Safety Equipment from *Summit English Language Arts 4 Activity Book*.

LEARNING COACH CHECK-IN   This activity page contains an open-ended question, so it's important that you review students' responses. Give students feedback, using the sample answers provided to guide you.

WRAP-UP

Question About Safety Equipment

Students will answer a question to show that they understand web page navigation and can analyze the text of a web page.

Staying Safe While Being Active Wrap-Up

Lesson Overview

ACTIVITY	ACTIVITY TITLE	TIME	ONLINE/OFFLINE
GET READY	Introduction to Staying Safe While Being Active Wrap-Up	**1** minute	
TRY IT	Design a Web Page **LEARNING COACH CHECK-IN**	**30** minutes	
	Read and Record	**10** minutes	
	Review Staying Safe While Being Active	**20** minutes	
QUIZ	Staying Safe While Being Active	**30** minutes	
	Spelling List 22	**10** minutes	
WRAP-UP	More Language Arts Practice	**19** minutes	

Lesson Goals

- Design a web page.
- Practice reading aloud to develop fluency.
- Review interactive web page elements, including hyperlinks, text, and visual elements.
- Take a quiz on defining and using interactive web pages.
- Take a spelling quiz.

MATERIALS

Supplied
- *Summit English Language Arts 4 Activity Book*
  - Design a Web Page

GET READY

Introduction to Stay Safe While Being Active Wrap-Up

Students will read the lesson goals.

TRY IT

Design a Web Page

Students will complete Design a Web Page from *Summit English Language Arts 4 Activity Book*. Students will choose a sport or activity they enjoy participating in and determine the safety equipment needed for the activity. They should then draw a web page layout and include the safety equipment information for the activity they have chosen. Allow students to use the Safety Equipment web page as a model if necessary. A website title and navigation bar have been included on the activity page so that students can imagine their web page is part of a website titled My Favorite Activities.

LEARNING COACH CHECK-IN This activity page contains open-ended questions, so it's important that you review students' responses. Give students feedback, using the sample answers provided to guide you.

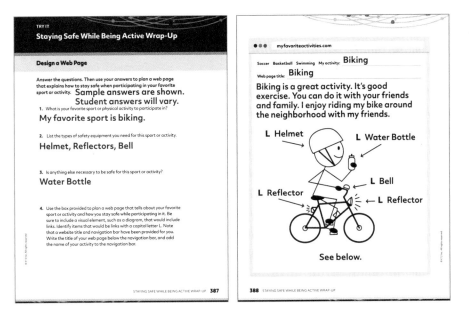

Additional answers

Helmet: A helmet protects my head if I fall off my bike.

Bell: A bell keeps me and others safe because I can use the bell to alert others that I'm near.

Reflector: Reflectors protect me from getting hit by a car if I ride my bike when it's dark. The cars' lights shine on the reflectors so the drivers see me.

Water Bottle: It's important to drink water when you're active. Having water when I ride my bike keeps me from getting dehydrated.

Read and Record

Good readers read quickly, smoothly, and with expression. This is called *fluency*. Students will record themselves reading aloud. They will listen to their recording and think about how quick, smooth, and expressive they sound.

TIP Encourage students to rerecord as needed.

Review Staying Safe While Being Active

Students will answer questions to review identifying and using interactive web pages, identifying details that support the main idea, and analyzing information and visual elements found on a web page.

Staying Safe While Being Active

Students will complete the Staying Safe While Being Active quiz.

Spelling List 22

Students will complete the Spelling List 22 quiz.

More Language Arts Practice

Students will practice skills according to their individual needs.

Keeping Safe from Rabies

Lesson Overview

ACTIVITY	ACTIVITY TITLE	TIME	ONLINE/OFFLINE
GET READY	Introduction to Keeping Safe from Rabies	**1** minute	🖥️
	Spelling List 23 Pretest **LEARNING COACH CHECK-IN**	**10** minutes	🖥️ and 📄
	Before You Read Rabies	**14** minutes	🖥️
READ	Rabies	**30** minutes	🖥️
	Check-In: Rabies	**5** minutes	🖥️
LEARN AND **TRY IT**	Find the Main Idea	**10** minutes	🖥️
	Find Main Ideas and Supporting Details	**10** minutes	🖥️
	Apply: Main Idea and Supporting Details	**15** minutes	🖥️
	Write About the Main Idea and Supporting Details **LEARNING COACH CHECK-IN**	**15** minutes	🖥️ and 📄
	Practice Words from Rabies	**8** minutes	🖥️
WRAP-UP	Question About Rabies	**2** minutes	🖥️

Content Background

Students will explore the Centers for Disease Control and Prevention's Rabies website. Students will learn that, just like text in a book, text on web pages can have a main idea and supporting details. The main idea is the most important point an author makes. Readers can determine the main idea by figuring out what most of the information in a text is about. Supporting details give more information about the main idea. Supporting details are usually the most important details in a text. If the main idea of a text is not directly stated, readers can analyze the supporting details to determine the main idea.

MATERIALS

Supplied
- *Summit English Language Arts 4 Activity Book*
  - Spelling List 23 Pretest
  - Write About the Main Idea and Supporting Details

Lesson Goals

- Take a spelling pretest.
- Describe interactive web pages.
- Determine the main idea and supporting details of a media message.
- Use elements of digital text, such as symbols or graphics, and interpret information presented on a web page.
- Determine meanings of unfamiliar words in the reading.

GET READY

Introduction to Keeping Safe from Rabies

Students will get a glimpse of what they will learn about in the lesson. They will also read the lesson goals and keywords. Have students select each keyword and preview its definition.

Spelling List 23 Pretest

Students will take a spelling pretest.

LEARNING COACH CHECK-IN   Have students turn to Spelling List 23 Pretest in *Summit English Language Arts 4 Activity Book* and open the online Spelling Pretest activity. Online, students will listen to the spelling word, type the word in the space indicated, and then check their answer. In the activity book, students will write the correct spelling of the word in the tables provided and indicate with a ✓ or an ✗ if they spelled the word correctly or incorrectly online. Students will repeat this process with the remaining words.

As needed, help students with the interaction between the online activity and the activity book page until they become comfortable with what they need to do. As students practice their spelling words throughout the workshop, they should pay special attention to words they spelled incorrectly on the pretest.

This is the complete list of words students will be tested on.

Words with /ow/ Spelled ow or ou	Suffix –ous	Suffix –ness	Heart Words
allow	furious	awareness	Florida
blouse	glorious	closeness	Nebraska
bound	various	forgiveness	
clownish	victorious	goodness	
drown	harmonious	illness	
drowsy			
bounced			
rowdy			
scoundrel			
surround			
howling			
vowels			
cloudy			

NOTE Have students keep their completed activity page in a safe place so they can refer to it later.

Before You Read Rabies

Students will be introduced to key vocabulary words that they will encounter in the upcoming reading.

READ

Rabies

Students will read Rabies, a Centers for Disease Control and Prevention website.

Check-In: Rabies

Students will answer questions to demonstrate their comprehension of information from the Rabies website.

LEARN AND TRY IT

LEARN   Find the Main Idea

Students will learn that some elements on interactive web pages function like features found in books. They will also learn how to use key details to determine the main idea of text found on a web page, how supporting details are usually the most important details, and how to use details to confirm what they believe to be the main idea of a text.

TRY IT   Find Main Ideas and Supporting Details

Students will analyze text from the Rabies website and answer questions about the main ideas and supporting details in the reading.

TRY IT   Apply: Main Idea and Supporting Details

Students will apply to a new work what they've learned about determining the main idea and supporting details of text from a web page.

TRY IT   Write About the Main Idea and Supporting Details

Students will complete Write About the Main Idea and Supporting Details from *Summit English Language Arts 4 Activity Book*. Students will need to review the information from one of the web pages of the Rabies website. They will then write a paragraph that explains the main idea and supporting details of that particular web page.

LEARNING COACH CHECK-IN   This activity page contains an open-ended question, so it's important you review students' responses. Give students feedback, using the sample answer provided to guide you.

TRY IT
Keeping Safe from Rabies

Write About the Main Idea and Supporting Details

On the home page of the Rabies website, select the link for the web page "How do you know if an animal has rabies?" Read the information on the web page, and use it to write a response in complete sentences.

Write a paragraph that states the main idea and supporting details of the text on the web page that answers the question "How do you know if an animal has rabies?"

The main idea is that you can tell an animal has rabies from the way it acts. The supporting details explain different ways an animal with rabies might act. Some animals might act mad. They might try to bite you or other animals. Animals with rabies have a lot of saliva. They drool a lot. A wild animal might move slowly or act tame. That's not how a wild animal usually acts, so it could have rabies. A doctor can find out if an animal has rabies by doing a laboratory test.

I learned a lot about rabies from this website.

TRY IT Practice Words from Rabies

Students will answer questions to demonstrate their understanding of the vocabulary words from the reading.

WRAP-UP

Question About Rabies

Students will answer a question to show that they understand how to determine the main idea of a text.

Keeping Safe from Rabies Wrap-Up

Lesson Overview

ACTIVITY	ACTIVITY TITLE	TIME	ONLINE/OFFLINE
GET READY	Introduction to Keeping Safe from Rabies Wrap-Up	**1** minute	🖥️
	Spelling List 23 Activity Bank	**10** minutes	📄
TRY IT	Make a Flyer About the Rabies Virus **LEARNING COACH CHECK-IN**	**30** minutes	🖥️ and 📄
	Read and Record	**10** minutes	🖥️
	Review Keeping Safe from Rabies	**20** minutes	🖥️
QUIZ	Keeping Safe from Rabies	**30** minutes	🖥️
WRAP-UP	More Language Arts Practice	**19** minutes	🖥️

Advance Preparation

Gather students' completed Spelling List 23 Pretest activity page from Keeping Safe from Rabies. Students will refer to this page during Get Ready: Spelling List 23 Activity Bank.

Lesson Goals

- Practice all spelling words.

- Design a flyer that includes the main idea and supporting details of a web page.

- Practice reading aloud to develop fluency.

- Review text and visual elements presented on an interactive web page.

- Review finding the main idea and supporting details of a media message.

- Take a quiz on interactive web pages and main idea and supporting details.

MATERIALS

Supplied
- *Summit English Language Arts 4 Activity Book*
  - Spelling List 23 Activity Bank
  - Make a Flyer About the Rabies Virus

Also Needed
- completed Spelling List 23 Pretest activity page from Keeping Safe from Rabies

Introduction to Keeping Safe from Rabies Wrap-Up

Students will read the lesson goals.

Spelling List 23 Activity Bank

Students will practice all spelling words from the workshop by completing Spelling List 23 Activity Bank from *Summit English Language Arts 4 Activity Book*. Make sure students have their completed Spelling List 23 Pretest activity page from Introduction to Keeping Safe from Rabies to refer to during this activity.

Remind students to pay special attention to words they spelled incorrectly on the Spelling Pretest.

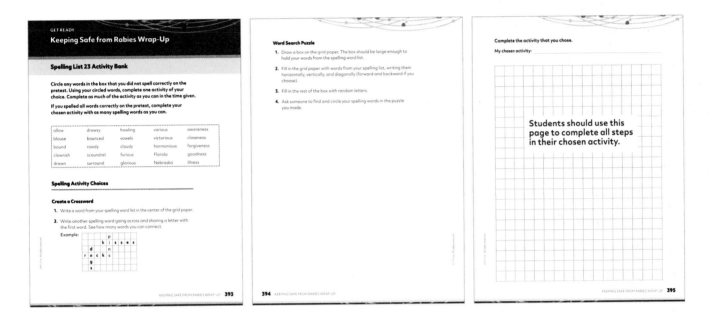

TRY IT

Make a Flyer About the Rabies Virus

Students will complete Make a Flyer About the Rabies Virus from *Summit English Language Arts 4 Activity Book*. Students will need to access the Rabies Virus web page. They should select the Rabies Virus link in the navigation bar of the Rabies website. Students are free to design their flyer as they wish, but it must include the main idea and supporting details of the text on the Rabies Virus web page.

LEARNING COACH CHECK-IN   This activity page contains an open-ended prompt, so it's important you review students' responses. Give students feedback, using the sample answers provided to guide you.

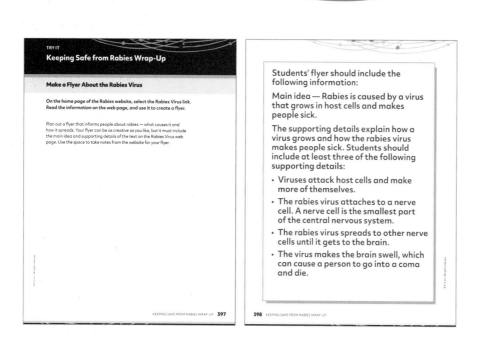

Read and Record

Good readers read quickly, smoothly, and with expression. This is called *fluency*. Students will record themselves reading aloud. They will listen to their recording and think about how quick, smooth, and expressive they sound.

TIP   Encourage students to rerecord as needed.

Review Keeping Safe from Rabies

Students will answer questions to review interactive elements, text, and visual elements found on web pages. They will also review identifying the main idea and supporting details of text from a website.

QUIZ

Keeping Safe from Rabies

Students will complete the Keeping Safe from Rabies quiz.

WRAP-UP

More Language Arts Practice

Students will practice skills according to their individual needs.

Elizabeth Blackwell

Lesson Overview

ACTIVITY	ACTIVITY TITLE	TIME	ONLINE/OFFLINE
GET READY	Introduction to Elizabeth Blackwell	**1** minute	
	Spelling List 23 Practice	**10** minutes	
	Before You Read Texts About Elizabeth Blackwell	**14** minutes	
READ	Texts About Elizabeth Blackwell	**30** minutes	
	Check-In: Elizabeth Blackwell	**5** minutes	
LEARN AND **TRY IT**	Comparing Texts About Elizabeth Blackwell	**10** minutes	
	Primary and Secondary Sources	**10** minutes	
	Apply: Primary and Secondary Sources	**15** minutes	
	Prepare to Write a Primary Source of Information	**15** minutes	
	Practice Words from Texts About Elizabeth Blackwell	**8** minutes	
WRAP-UP	Question About Texts About Elizabeth Blackwell	**2** minutes	

Content Background

Students will explore two sources of information about Elizabeth Blackwell, the first woman to become a doctor in the United States. Students will read a secondary source of information, a biography about Blackwell. They will also listen to and read a primary source of information, an excerpt from Blackwell's autobiography. Students will learn how information in primary and secondary sources is similar and different.

Students will learn that a primary source of information is a firsthand account created by someone who directly participated in or witnessed the events about which he or she wrote. The Declaration of Independence is an example of a primary source. Other examples include letters, diaries, and autobiographies.

A secondary source is created by someone who did not directly experience the events about which he or she wrote. History books and biographies are examples of secondary sources of information.

Students will also learn that authors' perspectives influence what they write. For example, the author of the secondary source of information, "Elizabeth

MATERIALS

Supplied
- *Summit English Language Arts 4 Expeditions in Reading*
- *Summit English Language Arts 4 Activity Book*
  - Prepare to Write a Primary Source of Information

Blackwell: A Pioneering Physician," wrote in depth about the Blackwell family's voyage to New York. The author's viewpoint seems to be that the voyage was a defining moment for Blackwell, one during which she decides she will become a doctor.

"Elizabeth Blackwell: A Pioneering Physician" Synopsis

In 1832, young Elizabeth Blackwell and her family sailed from England to New York to start a new life. Many of the steerage passengers on their ship died from cholera, which greatly affected Elizabeth. She decided that she would become a doctor. But in Elizabeth's time women rarely attended college and certainly did not become doctors. She had to overcome many obstacles, but she finally attended medical school and graduated at the top of her class. She became the first woman to earn a medical degree in the United States. She followed this success by building her medical practice from a small room in the poorest neighborhood in New York City to a thriving hospital for women and children.

Excerpts from Elizabeth Blackwell's Autobiography Synopsis

In this text, Blackwell describes some of her experiences seeking advice from medical professors on applying to medical school. In Blackwell's day, women usually did not receive higher education. Even Blackwell's supporters thought it would be so difficult in America that they suggested she dress as a man and attend school in Paris.

Lesson Goals

- Practice all spelling words.
- Define what makes a source of information a primary source or secondary source.
- Describe how an author's perspective influences an informational text.
- Compare and contrast information in primary and secondary sources.
- Plan for writing an autobiography, a primary source text about yourself.
- Determine meanings of unfamiliar words in the reading.

Introduction to Elizabeth Blackwell

Students will get a glimpse of what they will learn about in the lesson. They will also read the lesson goals and keywords. Have students select each keyword and preview its definition.

Spelling List 23 Practice

Students will practice all spelling words from the workshop.

Before You Read Texts About Elizabeth Blackwell

Students will be introduced to some key vocabulary words that they will encounter in the upcoming reading and learn some important background related to the reading.

READ

Texts About Elizabeth Blackwell

Students will read "Elizabeth Blackwell: Pioneering Physician" in *Expeditions in Reading*. This is a secondary source of information.

Students will also listen to and read along in their reading book as an excerpt from Blackwell's autobiography is read aloud.

NOTE The excerpt from Blackwell's autobiography is above a grade 4 reading level. Students will hear it read aloud. However, you may want to be available to answer students' questions about terminology and speech patterns in the text that were more common in the mid-1800s than in the present day.

Check-In: Texts About Elizabeth Blackwell

Students will answer questions to demonstrate their comprehension of "Elizabeth Blackwell: A Pioneering Physician" and the excerpt from Blackwell's autobiography.

LEARN AND TRY IT

LEARN Comparing Texts About Elizabeth Blackwell

Students will learn about the similarities and differences between a primary source of information and a secondary source of information on the same topic—Elizabeth Blackwell. They will also learn how an author's perspective influences what he or she writes.

TRY IT Primary and Secondary Sources

Students will analyze passages to determine similarities and differences between information in a primary source and secondary source. They will also analyze texts to determine the author's perspective.

TRY IT   Apply: Primary and Secondary Sources

Students will apply to new works what they've learned about primary and secondary sources of information and determining an author's perspective.

TRY IT   Prepare to Write a Primary Source of Information

Students will complete Prepare to Write a Primary Source of Information from *Summit English Language Arts 4 Activity Book*. Students will record information about themselves in a graphic organizer.

NOTE   Have students keep their completed activity page in a safe place so they can refer to it later.

TRY IT
Elizabeth Blackwell

Prepare to Write a Primary Source of Information

An autobiography is a primary source of information. Prepare to write a brief autobiography about yourself by completing the graphic organizer.   **Answers will vary.**

Facts About Me

I am _____ years old.

My birthday is

Where I was born:

Family members:

Friends:

My Favorite Activity

Something I love to do is

My Favorite Things

Food:

Movie:

Book:

Sport:

Singer or Song:

ELIZABETH BLACKWELL **399**

---

400   ELIZABETH BLACKWELL

Interesting Facts

Two things I'd like you to know about me:

The Best Thing

The best thing that ever happened to me:

WRAP-UP

Question About Texts About Elizabeth Blackwell

Students will answer a question to show that they understand how to identify primary and secondary sources of information.

Elizabeth Blackwell Wrap-Up

Lesson Overview

ACTIVITY	ACTIVITY TITLE	TIME	ONLINE/OFFLINE
GET READY	Introduction to Elizabeth Blackwell Wrap-Up	**1** minute	
	Spelling List 23 More Practice	**10** minutes	
TRY IT	Write Your Autobiography **LEARNING COACH CHECK-IN**	**30** minutes	
	Read and Record	**10** minutes	
	Review Texts About Elizabeth Blackwell	**20** minutes	
QUIZ	Elizabeth Blackwell	**30** minutes	
WRAP-UP	More Language Arts Practice	**19** minutes	

Advance Preparation

Gather students' completed Prepare to Write a Primary Source of Information activity page from Elizabeth Blackwell. Students will refer to this page during Try It: Write Your Autobiography.

Lesson Goals

- Practice all spelling words.

- Write a brief autobiography, using a completed graphic organizer as a reference.

- Practice reading aloud to develop fluency.

- Review the traits of primary and secondary sources of information and the similarities and differences among information given in primary and secondary sources.

- Review how authors' perspectives influence what they write.

- Take a quiz on primary and secondary sources of information and how authors' perspectives influence what they write.

MATERIALS

Supplied

- *Summit English Language Arts 4 Activity Book*
  - Write Your Autobiography

Also Needed

- completed Prepare to Write a Primary Source of Information activity page from Elizabeth Blackwell

Introduction to Elizabeth Blackwell Wrap-Up

Students will read the lesson goals.

Spelling List 23 More Practice

Students will practice all spelling words from the workshop.

Write Your Autobiography

Students will complete Write Your Autobiography from *Summit English Language Arts 4 Activity Book*. Make sure students have their completed Prepare to Write a Primary Source of Information from Elizabeth Blackwell to refer to during this activity.

LEARNING COACH CHECK-IN This activity page contains open-ended questions, so it's important that you review students' responses. Give students feedback, using the sample answers provided to guide you.

TRY IT
Elizabeth Blackwell Wrap-Up

Write Your Autobiography

Gather the activity book page Prepare to Write a Primary Source of Information from Elizabeth Blackwell. Use the information recorded on the activity book page to complete the following tasks. Use complete sentences in your response.
Sample answers are shown.

1. Use the information in the Facts About Me box to write 3–4 sentences that introduce your autobiography.

My name is Jane Smith. I am 10 years old, and I was born on February 29, 2008, in Houston, TX. I have a mom and dad, a younger brother named Miguel, and an older sister named Mary. My best friends are Abigail and Jade.

ELIZABETH BLACKWELL WRAP-UP **401**

2. Use the information in the Favorite Things and My Favorite Activity boxes to write 3–4 sentences.

Some of my favorite things are spaghetti, the movie *The Incredibles 2*, and the book *Pax* by Sara Pennypacker. I also really like the singer Beyoncé. I love to play basketball. I play in a league at the YMCA with a lot of my friends.

3. Use the information in the Interesting Facts box to write 3–4 sentences.

One interesting fact about me is that I was born on February 29...in a leap year. That means that my real birthday only happens every four years. Another interesting fact is that my mother is from France. She taught me how to speak a lot of French.

402 ELIZABETH BLACKWELL WRAP-UP

4. Use the information in The Best Thing box to write 3–4 sentences.

The best thing that ever happened to me was when Jade Baker moved into the house next to mine. We were both five years old when she moved in. She has become one of my best friends. When I spend time with Jade, I feel like I have another sister.

ELIZABETH BLACKWELL WRAP-UP **403**

Read and Record

Good readers read quickly, smoothly, and with expression. This is called *fluency*. Students will record themselves reading aloud. They will listen to their recording and think about how quick, smooth, and expressive they sound.

TIP Encourage students to rerecord as needed.

Review Texts About Elizabeth Blackwell

Students will answer questions to review what they have learned about primary and secondary sources of information and how authors' perspectives influence what they write.

QUIZ

Elizabeth Blackwell

Students will complete the Elizabeth Blackwell quiz.

WRAP-UP

More Language Arts Practice

Students will practice skills according to their individual needs.

"Louis Pasteur: Battle with Death"

Lesson Overview

ACTIVITY	ACTIVITY TITLE	TIME	ONLINE/OFFLINE
GET READY	Introduction to "Louis Pasteur: Battle with Death"	**1** minute	
	Spelling List 23 Review Game	**10** minutes	
	Before You Read "Louis Pasteur: Battle with Death"	**14** minutes	
READ	"Louis Pasteur: Battle with Death"	**30** minutes	
	Check-In: "Louis Pasteur: Battle with Death"	**5** minutes	
LEARN AND **TRY IT**	Elements of Narrative Nonfiction	**10** minutes	
	Determine Elements of Narrative Nonfiction	**10** minutes	
	Apply: Words Shape Meaning	**15** minutes	
	Write to Clarify the Meaning	**15** minutes	
	Practice Words from "Louis Pasteur: Battle with Death"	**8** minutes	
WRAP-UP	Question About "Louis Pasteur: Battle with Death"	**2** minutes	

Content Background

Students will read a narrative nonfiction story about Dr. Louis Pasteur, the French scientist whose many accomplishments include inventing pasteurization, which is still used today, and developing a vaccine against rabies.

Students will learn that narrative nonfiction is a type of informational text that shares many elements with fiction. One common element is the use of language to shape and clarify meaning. For example, in the story about Pasteur, the author writes, "A maddened, snarling wolf, foaming at the mouth, charged down the street. Panic-stricken people scattered before it." The language helps the reader understand the symptoms of an animal with rabies and visualize the horrific scene that strikes fear into the hearts of the townsfolk.

While the information in the story is true, it is organized in the same way as a fictional story. That means the story has a beginning, middle, and end. It also has a problem and solution. For example, at the beginning of a fictional story, readers usually meet main characters and learn about a problem the characters must solve. At the beginning of the narrative nonfiction "Louis

MATERIALS

Supplied
- *Summit English Language Arts 4 Expeditions in Reading*
- *Summit English Language Arts 4 Activity Book*
  - Write to Clarify the Meaning

Pasteur: Battle with Death," readers meet the main character, Louis Pasteur, and learn that the story's main problem is that there is no cure for rabies.

Finally, students will learn that, as in other informational texts, narrative nonfiction contains main ideas and supporting details. The main idea is the most important point the author conveys. Students will learn how key details support, or prove, the main idea.

Lesson Goals

- Practice all spelling words.

- Explain how an author uses language to shape and clarify meaning in text.

- Describe the organization of a narrative nonfiction text.

- Determine the main idea of an informational text and how key details support that main idea.

- Determine meanings of unfamiliar words in the reading.

GET READY

Introduction to "Louis Pasteur: Battle with Death"

Students will get a glimpse of what they will learn about in the lesson. They will also read the lesson goals and keywords. Have students select each keyword and preview its definition.

Spelling List 23 Review Game

Students will practice all spelling words from the workshop.

Before You Read "Louis Pasteur: Battle with Death"

Students will be introduced to some key vocabulary words that they will encounter in the upcoming reading and learn some important historical background related to the reading.

READ

"Louis Pasteur: Battle with Death"

Students will read "Louis Pasteur: Battle with Death" in *Expeditions in Reading*.

Check-In: "Louis Pasteur: Battle with Death"

Students will answer questions to demonstrate their comprehension of "Louis Pasteur: Battle with Death."

LEARN AND TRY IT

LEARN   Elements of Narrative Nonfiction

Students will learn that narrative nonfiction is a nonfiction text written like a fictional story. It can have descriptive language that shapes and clarifies meaning. It is organized like a work of fiction with a beginning, middle, and end, and it contains a problem that the main character works to solve. They will also learn that narrative nonfiction has main ideas and supporting details.

TRY IT   Determine Elements of Narrative Nonfiction

Students will analyze passages to determine how the author's words and phrases help shape and clarify meaning and how passages are organized. They will also determine the main idea of a passage and how the details support that main idea.

TIP   Remind students that they can test the statement that they believe is the main idea of a passage by checking that most sentences in the passage focus on that idea.

TRY IT   Apply: Words Shape Meaning

Students will apply to a new work what they've learned about how an author uses words and phrases to shape and clarify meaning.

TRY IT   Write to Clarify the Meaning

Students will complete Write to Clarify the Meaning from *Summit English Language Arts 4 Activity Book*.

SUPPORT   For students having difficulty understanding the target words or phrases, suggest that they refer to a dictionary.

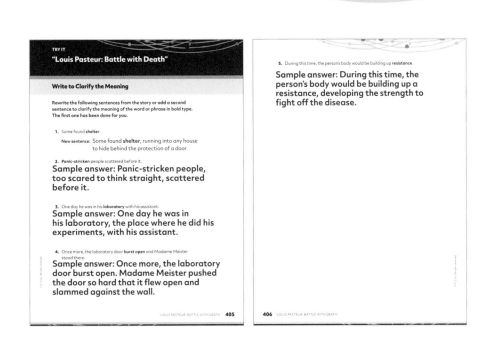

WRAP-UP

Question About "Louis Pasteur: Battle with Death"

Students will answer a question to show that they understand how an author uses language to clarify meaning in an informational text.

"Louis Pasteur: Battle with Death" Wrap-Up

Lesson Overview

ACTIVITY	ACTIVITY TITLE	TIME	ONLINE/OFFLINE
GET READY	Introduction to "Louis Pasteur: Battle with Death" Wrap-Up	**1** minute	🖥
TRY IT	Write a Summary of "Louis Pasteur: Battle with Death" **LEARNING COACH CHECK-IN**	**30** minutes	📄
	Read and Record	**10** minutes	🖥
	Review "Louis Pasteur: Battle with Death"	**20** minutes	🖥
QUIZ	"Louis Pasteur: Battle with Death"	**30** minutes	🖥
	Spelling List 23	**10** minutes	🖥
WRAP-UP	More Language Arts Practice	**19** minutes	🖥

Lesson Goals

- Write a summary of a story that includes a main idea and supporting details.

- Practice reading aloud to develop fluency.

- Review how an author uses language to shape and clarify meaning, the organization of narrative nonfiction, the main idea, and how details support the main idea.

- Take a quiz on how an author uses language to shape and clarify meaning, the organization of narrative nonfiction, the main idea, and how details support the main idea.

- Take a spelling quiz.

MATERIALS

Supplied
- *Summit English Language Arts 4 Expeditions in Reading*
- *Summit English Language Arts 4 Activity Book*
  - Write a Summary of "Louis Pasteur: Battle with Death"

GET READY

Introduction to "Louis Pasteur: Battle with Death" Wrap-Up

Students will read the lesson goals.

Write a Summary of "Louis Pasteur: Battle with Death"

Students will complete Write a Summary of "Louis Pasteur: Battle with Death" from *Summit English Language Arts 4 Activity Book*. The summary should include the main idea of the story and details that support the main idea.

LEARNING COACH CHECK-IN   This activity page contains an open-ended question, so it's important that you review students' responses. Give students feedback, using the sample answer provided to guide you.

TRY IT
"Louis Pasteur: Battle with Death" Wrap-Up

Write a Summary of "Louis Pasteur: Battle with Death"

Answer the question, then write a summary of "Louis Pasteur: Battle with Death." Use complete sentences in your summary.

1. Which statement is the main idea of "Louis Pasteur: Battle with Death"?

    a. Louis Pasteur was haunted his whole life by the memory of a rabid wolf attacking people in his village.

    b. Louis Pasteur grew up to be a scientist whose work led to the prevention of many diseases, including rabies.

    c. Louis Pasteur spent many long hours developing a 14-day treatment that cured rabies.

2. Write a summary of "Louis Pasteur: Battle with Death." Be sure to include the main idea of the story and details that support the main idea.

Sample answer: When Louis Pasteur was a little boy in France, he saw a wolf with rabies bite people in his village. Those people died, and Pasteur remembered how horrible that was. When Pasteur grew up, he became a scientist. He figured out how to prevent many diseases, including rabies. He developed a vaccine to keep cattle and sheep from getting anthrax. He invented a method for making milk safe that is still used today. It's called pasteurization. Pasteur wanted to

"LOUIS PASTEUR: BATTLE WITH DEATH" WRAP-UP **407**

408 "LOUIS PASTEUR: BATTLE WITH DEATH" WRAP-UP

solve the problem of rabies. But nobody knew what caused it. He discovered that the rabies virus was concentrated in nerve tissue. Then he used weak nerve tissue to make a dog immune to rabies. Pasteur tried the treatment on a boy. A dog with rabies had bitten the boy. The treatment was a success, and the boy lived. Pasteur finally solved the problem of dying from rabies.

Read and Record

Good readers read quickly, smoothly, and with expression. This is called *fluency*. Students will record themselves reading aloud. They will listen to their recording and think about how quick, smooth, and expressive they sound.

TIP   Encourage students to rerecord as needed.

Review "Louis Pasteur: Battle with Death"

Students will answer questions to review what they have learned about how an author uses language to shape and clarify meaning, the organization of narrative nonfiction, the main idea, and how details support the main idea.

QUIZ

"Louis Pasteur: Battle with Death"

Students will complete the "Louis Pasteur: Battle with Death" quiz.

Spelling List 23

Students will complete the Spelling List 23 quiz.

WRAP-UP

More Language Arts Practice

Students will practice skills according to their individual needs.

Greek Affixes

Lesson Overview

ACTIVITY	ACTIVITY TITLE	TIME	ONLINE/OFFLINE
GET READY	Introduction to Greek Affixes	**1** minute	🖥️
LEARN AND **TRY IT**	Look Back at Affixes	**4** minutes	🖥️
	Words with Greek Affixes	**10** minutes	🖥️
	Define Words with Greek Affixes	**10** minutes	🖥️
	Apply: Greek Affixes **LEARNING COACH CHECK-IN**	**15** minutes	📄
	Go Write!	**15** minutes	📄
	Review Greek Affixes	**15** minutes	🖥️
QUIZ	Greek Affixes	**15** minutes	🖥️
WRAP-UP	More Language Arts Practice	**20** minutes	🖥️
	Go Read!	**15** minutes	🖥️ or 📄

Content Background

Students learn will about words that have the Greek affixes *gram*, *mono*, and *auto*. They will learn how knowing the meaning of a word's affix can help them to determine the meaning of the word. They will also learn how context clues can help them to determine the meaning of a word with a Greek affix.

An affix is a word part that has a special meaning and that can be found at the beginning or ending of a word. An affix is not a word on its own. It must be attached to a base word or root to make a word. Many affixes commonly used in English have come from the Greek language.

Prefixes and suffixes fall under the category of affixes. A prefix is an affix that comes at the beginning of a word. For example, the prefix *mono* comes at the beginning of the word *monochrome*. Since the prefix *mono* means "one," the word *monochrome* means "one color."

A suffix is an affix that comes at the end of a word. For example, the suffix *gram* comes at the end of the word *diagram*. Since the suffix *gram* means "something written or drawn," the word *diagram* means "a drawing that communicates information."

Advance Preparation

During the Go Read! activity, students will have the option of using the digital library. Allow extra time for students to make their reading selection, or have students make a selection before beginning the lesson.

Lesson Goals

- Use Greek affixes to determine the meanings of words.
- Use context clues to determine the meanings of words.
- Read and write for pleasure.

KEYWORDS

affix – a word part attached to a root or base word to create a new word

prefix – a word part with its own meaning that can be added to the beginning of a base word or root to make a new word with a different meaning

suffix – a word part added to the end of a base word or root that changes the meaning or part of speech of a word

GET READY

Introduction to Greek Affixes

Students will get a glimpse of what they will learn about in the lesson. They will also read the lesson goals and keywords. Have students select each keyword and preview its definition.

Look Back at Affixes

Students will review the definition of an affix. They will also practice the prerequisite skill of identifying words with an affix and identifying the definition of a word with a common affix.

LEARN AND TRY IT

LEARN   Words with Greek Affixes

Students will learn the definition of several words that have Greek affixes. They will also learn that knowing the meaning of an affix can help them define an unknown word and how context clues can help them define a word with a Greek affix.

TRY IT   Define Words with Greek Affixes

Students will answer questions to demonstrate their understanding of how to use Greek affixes and context clues to determine the meanings of words.

TRY IT   Apply: Greek Affixes

Students will complete Apply: Greek Affixes from *Summit English Language Arts 4 Activity Book*.

LEARNING COACH CHECK-IN   This activity page contains an open-ended question, so it's important that you review students' responses. Give students feedback, using the sample answers provided to guide you.

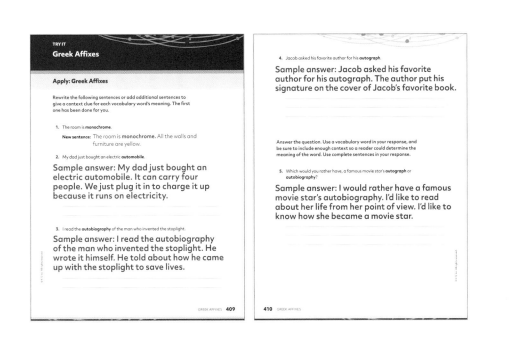

TRY IT   Go Write!

Students will write independently for pleasure. As they write, they should think about using words with Greek affixes in their writing.

TRY IT   Review Greek Affixes

Students will answer questions to review what they have learned about words with Greek affixes.

Greek Affixes

Students will complete the Greek Affixes quiz.

More Language Arts Practice

Students will practice skills according to their individual needs.

Go Read!

Students will read for pleasure. They should choose a book or a magazine that interests them, or they may choose a selection from the digital library, linked in the online lesson.

Students should read for the entire time. Have students select something to read ahead of time to help them stay focused.

Big Ideas: Mini-Project

Lesson Overview

Big Ideas lessons provide students the opportunity to further apply the knowledge acquired and skills learned throughout the unit workshops. Each Big Ideas lesson consists of these parts:

1. **Cumulative Review:** Students keep their skills fresh by reviewing prior content.

2. **Preview:** Students practice answering the types of questions they will commonly find on standardized tests.

3. **Synthesis:** Students complete an assignment that allows them to connect and apply what they have learned. Synthesis assignments vary throughout the course.

   In the Synthesis portion of this Big Ideas lesson, students will complete a small creative project that ties together concepts and skills they have encountered across workshops. These small projects are designed to deepen students' understanding of those concepts and skills.

   LEARNING COACH CHECK-IN   Make sure students complete, review, and submit the assignment to their teacher.

All materials needed for this lesson are linked online and not provided in the Activity Book.

Underwater
Adventures

Marine Biology Words

Lesson Overview

ACTIVITY	ACTIVITY TITLE	TIME	ONLINE/OFFLINE
GET READY	Underwater Adventures Unit Overview	**1** minute	🖥️
	Introduction to Marine Biology Words	**1** minute	🖥️
	Look Back at Root Words	**5** minutes	🖥️
LEARN AND **TRY IT**	Discover Word Meanings	**10** minutes	🖥️
	Determine Word Meanings	**10** minutes	🖥️
	Apply: Marine Biology Words **LEARNING COACH CHECK-IN**	**15** minutes	📄
	Go Write!	**15** minutes	🖥️ or 📄
	Review Marine Biology Words	**15** minutes	🖥️
QUIZ	Marine Biology Words	**15** minutes	🖥️
WRAP-UP	More Language Arts Practice	**18** minutes	🖥️
	Go Read!	**15** minutes	🖥️ or 📄

Content Background

Authors use all types of words in their writing. As readers, we need to use the resources that are provided, like a glossary, to help us understand the words. Other times, we need to use our knowledge of different word parts, such as Greek and Latin roots, to determine meaning.

Advance Preparation

During the Go Read! activity, students will have the option of using the digital library. Allow extra time for students to make their reading selection, or have students make a selection before beginning the lesson.

MATERIALS

Supplied
- *Summit English Language Arts 4 Activity Book*
  - Apply: Marine Biology Words

Also Needed
- reading material for Go Read!

Lesson Goals

- Figure out meanings of words using print and digital resources or word parts.

- Demonstrate knowledge on a quiz.

- Read and write for pleasure.

GET READY

Underwater Adventures Unit Overview

Students will read a summary of what they will learn in the Underwater Adventures unit.

Introduction to Marine Biology Words

Students will get a glimpse of what they will learn about in the lesson. They will also read the lesson goals.

Look Back at Root Words

Students will practice the prerequisite skill of using root words to determine meaning.

LEARN AND TRY IT

LEARN   Discover Word Meanings

Students will be introduced to the vocabulary words for the lesson. Then they will discover meanings of words using print or digital resources or parts of the word.

TRY IT   Determine Word Meanings

Students will continue to use their knowledge of word parts and language resources to determine meanings of unknown words.

TRY IT   Apply: Marine Biology Words

Students will complete Apply: Marine Biology Words from *Summit English Language Arts 4 Activity Book*.

TIP   Remind students to use the root word and context to help them determine the meanings of new words.

LEARNING COACH CHECK-IN   This activity page contains open-ended questions, so it's important that you review students' responses. Give students feedback, using the sample answers provided to guide you.

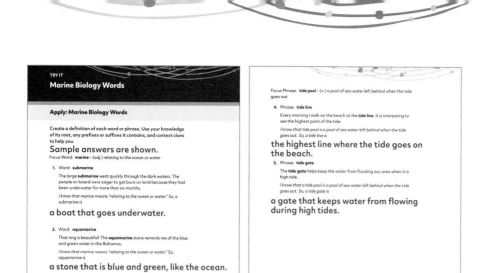

TRY IT Go Write!

Students will write independently for pleasure. As they write, they should think about using words related to marine biology.

TRY IT Review Marine Biology Words

Students will answer questions to review what they have learned about marine biology words.

QUIZ

Marine Biology Words

Students will complete the Marine Biology Words quiz.

WRAP-UP

More Language Arts Practice

Students will practice skills according to their individual needs.

Go Read!

Students will read for pleasure. They should choose a book or a magazine that interests them, or they may choose a selection from the digital library, linked in the online lesson.

Students should read for the entire time. Have students select something to read ahead of time to help them stay focused.

Presentation: Digital Tools

Lesson Overview

ACTIVITY	ACTIVITY TITLE	TIME	ONLINE/OFFLINE
GET READY	Introduction to Presentation: Digital Tools	**2** minutes	🖥
	Spelling List 24 Pretest **LEARNING COACH CHECK-IN**	**10** minutes	🖥 and 📄
	Look Back at Choosing Effective Language	**5** minutes	🖥
LEARN AND **TRY IT**	Precise Language	**15** minutes	🖥
	Use Precise Language	**10** minutes	🖥
	Presentation Software	**15** minutes	🖥
	Use Presentation Software **LEARNING COACH CHECK-IN**	**40** minutes	🖥 and 📄
WRAP-UP	Question About Using Presentation Software	**3** minutes	🖥
	Go Read!	**20** minutes	🖥 or 📄

Content Background

Students will learn how to use presentation software. Through a demonstration, they will learn fundamentals, such as opening the software and saving a new file. They will also learn some basic skills: creating a new slide, adding text, adding a picture, and adding an audio file.

The focus of this lesson is familiarity with the software itself (as opposed to writing or giving a presentation).

Grammar, Usage, and Mechanics Precise language is specific and exact. By using precise language, writers and speakers express their ideas clearly and help ensure that their audience understands their message. The opposite of precise language is vague language.

In these three sentences, notice how the precise verb best describes how Mina moved down the path.

Precise verb: Mina **strolled** down the path.

Less precise verb: Mina **walked** down the path.

Vague verb: Mina **went** down the path.

MATERIALS

Supplied
- *Summit English Language Arts 4 Activity Book*
  - Spelling List 24 Pretest
  - Use Presentation Software
- Use Presentation Software Answer Key (PowerPoint file)

Also Needed
- reading material for Go Read!

KEYWORDS

precise language – language that is specific and exact

Advance Preparation

During the Go Read! activity, students will have the option of using the digital library. Allow extra time for students to make their reading selection, or have students make a selection before beginning the lesson.

Lesson Goals

- Take a spelling pretest.
- Learn how to use precise language.
- Learn how to use presentation software.
- Practice using presentation software.
- Read for pleasure.

GET READY

Introduction to Presentation: Digital Tools

Students will get a glimpse of what they will learn about in the lesson. They will also read the lesson goals and keywords. Have students select each keyword and preview its definition.

Spelling List 24 Pretest

Students will take a spelling pretest.

LEARNING COACH CHECK-IN Have students turn to Spelling List 24 Pretest in *Summit English Language Arts 4 Activity Book* and open the online Spelling Pretest activity. Online, students will listen to the spelling word, type the word in the space indicated, and then check their answer. In the activity book, students will write the correct spelling of the word in the tables provided and indicate with a ✓ or an ✗ if they spelled the word correctly or incorrectly online. Students will repeat this process with the remaining words.

As needed, help students with the interaction between the online activity and the activity book page until they become comfortable with what they need to do. As students practice their spelling words throughout the workshop, they should pay special attention to words they spelled incorrectly on the pretest.

This is the complete list of words students will be tested on.

/us/ Spelled *ice* or *ace*	Root *ten*	Heart Words	Suffix *–ous*
apprentice	antenna	North Dakota	desirous
furnace	extend	Utah	famous
justice	tension		nervous
menace	tent		ridiculous
notice			
novice			
palace			
service			
lattice			
terrace			
surface			

NOTE   Have students keep their completed activity page in a safe place so they can refer to it later.

Look Back at Choosing Effective Language
Students will practice the prerequisite skill of choosing words and phrases for effect.

LEARN AND TRY IT

LEARN   Precise Language

Students will learn how to use precise language to improve writing and speech.

TRY IT   Use Precise Language

Students will answer questions about using precise language to improve writing and speech. They will receive feedback on their answers.

LEARN   Presentation Software

Students will learn how to use presentation software. They will learn how to open a new presentation; give the presentation a file name and save it; create new slides; add titles, text, pictures, and audio; and view the presentation as a slide show.

TIP   The presentation software used in this activity is PowerPoint. The skills shown can be applied to other types of presentation software with some modification.

TRY IT   Use Presentation Software

Students will complete Use Presentation Software from *Summit English Language Arts 4 Activity Book*. Use Presentation Software Answer Key, which is a sample completed presentation, is available online.

NOTE   Students will follow the directions on the activity page to practice using presentation software. Ensure that students have access to a computer while completing the activity.

LEARNING COACH CHECK-IN   Assist students as needed as they complete this activity, especially if this is their first time using presentation software. Give students feedback, using the sample completed presentation provided online to guide you.

TRY IT
Presentation: Digital Tools

Use Presentation Software

Use presentation software to complete this activity. **A sample completed presentation can be found online.**

1. Open the presentation software and select **Blank Presentation.**

2. Go to **File > Save As**, and select a location on your computer in which to save your presentation. Give your presentation a name. Do not delete the file extension (for example, ".pptx") from your name.

3. Create the slides of your presentation.
   a. **Slide 1:** Add a title to the first slide of your presentation. The title can be anything you like (for example, "Gymnastics"). If you wish, add a subtitle.
   b. **Slide 2:** Select **New Slide** from the Home tab to create a second slide. Add a title and at least two bullets with text next to them to your slide. Your bullets should relate to your title.
   c. **Slide 3:** Select **New Slide** to create a third slide. Add a title to your slide. Then add a picture by selecting the Pictures icon on the slide or by going to **Insert > Pictures**. Select a picture that is on your computer (for example, a picture from the Sample Pictures folder). If you can't find a picture that relates to your title, that's okay.
   d. **Slide 4:** Select **New Slide** to create a fourth slide. Add a title to your slide. Then go to **Insert > Audio > Record Audio**. Press the record button (a red circle), and talk for about twenty seconds. When you're finished recording, press the stop button (a blue square). Then press OK. Move the speaker icon next to the title. If you wish, add bullets and text to the slide.

4. Select **Slide Show > From Beginning**. Review your presentation!

5. Save your presentation to your computer using **File > Save** or the Save icon.

PRESENTATION: DIGITAL TOOLS **415**

Question About Using Presentation Software

Students will answer a question to show that they understand a skill related to using presentation software.

Go Read!

Students will read for pleasure. They should choose a book or a magazine that interests them, or they may choose a selection from the digital library, linked in the online lesson.

Students should read for the entire time. Have students select something to read ahead of time to help them stay focused.

Presentation: Planning

Lesson Overview

ACTIVITY	ACTIVITY TITLE	TIME	ONLINE/OFFLINE
GET READY	Introduction to Presentation: Planning	**2** minutes	🖥️
	Spelling List 24 Activity Bank	**10** minutes	📄
LEARN AND **TRY IT**	Punctuation for Effect	**10** minutes	🖥️
	Use Punctuation for Effect	**10** minutes	🖥️
	Explore a Student's Presentation	**15** minutes	🖥️
	Planning a Presentation	**15** minutes	🖥️
	Plan Your Presentation **LEARNING COACH CHECK-IN**	**35** minutes	📄
WRAP-UP	Question About Planning a Presentation	**3** minutes	🖥️
	Go Read!	**20** minutes	🖥️ or 📄

Content Background

Students will begin working on a **public service announcement** that they will create using presentation software. They will complete this assignment over the course of several lessons by following the writing process. Students will begin by prewriting, or planning.

Writing Process

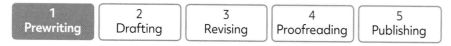

| 1 Prewriting | 2 Drafting | 3 Revising | 4 Proofreading | 5 Publishing |

During this step of the writing process, students will brainstorm and choose a topic and message for their public service announcement. Additionally, they will identify the audience and purpose of their public service announcement and use that information to begin planning how they will present their message.

Grammar, Usage, and Mechanics   In some cases, there are multiple correct ways to punctuate text. Students will learn that good writers think about how punctuation affects the meaning of text.

MATERIALS

Supplied
- *Summit English Language Arts 4 Activity Book*
  - Spelling List 24 Activity Bank
  - Plan Your Presentation
- Presentation Instructions (printout)

Also Needed
- completed Spelling List 24 Pretest activity page from Presentation: Digital Tools
- folder in which students are storing presentation assignment pages
- reading material for Go Read!

In the following example, the writer wants to show that Marshall is yelling. While both sentences are correctly punctuated, the sentence that uses the exclamation point more effectively captures the writer's intent.

Shows Marshall is yelling: "Stop!" said Marshall.

Correct but less effective: "Stop," said Marshall.

In the following example, the writer wants to build suspense. By using two separate sentences, the writer causes readers to pause and wait.

Builds suspense: He stopped. He listened closely.

Correct but less effective: He stopped, and he listened closely.

KEYWORDS

brainstorming – before writing, a way for the writer to come up with ideas

prewriting – the stage or step of writing in which a writer chooses a topic, gathers ideas, and plans what to write

Advance Preparation

Gather students' completed Spelling List 24 Pretest activity page from Presentation: Digital Tools. Students will refer to this page during Get Ready: Spelling List 24 Activity Bank.

Gather a folder that students can use to keep all notes and activity pages related to their presentation.

During the Go Read! activity, students will have the option of using the digital library. Allow extra time for students to make their reading selection, or have students make a selection before beginning the lesson.

Lesson Goals

- Practice spelling words offline.
- Choose the most effective way to punctuate text.
- Explore a model presentation.
- Begin planning your presentation.
- Read for pleasure.

GET READY

Introduction to Presentation: Planning

Students will get a glimpse of what they will learn about in the lesson. They will also read the lesson goals and keywords. Have students select each keyword and preview its definition.

Spelling List 24 Activity Bank

Students will practice all spelling words from the workshop by completing Spelling List 24 Activity Bank from *Summit English Language Arts 4 Activity*

Book. Make sure students have their completed Spelling List 24 Pretest activity page from Presentation: Digital Tools to refer to during this activity.

Remind students to pay special attention to words they spelled incorrectly on the Spelling Pretest.

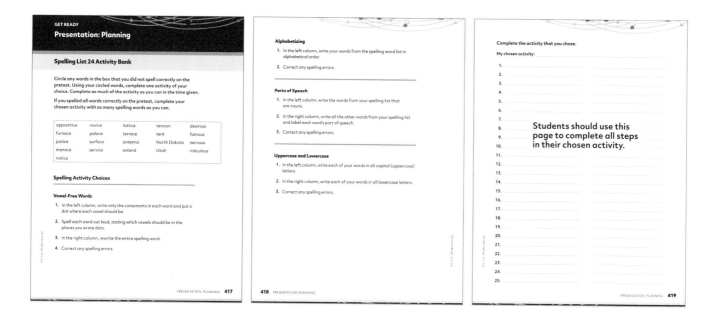

LEARN AND TRY IT

LEARN   Punctuation for Effect

Students will learn to think critically about how punctuation affects the meaning of a sentence. They will learn how to use punctuation for effect in writing.

TRY IT   Use Punctuation for Effect

Students will answer questions about using punctuation for effect in writing. They will receive feedback on their answers.

LEARN   Explore a Student's Presentation

Students will be introduced to their assignment, which is to create a public service announcement using presentation software. To help them better understand the assignment, students will explore a model presentation and think about the elements that make it successful.

TIP   Use an Internet search to locate age-appropriate public service announcements online. Watch them with students to help them understand the purpose of public service announcements and the types of topics they address.

TRY IT   Planning a Presentation

Students will investigate how a student chooses a topic and begins planning a presentation.

TRY IT Plan Your Presentation

Students will complete Plan Your Presentation from *Summit English Language Arts 4 Activity Book*.

LEARNING COACH CHECK-IN Review students' responses. Ensure that students have selected a topic for their presentation that meets the criteria listed in Question 3 of the activity page. When students have completed the page, they should store it in a folder so that they can refer to it throughout the writing process.

NOTE In addition to the planning activity, this activity page contains the instructions for the presentation. Students should read the instructions carefully, but in this lesson, they should complete the planning activity only (not the entire presentation assignment). If you or students wish, you can download and print another copy of the Presentation Instructions online.

TRY IT
Presentation: Planning

Plan Your Presentation

Read the assignment. You will complete the assignment in steps over multiple lessons.

Prompt: Use presentation software to create a public service announcement about a topic of your choice.

Requirements:

Use the template provided to create the following slides:

- A **title** slide
- A **hook** slide that catches the audience's attention about your topic; includes a heading, picture, and audio
- An **introduction** slide that states your message and shows its importance; includes a heading, picture, and audio
- Three **body** slides each organized on a subtopic that provide facts and details that support your message; each slide includes a heading, bulleted talking points, a picture, and audio
- A **conclusion** slide that restates and emphasizes your message; includes a heading, picture, and audio
- A **sources** slide that lists at least two trustworthy research sources

Be sure to do the following:

- Speak clearly and at an appropriate pace.
- Include relevant information from your research and your personal experience.
- Include the **URLs** of any pictures used in the presentation that you found online.
- Use correct **grammar**, **usage**, and **mechanics**.

PRESENTATION: PLANNING **421**

Audience: You will identify an appropriate audience for your presentation based on your message.

Purpose: Persuade your audience to listen to your message.

Brainstorm and choose a topic for your presentation.

1. Think about issues that are important to you. List as many topics as you can think of.

2. Read your answers to Question 1.
   a. Circle two topics that interest you the most.
   b. For each topic you chose, try stating a message related to the topic. Two sample topics and messages are shown.

422 PRESENTATION: PLANNING

Topic 1: litter from plastic water bottles

Message: Use a reusable water bottle instead of plastic water bottles.

Topic 2: animals in shelters

Message: Adopt a dog from a shelter instead of getting a dog from a breeder.

Topic 1:

Message:

Topic 2:

Message:

PRESENTATION: PLANNING **423**

---

3. Decide which message you wrote in Question 2 interests you more. Then answer Yes or No to each question.
   a. Is your message something that can be covered well in a six-slide presentation?
   b. Is your message something you can expand upon with at least three supporting subtopics?
   c. Is your message something that you can support with research?

4. Did you answer Yes to Parts A–C of Question 3? You have found your presentation topic! If not, go back to the topics you listed in Question 1, choose a different topic, and follow the process described in Questions 2 and 3.

5. Think about your message. Who is the audience for your message? Explain. (The *actual* audience will be your teacher, but you should target an audience that you feel is appropriate for your message.)

6. The purpose of a public service announcement is to persuade your audience to listen to your message. Based on your audience and purpose, list three subtopics that best support your message. Your subtopics should help your audience understand and then agree with your message.

Answers will vary. By the time they complete this activity page, students should have chosen a topic, message, audience, and supporting subtopics for their presentation.

424 PRESENTATION: PLANNING

Question About Planning a Presentation

Students will answer a question to show that they understand how to plan a presentation.

Go Read!

Students will read for pleasure. They should choose a book or a magazine that interests them, or they may choose a selection from the digital library, linked in the online lesson.

Students should read for the entire time. Have students select something to read ahead of time to help them stay focused.

Presentation: Research

Lesson Overview

ACTIVITY	ACTIVITY TITLE	TIME	ONLINE/OFFLINE
GET READY	Introduction to Presentation: Research	**2** minutes	
	Spelling List 24 Practice	**10** minutes	
	Don't Use Plastic Water Bottles	**10** minutes	
LEARN AND **TRY IT**	Researching a Presentation	**20** minutes	
	Research Your Presentation **LEARNING COACH CHECK-IN**	**55** minutes	and
WRAP-UP	Question About Researching a Presentation	**3** minutes	
	Go Read!	**20** minutes	or

Content Background

Students will continue working on a **public service announcement** that they will create using presentation software. They will complete this assignment over the course of several lessons by following the writing process.

Writing Process

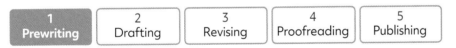

| 1 Prewriting | 2 Drafting | 3 Revising | 4 Proofreading | 5 Publishing |

In this lesson, students will continue prewriting, on planning, by conducting research. They will learn techniques that will help them research quickly and effectively. For instance, they will learn to skim a research source for important words and phrases. They will also learn how to use text features, such as headings and words in bold, to quickly locate information.

This lesson also emphasizes another important part of research: reflection. After students finish researching, they will answer questions to help them draw conclusions and evaluate how well they answered their research questions. Students will then decide whether, based on their reflection, they should revise any part of their plan for their presentation.

MATERIALS

Supplied
- *Summit English Language Arts 4 Activity Book*
  - Research Your Presentation
- Presentation Instructions (printout)
- Research Notes (printout)

Also Needed
- folder in which students are storing presentation assignment pages
- reading material for Go Read!

Advance Preparation

Gather the folder that students are using to store the activity pages related to their presentation. The folder should contain the following:

- Students' completed Plan Your Presentation activity page from Presentation: Planning

Students will need to complete their own research during Try It: Research Your Presentation. Make sure students have access to trustworthy research sources. You may choose to complete the activity at a library.

During the Go Read! activity, students will have the option of using the digital library. Allow extra time for students to make their reading selection, or have students make a selection before beginning the lesson.

Lesson Goals

- Practice spelling words online.
- Practice grammar skills by editing a passage.
- Learn how to conduct research for a presentation.
- Research for your presentation.
- Read for pleasure.

GET READY

Introduction to Presentation: Research

Students will get a glimpse of what they will learn about in the lesson. They will also read the lesson goals and keywords. Have students select each keyword and preview its definition.

Spelling List 24 Practice

Students will practice all spelling words from the workshop.

Don't Use Plastic Water Bottles

Students will edit a short passage to practice applying grammar skills. This passage contains opportunities to improve the writing related to using precise language, punctuation for effect, and words and phrases for effect.

LEARN   Researching a Presentation

Students will learn techniques that will help them research more efficiently and effectively, such as skimming, using text features, and taking notes on graphics and other visuals (such as charts and maps). They will learn how good researchers reflect on their findings and adjust their research questions and writing plans accordingly. They will also review other important research skills.

TIP   Tell students that major newspapers, such as the *New York Times*, the *Washington Post*, and the *Chicago Tribune* are all trustworthy sources. Likewise, government websites, such as those run by the Library of Congress and other agencies, contain reliable and useful information. Print reference books, such as *Encyclopedia Britannica* and the *World Book Encyclopedia*, are also credible sources of information.

TRY IT   Research Your Presentation

Students will complete Research Your Presentation from *Summit English Language Arts 4 Activity Book*. Make sure students have their completed Plan Your Presentation activity page from Presentation: Planning to refer to during this activity.

LEARNING COACH CHECK-IN   Assist students as needed in finding relevant, appropriate, and trustworthy research sources. When students have completed their research notes, they should store them in the folder they are using to organize their presentation assignment pages.

NOTE   If you or your students wish, you can download and print another copy of the Presentation Instructions online. Additional sheets for Research Notes are also available online.

Research Notes

Source

Title: _____

Author: _____

Published by: _____

URL (if necessary): _____

Notes

Key Information Written in Your Own Words:

_____
_____
_____
_____
_____

Direct Quotation:

_____
_____

Person Quoted: _____

Research Notes

Source

Title: _____

Author: _____

Published by: _____

URL (if necessary): _____

Notes

Key Information Written in Your Own Words:

_____
_____
_____
_____
_____

Direct Quotation:

_____
_____

Person Quoted: _____

Reflect on your research.

5. What general conclusions can you draw from your research? Summarize your research in 1 or 2 sentences.

_____
_____

6. Look back at your research questions.

a. How well does your research answer each of your questions?

_____
_____

b. Did you answer any questions that you didn't originally ask? If so, what?

_____
_____

c. Based on your research, revise your subtopics, or even your message. If you don't have any revisions to make, explain why.

_____
_____

WRAP-UP

Question About Researching a Presentation

Students will answer a question to show that they understand how to research a presentation.

Go Read!

Students will read for pleasure. They should choose a book or a magazine that interests them, or they may choose a selection from the digital library, linked in the online lesson.

Students should read for the entire time. Have students select something to read ahead of time to help them stay focused.

Presentation: Drafting (A)

Lesson Overview

ACTIVITY	ACTIVITY TITLE	TIME	ONLINE/OFFLINE
GET READY	Introduction to Presentation: Drafting (A)	**2** minutes	
	Spelling List 24 Review Game	**10** minutes	
	Everyone Should Learn to Code	**10** minutes	
LEARN AND **TRY IT**	Drafting and Choosing Images for a Presentation	**20** minutes	
	Draft Your Presentation **LEARNING COACH CHECK-IN**	**55** minutes	
WRAP-UP	Question About Drafting a Presentation	**3** minutes	
	Go Read!	**20** minutes	or

Content Background

Students will continue working on a **public service announcement**, an assignment that they will complete over the course of several lessons by following the writing process. In this lesson, students will begin drafting their presentation in PowerPoint.

Writing Process

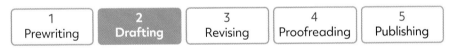

During **drafting**, students will use their research notes and other planning work to create a rough draft of their presentation. Students will draft directly in the presentation software—not on drafting paper. They will use a provided template that includes directions for what students need to do on each slide of the presentation.

Students will learn guidelines for how to find images online that they can use in their presentations. Since copyright law is complicated and image rights sometimes change, **ensure that students do not publish their completed presentations online.** That includes sharing the presentation on a personal or family website or on social media. Students should share their presentation with their teacher and classmates only.

MATERIALS

Supplied
- Model Presentation (PowerPoint file)
- Presentation Template (PowerPoint file)
- Presentation Instructions (printout)

Also Needed
- folder in which students are storing presentation assignment pages
- reading material for Go Read!

KEYWORDS

copyright – the right held by one person or company to publish, sell, distribute, and reproduce a work of art, literature, or music

draft – an early effort at a piece of writing, not the finished work

Students are expected to write about half of their rough draft in this lesson (although they may write more, if they wish). They will have time to finish and submit their draft in Presentation: Drafting (B).

Advance Preparation

Gather the folder that students are using to store the activity pages related to their presentation. The folder should contain the following:

- Students' completed Plan Your Presentation activity page from Presentation: Planning

- Students' completed research notes from Presentation: Research

During the Go Read! activity, students will have the option of using the digital library. Allow extra time for students to make their reading selection, or have students make a selection before beginning the lesson.

Lesson Goals

- Practice spelling words online.

- Practice grammar skills by editing a passage.

- Learn how to create your presentation using a template.

- Learn how to choose images to include in a presentation.

- Begin to draft your presentation.

- Read for pleasure.

GET READY

Introduction to Presentation: Drafting (A)
Students will get a glimpse of what they will learn about in the lesson. They will also read the lesson goals and keywords. Have students select each keyword and preview its definition.

Spelling List 24 Review Game
Students will practice all spelling words from the workshop.

Everyone Should Learn to Code
Students will edit a short passage to practice applying grammar skills. This passage contains opportunities to improve the writing related to using precise language, punctuation for effect, and words and phrases for effect.

LEARN   Drafting and Choosing Images for a Presentation

Students will learn how to use a template to create their public service announcement using presentation software. Students will also learn guidelines for finding images online that they can use in their presentation.

TIP   Students don't necessarily need to find images for their presentation online. They can use photos they take themselves (or photos for which they have a friend's or family member's permission to use). They can also create images, such as drawings, charts, and graphs, on the computer. Finally, students can draw on paper and then photograph or scan those drawings.

TRY IT   Draft Your Presentation

Students will use the Presentation Template to begin drafting their presentation. Students should complete about half of their draft during this activity. If students wish, they may complete more than half of their draft.

Make sure students have their completed Plan Your Presentation activity page from Presentation: Planning and their research notes from Presentation: Research to refer to during this activity.

LEARNING COACH CHECK-IN   Ensure that students understand how to use the template (you may wish to supervise them as they complete one slide). If necessary, remind students not to focus on perfection at this stage of the writing process.

TIP   Help students create a folder on the computer in which to save their in-progress presentation.

NOTE   If you or students wish, you can download and print another copy of the Presentation Instructions online. The Model Presentation is also available online as a reference.

Question About Drafting a Presentation

Students will answer a question to show that they understand how to draft a presentation.

Go Read!

Students will read for pleasure. They should choose a book or a magazine that interests them, or they may choose a selection from the digital library, linked in the online lesson.

Students should read for the entire time. Have students select something to read ahead of time to help them stay focused.

Presentation: Drafting (B)

Lesson Overview

ACTIVITY	ACTIVITY TITLE	TIME	ONLINE/OFFLINE
GET READY	Introduction to Presentation: Drafting (B)	**1** minute	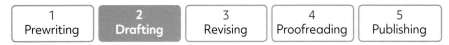
TRY IT	Review Precise Language and Punctuation for Effect	**10** minutes	
QUIZ	Precise Language and Punctuation for Effect	**20** minutes	
	Spelling List 24	**10** minutes	
TRY IT	Finish Drafting Your Presentation LEARNING COACH CHECK-IN	**60** minutes	
WRAP-UP	Turn In Your Presentation Draft	**1** minute	
	More Language Arts Practice	**8** minutes	
	Go Read!	**10** minutes	or

Content Background

Students will continue working on a **public service announcement**, an assignment that they will complete over the course of several lessons by following the writing process. In this lesson, students will finish drafting their presentation in PowerPoint. They will complete the remaining steps of the writing process in a future workshop.

Writing Process

| 1 Prewriting | 2 **Drafting** | 3 Revising | 4 Proofreading | 5 Publishing |

Advance Preparation

Help students locate their in-progress presentation that they saved to the computer in Presentation: Drafting (A).

Gather the folder that students are using to store the activity pages related to their presentation. The folder should contain the following:

- Students' completed Plan Your Presentation activity page from Presentation: Planning

- Students' completed research notes from Presentation: Research

MATERIALS

Supplied
- Model Presentation (PowerPoint file)
- Presentation Template (PowerPoint file)
- Presentation Instructions (printout)

Also Needed
- students' in-progress presentation from Presentation: Drafting (A)
- folder in which students are storing presentation assignment pages

Lesson Goals

- Review how to use precise language and punctuation for effect.
- Take a quiz on using precise language and punctuation for effect.
- Take a spelling quiz.
- Finish and submit the rough draft of your presentation.

GET READY

Introduction to Presentation: Drafting (B)

Students will read the lesson goals.

TRY IT

Review Precise Language and Punctuation for Effect

Students will answer questions to review what they have learned about using precise language and punctuation for effect.

QUIZ

Precise Language and Punctuation for Effect

Students will complete the Precise Language and Punctuation for Effect quiz.

Spelling List 24

Students will complete the Spelling List 24 quiz.

TRY IT

Finish Drafting Your Presentation

Students will complete the rough draft of their presentation. Students should open the PowerPoint file they saved in Presentation: Drafting (A) and complete their draft.

Make sure students have their completed Plan Your Presentation activity page from Presentation: Planning and their research notes from Presentation: Research to refer to during this activity.

LEARNING COACH CHECK-IN   Review students' presentation draft. Ensure that students' draft is in line with the assignment criteria outlined on the Plan Your Presentation activity page. Students should save a copy of their presentation on their computer.

NOTE   If you or students wish, you can download and print another copy of the Presentation Instructions online. The Presentation Template and Model Presentation are also available online.

WRAP-UP

Turn In Your Presentation Draft
Students will submit their presentation draft to their teacher.

More Language Arts Practice
Students will practice skills according to their individual needs.

Go Read!
Students will read for pleasure. They should choose a book or a magazine that interests them, or they may choose a selection from the digital library, linked in the online lesson.

Students should read for the entire time. Have students select something to read ahead of time to help them stay focused.

Coral Reefs (A)

Lesson Overview

ACTIVITY	ACTIVITY TITLE	TIME	ONLINE/OFFLINE
GET READY	Introduction to Coral Reefs (A)	**1** minute	🖥️
	Spelling List 25 Pretest **LEARNING COACH CHECK-IN**	**10** minutes	🖥️ and 📄
	Coral Reefs in 60 Seconds	**1** minute	🖥️
	Before You Read *National Geographic Kids: Coral Reefs*	**14** minutes	🖥️
READ	*National Geographic Kids: Coral Reefs*	**30** minutes	📄
	Check-In: *National Geographic Kids: Coral Reefs*	**5** minutes	🖥️
LEARN AND **TRY IT**	Learn About Coral Reef Content-Area Vocabulary	**10** minutes	🖥️
	Identify Coral Reef Life Word Meanings	**10** minutes	🖥️
	Apply: Content-Area Vocabulary	**15** minutes	🖥️
	Write About Coral Reefs and Camouflage **LEARNING COACH CHECK-IN**	**14** minutes	📄
	Practice Words from *National Geographic Kids: Coral Reefs*	**8** minutes	🖥️
WRAP-UP	Question About *National Geographic Kids: Coral Reefs*	**2** minutes	🖥️

Content Background

Students will read *National Geographic Kids: Coral Reefs* by Kristin Baird Rattini. They will learn how to determine the meaning of important academic and domain-specific words in a nonfiction text about marine biology.

Authors use a variety of ways to helps students understand key, but complex, academic terms as they read. Using context clues, such as looking for definitions, synonyms, antonyms, explanations, and restatements are all useful as students read. Being able to break down words into individual word parts (such as roots and affixes) as well as understanding that words have origins in other languages, can assist students as well. Finally, students can use text features provided by the author in a nonfiction text, such as glossaries and side bars, to help them define and find the meaning of

MATERIALS

Supplied
- *National Geographic Kids: Coral Reefs* by Kristin Baird Rattini
- *Summit English Language Arts 4 Activity Book*
  - Spelling List 25 Pretest
  - Write About Coral Reefs and Camouflage

important vocabulary words. All these features and details assist students with exploring the topic and making inferences to develop the meaning of content vocabulary.

National Geographic Kids: Coral Reefs Synopsis

National Geographic Kids: Coral Reefs takes us on a journey through the coral reefs, an important part of marine life's ecosystem. Through different pictures, graphics, humorous Q&As, and descriptive captions and sidebars, students learn how coral reefs are made, why they are important for other marine life and the environment, and what humans are doing to ensure they are preserved.

Lesson Goals

- Take a spelling pretest.
- Read *National Geographic Kids: Coral Reefs.*
- Determine word meanings using text features and word-part strategies.
- Make inferences to determine word meanings.

KEYWORDS

academic word – a word used in educational settings more than in conversation; often a more precise word in place of a more common word

glossary – a list of important terms and their meanings that is usually found in the back of a book

infer – to use clues and what you already know to make a guess

inference – a guess that readers make using the clues that an author gives them in a piece of writing

jargon – specialized language used by a particular group or activity

nonfiction – writing that presents facts and information to explain, describe, or persuade; for example, newspaper articles and biographies are nonfiction

root – a word part with a special meaning to which prefixes and suffixes can be added; for example, *spec* is a root that means "see"

text feature – part of a text that helps a reader locate information and determine what is most important; some examples are the title, table of contents, headings, pictures, and glossary

GET READY

Introduction to Coral Reefs (A)

Students will get a glimpse of what they will learn about in the lesson. They will also read the lesson goals and keywords. Have students select each keyword and preview its definition.

Spelling List 25 Pretest

Students will take a spelling pretest.

LEARNING COACH CHECK-IN   Have students turn to Spelling List 25 Pretest in *Summit English Language Arts 4 Activity Book* and open the online Spelling Pretest activity. Online, students will listen to the spelling word, type the word in the space indicated, and then check their answer. In the activity book, students will write the correct spelling of the word in the tables provided and indicate with a ✓ or an ✗ if they spelled the word correctly or incorrectly online. Students will repeat this process with the remaining words.

As needed, help students with the interaction between the online activity and the activity book page until they become comfortable with what they need

to do. As students practice their spelling words throughout the workshop, they should pay special attention to words they spelled incorrectly on the pretest.

This is the complete list of words students will be tested on.

Contractions	Root *fer*	Suffix *–ship*	Heart Words
couldn't	conference	friendship	Iowa
doesn't	ferry	horsemanship	Michigan
let's	prefer	leadership	
shouldn't	transfer	relationship	
there's			
they're			
who's			
won't			
wouldn't			
you're			
aren't			

NOTE   Have students keep their completed activity page in a safe place so they can refer to it later.

Coral Reefs in 60 Seconds

Students will watch a short video designed to spark their interest in upcoming topics.

Before You Read *National Geographic Kids: Coral Reefs*

Students will be introduced to some key vocabulary words that they will encounter in the upcoming reading and learn some important background information about nonfiction texts related to the reading.

READ

National Geographic Kids: Coral Reefs

Students will read *National Geographic Kids: Coral Reefs* by Kristin Baird Rattini.

Check-In: *National Geographic Kids: Coral Reefs*

Students will answer several questions to demonstrate their comprehension of *National Geographic Kids: Coral Reefs*.

LEARN AND TRY IT

LEARN   Learn About Coral Reef Content-Area Vocabulary

Students will be introduced to the different ways that they can use nonfiction text features and word strategies to understand the meaning of important content-area vocabulary.

TRY IT   Identify Coral Reef Word Meanings

Students will apply what they learned about determining content-area vocabulary meanings to other passages from the reading.

TRY IT   Apply: Content-Area Vocabulary

Students will apply to a new work what they've learned about determining the meaning of content-area vocabulary.

TRY IT   Write About Coral Reefs and Camouflage

Students will complete Write About Coral Reefs and Camouflage from *Summit English Language Arts 4 Activity Book*.

LEARNING COACH CHECK-IN   This activity page contains open-ended questions, so it's important that you review students' responses. Give students feedback, using the sample answers provided to guide you.

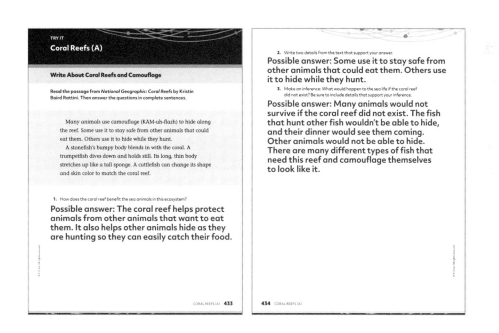

TRY IT Practice Words from *National Geographic Kids: Coral Reefs*

Students will answer questions to demonstrate their understanding of the vocabulary words from the reading.

WRAP-UP

Question About *National Geographic Kids: Coral Reefs*

Students will answer a question to show that they can recall important information about coral reefs.

Coral Reefs (B)

Lesson Overview

ACTIVITY	ACTIVITY TITLE	TIME	ONLINE/OFFLINE
GET READY	Introduction to Coral Reefs (B)	**1** minute	📶
	Spelling List 25 Activity Bank	**10** minutes	📄
	Recall *National Geographic Kids: Coral Reefs*	**5** minutes	📶
	Before You Read *Who Eats What? Coral Reef Food Chains*	**10** minutes	📶
READ	*Who Eats What? Coral Reef Food Chains*	**30** minutes	📶 or 📄
	Check-In: *Who Eats What? Coral Reef Food Chains*	**5** minutes	📶
LEARN AND **TRY IT**	Making Connections, Inferences, and Conclusions	**10** minutes	📶
	Identify Connections, Inferences, and Conclusions	**10** minutes	📶
	Apply: Making Connections to the Text	**15** minutes	📶
	Write About the Food Chain in Coral Reefs LEARNING COACH CHECK-IN	**15** minutes	📄
	Practice Words from *Who Eats What? Coral Reef Food Chains*	**7** minutes	📶
WRAP-UP	Question About *Who Eats What? Coral Reef Food Chains*	**2** minutes	📶

Content Background

Students will read *Who Eats What? Coral Reefs Food Chains* by Rebecca Pettiford. They will learn how to make connections and inferences and draw conclusions from the text.

Authors include important ideas and supporting details in their writing. This helps readers better understand and connect to the text. Sometimes, connections are easy to make because the information is stated directly in the text. Other times, readers need to make inferences or draw conclusions to connect to the important ideas.

Advance Preparation

Gather students' completed Spelling List 25 Pretest activity page from Coral Reefs (A). Students will refer to this page during Get Ready: Spelling List 25 Activity Bank.

MATERIALS

Supplied
- *Who Eats What? Coral Reef Food Chains* by Rebecca Pettiford
- *Summit English Language Arts 4 Activity Book*
  - Spelling List 25 Activity Bank
  - Write About the Food Chain in Coral Reefs

Also Needed
- completed Spelling List 25 Pretest activity page from Coral Reefs (A)

Who Eats What? Coral Reef Food Chains Synopsis

Who Eats What? Coral Reef Food Chains takes us on an exciting journey into coral reefs, where many marine animals and plants live. The author explains how coral reefs are made and how vital they are to ensuring the survival of all in the ecosystem. The coral reef is just one part of a large food chain, which is made up of different types of plants and animals. The author explains each part of the food chain, pointing out how each aspect is a vital part of the food chain as a whole.

Lesson Goals

- Practice all spelling words offline.
- Read *Who Eats What? Coral Reef Food Chains*.
- Determine connections to ideas in a text by making inferences and drawing conclusions.
- Determine the meaning of words using context.

KEYWORDS

conclusion – a decision made, or opinion formed, about something not stated, using information provided and what is already known

infer – to use clues and what you already know to make a guess

inference – a guess that readers make using the clues that an author gives them in a piece of writing

main idea – the most important point the author makes; it may be stated or unstated

supporting detail – a detail that gives more information about a main idea

GET READY

Introduction to Coral Reefs (B)

Students will get a glimpse of what they will learn about in the lesson. They will also read the lesson goals and keywords. Have students select each keyword and preview its definition.

Spelling List 25 Activity Bank

Students will practice all spelling words from the workshop by completing Spelling List 25 Activity Bank from *Summit English Language Arts 4 Activity Book*. Make sure students have their completed Spelling List 25 Pretest activity page from Coral Reefs (A) to refer to during this activity.

Remind students to pay special attention to words they spelled incorrectly on the Spelling Pretest.

Recall *National Geographic Kids: Coral Reefs*

Students will answer some questions to review the reading that they have already completed.

Before You Read *Who Eats What? Coral Reef Food Chains*

Students will be introduced to some key vocabulary words that they will encounter in the upcoming reading.

READ

Who Eats What? Coral Reef Food Chains

Students will read *Who Eats What? Coral Reef Food Chains* by Rebecca Pettiford.

NOTE Students have the option to read this text online on Big Universe. To locate the text in Big Universe, search for "Coral Reef Food Chains."

Check-In: *Who Eats What? Coral Reef Food Chains*

Students will answer several questions to demonstrate their comprehension of *Who Eats What? Coral Reef Food Chains*.

LEARN AND TRY IT

LEARN   Make Connections, Inferences, and Conclusions

Students will learn how to make connections to main ideas in a text using supporting details, their own inferences, and conclusions they draw.

TRY IT Identify Connections, Inferences, and Conclusions

Students will analyze passages and answer questions about connections, inferences, and conclusions that can be made in a text.

TRY IT Apply: Making Connections to the Text

Students will apply to a new work what they've learned about making connections.

TRY IT Write About the Food Chain in Coral Reefs

Students will complete Write About the Food Chain in Coral Reefs from *Summit English Language Arts 4 Activity Book*.

LEARNING COACH CHECK-IN   This activity page contains an open-ended question, so it's important that you review students' responses. Give students feedback, using the sample answer provided to guide you.

TRY IT
Coral Reefs (B)

Write About the Food Chain in Coral Reefs

Read the passage from *Who Eats What? Coral Reef Food Chains* by Rebecca Pettiford. Then answer the questions in complete sentences.

Plant plankton and sea grass are **producers**. They are the first link in the coral reef food chain. These plants use the sun's energy to make their own food.

Small fish and green sea turtles eat the plants. They are the next link in the chain. They are **consumers**.

Large fish, octopuses, and sharks eat consumers. They are **predators**, the next link in the chain.

Sharks are a top predator. They eat smaller predators.

When an animal dies, **decomposers** such as **bacteria** break down its body. They change the dead matter into **nutrients**. The nutrients return to the sea floor.

1. How do the parts of the coral reef food chain depend on each other? Include details from the text to support your answer.

Each part of the food chain depends on something else for its survival. For example, producers depend on the sun to help them make their own food and energy. Consumers depend on those producers for food. Then predators eat

CORAL REEFS (B) **439**

consumers and smaller predators so that they can survive. Finally, decomposers get their energy from dead matter that falls to the sea floor, where the producers grow.

440 CORAL REEFS (B)

TRY IT Practice Words from *Who Eats What? Coral Reef Food Chains*

Students will answer questions to determine their understanding of the vocabulary words from the reading.

WRAP-UP

Question About *Who Eats What? Coral Reef Food Chains*

Students will answer a question to demonstrate they understand what they read in *Who Eats What? Coral Reef Food Chains*.

Coral Reefs (C)

Lesson Overview

ACTIVITY	ACTIVITY TITLE	TIME	ONLINE/OFFLINE
GET READY	Introduction to Coral Reefs (C)	**1** minute	🛜
	Spelling List 25 Practice	**10** minutes	🛜
	Recall *Who Eats What? Coral Reef Food Chains*	**5** minutes	🛜
	Before You Read *Coral Reefs*	**10** minutes	🛜
READ	*Coral Reefs*	**30** minutes	📄
	Check-In: *Coral Reefs*	**5** minutes	🛜
LEARN AND **TRY IT**	Comparing and Contrasting Nonfiction Texts	**10** minutes	🛜
	Compare and Contrast Nonfiction Texts	**10** minutes	🛜
	Apply: Compare and Contrast Details	**15** minutes	🛜
	Write About Coral Reefs **LEARNING COACH CHECK-IN**	**15** minutes	📄
	Practice Words from *Coral Reefs*	**7** minutes	🛜
WRAP-UP	Question About Coral Reefs	**2** minutes	🛜

Content Background

Students will read *Coral Reefs* by Jason Chin. They will learn how to compare and contrast details from nonfiction texts that are written about the same topic.

There are many books written to inform readers about one topic. When reading a variety of texts on one topic, as students do in this workshop, readers should be able to identify information that is similar across the texts. Sometimes authors may show ideas using different text structures and features, or prioritize different information. When readers can identify these similarities and differences, they are practicing the important skill of comparing and contrasting texts.

MATERIALS

Supplied
- *Coral Reefs* by Jason Chin
- *Who Eats What? Coral Reef Food Chains* by Rebecca Pettiford
- *National Geographic Kids: Coral Reefs* by Kristin Baird Rattini
- *Summit English Language Arts 4 Activity Book*
  - Write About Coral Reefs

Coral Reefs Synopsis

Coral Reefs takes the reader on a vividly illustrated journey through a coral reef and intertwines the experience with that of a young girl visiting the library to read about coral reefs in a book. Readers learn about the intricate relationship between plants and animals in a coral reef as members work to adapt and survive in this underwater biome.

Lesson Goals

- Practice all spelling words online.
- Read *Coral Reefs*.
- Compare and contrast details in nonfiction texts on the same topic.

GET READY

Introduction to Coral Reefs (C)
Students will get a glimpse of what they will learn about in the lesson. They will also read the lesson goals and keywords. Have students select each keyword and preview its definition.

Spelling List 25 Practice
Students will practice all spelling words from the workshop.

Recall *Who Eats What? Coral Reef Food Chains*
Students will answer some questions to review the reading that they have already completed.

Before You Read *Coral Reefs*
Students will be introduced to some key vocabulary words that they will encounter in the upcoming reading.

READ

Coral Reefs
Students will read *Coral Reefs* by Jason Chin.

Check-In: *Coral Reefs*
Students will answer several questions to demonstrate their comprehension of *Coral Reefs*.

LEARN   Comparing and Contrasting Nonfiction Texts

Students will learn how to compare and contrast details in the three nonfiction texts they have read.

TRY IT   Compare and Contrast Nonfiction Texts

Students will answer questions comparing and contrasting three nonfiction texts.

TRY IT   Apply: Compare and Contrast Details

Students will apply to a new work what they've learned about comparing and contrasting details in multiple texts.

TRY IT   Write About Coral Reefs

Students will complete Write About Coral Reefs from *Summit English Language Arts 4 Activity Book*.

LEARNING COACH CHECK-IN   This activity page contains open-ended questions, so it's important that you review students' responses. Give students feedback, using the sample answers provided to guide you.

TRY IT
Coral Reefs (C)

Write About Coral Reefs

Pretend you are being interviewed for a friend's project on marine life. Answer the questions about coral reefs using complete sentences. Be sure to use details from the different books you've read to support your answers.

1. Why are coral reefs so important?

Answers will vary. Sample answer: Coral reefs are important because they are home to diverse aquatic plants and animals. In the text *Coral Reefs* by Jason Chin, the author explains that coral reefs are "cities of the sea." Like our cities, coral reefs give plants and animals food, shelter, and protection.

2. What are the top three facts you learned about coral reefs?

See below.

CORAL REEFS (C)   **441**

---

3. How do coral reefs help animals and plants survive?

Answers will vary. Sample answer: In *Who Eats What? Coral Reef Food Chains* by Rebecca Pettiford, I learned that some plants and animals need the coral reef for food. For example, parrot fish eat the polyps in coral reefs. Other animals use the coral reef to hide from predators. Squirrelfish use the reef to hide from grouper. A cuttlefish hides by changing its color, so it matches with the reef.

I would love to visit the Great Barrier Reef someday.

442   CORAL REEFS (C)

Additonal answers

2. Answers will vary. Sample answer: In *National Geographic Kids: Coral Reefs* by Kristin Baird Rattini, I learned that a reef can have 800 different types of coral polyps. My favorite is the brain coral because it really looks like a brain. Another interesting fact I learned is that cool animals live in the coral reefs. In *Coral Reefs* by Jason Chin, I read about a fish called the whale shark that visits the coral reef once a year. Finally, in *Who Eats What? Coral Reef Food Chains* by Rebecca Pettiford, I learned that coral reefs take a long time to grow. They only grow 2.5 centimeters a year!

TRY IT   Practice Words from *Coral Reefs*

Students will answer questions to determine their understanding of the vocabulary from the reading.

WRAP-UP

Question About *Coral Reefs*

Students will answer a question to show that they understand comparing and contrasting details in *Coral Reefs*.

Coral Reefs (D)

Lesson Overview

ACTIVITY	ACTIVITY TITLE	TIME	ONLINE/OFFLINE
GET READY	Introduction to Coral Reefs (D)	**1** minute	
	Spelling List 25 Review Game	**10** minutes	
	Recall *Coral Reefs*	**5** minutes	
	Before You Read "Choose a Sunscreen Right for Reefs"	**10** minutes	
READ	"Choose a Sunscreen Right for Reefs"	**15** minutes	
	Check-In: "Choose a Sunscreen Right for Reefs"	**5** minutes	
LEARN AND **TRY IT**	Identifying Details and Techniques in Persuasive Texts	**10** minutes	
	Identify Details and Techniques in Persuasive Texts	**10** minutes	
	Apply: Author's Word Choice	**15** minutes	
	Plan to Write a Persuasive Essay **LEARNING COACH CHECK-IN**	**29** minutes	
	Practice Words from "Choose a Sunscreen Right for Reefs"	**8** minutes	
WRAP-UP	Question About "Choose a Sunscreen Right for Reefs"	**2** minutes	

Content Background

Students will learn about how authors convince readers to believe their point of view in a persuasive essay. Students will also learn about the different techniques authors use to convey their ideas and beliefs to their audience.

"Choose a Sunscreen Right for Reefs" Synopsis

This persuasive essay argues why people should use "reef-safe" sunscreen to help protect the coral reefs and all animals and plants associated with them. The author supports his position using evidence. He also uses specific techniques to grab readers' attention and convince them of his beliefs on the issue.

Lesson Goals

- Practice all spelling words online.
- Identify important details and techniques in a persuasive text.
- Plan to write a persuasive essay.

KEYWORDS

persuasive essay – an essay in which the writer tries to convince readers to agree with a stance on an issue

point of view – the perspective a story, or text, is told from

GET READY

Introduction to Coral Reef (D)

Students will get a glimpse of what they will learn about in the lesson. They will also read the lesson goals and keywords. Have students select each keyword and preview its definition.

Spelling List 25 Review Game

Students will practice all spelling words from the workshop.

Recall *Coral Reefs*

Students will answer some questions to review the reading that they have already completed.

Before You Read "Choose a Sunscreen Right for Reefs"

Students will be introduced to some key vocabulary words that they will encounter in the upcoming reading and learn some important information about persuasive texts before they read.

READ

"Choose a Sunscreen Right for Reefs"

Students will read "Choose a Sunscreen Right for Reefs" in *Expeditions in Reading*.

Check-In: "Choose a Sunscreen Right for Reefs"

Students will answer several questions to demonstrate their comprehension of "Choose a Sunscreen Right for Reefs."

LEARN AND TRY IT

LEARN   Identifying Details and Techniques in Persuasive Texts

Students will learn how to analyze details and the author's techniques in a persuasive essay.

TRY IT   Identify Details and Techniques in Persuasive Texts

Students will answer several questions to demonstrate their ability to identify important details and techniques, make inferences, and draw conclusions about information in a persuasive essay.

TRY IT   Apply: Author's Word Choice

Students will apply to a new work what they've learned about identifying important details and techniques, making inferences, and drawing conclusions in persuasive essays.

TRY IT   Plan to Write a Persuasive Essay

Students will complete Plan to Write a Persuasive Essay from *Summit English Language Arts 4 Activity Book*.

LEARNING COACH CHECK-IN   This activity page contains open-ended questions, so it's important that you review students' responses. Give students feedback, using the sample answers provided to guide you.

NOTE   Have students keep their completed activity page in a safe place so they can refer to it later.

TRY IT
Coral Reefs (D)

Plan to Write a Persuasive Essay

Use the prompt to answer the questions.

Prompt: Write a persuasive essay about an issue that's important to you.

1. Brainstorm topics for your essay. List as many topics as you can in the box. Use these sentence starters to help you think of ideas:
   • I believe that . . .
   • It is important that . . .
   • Everyone should . . .
   • All children should be able to . . .

   Answers will vary.

2. Read your list from Question 1 and choose a topic for your essay. Complete the sentence to clearly state the topic of your essay.

   I believe that _____ because

   Sample answer: I believe that everyone should use reusable water bottles because plastic water bottles pollute the earth.

   CORAL REEFS (D)   **443**

---

3. Who do you imagine as the audience of your persuasive essay? Why?

   Sample answer: I imagine both adults and children as my audience. Adults are usually the ones who buy water bottles. But children can help adults make good decisions.

4. List three reasons that support your opinion. For each reason, list supporting details. Choose reasons and details that will help you persuade your audience to agree with your opinion. You do not need to use complete sentences.

   Reason 1:   See below.

   Supporting details:

   Reason 2:

   Supporting details:

   444   CORAL REEFS (D)

   Reason 3:

   Supporting details:

   CORAL REEFS (D)   **445**

Additional answers

4. Answers will vary. One sample reason and details that support it are shown.

   Reason 1:

   Plastic water bottles take hundreds of years to break down.

   Supporting details:

   – landfills will become full if we use them

   – at some point, we won't have space for landfills

   – landfills take up animal habitats

Question About "Choose a Sunscreen Right for Reefs"

Students will answer a question to show that they understand how to identify important details and techniques in persuasive essays.

Coral Reefs Wrap-Up

Lesson Overview

ACTIVITY	ACTIVITY TITLE	TIME	ONLINE/OFFLINE
GET READY	Introduction to Coral Reefs Wrap-Up	**1** minute	
TRY IT	Write a Persuasive Essay LEARNING COACH CHECK-IN	**30** minutes	
	Read and Record	**10** minutes	
	Review Coral Reefs	**20** minutes	
QUIZ	Coral Reefs	**30** minutes	
	Spelling List 25	**10** minutes	
WRAP-UP	More Language Arts Practice	**19** minutes	

Advance Preparation

Gather students' completed Plan to Write a Persuasive Essay activity page from Coral Reefs (D). Students will refer to this page during Try It: Write a Persuasive Essay.

Lesson Goals

- Write a persuasive essay.
- Compare and contrast nonfiction texts on the same topic.
- Make connections to ideas in a text by making inferences and drawing conclusions.
- Determine word meanings using text features and word-part strategies.
- Take a quiz on coral reefs.
- Take a spelling quiz.

MATERIALS

Supplied
- *Summit English Language Arts 4 Activity Book*
  - Write a Persuasive Essay

Also Needed
- completed Plan to Write a Persuasive Essay activity page from Coral Reefs (D)

Introduction to Coral Reefs Wrap-Up

Students will read the lesson goals.

TRY IT

Write a Persuasive Essay

Students will complete Write a Persuasive Essay from *Summit English Language Arts 4 Activity Book*. Make sure students have their completed Plan to Write a Persuasive Essay activity page from Coral Reefs (D) to refer to during this activity.

LEARNING COACH CHECK-IN   This activity page contains an open-ended assignment, so it's important that you review students' responses.

Read and Record

Good readers read quickly, smoothly, and with expression. This is called *fluency*. Students will record themselves reading aloud. They will listen to their recording and think about how quick, smooth, and expressive they sound.

Review Coral Reefs

Students will answer questions to review what they have learned about coral reefs.

QUIZ

Coral Reefs

Students will complete the Coral Reefs quiz.

Spelling List 25

Students will complete the Spelling List 25 quiz.

WRAP-UP

More Language Arts Practice

Students will practice skills according to their individual needs.

Big Ideas: Critical Skills Assignment

Lesson Overview

Big Ideas lessons provide students the opportunity to further apply the knowledge acquired and skills learned throughout the unit workshops. Each Big Ideas lesson consists of these parts:

1. **Cumulative Review:** Students keep their skills fresh by reviewing prior content.

2. **Preview:** Students practice answering the types of questions they will commonly find on standardized tests.

3. **Synthesis:** Students complete an assignment that allows them to connect and apply what they have learned. Synthesis assignments vary throughout the course.

   In the Synthesis portion of this Big Ideas lesson, students will read new selections. They will answer literal and inferential comprehension questions and complete writing questions that ask for short responses about the reading selections. Students should refer to the selections while answering the questions, because the questions emphasize using textual evidence. The questions call for students to demonstrate critical thinking, reading, and writing skills.

   LEARNING COACH CHECK-IN   This is a graded assessment. Make sure students complete, review, and submit the assignment to their teacher.

All materials needed for this lesson are linked online and not provided in the Activity Book.

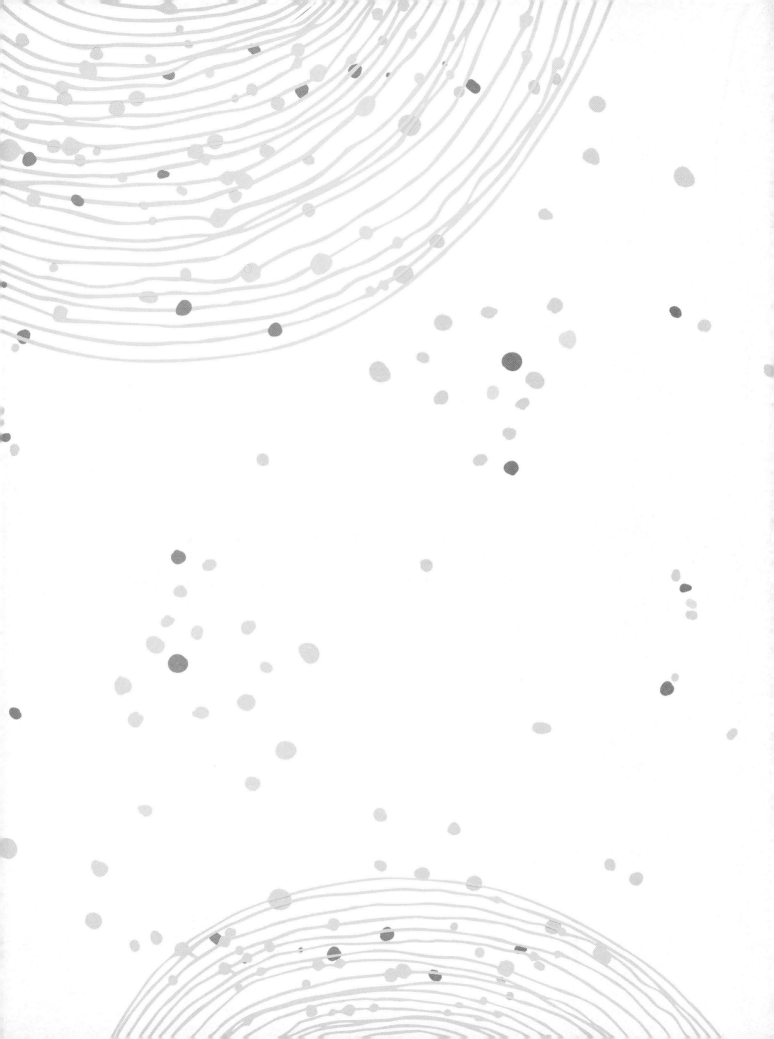

Life Choices

Presentation: Revising

Lesson Overview

ACTIVITY	ACTIVITY TITLE	TIME	ONLINE/OFFLINE
GET READY	Life Choices Unit Overview	**1** minute	🖥️
	Introduction to Presentation: Revising	**1** minute	🖥️
	Look Back at a Public Service Announcement	**15** minutes	🖥️
LEARN AND **TRY IT**	Revising a Presentation	**20** minutes	🖥️
	Revise Your Presentation **LEARNING COACH CHECK-IN**	**60** minutes	🖥️ and 📄
WRAP-UP	Question About Revising a Presentation	**3** minutes	🖥️
	Go Read!	**20** minutes	🖥️ or 📄

Content Background

Students will continue working on the **public service announcement**, a presentation that they created in PowerPoint. In this lesson, students will **revise** their presentation in PowerPoint.

Writing Process

| 1 Prewriting | 2 Drafting | 3 Revising | 4 Proofreading | 5 Publishing |

To revise their presentation, students will use a checklist. The checklist focuses on content (*Do the headings capture the main idea of each slide?*) and organization (*Do the bullets support the main idea of each slide? Should any bullets be moved to a different slide?*). Using the checklist, students will revise the content and organization of all aspects of their presentation: the text, the pictures, and the audio that they recorded.

Students may not understand the difference between revising and proofreading. When revising, writers and speakers focus on large issues, such as the order of ideas. When proofreading, writers and speakers fix errors in grammar, usage, and mechanics, such as spelling or punctuation mistakes.

Encourage students to focus on revision during this lesson. In the next lesson (Presentation: Proofreading), students will proofread. Additionally, students should not focus on the clarity or pace of the audio in this lesson. Those speaking skills are included on the checklist in Presentation: Proofreading.

MATERIALS

Supplied
- *Summit English Language Arts 4 Activity Book*
  - Revise Your Presentation
- Model Presentation (PowerPoint file)
- Presentation Template (PowerPoint file)
- Public Service Announcement: Revision Feedback Sheet (printout)
- Presentation Instructions (printout)

Also Needed
- students' presentation draft from Presentation: Drafting (B)
- folder in which students are storing presentation assignment pages
- reading material for Go Read!

Advance Preparation

Help students locate their draft presentation that they saved to the computer in Presentation: Drafting (B).

Gather the folder that students are using to store the activity pages related to their presentation. The folder should contain the following:

- Students' completed Plan Your Presentation activity page from Presentation: Planning

- Students' completed research notes from Presentation: Research

Prior to the Revise Your Presentation activity in this lesson, review students' draft presentation, and then complete Public Service Announcement: Revision Feedback Sheet.

During the Go Read! activity, students will have the option of using the digital library. Allow extra time for students to make their reading selection, or have students make a selection before beginning the lesson.

KEYWORDS

revising – the stage or step of the writing process in which the writer rereads and edits the draft, correcting errors and making changes in content or organization that improve the piece

Lesson Goals

- Use a checklist to revise your presentation.
- Read for pleasure.

GET READY

Life Choices Unit Overview
Students will read a summary of what they will learn in the Life Choices unit.

Introduction to Presentation: Revising
Students will get a glimpse of what they will learn about in the lesson. They will also read the lesson goals and keywords. Have students select each keyword and preview its definition.

Look Back at a Public Service Announcement
Students will review a model public service announcement and revisit what makes it successful.

LEARN   Revising a Presentation

Through a guided activity, students will explore how to revise a sample student public service announcement.

TRY IT   Revise Your Presentation

Students will complete Revise Your Presentation from *Summit English Language Arts 4 Activity Book*. They will need the draft of their public service announcement, which they completed and saved to the computer in Presentation: Drafting (B).

LEARNING COACH CHECK-IN   Guide students through the revision process.

1. Gather and use the Public Service Announcement: Revision Feedback Sheet that you filled out to guide a discussion with students.

   - Tell students the strengths of their presentation. Provide positive comments about the ideas, language, detail, or other elements of the presentation that you enjoyed.

   - Walk through your feedback with students.

   - As you discuss your feedback, encourage students to actively revise their draft in response. Reassure students that it's okay to remove or move around text, images, and even slides. Students should revise their draft directly in PowerPoint. That includes revising audio as necessary by using the PowerPoint recording tool.

2. Have students review and revise their presentation draft once more, using the Revise Your Presentation activity page to guide them.

   - For students having difficulty recognizing areas they should revise, suggest a revision, and think aloud to model your revising. For example: *This fact doesn't sound right here. It really goes with the ideas on the next slide. Let's move it there, or else the audience might get confused. Can you find any other facts or details that are out of place?*

3. Make sure students save their revised draft in a folder on the computer. Help students give their revised draft a new file name in case they want to revisit their original draft.

TIP   Remind students to focus on the checklist questions. Emphasize that they should not worry about spelling, punctuation, grammar, and so on.

NOTE   If you or students wish, you can download and print another copy of the Presentation Instructions online. The Model Presentation and Presentation Template are also available online as references.

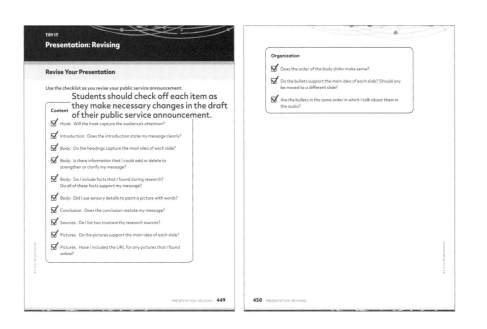

WRAP-UP

Question About Revising a Presentation

Students will answer a question to show that they understand a key revision skill.

Go Read!

Students will read for pleasure. They should choose a book or a magazine that interests them, or they may choose a selection from the digital library, linked in the online lesson.

Students should read for the entire time. Have students select something to read ahead of time to help them stay focused.

Presentation: Proofreading

Lesson Overview

ACTIVITY	ACTIVITY TITLE	TIME	ONLINE/OFFLINE
GET READY	Introduction to Presentation: Proofreading	**2** minutes	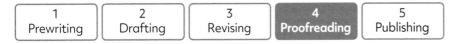
	Look Back at Clarity and Pace	**15** minutes	
LEARN AND **TRY IT**	Proofreading a Presentation	**20** minutes	
	Proofread Your Presentation LEARNING COACH CHECK-IN	**60** minutes	and
WRAP-UP	Question About Proofreading a Presentation	**3** minutes	
	Go Read!	**20** minutes	or

Content Background

Students will continue working on the **public service announcement**, a presentation that they created in PowerPoint. In this lesson, students will **proofread** their revised presentation in PowerPoint.

Writing Process

1 Prewriting	2 Drafting	3 Revising	4 Proofreading	5 Publishing

To proofread their presentation, students will use a checklist. The checklist focuses on grammar (*Are all sentences complete and correct?*), usage (*Are the words I use precise?*), and mechanics (*Is every word spelled correctly, including frequently confused words?*).

The checklist also focuses on the speaking skills of pace and clarity. *Pace* refers to how quickly or slowly someone speaks. *Clarity* refers to correct pronunciation of words, as well as appropriate volume.

Proofreading is sometimes called *editing*.

Advance Preparation

Help students locate their revised presentation that they saved to the computer in Presentation: Revising.

Gather the folder that students are using to store the activity pages related to their presentation. The folder should contain the following:

MATERIALS

Supplied
- *Summit English Language Arts 4 Activity Book*
  - Proofread Your Presentation
- Model Presentation (PowerPoint file)
- Presentation Template (PowerPoint file)
- Public Service Announcement: Proofreading Feedback Sheet (printout)
- Presentation Instructions (printout)

Also Needed
- students' revised presentation from Presentation: Revising
- folder in which students are storing presentation assignment pages
- reading material for Go Read!

- Students' completed Plan Your Presentation activity page from Presentation: Planning

- Students' completed research notes from Presentation: Research

Prior to the Proofread Your Presentation activity in this lesson, review students' revised presentation and complete Public Service Announcement: Proofreading Feedback Sheet.

During the Go Read! activity, students will have the option of using the digital library. Allow extra time for students to make their reading selection, or have students make a selection before beginning the lesson.

Lesson Goals

- Use a checklist to proofread your presentation.

- Read for pleasure.

GET READY

Introduction to Presentation: Proofreading

Students will get a glimpse of what they will learn about in the lesson. They will also read the lesson goals and keywords. Have students select each keyword and preview its definition.

Look Back at Clarity and Pace

Students will review what it means to speak clearly and at an understandable pace.

LEARN AND TRY IT

LEARN Proofreading a Presentation

Through a guided activity, students will explore how to proofread a sample student public service announcement.

TRY IT Proofread Your Presentation

Students will complete Proofread Your Presentation from *Summit English Language Arts 4 Activity Book*. They will need their revised public service announcement, which they saved to the computer in Presentation: Revising.

LEARNING COACH CHECK-IN Guide students through the proofreading process.

1. Have students proofread the text in their presentation for grammar, usage, and mechanics.

   - Have students slowly read the text aloud on each slide, listening for errors such as missing words, incomplete sentences, and agreement errors. As students catch errors, have them fix the errors in PowerPoint.

2. Have students review the audio for pace and clarity. Follow this process for each slide.

   - Have students listen to the audio that they recorded. As they listen, they should note any words that they did not pronounce clearly, as well as any issues with pace or volume.

   - Have students practice their speech before they rerecord it. Give students feedback to help them fix issues related to pronunciation, pace, and volume.

   - When students are ready, have them rerecord the audio.

   SUPPORT   For the audio on the first slide, point out and explain ways that students can make improvements.

3. Have students review their presentation once more, using the Proofread Your Presentation activity page. Students should fix any additional errors that they find.

4. Have students save their presentation in a folder on the computer. Help students give their edited presentation a new file name in case they want to revisit their previous version.

   OPTIONAL   Have students exchange presentations with a peer and use the Public Service Announcement: Proofreading Feedback Sheet to proofread the other student's presentation.

   NOTE   If you or students wish, you can download and print another copy of the Presentation Instructions online. The Model Presentation and Presentation Template are also available online as references.

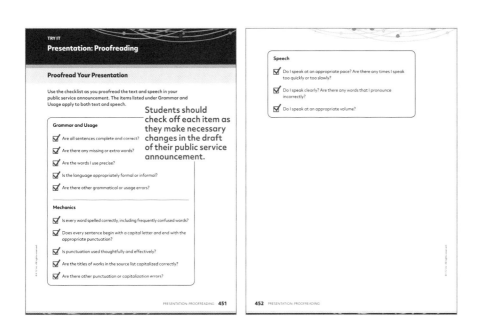

TRY IT

Presentation: Proofreading

Proofread Your Presentation

Use the checklist as you proofread the text and speech in your public service announcement. The items listed under Grammar and Usage apply to both text and speech.

Students should check off each item as they make necessary changes in the draft of their public service announcement.

Grammar and Usage

☑ Are all sentences complete and correct?

☑ Are there any missing or extra words?

☑ Are the words I use precise?

☑ Is the language appropriately formal or informal?

☑ Are there other grammatical or usage errors?

Mechanics

☑ Is every word spelled correctly, including frequently confused words?

☑ Does every sentence begin with a capital letter and end with the appropriate punctuation?

☑ Is punctuation used thoughtfully and effectively?

☑ Are the titles of works in the source list capitalized correctly?

☑ Are there other punctuation or capitalization errors?

Speech

☑ Do I speak at an appropriate pace? Are there any times I speak too quickly or too slowly?

☑ Do I speak clearly? Are there any words that I pronounce incorrectly?

☑ Do I speak at an appropriate volume?

PRESENTATION: PROOFREADING **451**

452 PRESENTATION: PROOFREADING

Question About Proofreading a Presentation

Students will answer a question to show that they understand a key proofreading skill.

Go Read!

Students will read for pleasure. They should choose a book or a magazine that interests them, or they may choose a selection from the digital library, linked in the online lesson.

Students should read for the entire time. Have students select something to read ahead of time to help them stay focused.

Presentation: Publishing

Lesson Overview

ACTIVITY	ACTIVITY TITLE	TIME	ONLINE/OFFLINE
GET READY	Introduction to Presentation: Publishing	**2** minutes	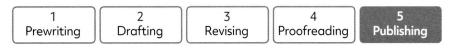
LEARN AND **TRY IT**	Reflecting on a Presentation	**20** minutes	
	Reflect on Your Presentation	**40** minutes	
	Present Your Public Service Announcement LEARNING COACH CHECK-IN	**25** minutes	
WRAP-UP	Turn In Your Presentation	**1** minute	
	More Language Arts Practice	**12** minutes	
	Go Read!	**20** minutes	

Content Background

Students will reflect on and share their **public service announcement**. In this lesson, they will also submit their public service announcement to their teacher.

Writing Process

1 Prewriting	2 Drafting	3 Revising	4 Proofreading	**5 Publishing**

NOTE During the reflection activities, students will think about ways they could share and publish their presentation. **Because of potential image copyright issues, however, students should not actually publish their presentations.** Publishing includes sharing their presentations online via social media or personal websites.

Advance Preparation

Help students locate their edited presentation that they saved to the computer in Presentation: Proofreading. They will need to refer to their presentation in several of the activities.

During the Go Read! activity, students will have the option of using the digital library. Allow extra time for students to make their reading selection, or have students make a selection before beginning the lesson.

MATERIALS

Supplied
- *Summit English Language Arts 4 Activity Book*
  - Reflect on Your Presentation

Also Needed
- students' edited presentation from Presentation: Proofreading
- reading material for Go Read!

Lesson Goals

- Reflect on the audience and purpose of your presentation.

- Learn about publishing a presentation.

- Share your presentation with your Learning Coach.

- Submit your presentation to your teacher.

GET READY

Introduction to Presentation: Publishing

Students will read the lesson goals.

LEARN AND TRY IT

LEARN   Reflecting on a Presentation

Students will explore how the author of a presentation reflects on audience and purpose. They will also learn how audience and purpose affect where an author might choose to share or publish a presentation.

TRY IT   Reflect on Your Presentation

Students will complete Reflect on Your Presentation from *Summit English Language Arts 4 Activity Book*. As they complete this activity, they will need to refer to their public service announcement, which they saved to the computer in Presentation: Proofreading.

NOTE   If students wish, they may make additional changes to their presentation after completing this activity.

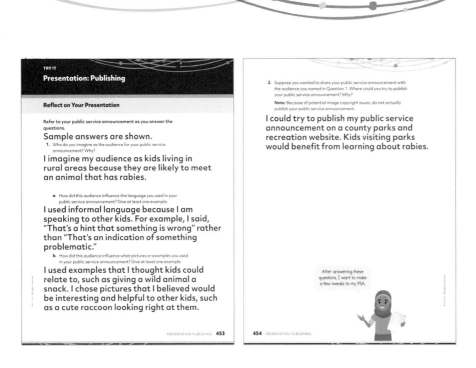

TRY IT   Present Your Public Service Announcement

Students will present their public service announcement to their Learning Coach.

LEARNING COACH CHECK-IN   Watch students present their public service announcement. After they finish, give specific praise and ask thoughtful questions.

For example:

- *That picture of a raccoon really caught my attention.*

- *That fact surprised me. Where did you learn that? Did anything you learned surprise you?*

WRAP-UP

Turn In Your Presentation

Students will submit their presentation to their teacher.

More Language Arts Practice

Students will practice skills according to their individual needs.

Go Read!

Students will read for pleasure. They should choose a book or a magazine that interests them, or they may choose a selection from the digital library, linked in the online lesson.

Students should read for the entire time. Have students select something to read ahead of time to help them stay focused.

"Tayo's Wishes"

Lesson Overview

ACTIVITY	ACTIVITY TITLE	TIME	ONLINE/OFFLINE
GET READY	Introduction to "Tayo's Wishes"	**1** minute	
	Spelling List 26 Pretest **LEARNING COACH CHECK-IN**	**10** minutes	and
	Wishes in 60 Seconds	**1** minute	
	Before You Read "Tayo's Wishes"	**14** minutes	
READ	"Tayo's Wishes"	**30** minutes	
	Check-In: "Tayo's Wishes"	**5** minutes	
LEARN AND **TRY IT**	Determine a Theme of "Tayo's Wishes"	**10** minutes	
	Find Themes and Supporting Evidence	**10** minutes	
	Apply: Determine the Theme	**15** minutes	
	Theme of a Legend **LEARNING COACH CHECK-IN**	**14** minutes	
	Practice Words from "Tayo's Wishes"	**8** minutes	
WRAP-UP	Question About "Tayo's Wishes"	**2** minutes	

Content Background

Students will learn about determining the theme of a story and using evidence from the text to support that theme.

A theme is a message the author conveys in the story. It is usually a universal lesson about life. A story's theme can be determined from characters' experiences and the results of those experiences. For example, one theme of "Tayo's Wishes" is that there is value in doing work that you can take pride in. The text details about Tayo's experiences provide the evidence for this theme.

MATERIALS

Supplied
- *Summit English Language Arts 4 Expeditions in Reading*
- *Summit English Language Arts 4 Activity Book*
  - Spelling List 26 Pretest
  - Theme of a Legend

"Tayo's Wishes" Synopsis

"Tayo's Wishes" is a legend about a hard-working yam farmer named Tayo who lives in Nigeria. He spends his days pulling yams out of the ground and stacking them in crates. As a result, he has constant back pain. One day, he takes a shortcut home and runs into a god named Eshu. Eshu is not supposed to be seen, so he grants Tayo three wishes. For his first wish, Tayo asks to have his work done for him by the time he reaches the field every morning. For his second wish, he asks to be free from his back pain. Eshu grants both wishes. At first, Tayo enjoys his work being done for him. But over time he grows bored, and the people stop calling him the hardest working man in all of Nigeria. Tayo decides to ask Eshu to grant his third and final wish: to undo the first wish. Eshu grants the wish, and Tayo once again enjoys being known as the hard-working yam farmer.

Lesson Goals

- Take a spelling pretest.

- Use details from the text to describe the characters, setting, and events of a story.

- Determine the theme of a story, and find evidence in the text to support the theme.

- Write about the theme of a story and evidence that supports the theme.

- Determine meanings of unfamiliar words in the reading.

GET READY

Introduction to "Tayo's Wishes"

Students will get a glimpse of what they will learn about in the lesson. They will also read the lesson goals and keywords. Have students select each keyword and preview its definition.

Spelling List 26 Pretest

Students will take a spelling pretest.

LEARNING COACH CHECK-IN   Have students turn to Spelling List 26 Pretest in *Summit English Language Arts 4 Activity Book* and open the online Spelling

Pretest activity. Online, students will listen to the spelling word, type the word in the space indicated, and then check their answer. In the activity book, students will write the correct spelling of the word in the tables provided and indicate with a ✓ or an ✗ if they spelled the word correctly or incorrectly online. Students will repeat this process with the remaining words.

As needed, help students with the interaction between the online activity and the activity book page until they become comfortable with what they need to do. As students practice their spelling words throughout the workshop, they should pay special attention to words they spelled incorrectly on the pretest.

This is the complete list of words students will be tested on.

Compound Words		Heart Words
anywhere	supermarket	Washington, D.C.
background	windshield	Puerto Rico
campground	wristwatch	Guam
earthquake	toothpick	
handshake	yardstick	
masterpiece	dishwasher	
overlook	homesick	

NOTE Have students keep their completed activity page in a safe place so they can refer to it later.

Wishes in 60 Seconds

Students will watch a short video designed to spark their interest in upcoming topics.

Before You Read "Tayo's Wishes"

Students will be introduced to some key vocabulary words that they will encounter in the upcoming reading and learn some important background related to the reading.

READ

"Tayo's Wishes"

Students will read "Tayo's Wishes" in *Expeditions in Reading*.

Check-In: "Tayo's Wishes"

Students will answer questions to demonstrate their comprehension of "Tayo's Wishes."

LEARN AND TRY IT

LEARN   Determine a Theme of "Tayo's Wishes"

Students will learn about determining the theme of a story and how evidence from the text supports the theme.

TRY IT   Find Themes and Supporting Evidence

Students will analyze a passage to determine themes and textual evidence that supports the themes.

TRY IT   Apply: Determine the Theme

Students will apply to a new work what they've learned about determining theme and evidence to support a theme.

TRY IT   Theme of a Legend

Students will complete Theme of a Legend from *Summit English Language Arts 4 Activity Book*.

LEARNING COACH CHECK-IN   This activity page contains open-ended questions, so it's important that you review students' responses. Give students feedback, using the sample answers provided to guide you.

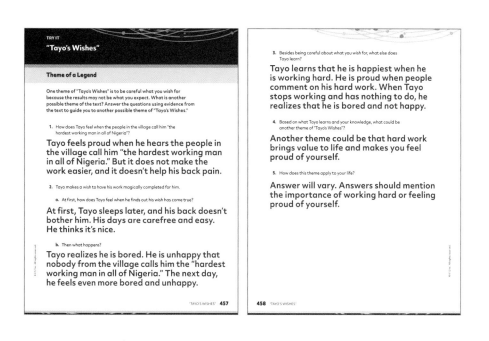

TRY IT   Practice Words from "Tayo's Wishes"

Students will answer questions to demonstrate their understanding of the vocabulary words from the reading.

WRAP-UP

Question About "Tayo's Wishes"

Students will answer a question to show that they understand how to determine themes and evidence to support themes.

"Tayo's Wishes" Wrap-Up

Lesson Overview

ACTIVITY	ACTIVITY TITLE	TIME	ONLINE/OFFLINE
GET READY	Introduction to "Tayo's Wishes" Wrap-Up	**1** minute	🖥️
	Spelling List 26 Activity Bank	**10** minutes	📄
TRY IT	Analyze a Character **LEARNING COACH CHECK-IN**	**30** minutes	📄
	Read and Record	**10** minutes	🖥️
	Review "Tayo's Wishes"	**20** minutes	🖥️
QUIZ	"Tayo's Wishes"	**30** minutes	🖥️
WRAP-UP	More Language Arts Practice	**19** minutes	🖥️

Advance Preparation

Gather students' completed Spelling List 26 Pretest activity page from "Tayo's Wishes." Students will refer to this page during Spelling List 26 Activity Bank.

Lesson Goals

- Practice all spelling words.

- Write a character analysis of a story's main character.

- Practice reading aloud to develop fluency.

- Review finding a theme and textual evidence that supports the theme.

- Review using text details to support inferences and describing characters, setting, and events of a story.

- Take a quiz on determining theme, finding textual evidence to support theme, and using details to support inferences and describe characters, setting, and events of a story.

Introduction to "Tayo's Wishes" Wrap-Up

Students will read the lesson goals.

Spelling List 26 Activity Bank

Students will practice all spelling words from the workshop by completing Spelling List 26 Activity Bank from *Summit English Language Arts 4 Activity Book*. Make sure students have their completed Spelling List 26 Pretest activity page from "Tayo's Wishes" to refer to during this activity.

Remind students to pay special attention to words they spelled incorrectly on the Spelling Pretest.

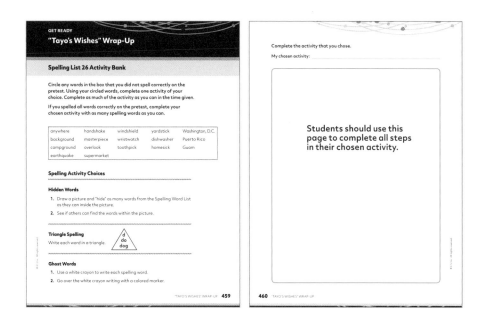

Analyze a Character

Students will complete Analyze a Character from *Summit English Language Arts 4 Activity Book*.

LEARNING COACH CHECK-IN   This activity page contains open-ended questions, so it's important that you review students' responses. Give students feedback, using the sample answers provided to guide you.

TRY IT   Read and Record

Good readers read quickly, smoothly, and with expression. This is called *fluency*. Students will record themselves reading aloud. They will listen to their recording and think about how quick, smooth, and expressive they sound.

TIP   Encourage students to rerecord as needed.

TRY IT   Review "Tayo's Wishes"

Students will answer questions to review what they have learned about "Tayo's Wishes."

QUIZ

"Tayo's Wishes"

Students will complete the "Tayo's Wishes" quiz.

WRAP-UP

More Language Arts Practice

Students will practice skills according to their individual needs.

"The Green Glass Ball"

Lesson Overview

ACTIVITY	ACTIVITY TITLE	TIME	ONLINE/OFFLINE
GET READY	Introduction to "The Green Glass Ball"	**1** minute	🖥️
	Spelling List 26 Review Game	**10** minutes	🖥️
	Before You Read "The Green Glass Ball"	**14** minutes	🖥️
READ	"The Green Glass Ball"	**30** minutes	📄
	Check-In: "The Green Glass Ball"	**5** minutes	🖥️
LEARN AND **TRY IT**	Elements of Drama	**10** minutes	🖥️
	Explore Elements of a Play	**10** minutes	🖥️
	Apply: Structure of Drama	**15** minutes	🖥️
	Parts of a Drama **LEARNING COACH CHECK-IN**	**15** minutes	📄
	Practice Words from "The Green Glass Ball"	**8** minutes	🖥️
WRAP-UP	Question About "The Green Glass Ball"	**2** minutes	🖥️

Content Background

Students will learn about the genre of drama, or plays. They will learn the elements that are unique to a play, which include a cast of characters, settings, scenes, and stage directions. Students will learn terminology related specifically to plays. They will also learn about characterization, or how the playwright reveals characters' traits. In a play, character traits typically must be inferred from what characters say and do.

In a play, the story is told mainly through the dialogue of the characters instead of through descriptions like one would find in a novel. Readers also learn that a play tells a story, like a novel; however, plays are organized into scenes and acts instead of chapters.

It is important for readers to understand how to read a play and how the parts come together to tell a story. For example, it is important to read the stage directions to pick up additional information about a character and how the action progresses.

MATERIALS

Supplied
- *Summit English Language Arts 4 Expeditions in Reading*
- *Summit English Language Arts 4 Activity Book*
  - Parts of a Drama

"The Green Glass Ball" Synopsis

"The Green Glass Ball" is an Irish folktale written as a play. The main characters are an optimistic Tinker and his pessimistic friend, Donkey. The play begins with the two going into town in search of work. Tinker carries on conversations with many individuals and repairs a variety of items. Despite Donkey's protests, Tinker continues fixing items in exchange for food instead of money. Tinker and Donkey encounter an Old Woman who asks for Tinker to repair her kettle. She is impressed by his work and pays him with a green glass ball instead of food or money. The Old Woman tells them that the green glass ball is magical and can grant them one wish. She encourages them to think well before they wish because wishes can be dangerous. In Scene 2, Tinker and Donkey return home and discuss the day's events with Tinker's nephew, Tim. They discuss possible wishes, and Tinker and Donkey have a disagreement. By accident, Tinker wishes for Donkey to disappear. He immediately regrets his wish. Rather than making a wish for himself, Tim wants to make his uncle happy and so wishes for Donkey to return. Donkey returns and makes peace with Tinker. The Old Woman reappears and takes the green glass ball. She gets rid of it and reminds them of a lesson learned: it is best to make a kind or generous wish.

KEYWORDS

characterization – the techniques an author uses to reveal character traits; characters are revealed by their words, thoughts, actions, and what other characters say about them

dialogue – the words that characters say in a written work

drama – another word for *play*

scene (drama) – a subdivision of an act of a play that happens at a fixed time and place

stage directions – instructions from a playwright that tell the actors what to do during the play

Lesson Goals

- Practice all spelling words.
- Identify and describe structural elements unique to a play using appropriate terminology.
- Determine characteristics of a play's elements and why an author uses those elements.
- Describe the characterization of characters in a play.
- Explain how scenes fit together in a play.
- Determine meanings of unfamiliar words in the reading.

GET READY

Introduction to "The Green Glass Ball"

Students will get a glimpse of what they will learn about in the lesson. They will also read the lesson goals and keywords. Have students select each keyword and preview its definition.

Spelling List 26 Review Game

Students will practice all spelling words from the workshop.

Before You Read "The Green Glass Ball"

Students will be introduced to some key vocabulary words that they will encounter in the upcoming reading and learn some important background related to the reading.

READ

"The Green Glass Ball"

Students will read "The Green Glass Ball" in *Expeditions in Reading*.

Check-In: "The Green Glass Ball"

Students will answer questions to demonstrate their comprehension of "The Green Glass Ball."

LEARN AND TRY IT

LEARN   Elements of Drama

Students will learn about the elements of a play and the terminology used in this genre.

TRY IT   Explore Elements of a Play

Students will analyze excerpts from a play to demonstrate knowledge of the elements of plays and the purpose of those elements, traits of characters, and the play's structure.

TRY IT   Apply: Structure of Drama

Students will apply to a new work what they've learned about identifying the structure of a drama and how the scenes fit together.

TRY IT Parts of a Drama

Students will complete Parts of a Drama from *Summit English Language Arts 4 Activity Book*.

TIP Remind students to focus on purposes of the parts of a drama.

LEARNING COACH CHECK-IN This activity page contains open-ended questions, so it's important that you review students' responses. Give students feedback, using the sample answers provided to guide you.

TRY IT
"The Green Glass Ball"

Parts of a Drama

Read the excerpt of "The Green Ball."
Possible answers are shown.

"The Green Ball"

Cast of Characters

CASSIE, the talking dog
CONNOR, the boy

Present day, by the ocean

Scene 1

CONNOR: *(smiling)* Another beautiful day at the ocean, huh, Cassie?
CASSIE: *(jumping up and down)* Ruff, ruff! Yes, I love the beach so much! Can you throw the green ball please?
CONNOR: *(throws the ball)* Go, get it Cassie!
CASSIE: *(jumps into the water with a splash)* Oh, I love to swim! I love to swim! Hey, where did that ball go?
CONNOR: Cassie, where is that ball?
CASSIE: *(looking around the water)* I can't find it anywhere!

"THE GREEN GLASS BALL" **463**

Answer the questions using complete sentences and the appropriate word from the word bank.

Parts of a Play Word Bank

cast of characters	description	stage directions
setting	dialogue	scenes

1. Who is in "The Green Ball"?
The <u>cast of characters</u> includes Cassie, the talking dog, and Connor, the boy.

2. Where does it take place?
The <u>setting</u> is present day, by the ocean.

3. What is in parentheses ( )?
The <u>stage directions</u> are included in parentheses.

a. Why are stage directions needed in a play?

See below.

b. What information do we learn about Cassie from the stage directions?
We learn that Cassie jumps up and down with excitement. We also learn she looks around for her ball.

464 "THE GREEN GLASS BALL"

---

c. What information do we learn about Connor from the stage directions?
Connor starts the play with a smile. This shows how happy he is to be at the beach playing ball with his dog. We also learn that he throws the ball for Cassie.

What happens next? Continue the play in your own words. Write four lines that include stage directions for Cassie and Connor.

Students should continue the story in the format of a play. They may include finding the ball that went missing in the water. It is important that students include stage directions. These stage directions might include information that describe the optimistic character traits that Cassie and Connor exhibit in the first part of the play.

"THE GREEN GLASS BALL" **465**

Additional answers

3a. The stage directions give the actors more information. The stage directions might tell the actors where they need to be on the stage and what actions need to happen to move the scene along. They also provide a picture in the reader's mind of what is happening on the stage.

TRY IT Practice Words from "The Green Glass Ball"

Students will answer questions to demonstrate their understanding of the vocabulary words from the reading.

WRAP-UP

Question About "The Green Glass Ball"

Students will answer a question to show that they understand the structural elements of a play.

"The Green Glass Ball" Wrap-Up

Lesson Overview

ACTIVITY	ACTIVITY TITLE	TIME	ONLINE/OFFLINE
GET READY	Introduction to "The Green Glass Ball" Wrap-Up	**1** minute	🖥️
TRY IT	Write About How Characters Change **LEARNING COACH CHECK-IN**	**30** minutes	📄
	Read and Record	**10** minutes	🖥️
	Review "The Green Glass Ball"	**20** minutes	🖥️
QUIZ	"The Green Glass Ball"	**30** minutes	🖥️
	Spelling List 26	**10** minutes	🖥️
WRAP-UP	More Language Arts Practice	**19** minutes	🖥️

Lesson Goals

- Write about how a character changes from the beginning of a play to the end.
- Practice reading aloud to develop fluency.
- Review structural elements of a play, characterization, how a character changes, and how scenes provide the structure of a play.
- Take a quiz on the structural elements of a play, characterization, how characters change, and how scenes provide the structure of a play.
- Take a spelling quiz.

GET READY

Introduction to "The Green Glass Ball" Wrap-Up

Students will read the lesson goals.

Write About How Characters Change

Students will complete Write About How Characters Change from *Summit English Language Arts 4 Activity Book*. Students will use evidence from the text to explain how a character changes from the beginning to the end of the play.

TIP Remind students to take notes in the chart so they can focus on writing a concise paragraph describing the characters' changes in the play.

LEARNING COACH CHECK-IN This activity page contains open-ended questions, so it's important that you review students' responses. Give students feedback, using the sample answers provided to guide you.

Additional answers

Text Evidence	Notes About Donkey
Beginning "The usual thing. I can't teach him anything. He works for nothing. Today, we did not even take in one coin."	**Beginning** Is annoyed with Tinker for not making money
End "Why don't you wish to be a king? Then I could be the king's donkey. I could have a fine stable to live in, and grooms to care for me. What a life!"	**End** Wishes for a better life
End (*Thoughtfully*) "Yes, I guess I'm all right. It's too bad we lost the wishes. It was my fault. I complained too much."	**End** Realized he was wrong and feels bad; Wants to make things better

Read and Record

Good readers read quickly, smoothly, and with expression. This is called *fluency*. Students will record themselves reading aloud. They will listen to their recording and think about how quick, smooth, and expressive they sound.

 TIP Encourage students to rerecord as needed.

Review "The Green Glass Ball"

Students will answer questions to review what they have learned about elements of plays, characterization, and the structure of a play.

QUIZ

"The Green Glass Ball"

Students will complete the "The Green Glass Ball" quiz.

Spelling List 26

Students will complete the Spelling List 26 quiz.

WRAP-UP

More Language Arts Practice

Students will practice skills according to their individual needs.

"The Gold Coin"

Lesson Overview

ACTIVITY	ACTIVITY TITLE	TIME	ONLINE/OFFLINE
GET READY	Introduction to "The Gold Coin"	**1** minute	
	Spelling List 27 Pretest **LEARNING COACH CHECK-IN**	**10** minutes	and
	Before You Read "The Gold Coin"	**14** minutes	
READ	"The Gold Coin"	**30** minutes	
	Check-In: "The Gold Coin"	**5** minutes	
LEARN AND **TRY IT**	How a Story's Plot Develops	**10** minutes	
	Identify Plot Development	**10** minutes	
	Apply: Conflict and Resolution	**15** minutes	
	Developing a Character **LEARNING COACH CHECK-IN**	**15** minutes	
	Practice Words from "The Gold Coin"	**8** minutes	
WRAP-UP	Question About "The Gold Coin"	**2** minutes	

Content Background

The plot is what happens in a literary text. Each event causes another event, driven by the actions of the characters in a text. Within the plot of the story, there is a conflict or problem that eventually is resolved in the resolution.

MATERIALS

Supplied
- *Summit English Language Arts 4 Expeditions in Reading*
- *Summit English Language Arts 4 Activity Book*
  - Spelling List 27 Pretest
  - Developing a Character

"The Gold Coin" Synopsis

"The Gold Coin" is a folktale about a thief named Juan. One night, he sees a woman sitting in her hut admiring a gold coin and decides he must have it. He attempts to steal it, but he discovers the woman and the gold coin are nowhere to be found. Juan follows the trail and comes upon farmers working by a river. Juan hasn't talked to people in years, but because he is eager to get the gold coin, he talks to them. The farmers promise to help him cross the river if he helps them for the day. That night he joins them for dinner, something else he has not done in years. Over dinner, he learns that the woman, Doña Josefa, travels around to heal people and offers a gold coin to those who need it. The story continues with Juan always a few steps behind Doña Josefa, meeting new people, helping people with work, and noticing the good things in life. In turn, the people help him move on in his journey. Finally, Juan catches up with Doña Josefa and asks for the gold coin. She gives Juan the gold coin. Just then, a girl comes asking for Doña Josefa's help with delivering her mother's baby. Doña Josefa is hesitant to leave her house because of the impending storm. Juan decides to stay behind to protect her house and decides to give the gold coin back to Doña Josefa. He says the newborn will need it more than him.

KEYWORDS

conflict – a problem or issue that a character faces in a story

homophone – a word that sounds the same as another word but has a different spelling and meaning

plot – what happens in a story; the sequence of events

resolution – the outcome of a story

Lesson Goals

- Take a spelling pretest.
- Describe how the plot develops in a story.
- Describe the conflict and resolution of a story.
- Determine meanings of unfamiliar words in the reading.

GET READY

Introduction to "The Gold Coin"

Students will get a glimpse of what they will learn about in the lesson. They will also read the lesson goals and keywords. Have students select each keyword and preview its definition.

Spelling List 27 Pretest

Students will take a spelling pretest.

LEARNING COACH CHECK-IN　Have students turn to Spelling List 27 Pretest in *Summit English Language Arts 4 Activity Book* and open the online Spelling Pretest activity. Online, students will listen to the spelling word, type the word in the space indicated, and then check their answer. In the activity book, students will write the correct spelling of the word in the tables provided and indicate with a ✓ or an ✗ if they spelled the word correctly or incorrectly online. Students will repeat this process with the remaining words.

As needed, help students with the interaction between the online activity and the activity book page until they become comfortable with what they need to do. As students practice their spelling words throughout the workshop, they should pay special attention to words they spelled incorrectly on the pretest.

This is the complete list of words students will be tested on.

Homophones
berry, bury
groan, grown
mail, male
tail, tale
waist, waste
lessen, lesson
road, rode, rowed
close, clothes

NOTE　Have students keep their completed activity page in a safe place so they can refer to it later.

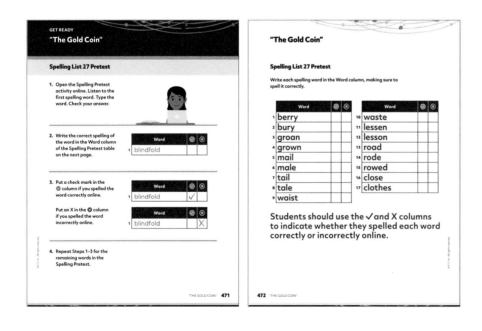

Before You Read "The Gold Coin"

Students will be introduced to some key vocabulary words that they will encounter in the upcoming reading.

READ

"The Gold Coin"

Students will read "The Gold Coin" in *Expeditions in Reading*.

Check-In: "The Gold Coin"

Students will answer several questions to demonstrate their comprehension of "The Gold Coin."

LEARN AND TRY IT

LEARN How a Story's Plot Develops

Students will learn how the plot of a story develops. They will also learn what happens in each part of a story's plot.

TRY IT Identify Plot Development

Students will answer questions in which they identify what happens in parts of the story's plot. They will also analyze passages to determine how a plot develops.

TRY IT Apply: Conflict and Resolution

Students will apply to a new work what they've learned about the conflict and resolution of a story.

TRY IT Developing a Character

Students will complete Developing a Character from *Summit English Language Arts 4 Activity Book*.

LEARNING COACH CHECK-IN This activity page contains open-ended questions, to it's important that you review students' responses. Give students feedback, using the sample answers provided to guide you.

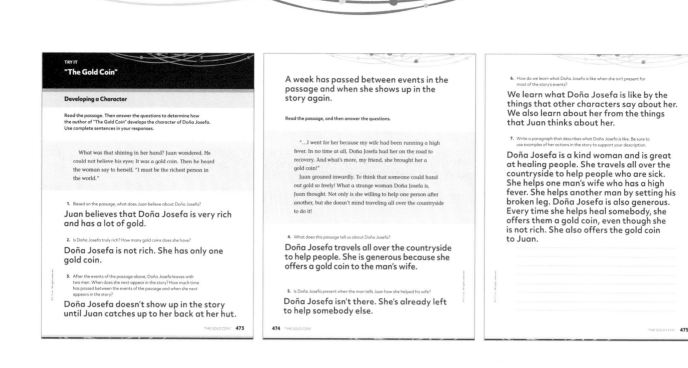

TRY IT   Practice Words from "The Gold Coin"

Students will answer questions to demonstrate their understanding of the vocabulary words from the reading.

WRAP-UP

Question About "The Gold Coin"

Students will answer a question to show that they understand the parts of a story's plot.

"The Gold Coin" Wrap-Up

Lesson Overview

ACTIVITY	ACTIVITY TITLE	TIME	ONLINE/OFFLINE
GET READY	Introduction to "The Gold Coin" Wrap-Up	**1** minute	
	Spelling List 27 Activity Bank	**10** minutes	
TRY IT	Compare and Contrast Events **LEARNING COACH CHECK-IN**	**30** minutes	
	Read and Record	**10** minutes	
	Review "The Gold Coin"	**20** minutes	
QUIZ	"The Gold Coin"	**30** minutes	
WRAP-UP	More Language Arts Practice	**19** minutes	

Advance Preparation

Gather students' completed Spelling List 27 Pretest activity page from "The Gold Coin." Students will refer to this page during Spelling List 27 Activity Bank.

Lesson Goals

- Practice all spelling words.

- Compare and contrast the patterns of events in two multicultural stories.

- Practice reading aloud to develop fluency.

- Review plot development, conflict, resolution, and theme.

- Review the story elements of character, setting, and plot, including the pattern of events.

- Take a quiz on plot development, conflict, resolution, theme, and story elements.

Introduction to "The Gold Coin" Wrap-Up

Students will read the lesson goals.

Spelling List 27 Activity Bank

Students will practice all spelling words from the workshop by completing Spelling List 27 Activity Bank from *Summit English Language Arts 4 Activity Book*. Make sure students have their completed Spelling List 27 Pretest activity page from "The Gold Coin" to refer to during this activity.

Remind students to pay special attention to words they spelled incorrectly on the Spelling Pretest.

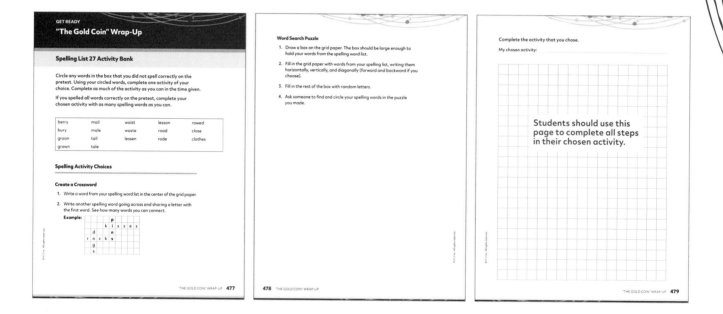

Compare and Contrast Events

Students will write about the similarities and differences in the plots of two multicultural stories.

SUPPORT   For students having difficulty recognizing similarities and differences, have students start with the differences.

LEARNING COACH CHECK-IN   This activity page contains open-ended questions, so it's important that you review students' responses. Give students feedback, using the sample answers provided to guide you.

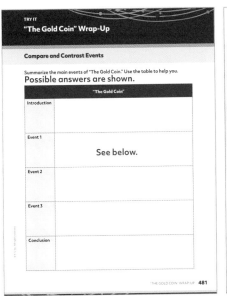

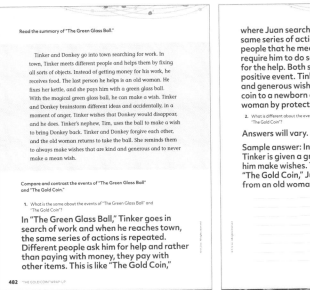

Additional answers

"The Gold Coin"	
Introduction	Juan wants an old woman's gold coin, but he can't find it.
Event 1	He searches for the old woman to get the gold coin. Along the way he helps different people, so they can help him continue on his journey.
Event 2	He learns that the old woman is continuing to give out gold coins to all the people she heals. Juan is confused and angry about this action.
Event 3	Finally, he meets up with the old woman. She explains that no one would keep the gold coin because they kept saying someone else would need it. She gives him the gold coin.
Conclusion	The old woman is called to deliver a baby. Juan stays to keep the old woman's house safe from the storm and gives the gold coin back to her to give to the newborn.

TRY IT Read and Record

Good readers read quickly, smoothly, and with expression. This is called *fluency*. Students will record themselves reading aloud. They will listen to their recording and think about how quick, smooth, and expressive they sound.

TIP Encourage students to rerecord as needed.

TRY IT Review "The Gold Coin"

Students will answer questions to review what they have learned about plot development, conflict, resolution, theme, and story elements.

QUIZ

"The Gold Coin"

Students will complete "The Gold Coin" quiz.

WRAP-UP

More Language Arts Practice

Students will practice skills according to their individual needs.

"The Grateful Stork"

Lesson Overview

ACTIVITY	ACTIVITY TITLE	TIME	ONLINE/OFFLINE
GET READY	Introduction to "The Grateful Stork"	**1** minute	
	Spelling List 27 Review Game	**10** minutes	
	Before You Read "The Grateful Stork"	**9** minutes	
READ	"The Grateful Stork"	**30** minutes	
	Check-In: "The Grateful Stork"	**5** minutes	
LEARN AND **TRY IT**	Compare and Contrast Topics, Plots, and Themes	**10** minutes	
	Analyze Topics, Plots, and Themes	**10** minutes	
	Apply: Themes Across Texts	**20** minutes	
	Compare and Contrast Themes LEARNING COACH CHECK-IN	**15** minutes	
	Practice Words from "The Grateful Stork"	**8** minutes	
WRAP-UP	Question About "The Grateful Stork"	**2** minutes	

Content Background

Students will read the Japanese folktale "The Grateful Stork." They will then learn about comparing and contrasting topics, plots, and themes found in "The Grateful Stork" to those found in stories from other cultures.

A *topic* is the subject of a story. Students will learn that while the same topic can be found across stories, the way that the topic is addressed can be different. For example, the topic of happiness is found in both "The Grateful Stork" and "The Gold Coin." But in "The Grateful Stork," the source of happiness is family bonds. In "The Gold Coin," happiness comes from developing ties to one's community. The source of happiness in each story also provides some insight into the culture each story comes from—Japan and Central America.

Students will also learn about patterns of events in stories, or how plots unfold and develop. Students will, again, compare and contrast. For example, the plot of "The Grateful Stork" develops through the repetitive events of the young girl weaving brocades. The plot of "The Gold Coin"

MATERIALS

Supplied
- *Summit English Language Arts 4 Expeditions in Reading*
- *Summit English Language Arts 4 Activity Book*
  - Compare and Contrast Themes

develops through the repetitive experiences of Juan as he attempts to catch up to Doña Josefa.

Theme is the author's message or a big idea that develops over the course of a story. It is a statement rather than just a word. For example, a theme found in both "The Grateful Stork" and "The Gold Coin" is that happiness does not come from being rich. While the theme may be the same in both stories, the way the theme is developed in each story is different.

"The Grateful Stork" Synopsis

"The Grateful Stork" is a Japanese folktale about a poor, old man who finds and releases a white stork caught in a trap in a snowstorm. A little while later, the old man and his wife have a visitor at their door, a young girl about seventeen years old. The young girl spends the night and ends up staying for some time. They appreciate her help in the house and grow fond of her. They decide she should live with them. The young girl asks for thread to weave something for them. She makes them promise to not look behind the screen while she is weaving. They both promise, and the young girl weaves a beautiful brocade that the old man sells in town for a lot of money. The old man returns home with more thread, presents, and good food. The young girl weaves another creation and again, the old man is successful in selling it. Then one day, as the young girl begins weaving, the old woman breaks her promise. She looks behind the screen and to her surprise, she finds a white stork rather than the young girl. The old woman is ashamed. The young girl, who had come to repay the old man for saving her life, now leaves because they know her disguise. The young girl turns into the stork and flies away.

Lesson Goals

- Practice all spelling words.

- Compare and contrast topics, plots, and themes of stories from different cultures.

- Determine meanings of unfamiliar words in the reading.

Introduction to "The Grateful Stork"

Students will get a glimpse of what they will learn about in the lesson. They will also read the lesson goals and keywords. Have students select each keyword and preview its definition.

Spelling List 27 Review Game

Students will practice all spelling words from the workshop.

Before You Read "The Grateful Stork"

Students will be introduced to some key vocabulary words that they will encounter in the upcoming reading.

READ

"The Grateful Stork"

Students will read "The Grateful Stork" in *Expeditions in Reading*.

Check-In: "The Grateful Stork"

Students will answer questions to demonstrate their comprehension of "The Grateful Stork."

LEARN AND TRY IT

LEARN   Compare and Contrast Topics, Plots, and Themes

Students will learn about comparing and contrasting the treatment of topics, plots, and themes of stories from different cultures.

TRY IT   Analyze Topics, Plots, and Themes

Students will answer questions in which they determine similarities and differences in how two stories treat topics, plots, and themes.

TRY IT   Apply: Compare Themes Across Texts

Students will apply to a new work what they've learned about comparing and contrasting the treatment of themes in stories.

TRY IT   Compare and Contrast Themes

Students will complete Compare and Contrast Themes from *Summit English Language Arts 4 Activity Book*.

This activity page contains open-ended questions, so it's important that you review students' responses. Give students feedback, using the sample answers provided to guide you.

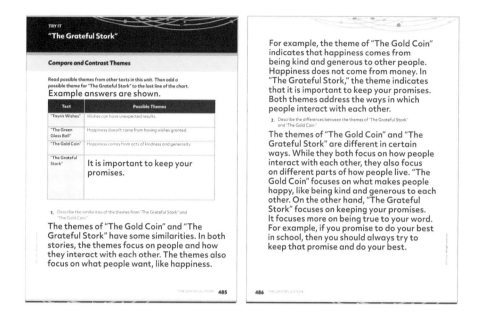

TRY IT
"The Grateful Stork"

Compare and Contrast Themes

Read possible themes from other texts in this unit. Then add a possible theme for "The Grateful Stork" to the last line of the chart.
Example answers are shown.

Text	Possible Themes
"Toya's Wishes"	Wishes can have unexpected results.
"The Green Glass Ball"	Happiness doesn't come from having wishes granted.
"The Gold Coin"	Happiness comes from acts of kindness and generosity.
"The Grateful Stork"	**It is important to keep your promises.**

1. Describe the similarities of the themes from "The Grateful Stork" and "The Gold Coin."

The themes of "The Gold Coin" and "The Grateful Stork" have some similarities. In both stories, the themes focus on people and how they interact with each other. The themes also focus on what people want, like happiness.

For example, the theme of "The Gold Coin" indicates that happiness comes from being kind and generous to other people. Happiness does not come from money. In "The Grateful Stork," the theme indicates that it is important to keep your promises. Both themes address the ways in which people interact with each other.

2. Describe the differences between the themes of "The Grateful Stork" and "The Gold Coin."

The themes of "The Gold Coin" and "The Grateful Stork" are different in certain ways. While they both focus on how people interact with each other, they also focus on different parts of how people live. "The Gold Coin" focuses on what makes people happy, like being kind and generous to each other. On the other hand, "The Grateful Stork" focuses on keeping your promises. It focuses more on being true to your word. For example, if you promise to do your best in school, then you should always try to keep that promise and do your best.

TRY IT Practice Words from "The Grateful Stork"

Students will answer questions to demonstrate their understanding of the vocabulary words from the reading.

WRAP-UP

Question About "The Grateful Stork"

Students will answer a question to show that they can determine the theme of a story.

"The Grateful Stork" Wrap-Up

Lesson Overview

ACTIVITY	ACTIVITY TITLE	TIME	ONLINE/OFFLINE
GET READY	Introduction to "The Grateful Stork" Wrap-Up	**1** minute	
TRY IT	Characters' Relationships Change **LEARNING COACH CHECK-IN**	**30** minutes	
	Read and Record	**10** minutes	
	Review "The Grateful Stork"	**20** minutes	
QUIZ	"The Grateful Stork"	**30** minutes	
	Spelling List 27	**10** minutes	
WRAP-UP	More Language Arts Practice	**19** minutes	

Lesson Goals

- Write about the interactions and relationships among characters in a story.

- Practice reading aloud to develop fluency.

- Review characters, setting, events, and theme of "The Grateful Stork."

- Review comparing and contrasting the treatment of topics, plots, and themes of stories from different cultures.

- Take a quiz on story elements of "The Grateful Stork" and comparing and contrasting stories from different cultures.

- Take a spelling quiz.

MATERIALS

Supplied

- *Summit English Language Arts 4 Expeditions in Reading*
- *Summit English Language Arts 4 Activity Book*
  - Characters' Relationships Change

GET READY

Introduction to "The Grateful Stork" Wrap-Up

Students will read the lesson goals.

Characters' Relationships Change

Students will complete Characters' Relationships Change from *Summit English Language Arts 4 Activity Book*.

LEARNING COACH CHECK-IN   This activity page contains open-ended questions, so it's important that you review students' responses. Give students feedback, using the sample answers provided to guide you.

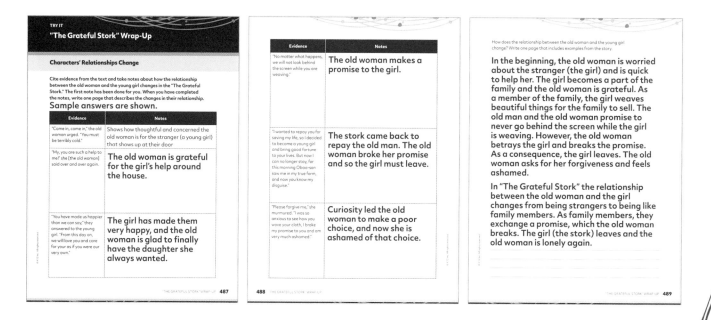

Read and Record

Good readers read quickly, smoothly, and with expression. This is called *fluency*. Students will record themselves reading aloud. They will listen to their recording and think about how quick, smooth, and expressive they sound.

TIP   Encourage students to rerecord as needed.

Review "The Grateful Stork"

Students will answer questions to review what they have learned about story elements and comparing and contrasting stories from different cultures.

QUIZ

"The Grateful Stork"

Students will complete "The Grateful Stork" quiz.

Spelling List 27

Students will complete the Spelling List 27 quiz.

WRAP-UP

More Language Arts Practice

Students will practice skills according to their individual needs.

Sayings

Lesson Overview

ACTIVITY	ACTIVITY TITLE	TIME	ONLINE/OFFLINE
GET READY	Introduction to Sayings	**1** minute	🖥
LEARN AND **TRY IT**	Identifying and Describing Sayings	**10** minutes	🖥
	More Sayings	**10** minutes	🖥
	Apply: Sayings **LEARNING COACH CHECK-IN**	**15** minutes	📄
	Go Write!	**15** minutes	📄
	Review Sayings	**15** minutes	🖥
QUIZ	Sayings	**15** minutes	🖥
WRAP-UP	More Language Arts Practice	**19** minutes	🖥
	Go Read!	**20** minutes	🖥 or 📄

Content Background

Students will learn about three types of figurative language—idioms, adages, and proverbs. These types of figurative language are also called *sayings*.

Every language has its own sayings. They provide a brief way of communicating an idea that would be understood by people that share the same language and culture.

Sayings include adages, proverbs, and idioms. Adages express a general truth, like *Birds of a feather flock together*, meaning that people with common interests or qualities tend to spend time together. A proverb expresses a general truth or offers advice. For example, *Better late than never* means that it is better to do something late or arrive late than to do nothing at all. An idiom is an expression that cannot be understood from the meanings of its separate words. You must learn the meaning of the expression as a whole. For example, *under the weather* is an idiom that means that somebody is not feeling well.

MATERIALS

Supplied
- *Summit English Language Arts 4 Activity Book*
  - Apply: Sayings

Also Needed
- reading material for Go Read!

Advance Preparation

During the Go Read! activity, students will have the option of using the digital library. Allow extra time for students to make their reading selection, or have students make a selection before beginning the lesson.

Lesson Goals

- Define *idioms*, *adages*, and *proverbs*.
- Identify and explain the meaning of idioms, adages, and proverbs.
- Identify and explain the meaning of idioms in a text.
- Take a quiz on idioms, adages, and proverbs.
- Read and write for pleasure.

KEYWORDS

adage – an old, familiar saying that describes a common truth

idiom – a group of words that does not actually mean what it says; for example, *raining cats and dogs, a month of Sundays*

proverb – a brief, popular saying that describes a wise thought

GET READY

Introduction to Sayings

Students will get a glimpse of what they will learn about in the lesson. They will also read the lesson goals and keywords. Have students select each keyword and preview its definition.

LEARN AND TRY IT

LEARN Identifying and Describing Sayings

Students will be introduced to the idioms, adages, and proverbs for the lesson. They will learn the definition of the terms *idiom*, *adage*, and *proverb* and how context clues can help them to determine the meanings of these sayings in a text.

TRY IT More Sayings

Students will answer questions in which they determine the meanings of idioms, adages, or proverbs.

TRY IT Apply: Sayings

Students will complete Apply: Sayings from *Summit English Language Arts 4 Activity Book*.

TIP   Remind students to use context to help them understand the meaning of each saying.

LEARNING COACH CHECK-IN   This activity page contains open-ended questions, so it's important that you review students' responses. Give students feedback, using the sample answers provided to guide you.

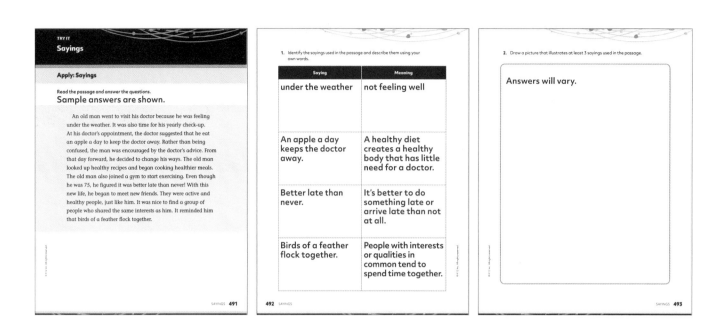

TRY IT   Go Write!

Students will write independently for pleasure. As they write, they should think about using idioms, adages, and proverbs in their writing.

TRY IT   Review Sayings

Students will answer questions to review what they have learned about idioms, adages, and proverbs.

QUIZ

Sayings

Students will complete the Sayings quiz.

WRAP-UP

More Language Arts Practice

Students will practice skills according to their individual needs.

Go Read!

Students will read for pleasure. They should choose a book or a magazine that interests them, or they may choose a selection from the digital library, linked in the online lesson.

Students should read for the entire time. Have students select something to read ahead of time to help them stay focused.

Big Ideas: Respond to a Prompt

Lesson Overview

Big Ideas lessons provide students the opportunity to further apply the knowledge acquired and skills learned throughout the unit workshops. Each Big Ideas lesson consists of these parts:

1. **Cumulative Review:** Students keep their skills fresh by reviewing prior content.

2. **Preview:** Students practice answering the types of questions they will commonly find on standardized tests.

3. **Synthesis:** Students complete an assignment that allows them to connect and apply what they have learned. Synthesis assignments vary throughout the course.

   In the Synthesis portion of this Big Ideas lesson, students will respond to an essay prompt based on reading selections. To respond meaningfully, students will need to use their own ideas as well as examples from the readings. Students' writing will be assessed in four categories: purpose and content; structure and organization; language and word choice; and grammar, usage, and mechanics.

   LEARNING COACH CHECK-IN   This is a graded assessment. Make sure students complete, review, and submit the assignment to their teacher.

All materials needed for this lesson are linked online and not provided in the Activity Book.

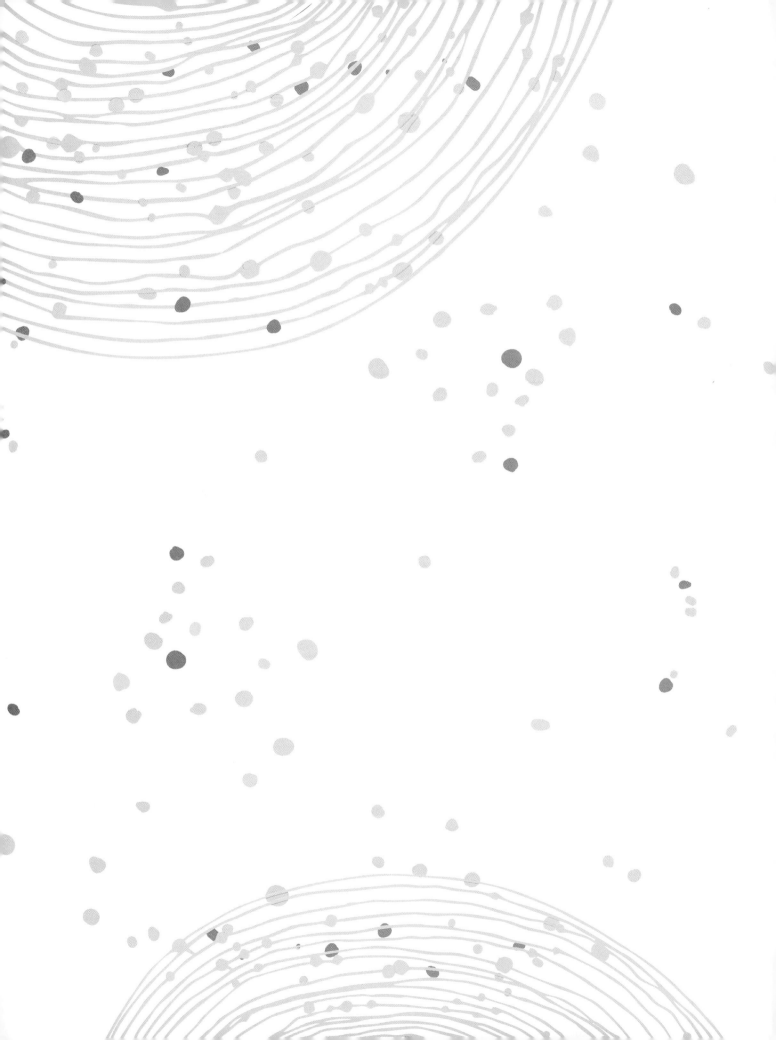